ASIAN VOICES IN CHRISTIAN THEOLOGY

Other books edited by Gerald H. Anderson:

The Theology of the Christian Mission
Sermons to Men of Other Faiths and Traditions
Christian Mission in Theological Perspective
Christ and Crisis in Southeast Asia
Studies in Philippine Church History
Concise Dictionary of the Christian World Mission (co-editor)
Mission Trends (co-editor)

ASIAN VOICES
IN
CHRISTIAN
THEOLOGY

Edited and with an Introduction by
GERALD H. ANDERSON

MARYKNOLL   NEW YORK

In memory of

DANIEL THAMBYRAJAH NILES

1908—1970

The Task of Theology
in the Asian Churches

It is out of the contemporary necessity to confess the Faith that there arises the task of theology for the churches in Asia. Theology is a living thing, having to do with our very existence as Christians and as churches. We cannot conceive of it in static or neatly defined final terms. A living theology must speak to the actual questions people in Asia are asking in the midst of their dilemmas; their hopes, aspirations, and achievements; their doubts, despair, and suffering. It must also speak in relation to the answers that are being given by Asian religions and philosophies, both in their classical forms and in new forms created by the impact on them of Western thought, secularism, and science. Christian theology will fulfill its task in Asia only as the Asian churches, as servants of God's Word and revelation in Jesus Christ, speak to the Asian situation and from involvement in it. Dogmatic theological statements from a church that stands on the sidelines as spectator or even interpreter of what God is doing in Asia can carry no conviction.

A living theology is born out of the meeting of a living church and its world. We discern a special task of theology in relation to the Asian renaissance and revolution, because we believe God is working out his purposes in these movements of the secular world. The Asian churches so far, and in large measure, have not taken their theological task seriously enough, for they have been largely content to accept the ready-made answers of Western theology or confessions. We believe, however, that today we can look for the development of authentic living theology in Asia.

A statement issued by an EACC consultation
December 1965, Kandy, Sri Lanka

CONTENTS

CONTRIBUTORS

Gerald H. Anderson, associate director, Overseas Ministries Study Center, Ventnor, New Jersey; formerly professor of church history and ecumenics, and academic dean of Union Theological Seminary, Manila, Philippines; and president of Scarritt College for Christian Workers, Nashville, Tennessee.

Mariano C. Apilado, a minister of the United Church of Christ in the Philippines, has an M. Theol. degree from the federated faculty of the South East Asia Graduate School of Theology, and is a doctoral candidate at Vanderbilt University, preparing to teach historical theology at Union Theological Seminary, Manila.

Douglas J. Elwood, professor of theology, Union Theological Seminary, Manila; was professor of theology and philosophy of religion at Silliman University Divinity School in the Philippines (1961–1971); and professor of theology at Tainan Theological College in Taiwan (1972–1975).

Kosuke Koyama, senior lecturer in religious studies, University of Otago in Dunedin, New Zealand; was a Japanese Kyodan missionary to the Church of Christ in Thailand, 1960–1968, teaching at Thailand Theological Seminary in Chiengmai. From 1968 to 1974 he was executive director of the Association of Theological Schools in Southeast Asia, dean of the Southeast Asia Graduate School of Theology, and editor of the *South East Asia Journal of Theology*, with headquarters in Singapore.

Yoshinobu Kumazawa, professor of theology, Tokyo Union Theological Seminary; was Henry W. Luce visiting professor at Union Theological Seminary, New York City, for 1973–1974.

Emerito P. Nacpil, executive director of the Association of Theological Schools in Southeast Asia, and dean of the Southeast Asia Graduate School of Theology; formerly professor of theology, academic dean, and president of Union Theological Seminary, Manila, Philippines.

Edward Nyhus, a doctoral candidate at University of Wisconsin, taught church history on the theological faculty of Nommensen University, Pematang Siantar, Indonesia, from 1959 to 1971.

Tongshik Ryu, professor of religion, Yonsei University, Seoul; formerly director of the editorial department, Christian Literature Society of Korea.

Lothar Schreiner, professor of missiology and history of religions at the Kirchliche Hochschule in Wuppertal, Germany, taught on the theological faculty of Nommensen University, Pematang Siantar, Indonesia, from 1956 to 1965.

Lynn A. de Silva, director of the Study Center for Religion and Society in Colombo, Sri Lanka (Ceylon); was visiting lecturer at Selly Oak Colleges, Birmingham, England, for 1970–1971.

T.B. Simatupang, presiding chairman and a president of the Christian Conference of Asia; member of the executive committee of the World Council of Churches; a president of the Council of Churches in Indonesia; retired general and former chief of staff of the Indonesian Armed Forces.

Choan-seng Song, associate director, Commission on Faith and Order of the World Council of Churches in Geneva, Switzerland; formerly professor of theology and principal of Tainan Theological College, Taiwan; and secretary for Asian Ministries of the Reformed Church in America.

U Kyaw Than, a Burmese layman, visiting professor of missions at the Divinity School of Yale University; was Asia secretary of the World Student Christian Federation (1950–1953), and associate general secretary (1953–1956); East Asia secretary of the World Council of Churches and International Missionary Council (1956–1959); associate general secretary of the East Asia Christian Conference (1959–1967), and general secretary (1968–1973).

M.M. Thomas, director of the Christian Insitute for the Study of Religion and Society in Bangalore, India; editor of the quarterly journal *Religion and Society;* chairman of the Central and Executive Committees of the World Council of Churches; was chairman of the World Council of Churches Conference on Church and Society at Geneva in 1966; Henry W. Luce visiting professor at Union Theological Seminary, New York City, for 1966–1967.

ASIAN VOICES IN CHRISTIAN THEOLOGY

INTRODUCTION

Gerald H. Anderson

A church historian in the Philippines wrote recently that "a radical shift of perspective" is now required to make the Church conscious of "the new center of gravity of the people of God."[1] The required shift is away from a North Atlantic tribalistic mentality, which assumes that everything of importance in the life and thought of the Church happens somewhere between Rome and Berkeley, California, toward an awareness that the areas of greatest church growth and theological vitality today are in the so-called Third World (actually the two-thirds world) of Asia, Africa, and Latin America—where the majority of Christians will be living in the year 2000.[2]

Christian theology has suffered from a state of "Teutonic captivity"—seldom getting "the chance to break out of the Western historical and cultural framework to which the Word of God in the Bible has been made captive," says Choan-seng Song.[3] A few years ago the editor of *The Christian Century* (the triumphalism of the title is an embarrassing reminder of the problem) pointed out that "the Aryan bias of Christian doctrine is perhaps the most serious intellectual obstacle to full ecumenical fellowship with the younger churches, to their own theological creativity, and to Christian evangelism in Asia, Africa, and Latin America."[4]

The great new fact of our time, however, is the break from Teutonic captivity by Christian theologians in the Third World as they seek to reconceptualize the God of biblical revelation within the context of their different cultures. This volume focuses upon that experience among Protestants in Asia and the emergence of "a third perspective" in Christian theology, in contrast to that of the Latin and Greek theological traditions which emanated from the Greco-Roman cultural matrix.[5]

Asian theologians are proposing today what they call the "critical Asian principle" as a method for doing theology in their situations. They are not yet very clear about it, but as they struggle to discover its

3

range and depth they see it operating at various methodological levels. "For one thing," says Dr. Emerito P. Nacpil, executive director of the Association of Theological Schools in Southeast Asia, "it is a way of saying where our area of responsibility is, namely, the varieties and dynamics of Asian realities. We are committed to understanding this context both sympathetically and critically. For another thing, it is a way of saying that we will approach and interpret the Gospel in relation to the needs and issues peculiar to the Asian situations. It functions therefore partly as hermeneutical principle. Thirdly, it is a way of saying that a theology worth its salt at this time in Asia must be capable not only of illuminating the Asian realities with the light of the Gospel, but also of helping manage the changes now taking place along lines more consonant with the Gospel."[6]

Various concepts describe the efforts to do theology this way in Asia—and elsewhere. It has been spoken of as theological adaptation, accommodation, inculturation, incarnation, or—most frequently —indigenization (meaning to grow out of the natural environment of a place). Most recently, however, the key concept in governing this process is spoken of as *contextualization*. The Theological Education Fund, headed by Dr. Shoki Coe from Taiwan, describes contextualization:

> It means all that is implied in the familiar term "indigenization" and yet seeks to press beyond. Contextualization has to do with how we assess the peculiarity of Third World contexts. Indigenization tends to be used in the sense of responding to the Gospel in terms of a traditional culture. Contextualization, while not ignoring this, takes into account the process of secularity, technology, and the struggle for human justice, which characterize the historical moment of the nations in the Third World.
>
> Yet a careful distinction must be made between authentic and false forms of contextualization. False contextualization yields to uncritical accommodation, a form of culture faith. Authentic contextualization is always prophetic, arising always out of a genuine encounter between God's Word and his world, and moves toward the purpose of challenging and changing the situation through rootedness in and commitment to a given historical moment.
>
> It is therefore clear that contextualization is a dynamic not a static process. It recognizes the continually changing nature of every human situation and of the possibility for change, thus opening the way for the future.[7]

Reflecting on the concept of contextualization, Kosuke Koyama—the Japanese missionary theologian who taught in Thailand for eight years—says, "there has been an alarming misunderstanding . . . that contextualization of theology means simply to take context seriously and adjust theology to fit into it. That would be 'uncritical accommodation.' . . . Context must not be viewed as something 'absolute' . . . as a tiger looks at the cage in which he is caged." Rather, says Koyama, context is "a dynamic relational concept. . . . Authentic contextualization is a prophetic mode of living in the given historical cultural situation. It challenges the context and attempts to make critical theological observations. . . . It is neither an easy accommodation nor an easy prophetism, but is both a serious accommodation and a serious prophetism. It aims at an accommodational prophetism and prophetic accommodation."[8]

A similar emphasis was sounded several years ago by M.M. Thomas when— speaking of the renaissance of traditional cultures in Asia—he said that the task of indigenization of the Gospel and the Church "is that of relevantly relating the Church and its word of judgment and redemption to the forces of cultural change which are at work in the present, and to the new cultural values which are emerging," to bring about "the Christian transformation and synthesis of traditional and modern cultures."[9]

Until rather recently, however, the churches in Asia were hindered in their theological development by two fundamental problems.[10] First, as one Asian expressed it to me a few years ago, "Christianity has been largely a 'potted plant' in Asia. It was transported without being transplanted. It is still viewed by Asians as a foreign importation and imposition." The fact that Christianity began in Asia (Jesus was an Asian!) did not matter; it travelled to Asia for the most part by way of the West. The challenge has been for the churches to relate themselves more fully to the soil of Asia—to get down to the rice-roots level of Asian civilization.

The second problem is that Christians have tended toward a ghetto mentality among themselves. A Catholic writer has observed that the Christian community in Asia has been more like glue than leaven. The churches have been preoccupied with their own existence and organization, and correspondingly they have lagged behind in prophetic concern for the social relevance and outreach of the Gospel into the mainstream task of nation-building. At best, in the view of one missionary, "the churches have been more resolutionary than revolutionary in their approach to the social problems of Asia; they have said more than they have done." Part of the reason for this isolation from national life has been a minority consciousness among many Christians, with an accompanying sense of security (and perhaps superiority) achieved by insulating themselves against involvement. Another part has been a pietistic heritage which has not taken social struggles seriously. In many instances, however, it has been a lack neither of courage nor of conviction. Rather, lack of understanding and knowledge about the dynamics of social change and the development of new forms of witness and service have kept Christians from responsible participation in the social problems inherent in the contemporary Asian revolution.

Circumstances and attitudes are rapidly changing, however, as is evident from the essays in this volume. Church leaders in Asia recognize that, as Bishop Nirmal Minz of the Evangelical Lutheran Church in India has pointed out, "Second-hand and derived theological thought cannot take a church too far in its life in a given environment. It must spring out of the peoples' life situation. Until its theology is the struggle of the church in a given situation in the proclamation of the Gospel, a church will remain isolated from the situation with an alien vision of Jesus Christ."[11]

At a consultation in Kandy, Ceylon, in 1965, Asian theologians said that a confessing theology would be "a theology which is the result of the wrestling of an Asian Church with its Asian environment." The first Asian Faith and Order Conference, sponsored by the East Asia Christian Conference (EACC) at Hong Kong in 1966 on the theme "Confessing the Faith in Asia Today," declared: "For the churches in Asia to confess the faith means that they speak out of their oneness given to them in Jesus Christ and that they speak also out of their solidarity with the world in which they live."[12] The Conference affirmed that

> confessing must be done from within the mainstream of the life of the larger community in which Christians participate. Confessing cannot be done from an isolated ghetto. Christian theology will fulfil its task in Asia only as the Asian churches, as servants of God's word and revelation in Jesus Christ, speak to the Asian situation and from involvement and participation in it.[13]

The fundamental idea of Christian solidarity with the world had already been affirmed at the Kuala Lumpur Assembly of the EACC in 1959 when it affirmed that it is the task of the churches to discern the presence of Jesus Christ in contemporary Asian history, so that they may respond to him and participate in his work for the world.[14] Thus, in response to the question, "What is God doing in and through the Asian revolution?" M.M. Thomas can say, "There is a general consensus among the churches in Asia that God in Christ is present in the Asian revolution and his creative, judging, and redemptive will is its essential dynamic."[15]

This incarnational/contextual approach to theological construction is exciting because it requires the churches in this period of profound change to penetrate and participate in the Asian revolution, which is "the most dynamic factor in the history of the twentieth century."[16] But, as the authors in this volume recognize, it also involves the risk of cultural captivity—the danger of identifying the Gospel too closely with a particular set of socioeconomic and political conditions or aspirations, as has happened all too often in the West. Yet, as Richard J. Neuhaus rightly observes, "A religion that affirms the Incarnation and the proposition that the finite can contain the infinite can afford to run some risks. In fact, it has little choice in the matter." Running the risk of cultural captivity, he says, "is inherent in the Church's mission."[17]

Theologically, there can be no unresolved conflict "between particularity and universality, between indigenity and catholicity" in the nature of the church "any more than there can be in Him Who was the eternal Word made flesh, the Universal localized in a certain time and place. But both the conditions and experience of selfhood and universality are liable to distortion and when this happens there are sure to be areas of tension."[18] Out of the tensions of theological creativity in Asia we may anticipate—with Arend Th. van Leeuwen—that there will likely "come to the fore some aspects of the biblical message which have been much neglected in the West; and some new heresies."[19] As these different expressions of Christian experience emerge, the question raised by Max Warren is timely: "Are we of the West prepared to trust the Holy Spirit to lead the Christians of Asia . . . or must a controlling Western hand be permanently resting on the Ark of God?"[20]

The essays which follow suggest something of the promise—and problems— of theological construction in Asia. Writing from very varied circumstances the authors describe the theological issues that confront the church in their respective lands—in light of their Christian heritage and national history—and discuss what is being done by the theologians there to articulate the Christian message in terms that are faithful to the biblical revelation, meaningful to their cultural traditions, and informed concerning the secular movements and ideologies which had their origins in the West but have now become more or less indigenous to most of the countries of Asia.[21] It is hoped that, taken together, the essays and the material in the Appendix and Bibliography may serve to increase our understanding and appreciation of the Asian response to Christ, and thereby enrich our own response to Him.

NOTES

1. John Schumacher, S.J., "The 'Third World' and the Twentieth-century Church," in Gerald H. Anderson and Thomas F. Stransky, C.S.P., eds., *Mission Trends No. 1* (New York: Paulist Press; and Grand Rapids, Mich.: Wm.B. Eerdmans Publishing Co., 1974), p. 213.

2. It is anticipated, for instance, that in A.D. 2000 there will be 395 million Christians (48.3 percent of the population) in Africa. David B. Barrett, "The Discipling of Africa in This Generation," in Alan R. Tippett, ed., *God, Man and Church Growth* (Grand Rapids, Mich.: Wm. B. Eerdmans Publishing Co., 1973), p. 397.

3. Choan-seng Song, "The New China and Salvation History—A Methodological Enquiry," *South East Asia Journal of Theology* XV, 2 (1974) 55–56.

4. Alan Geyer, "Toward a Convivial Theology," *The Christian Century*, April 23, 1969, p. 542.

5. Cf. Robin H.S. Boyd, *India and the Latin Captivity of the Church: The Cultural Context of the Gospel* (London: Cambridge University Press, 1974).

6. Emerito P. Nacpil, "The Question of Excellence," an address to the Foundation for Theological Education in Southeast Asia, New York City, December 6, 1974. Mimeographed.

7. Theological Education Fund, *Ministry in Context* (London: TEF, 1972), p. 20.

8. Kosuke Koyama, "Some Reflections on Contextualization" (Singapore: mimeographed, 1973), p. 2; cf. Kosuke Koyama, "Reflections on Association of Theological Schools in South East Asia," *South East Asia Journal of Theology* XV, 2 (1974), 18–19.

9. M.M. Thomas, "Indigenization and the Renaissance of Traditional Cultures," *International Review of Mission* LII, 206 (1963), 191, 194.

10. I have previously expressed some of these concerns in the Introduction and

Conclusion to *Christ and Crisis in Southeast Asia* (New York: Friendship Press, 1968), pp. 11, 165–66

11. Nirmal Minz, "The Freedom of the Indigenous Church Under the Holy Spirit and Communication of the Common Christian Heritage in the Context of This Freedom," in R. Pierce Beaver, ed., *The Gospel and Frontier Peoples* (South Pasadena, Calif.: William Carey Library, 1973), p. 109.

12. *Confessing the Faith in Asia Today*. Statement Issued by the Consultation Convened by the East Asia Christian Conference and Held in Hong Kong, October 26–November 3, 1966, p. 14.

13. *Ibid.*, p. 52.

14. *Witnesses Together*. The Official Report of the Inaugural Assembly of the EACC, Kuala Lumpur, Malaya, May 14–24, 1959. Rangoon: EACC, n.d., p. 60.

15. M.M. Thomas, *The Christian Response to the Asian Revolution* (London: SCM Press, 1966), p. 27.

16. Claude A. Buss, *The Arc of Crisis: Nationalism and Neutralism in Asia Today* (Garden City, N.Y.: Doubleday & Co., 1961), p. 19.

17. Richard J. Neuhaus, "Liberation Theology and the Captivities of Jesus," *Worldview* XVI, 6 (1973), 42, 43.

18. George H. Hood, "In Whole and in Part," *International Review of Mission* LXI, 243 (1972), 274–75. Cf. "Decree on the Church's Missionary Activity *(Ad Gentes)*," *Documents of Vatican II*, ed. by Walter M. Abbot (New York: Guild Press, America Press, Association Press, 1966), paragraphs 10 and 22, pp. 596–97, 612–13.

19. Arend Th. van Leeuwen, *Christianity in World History: The Meeting of the Faiths of East and West* (New York: Scribner's, 1967), p. 425.

20. Max A.C. Warren, "Introduction," in John V. Taylor, *The Primal Vision* (London: SCM Press, 1963), p. 9.

21. I am indebted to Charles West for his helpful observations on these matters in a report to the Foundation for Theological Education in Southeast Asia, New York City, November 27, 1972. Mimeographed.

I: INDIA

M. M. THOMAS

Toward an Indigenous Christian Theology

For over a decade now, the Indian Christian Theological Association and its organ, the *Indian Journal of Theology*, have been in existence. They have received a certain, though unofficial, recognition from the churches and theological colleges of India, and they represent the idea, affirmed by Christian theologians and church leaders in India, that as an expression of the Christian faith and as a tool of Christian witness against the Indian background, the Indian church should develop an indigenous Christian theology. As yet, the idea has not been actualized; but there are indications that the movement toward it has some promising dynamic features. Many streams of theological activity have contributed to the acknowledgment that, to be living, theology must reckon with the context of the traditional and contemporary life and thought of India. To understand the current Indian theological scene, it is necessary to look at some of the more important tributaries.

THEOLOGICAL EDUCATION

First, the continuous task of theological education of evangelists and ministers of the rural and the increasing number of urban churches in India through the theological and Bible schools has contributed in no small measure to the development of theological thought in India. The year 1968 marked the 150th anniversary of the founding of Serampore College for the education of Christian youth for spreading the Gospel in India. The training of the ordained ministry became the central emphasis of theological education later. The Serampore College Act of 1918—through which the senate of Serampore University

11

could affiliate theological schools under the leadership of colleges that grant bachelor of divinity degrees (Serampore, Bangalore, Jabalpur, and Calcutta, which use the English language; and other colleges using the regional languages, which have recently been added) and establish standards of theological education—and the NCC Board of Theological Education have helped the development of a standardized theological training for pastoral ministers in the country. The Christian Student's Library, designed primarily for theological students, has been widely used. Surveys of theological education made first by Charles Ranson[1] in 1943 and then a decade later by M.H. Harrison[2] have focused the attention of the churches on theological education as it relates to the training of the ministry. The National Consultation on Theological Education held in 1968 shows the extent of the awareness which exists among Indian theological educators concerning the need to orient the theology of evangelism and ministry to the contemporary religious and social situation of India. Speaking of the "ministry in retrospect," the report notes that Western models of ministry, which were introduced in India in the early mission days, are still faithfully followed by the churches and have been very slowly adapted to the Indian environment. "It is possible," says the report, "that one major factor in this failure is the fact that the large portion of the accession to the Christian church was from the depressed classes of society who do not have a predominantly priestly concern or function. The challenge of accommodation in ministerial patterns still remains."[3] And so far as the future is concerned, the consultation calls for a radical orientation of the patterns of the ministry "in response to the new situation of our times." What does this mean? To quote:

> It means sharing India's search for new meaning, for new humanity, not only ministering to men's poverty but also seeking to lead them out of poverty. It means specialized ministries to men in urban and rural situations.
>
> It means an open-minded encounter with the renascent religions of India, a readiness to discern values in them and to minister to the intellectual and religious aspirations of those involved in this renascence, along with its cultic expressions.
>
> It means learning to minister to men who face new and unprecedented decisions in their political, economic, intellectual, religious, and cultural life.
>
> In and through all the involvement with the world, the church's pri-

mary concern is to proclaim the Good News of Jesus Christ and to learn how to draw men to Him who alone is able to bring meaning and wholeness.[4]

This pattern of ministry is possible only by envisaging the pastor as "a member of a team which includes other pastors, professional workers, laymen and laywomen, married and celibates."[5] Here the ministry of lay Christian organizations, such as "the YMCA, YWCA, SCM, UESI, CASA community development services, and other agencies of social work," become integrated. Since "the whole church" is sent into the world for the unity of reconciliation "the training of its manifold ministries must have this missionary purpose constantly in view."[6]

DISCUSSION ON CHURCH UNION

A second stream of theological creativity in India has been the struggle of different confessional bodies and communions to formulate a basis of common faith and order for the union of churches. Thus the history of the movement toward the formation of the Church of South India and the subsequent dialogues of the CSI with Lutheran and Baptist churches have helped the denominations involved to look at the Western confessions to which they have adhered from a new perspective and to think out afresh the fundamentals of the faith and order of a united church in South India. A similar process has taken place in the emergence of the union of churches in North India. Bengt Sundkler's *Church of South India: The Movement Towards Union, 1900–1947*[7] and the chapter on the "United Churches and Union Schemes in India, Pakistan and Ceylon, with Special Reference to the Statements of Faith" in G. C. Oosthuizen's *Theological Battleground in Asia and Africa*[8] indicate the nature of the theological issues dealt with in these interchurch negotiations. The basic issue, of course, was the faith, the nature, and the function of the church. And the statements of the "Faith of the Church," included in the Constitution of the CSI, show the precise issues dealt with:

> The Church of South India accepts the Holy Scriptures of the Old and New Testaments as containing all things necessary to salvation and as the supreme and decisive standard of faith; and acknowledges that the church

must always be ready to correct and reform itself in accordance with the teaching of those Scriptures as the Holy Spirit shall reveal it.

It also accepts the Apostles' Creed and the Creed commonly called the Nicene, as witnessing to and safeguarding that faith; and it thankfully acknowledges that same faith to be continuously confirmed by the Holy Spirit in the experience of the Church of Christ.

Thus it believes in God, the Father, the Creator of all things, by whose love we are preserved;

It believes in Jesus Christ, the incarnate Son of God and Redeemer of the world, in whom alone we are saved by grace, being justified from our sins by faith in Him;

It believes in the Holy Spirit, by whom we are sanctified and built up in Christ and in the fellowship of his Body;

And in this faith it worships the Father, Son, and Holy Spirit, one God in Trinity and Trinity in Unity.[9]

The idea that the church in India should express the universal Christian faith in the thought-forms and life-forms of India has found acceptance from the very early days of the union negotiations and has found its place in the Constitution of CSI thus: "The Church of South India desires, therefore, conserving all that is of spiritual value in its Indian heritage, to express under Indian conditions and in Indian forms the spirit, the thought, and the life of the Church Universal." This, of course, is an idea which the CSI has yet to realize. But the acknowledgment of the idea is, in itself, significant.

CHRISTIAN APOLOGETICS

The third source of new theological thinking is the body of insights which has emerged in the encounter of Christian thinkers with the philosophical and religious systems of classical Hinduism and in their dialogue with the leaders of renascent Hinduism regarding their understanding of Christ and the relation between Christianity and other religions. In fact it is in Christian apologetics in the context of Hinduism that the crucial issues of an indigenous Christian theology have become clarified and its fundamentals formulated.

There is a history of Neo-Hindu views on Christ and Christianity and of the many attempts of the Christian church through its theologians and leading laymen to enter into controversy and/or dialogue with it to affirm the orthodox faith. Rajah Rammohan Roy was a monotheist fighting against the monism/polytheism of traditional Hinduism. In 1820 he produced his compilation from the synoptic Gospels under the title *Precepts of Jesus: The Guide to Peace and*

Happiness and interpreted Christ as the moral teacher and religious messenger par excellence. When Joshua Marshman of Serampore attacked Rammohan Roy for not explicitly acknowledging Christ's deity and atonement, Rammohan Roy reaffirmed his view of Christ as the pre-existent firstborn of *creatures* and his doctrine of forgiveness of sins through repentance without the atonement of Christ.[10] As the Brahmo Samaj became the spiritual home of many educated Hindus, the issues involved in the Rammohan Roy–Marshman controversy were kept alive in the defenses of the Christian faith against Brahmo theism. Lal Behari Day and Krishna Mohan Banerjee of Bengal, and Nehemiah Goreh and Pandita Ramabai of Maharashtra, continued to controvert not only classical Hinduism but also Brahmo theism, especially its rejection of revelation and atonement.[11] But Banerjee's *Arian Witness* in 1875, with its attempt to see in the Vedic idea of the Purusha sacrifice and Prajapathi the expectation of Jesus the Emmanuel and his sacrifice, and Day's "memorandum," *The Desirableness and Practicability of Organizing a National Church in Bengal*, addressed to the authorities of the Mission, which recommended the unification of all the churches, including the Roman Catholic, on the foundation of the Apostles' Creed, show their positive response to the challenge of Brahmoism to make Christianity indigenous. Among the Brahmo leaders, Keshub Chunder Sen, with his doctrines of Christ as "the divine humanity" and of "uni-Trinity," came nearest to the idea of the incarnation of the Logos in Christ:

> The New Testament commenced with the birth of the Son of God. The Logos was the beginning of creation and its perfection too was the Logos—the culmination of humanity in the Divine Son. We have arrived at the last link in the series of created organism. The last expression of Divinity is Divine Humanity. Having exhibited itself in endless varieties of progressive existence the primary creative force at last took the form of the Son in Christ Jesus.[12]

Keshub emphasized his Church of the New Dispensation as an expression of the universal Christ and as the fulfilment of Hinduism, in the dispensation of the Spirit. In his proposed harmony of all religions, he called for the affirmation of three points: that all religions are equally true, that all religions have truths which should be harmonized in the light of Christ, and that Keshub's own *adesh* (inspiration) was to be the criterion of harmonization. The Christian churches on the whole reacted against the religious syncretism in Keshub's theology. But the path opened up by his ideas of Christ and Christ-centered harmony of religions prompted Brahmobandhav Upadhyaya to join the Christian church and to accept baptism. Brahmobandhav became the pioneer of indigenous theology, and sought to establish a monastic order of Indian Christian Sanyasis, to employ Vedanta for the expression of Christian theology, and to obtain recognition of the Vedas as the Indian Old Testament.[13] Calling himself a Hindu Catholic, he used the categories of *Satchitananda* (being-knowledge-bliss) for the Trinity, with *chit* for Logos, which became incarnate in Jesus. He edited the *Sophia* and later the *Twentieth Century* for the spread of his indigenous theology. But the opposition of the Catholic hierarchy made him conclude that indigenous Christianity had no future except through India attaining independence. Accordingly, he became involved with the national agitation in Bengal, thus bringing his indigenous Christianity into relation with Indian nationalism. The Roman and non-Roman churches on the whole rejected not only Brahmobandhav but also Keshub as unorthodox. It was much later that Keshub's doctrine of Christ as divine humanity and the culmination of the creative process reappeared in Chenchiah's rethinking of theology.

With the emergence of Ramarkrishna Paramahamsa, Swami Vivekananda, and later Dr. S. Radhakrishnan, Brahmo theism lost its dominant position in Neo-Hinduism; and Advaita Vedanta, with its philosophy of self-realization through the mystic vision of nonduality, reasserted itself. Based on Sri Ramakrishna's "experience" of his identity with Kali, Rama, Brahman, Mohammed, and Christ, he propounded the idea of the equality of religions. He said:

> A lake has several ghats. At one the Hindus take water in pitchers and call it *jal*; at another the Musalmans take water in leather bags and call it *pani*. At a third, the Christians call it *water*. Can we imagine that it is not *jal*, but only *pani* or *water*? How ridiculous! The substance is one under different names, and everyone is seeking the same substance; only climate, temperament and name create differences.[14]

And Swami Vivekananda saw the religious experience of *dvaita* (duality), *visistadvaita* (qualified nondualism), and *advaita* (nondualism) as three phases, or stages, of a ladder in a single religious development of which advaita constitutes the ultimate goal. The experience of the personal God may be a step to the highest realization but not the goal, which is identity of the soul with Brahman. Jesus Christ himself went through these different stages to the experience of identity: "I and my Father are one." The historicity of the person of Jesus is the nonessential part of Christianity; it is the principle of Christhood, not the person of Christ, that is essential. Christ is only one of the many *avatars* (incarnations) appearing in the endless cycle of samsara to liberate man from the cycle through the vision of the ultimate One without a second. Vivekananda combines this approach of the religion of Vedanta with the practical Vedanta of active selfless service in society.

Radhakrishnan gave Vivekananda's religion of Advaita Vedanta and its practical humanism of service a sounder metaphysical basis.[15]

Christian apologetics have been concerned with the defense of the Christian faith against the onslaughts of Advaita Vedanta at three points: its idea of the essential oneness of all religions, its conception of the ultimate as impersonal and ahistorical, and the priority it gives to metaphysical evil over the moral. There is a long list of Western teachers in the theological colleges who have entered this field of Christian apologetics. E. W. Thompson's *The Word of the Cross to Hindus*[16] and Nicol Macnicol's *Is Christianity Unique?*[17] are illustrations of works clarifying the faith and doctrines of Christianity as contrasted with Vedanta, which has a different axis. Between Vedanta and Christianity there is an either/or choice to be made.

J. R. Chandran, in his unpublished thesis on Vivekananda's views of Christ and Christianity and the principles of Christian apologetics in relation to them in the light of Origen's *Against Celsus*, follows the same pattern but goes further. He rejects Vivekananda's harmony of religions as "virtually the abandonment of all principles of moral and religious discrimination" and his biblical exegesis of the verse "I and my Father are one" in terms of advaita as alien to the fundamentals of biblical religion. Chandran sees fundamental differences between the Christian understanding of "man as creature and the object of God's love, and as sinner who cannot be redeemed except through God's grace," and history as "a real and purposive unity in the hands of God," and the advaita view of "the essential divinity of the soul and the interpretation of history in terms of meaningless repetition of cycles." In fact, the dimensions of personality and history are the "sphere of morality," and Christian theology in India must defend the priority of the moral over the metaphysical by showing the challenging relevance of Christian faith to the "moral conflicts affecting individuals as well as groups in the social, economic and political relationships." But Chandran emphasizes that the Christian message must be communicated through those elements of Hinduism that express an awareness of the moral purposes and issues in the world. He adds:

> With sufficient caution the Gita doctrine of the Avatara as a voluntary act of the deity in order to destroy evil from the world may be interpreted as a rudimentary recognition by the Hindu of the reality of moral issues in the world. More important is the modern movement for social reform within Hinduism which, rightly valued, might lead to a reconsideration of its ultimate significance.[18]

In this setting, says Chandran, Christian theology has the task of grappling with the truth and meaning behind the advaitic assertion of the Impersonal Ultimate, and the ultimacy of the mystic experience of Brahman-atman identity. There is need to further clarify the Christian approach to the suprapersonal nature of God in the doctrine of the Trinity. He says:

> The Christian doctrine of the Trinity which speaks not only of God as at one level of His life (Three Persons) akin to but immeasurably greater than ourselves, also reminds us of the unity of substance, in which God overpasses all that we know of Him and recedes from our gaze into rich vistas of being which we can neither fathom nor plumb. It is therefore incorrect to speak of Christians as believing in a personal God; the central doctrine of their creed asserts belief in "personality plus"—a suprapersonal God.[19]

Bishop A.J. Appasamy has offered a Christian doctrine of immanence and mysticism as the answer to Advaita Vedanta. In his book *What Is Moksha?* he advocates speaking of Christ to the Hindus "from the inside, feeling with their intense feelings, longing with them their deepest longings, thinking with them through their most baffling problems, following with them their highest ideals, doing all these in that measure and to that degree which our loyalty to Christ permits."[20] And in the context of such an approach his response to advaita doctrine and realization in a more recent pamphlet shows that "the Mahavakya of the Christian religion is not 'I and my Father are one,' but 'Abide in me and I in you.' "[21] It is bhakti mysticism of interpersonal mutual indwelling that he emphasizes in contrast to the advaitic mysticism. The advaitic interpretation of Christ sees in him two levels—one a level of Christ's dependence on God and the other of unity with him. Appasamy affirms that dependence and unity were integral to Christ's mysticism. The church has always had mystics, even mystics whose experience obliterated distinctions between man and God. But in judging the orthodoxy of mystics, the test of the church was "impeccability: Do the devotees interpret that identity as rendering the soul permanently incapable of sin?" Appasamy considers this test "an excellent one and badly needed in India." He sees both the metaphysical and moral levels in the idea of sonship and fellowhip with God: It is both of "nature" and of "will." He also emphasizes the suprapersonal nature of God: "The Incarnation is but a working hypothesis helping and guiding men to reach a knowledge of the Divine and does not exhaust all the infinite grandeur of God."[22] In his doctrine of divine immanence he stresses that "God is immanent in different objects in different fashions and in different degrees"; otherwise it will cut at the root of morality.[23]

Surjit Singh's *Preface to Personality*[24] is a discussion of "Christology in relation to Radhakrishnan's philosophy." It is not only a Christian critique of Radhakrishnan's Christology, but also an attempt to use Radhakrishnan's more creative ideas for a new Christology. Radhakrishnan's philosophy is a restatement of advaita, with a view to saving the world and making room for a spiritual humanism, as a foundation for India's search for new political and social life. Therefore there is in Radhakrishnan the idea of an Absolute which does not annihilate personal values and plurality, though he reverts, off and on, to an abstract monism destructive of values. And Radhakrishnan defines his "dynamic monism" thus:

> The Absolute is not an abstract unit, but a concrete whole binding together the differences which are subordinate to it. The whole has existence through the parts and the parts are intelligible only through the whole. The values we find and enjoy while on the way to it are preserved and receive their full supplementation in it. They are not annihilated.[25]

This makes plurality "not the final truth" but an essential element in the picture of reality as a whole; and ultimate reality is involved in pluralism without being exhausted by it. "In this context individuality as laying claim to absolutism would be denied. But in so far as it aligns itself with the patterns of ultimate reality, it is affirmed and preserved."[26] This according to Surjit Singh corresponds to the conception of individuality as revealed in Jesus Christ. He says:

> The whole life of Jesus the Christ, and particularly the Cross, bears witness to the phenomenon of the destruction of individuality as laying claim to absolutism. On the other hand by positive righteousness he made himself so transparent to the divine that no contradiction remained between divinity and humanity. The relation of perfect union was achieved. By making humanity transparent, by stripping it off from any possibility of its asserting itself in its own right, the humanity was not by any means absorbed in the divinity, but only became completely responsive. Therefore the God-Man is not only a reality in history but is also beyond it.[27]

The significance of Christ's bodily resurrection lies in the fact that it represents a historical individuality which is spiritual. In it historical reality is "taken up into the consummation of things and is preserved in the essential structure of Reality."[28] He adds:

> Jesus Christ, the unity of God and man, represents that the picture of Ultimate Reality is not only divine but divine-human. Temporal and historical existence has made a difference. This is not to argue that this picture exhausts the depths of the divine being but that is how Ultimate Reality would appear to us. The God-Man is the representation of Ultimate Reality as it concerns us as we are related to it . . . the God-Man is the norm of Ultimate Reality. In him the criterion appears.[29]

D.G. Moses, in his study *Religious Truth and the Relation between Religions*,[30] gives a philosophic criticism of Radhakrishnan's doctrine of the equality of religions. Radhakrishnan denies the validity of creeds and religious symbols because they have only instrumental value. Moses points out that if they have an instrumental function to fulfil, then it is important to judge which are adequate instruments and which not, and it becomes a criterion of discrimination among creeds and dogmas. Ideas of God are important because they have an intimate connection with the experience of God. Even in mystic experience there is a credal counterpart. Commenting on the thesis of Radhakrishnan, that the different creeds are "the historical formulations of the formless truth," Moses says "the truth that can be known by man must have some form" and every religion cannot be "a perfect expression" of the divine.[31] On the use of the term "finality," which Radhakrishnan rejects in religion, Moses says:

If the term finality is understood in the sense of that which is *fundamental*, that which has to be included in whatever further progress is achieved, or, in other words, if finality is thought of in terms of that which is *elemental*, then it is possible to regard even a historical religion as final. . . . Thus, it is not necessary to regard finality as excluding progress or as incompatible with the finitude of man.[32]

And Moses affirms that truth has its exclusiveness, but it is an exclusiveness "that does not destroy, but fulfils," and therefore it "will not breed bigotry but promote humble sharing."[33]

Mahatma Gandhi's views of Christ and Christianity are expressed in two collections of his writings, *The Message of Jesus Christ*[34] and *Christian Missions*.[35] For Gandhi the message of Jesus was the Sermon on the Mount. Jesus represents not a person, but the personification of the moral and spiritual principle of nonviolence. Gandhi points out that "the example of Jesus' suffering is a factor in the composition of my underlying faith in non-violence, which rules in all my actions, worldly and temporal."[36] But the historical person of Jesus himself is not essential to the message. Gandhi could never believe that Jesus was the incarnate Son of God in any unique sense. He pays "equal homage to Jesus, Mohammed, Krishna, Buddha, Zoroaster and others that may be named."[37] He believes "all religions are true but imperfect" and need reform in the light of each other's truth and of the ultimate principle of nonviolence. Therefore he opposed all conversions from one faith to another and, in fact, all propaganda of religious truth. It was Gandhi's conviction that "the principal faiths of the world" are all based on "common fundamentals."[38]

There were many encounters between Christian evangelists and Gandhi. Even as they saw in the practice of *satyagraha* (resistance to evil through voluntary suffering) a new extension of the Christian ethics of agape to politics, they sought to emphasize the person of Christ as the center of the Gospel. E. Stanley Jones, in his *Mahatma Gandhi; An Interpretation*,[39] is typical of this approach. He admits Gandhi's great contribution toward making the cross real in India, and affirms that insofar as Gandhi lived by Christian principles he "discovered and lived by the Person of Christ however dimly and unconsciously." But his criticism was that Gandhi never penetrated through the principles to the Person. So he wrote in a letter to Gandhi:

I thought you had grasped the center of the Christian faith, but I am afraid
I must change my mind. I think you have grasped certain principles of the
Christian faith which have moulded you and have helped make you
great—you have grasped the principles but you have missed the
Person. . . . May I suggest that you penetrate through the principles to
the Person and then come back and tell us what you have found. I don't say
this as a mere Christian propagandist. I say this because we need you and
need the illustration you could give us if you really grasped the centre—
the Person.[40]

Mahatma considered the passion for evangelism as an expression of
lack of humility. Since he looked on salvation as an attainment
through moral self-discipline, he was right from his point of view,
says Jones. But salvation is different for the Christian—it is a gift of
Grace. And talking about it is not talking of oneself, but "laying the
tribute of my love and gratitude at the feet of Another. Not to talk
about it would be indelicate and would lack humility." Jones admits
that Christians should "take very seriously the rose perfume emphasis
[of Gandhi] as a corrective," but to rule out the evangelism of lips is
"onesided and unnatural." Jesus lived the Gospel but also com-
mended it in words. "It was all of a piece."

Regarding the identification of Christ with Western civilization
and Western Christianity which Gandhi also had in mind when he
opposed conversion, Jones says: "Our message is not the system, but
the Saviour," and India, "out of her rich cultural and religious past,"
should bring to the interpretation of the Universal Christ something
which will greatly enrich the total expression. He adds: "Especially
now that Mahatma Gandhi has lived and died we think you can
interpret Christ in terms in which we are lacking in the West."[41] Jones
had written his *Christ of the Indian Road*[42] and had been following this
emphasis on the Person transcending the system in his evangelistic
campaigns among the educated Hindus.

THINKING ON CHRISTIANITY AND OTHER RELIGIONS

We could speak of the theological ferment which took place among the
Christian thinkers, both Western and Indian, as arising partly in
response to the challenge of Neo-Hinduism and partly as the result of
the impact of liberal and Barthian theologies from the West.

Most early missionaries had thought of Hinduism simply as the work of the devil. But during the period of liberalism in theology, men like Max Müller (1823–1900) revealed its treasures. In India the lectures of William Miller (1838–1923) of Madras Christian College on "The Christian Conception of God's Dealings with Mankind" in 1890 and "The Place of Hinduism in the Story of the World" in 1895 were based on his acknowledgment of the divine education of mankind through all religions and nations. He spoke of the spiritual values of Hinduism which would be developed and fulfiled in Jesus Christ. He made the clearest distinction between Christ and Christianity, saying, "It is not with Christianity, it is with Christ alone, you have to do." Bernard Lucas (1860–1920) gave to his book *Our Task in India* the subtitle *Shall We Proselytise or Evangelise India?*[43] He spoke of the work of Christ and his Spirit transforming Hinduism, and of evangelism as working to further it rather than to win converts to a churchly Christianity.[44] This was in line with the Neo-Hindu demand that the religious development of a people should be one of organic growth from within their own traditional religion, without a radical break with it. Christian liberalism affirmed the necessity of Hinduism to acknowledge Jesus Christ as the criterion and fulfilment of Hinduism. Some liberals maintained that this acknowledgment of Christ did not require a change of religious affiliation from Hinduism to Christianity. Therefore baptism came to be questioned. O. Kandasamy Chetty considered himself an unbaptized Christian in the Hindu fold. His example has been followed by many up to this day. The current Christian movement of Subba Rao of Andhra Pradesh is of Hindus who accept Jesus Christ as Lord and Savior and still remain unbaptized within the Hindu fold.[45] The question of whether baptism in India has become like the Jewish circumcision, the mark of entry from one communal group or caste to another, is a subject that has been raised off and on in the history of the Indian Church. A few years ago Kaj Baago, former Professor of Church History at United Theological College, Bangalore, initiated some lively discussion on it among Christian theologians. Men with deep evangelistic concern have all along been exercised about it. Narayan Varma Tilak, the Christian poet of Maharashtra, in his old age visualized an Indian pattern of discipleship of Christ and of a church of Christ transcending the community of the baptized. His idea of "God's Durbar" was to build up "a brotherhood of the baptised and unbaptised disciples of Christ." Tilak, who said he came to Christ "over the bridge of

Tukaram's verse," and who considered the poetry and sayings of the
Marathi Hindu saints as "our first Old Testament," wrote in 1916:
"India needs Christ, not so much Christianity."

T. E. Slater and J. N. Farquhar were more conservative representatives of Christian liberalism. Farquhar's *The Crown of Hinduism*[46] gave
classical expression to it. He saw Christianity as the crown of Hinduism, and said, "It is the duty of the Hindus to give up Hinduism so
that Christianity may take its place, and may thereby fulfil all that is
in it of good." Farquhar's *Modern Religious Movements in India*,[47] and
the *Heritage of India Series* which he edited,[48] caught the imagination of
Christian theologians and Hindu thinkers alike. There were others
like the Anglican fathers of the Oxford (Calcutta) and Cambridge
(Delhi) missions, and of the Poona and the Kanpur brotherhoods;
teachers at the United Theological College, Bangalore; scholars of the
caliber of Nicol Macnicol, A. G. Hogg, and others, who entered the
debate. Whether they accepted Farquhar's crown theory or not, they
approached the world of Hindu spirituality and philosophy sympathetically, and clarified the truth and meaning of the Christian
Gospel in their categories. For most it was probably no more than an
effort at communication, and there was little recognition that Hinduism itself would help to provide a new understanding of the Gospel. A. G. Hogg's *Karma and Redemption*[49] deserves special mention,
since it took the problem of understanding and communicating the
Christian faith within the framework of Hindu spirituality and
philosophy to a new dimension. Hogg examined and recognized the
spiritual questions and the relative validity of the answer behind the
doctrine of Karma, and moved beyond this to the necessity of unmer-
ited and vicarious suffering in a moral universe. Gandhi's *satyagraha*,
with its doctrine of vicarious suffering, had already made the issue of
Karma and vicarious suffering central in reformed Hinduism.

The Report of the Laymen's Foreign Missions Inquiry Commission, led by W. E. Hocking, with its emphasis on religious relativism
and the sharing of religious values among the religions, and the
Jerusalem IMC meeting in 1928, which proposed an interreligious
united front against secularism, were milestones in the march of
liberal theology in India. But Kraemer's *The Christian Message in a
Non-Christian World*[50] and the discussion of its "biblical realism" at
Tambaram in 1938 and afterwards, put an end to the idea of a

common religious basis for interreligious fellowship, and placed the Christian Gospel in radical discontinuity with the religions of man and all religious syncretism. There was also the rediscovery of the church as a constitutive aspect of the Gospel. As a result there was a new tendency to absolutize the Christian religion over against other religions. The theological insights of biblical realism had come to stay, but after World War II the new demands of interreligious cooperation on a secular human basis and for a secular society, and the emphasis on the presence of the ferment of the Gospel in Neo-Hinduism, led to a post-liberal post-Kraemer stance in interreligious relations. This has found expression in the approach of the Christian Institute for the Study of Religion and Society at Bangalore, with its studies on the living faiths of India and on interreligious dialogues. The symposium "Inter-religious Dialogue" in 1967 argued the theology of interreligious relation from fundamentals, and the various points of view expressed in it show that a consensus on a theology of interreligious dialogue is far from realized.

THEOLOGY OF NATIONALISM

The thinking about the Christian significance of Indian nationalism has been led mainly by laymen, but laymen capable of theological reflection. I have in mind men like C. F. Andrews and S. K. Rudra of St. Stephen's College, Delhi, and S. K. Datta and K. T. Paul of the YMCA of India. C. F. Andrews' pamphlet *The Ideal of Indian Nationality*[51] and his book *The Renaissance in India: Its Missionary Aspect*;[52] S. K. Rudra's pamphlet *Christ and Modern India*;[53] S.K. Datta's *The Desire of India*;[54] and K.T. Paul's *The British Connection With India*[55] and his lectures on Christian nationalism all deal with the theology of Indian nationalism. They see the hand of divine providence in the history of the British connection with India, with the impact of Western culture on Indian life and thought and the awakening of the Indian people to new aspirations of freedom and justice. For K.T. Paul the emergence of nation and nationalism is in the design of God; he sees new creativeness and destructiveness in Indian nationalism, and it is the task of the Christian nationalist to bring it under the "searching scrutiny" of the light of Christ and to promote the good and the creative. Britain should also realize the providential design of the British Indian connection, for "there are forces embedded in Indian personality and treasures enshrined in Indian culture which are waiting to be tapped by the seeker after better things." The Indian awakening was providential also because it was a *preparatio evangelica*. Alexander Duff, John Wilson and William Miller, the educational missionaries, saw a cultural preparation for the Gospel in the substitution of Western culture for Indian culture. But the Indian Christian nationalists saw it in the assimilation of Western cultural values by Hindu religion and culture. The national movement, says K. T. Paul, has been the result of "a widespread process brought about by a tacit recognition of the values that are in the mind of Christ as the supreme criterion for all human conduct, public and private." Of course, in the past the religious message was "vitiated by reason of the superior plane from which it was presented as much as by its foreign flavour and concomitants."[56] But Indian nationalism calls for a more correct thinking about the distinction and interrelation between Christ, Christianity, and Western civilization, so that the Christian message may be disentangled from religion and culture and enabled to become indigenous to the religion and culture of India and to speak to the universal human.

Andrews, Rudra, Datta, and Paul were most conscious of the contribution of the Gospel of Christ and the practice of fellowship in Christ to the breaking-down of caste, class, and communal exclusiveness and the building-up of a new society and national community. They rejected outright the suggestion that Christian spirituality is purely a cult of the inner life that leaves the traditional social relations unaffected. The Gospel of Christ was a message of renewal of society. S.K. Rudra speaks of the great task of building up one Indian nation out of all the diverse races and divisions, and offers the person of Christ as the source of the new Indian nation:

> That living Person in the plenitude of His spiritual power embodies in Himself all the moral forces which go to create a vital and progressive organism—an organism which may find its goal in a united and independent nation. He embodies them, not merely as being the teacher, but as being Himself the Living Motive Power behind them, the Power who gives new moral life to those who come to Him. . . . In Him, the living Person, and not in any human philosophy or system, lies the key to India's future. For Christ stands out before all mankind for faith and belief in the one Invisible and Incomprehensible God, in whom He Himself

dwells, and whom He has revealed as the Father, implying thereby the sonship of men to God, and their brotherhood with one another. . . . India's children would gain in Christ the full function of their new-formed national consciousness. A great Indian Church would become possible and therefore a great Indian nation.[57]

And for C. F. Andrews, the challenge of Indian nationalism was a call to a deeper realization of

Christ the Eternal Word, the Life and Light of millions who have not yet consciously known Him; Christ the Son of Man suffering in each indignity offered to the least of His brethren; Christ the Giver of more abundant life to noble and aspiring souls; Christ the Divine Head of Humanity, in whom all the races of mankind are gathered into One.[58]

The Christian Nationalists have also given a great deal of thought to "the place of the church in the currents of India's thought and feeling and aspirations and action," and to the manner in which the church can become "an effective factor in determining India's standards, in the evolution of its corporate conscience." Paul asks, "What is the contribution of Christian citizenship to public opinion in India?" He sees it expressed by Christians "not merely through direct religious work, but through the multitudinous responsibilities which are called secular." And both Datta and Paul fought the communal representation of Indian Christians in political life on the grounds that it would turn the church into a political group, organizing itself around communal self-interest when it ought to be cementing and renewing influence among all the communities constituting the national community.

The CISRS study summed up the theology of nation-building after Indian independence in the book *Christian Participation in Nation-Building*.[59] It is a continuation of the theology of nationalism started by the Christian Nationalists of the earlier period.

An Indigenous Theology

The five streams dealt with in the preceding pages have contributed to the development of the idea of an Indian church witnessing to Christ within the context of the Indian realities of life, and in this sense, indigenous. It must be immediately pointed out that the contemporary Indian reality is not the traditional one, but the traditional one renewed under the impact of the West and of the awakening. The Christian Asram movement led by the pioneers of the Christa-Kula Asram at Tiruppattur, Dr. S. Jesudason and Dr. Forrester Paton; the National Christian Council for cooperation among the missions and churches in the national context; the National Missionary Society of India under the leadership of Azariah (later Bishop), K. T. Paul, and others; the Student Christian Movement, formed as wings of the YMCA and YWCA, and later as an independent movement, under the leadership of a Christian nationalist, A. Ralla Ram; and the movement of church unions in South India and North India—all were influenced by the thought of an indigenous Indian church. And the idea of an indigenous theology was inherent in it. The leaders who contributed to the book *Rethinking Christianity in India*—[60] Justice P. Chenchiah, V. Chakkarai, A.N. Sudarisanam, Eddy Asirvatham, G.V. Job, S. Jesudason, and D.M. Devasahayam—have been exercised about an indigenous theology both before and after Tambaram in 1938, in what was called the Bangalore Conference Continuation, and through the columns of the weekly *Guardian*. Chakkarai was the most systematic theologian among them, as is evident in his books, *Jesus the Avatar*[61] and *The Cross and Indian Thought*.[62] But Chenchiah was the more creatively original. *The Theology of Chenchiah*[63] and *The Theology of Chakkarai*[64] are selections from their writings. Paul D. Devanandan was associated with the Rethinking Christianity group and shared their concerns; and since he absorbed the challenge of Kraemer's "biblical realism," he led the movement in Independent India for a post-Kraemer Indian theology.

The debates taking place in and around the Indian Christian Theological Association on the theological task in India have helped to crystallize the principles of an indigenous theology. Marcus Ward's *Our Theological Task*[65] sums up the results of the first conference in Poona. As Chenchiah said in his review of this work, it has a rather narrow view of the Indian theological task, in which "with three absolutes of unchanging core, unalterable faith and essential deposit, allots to theology the limited function of translating the fixed faith into a variety of languages, seeking proper ideas and words to express the three absolutes."[66] The Poona conference in 1942 stated, "Here we would stress our opinion that the 'Indianisation' of Christianity refers only to such changes in external forms and terms as will make the unchanging Gospel intelligible in India."[67] But it emphasized the necessity for the Church's discernment of the Indian situation as well as learning from the heritage of the universal church. So the theological task calls for "study (a) of the Bible; (b) of the Patristic Age, for methods of interpreting Christian dogma in the context of a non-Christian environment; (c) of church history with a view to understanding our Christian heritage; (d) of Indian and non-Christian religious thought, with a view to understanding our non-Christian heritage and reinterpreting it in the light of Christ; (e) of contemporary life and thought, particularly in India, with a view to indicating the relevance to our age of the Christian doctrine of man, the Christian interpretation of history, and of the Christian ideal of society."[68] Clearly, Poona 1942 opened the door very little to the outside world, but was in itself a recognition of the restlessness of Indian Christians regarding the domination of Western formulations of theology. Later conferences, however, have, on the basis of deeper biblical scholarship, opted for the broader view. Jabalpur 1964 followed W.M. Roth in affirming that the question "Who is Jesus?" cannot be answered "by one or several standard formulae, to be held exclusively and perpetually valid, but in the actual confrontation of Christ with the world in preaching and teaching in each period and place." And faithfulness to the Bible and the church Fathers was defined, not as "adherence" to a dogma with its given terms, giving the Indian church only the task of "translation" to the situation in theology, but "continuity" with their living core and spirit, releasing the Indian church to consider theology as a creative endeavor, to bring out new facets of the truth and meaning of the person of Jesus Christ and his salvation.

The Doctrine of New Creation

After this survey of the development of Indian thinking on theology, we may end by outlining the doctrine of new creation and new humanity which has emerged as an indigenous tradition in India. We have already referred to Keshub Chunder Sen's doctrine of Christ as divine humanity, and C.F. Andrews' doctrine of Christ as the divine head of a new humanity; and Surjit Singh's concept of God-Man within the framework of a dynamic monism has already been dealt with. It may not be inappropriate to conclude this paper with brief surveys of Chenchiah's doctrine of the new man, which is clothed in the categories of emergent evolution of the creative process and of Devanandan's reinterpretation of the same in the terms of a theology of eschatological hope and its historical fulfilment.

Chenchiah says, "Viewed as an outburst or inrush into history, Jesus is the manifestation of a new creative effort of God, in which the cosmic energy or *sakti* is the Holy Spirit, the new creation is Christ, and the new life order, the Kingdom of God."[69] He found support for his views in the philosophical excursions of two of his contemporaries in India—Sri Aurobindo of Pondicherry, and Master C.V. V. (C. V. Venkatasami Rao of Kumbakonam). The influence of Henri Bergson may also be traced. But Chenchiah was also standing squarely on the biblical and patristic traditions. He says that Indian Christology should be based on the discovery and the recovery of the Pauline theology of incarnation as new Adam, and should work along the lines of the Eastern theology of the Son of Man, linking it with the incarnation and the resurrection. Jesus, according to Chenchiah, can be understood only with the "larger development of world thought, the reaching of world concepts in politics and history, the processes of science,"[70] and in the perspective of the cosmic process:

> Jesus is the "first fruits of a new creation," holds Paul. "Jesus is the first of a new race, the sons of God," propounds St. John. The flash of illumination places Jesus in creation as its pinnacle and crown and demands from us a study of him in the context of creation along with its major terms, atom, amoeba, man. Before we can grasp the true significance of Jesus, we have to study Him in the context of the antecedent terms of creation.[71]

God's assumption of humanity, including the body, was a permanent one, and from now on Jesus is the Power of God and the first fruits of a new creation, a divine humanity transcending mankind. In this connection Chenchiah makes a clear distinction between the Hindu and Christian views of the incarnation; indeed, his criticism of Barthian theology is precisely that it is more akin to the Hindu than to the Christian view:

> Incarnation is perfected human body receiving the full divinity of God into permanent integration. (It is essential for our doctrine of incarnation to hold that Jesus assumed body permanently as the consummation of creative human process.) In Indian Christian theology Jesus belongs to

man and even though he may sojourn in heaven, he will return to earth, for here lies his home. A type of Christian theology approximates his function to that of Hindu *avatar*. The Son became Jesus to offer his life on the Cross as propitiation and went to his home in Heaven after his Mission was fulfilled. In that case incarnation will be an adventure, an interlude in the Eternal Son's life, leaving no permanent deposit on earth or in heaven. He assumed the body for a purpose and when it was over, he resumed his former status. Our conception of the Son of Man radically differs from this. Jesus, on the view controverted, does not remain unchanged. He reverts to his place as second person in Trinity. . . . Indian Christian theology probes deeply into the meaning of the fact that Jesus ascended into Heaven as Jesus and never resumed his place as the second person in Trinity. After ascension the Trinity was no longer Father, Son and Holy Ghost, but Father, Jesus and Holy Spirit. . . . Humanity did not borrow Jesus to stay a while on earth. We have lent him to heaven to stay there for a while.[72]

Jesus represents not merely the meeting, but the fusion into unity, of God and man so that man may partake of it. It is thus that he becomes "God permanently residing in creation" bringing to birth "a new order in creation." Here incarnation and resurrection are linked.

For Devanandan, too, the Gospel was essentially the Good News of new creation in Jesus Christ, which has "personal, social and cosmic dimensions." He said:

At the threshold of this century, we talked of evangelism in terms of a Social Gospel. Though we erred in our understanding of its true nature, we have come to admit that God's redemptive work must radically affect human relations in society. Perhaps as we reach the middle of this century, we are coming to realize that the total sweep of the Good News envelopes God's entire creation. The ultimate end is a new heaven and a new earth, a new creation. How utterly impossible can it be for any fragment of mankind to be changed or even for all humanity to be transformed, unless the grossly material and purely animal content of world life is also transformed! Is that not why the fact of the Risen Lord forms the core of the Gospel we proclaim? It was so from the beginning of the apostolic ministry.[73]

This new creation is for Devanandan "a reality in the present, while its consummation is in the future." The "present" in Christ is the extension of the incarnation and the anticipation of his second-coming; and the "contemporary Christ" and his creative and redemptive work is the real history underlying the happenings of contemporary life and world events. Devanandan sees the pledge of the new creation both within the Church and without it. For all persons now share in the new creation in Christ. A new humanity is now in the making, in which all persons are being reconciled to God, one to another, and each to his own self.

Like Chenchiah, Devanandan emphasized that the new creation in Christ is not merely something that touches human history from without as a tangent touches a circle; instead it becomes a process that takes hold of the process of human history from within, and gives it shape and direction. It makes it possible for faith to look for the signs of God's new creation in Christ, not only in the transformed lives of individuals, but also in the struggles and purposes of men to renew structures of society, culture, and religion and to transform earth and heaven in the name of the dignity and destiny of man. Further, he affirms that not only the ultimate end but also the pattern of God's judging and saving action to renew creation here and now is revealed in some measure to faith. This is the basis of prophecy and service. Thus, through the forgiveness and reconciling power of God in Jesus Christ, the process is held within the judgment and fulfilment of the process of the new creation, inaugurated in the cross and in the resurrection of Christ and moving forward to its consummation.

NOTES

1. Charles Ranson, *The Christian Minister in India* (London: Lutterworth Press, 1946).

2. M.H. Harrison, *After Ten Years* (Nagpur: NCC of India, 1957).

3. See *Theological Education in India: Report of Study Programme and Consultation, 1967–68* (Board of Theological Education of the NCC of India and Senate of Serampore College, 1968), p. 6.

4. *Ibid.*, p. 7.

5. *Ibid.*

6. *Ibid.*, p. 8.

7. Bengt Sundkler, *Church of South India: The Movement Towards Union, 1900–1947* (London: Lutterworth Press, 1954).

8. G.C. Oosthuizen, *Theological Battleground in Asia and Africa* (London: Hurst, 1972).

9. "The Church of South India is competent to issue supplementary statements concerning the faith for the guidance of its teachers and the edification of the faithful, provided that such statements are not contrary to the truths of our religion revealed in the Holy Scriptures." *The Constitution of the Church of South India* (Madras: CLS, 1952), p. 5.

10. Sophia Dobson Collet, ed., *The Life and Letters of Raja Rammohun Roy* (London, 1900). Also see Joshua Marshman, *A Defence of the Deity and Atonement of Jesus Christ in Reply to Rammohun Roy of Calcutta* (London, 1822).

11. L.B. Day, *An Antidote to Brahmoism in Four Lectures*, 1867; K.M. Banerjee, *Dialogues on Hindu Philosophy*, 1861; N. Goreh, *Theism and Christianity*, 1882; P. Ramabai, *A Testimony*, 1917.

12. Keshub Chunder Sen, "That Marvellous Mystery—The Trinity" (1882) in Manilal C. Parekh, *Bramarshi Keshub Chunder Sen* (Rajkot, 1931), pp. 152–67.

13. See J. Russell Chandran's unpublished thesis (Oxford University, 1949), "Christian Apologetics in Relation to Vivekananda in the Light of Origen, *Contra Celsum*," Appendix C, p. 216.

14. *The Gospel of Ramakrishna* (New York: Ramakrishna Vivekananda Center, 1942), p. 35.

15. See S. Radhakrishnan, *Eastern Religions and Western Thought* (Oxford: Clarendon Press, 1939).

16. E.W. Thompson, *The Word of the Cross to Hindus* (London: Epworth Press, 1933).

17. Nicol Macnicol, *Is Christianity Unique?* (London: SCM Press, 1936).

18. Chandran, *op. cit.*, p. 347.

19. *Ibid.*, p. 340. Chandran is here referring to C.C.J. Webb, *God and Personality* (London, Allen and Unwin, 1918), pp. 61–88, 241–75.

20. A.J. Appasamy, *What Is Moksha?* (Madras: CLS, 1931), p. 9.

21. A.J. Appasamy, *My Theological Quest* (Bangalore: CISRS, 1964).

22. Appasamy, *What Is Moksha?*, p. 112.

23. Appasamy, *My Theological Quest*, p. 32.

24. Surjit Singh, *Preface to Personality* (Madras: CLS, 1952).

25. S. Radhakrishnan, *The Reign of Religion in Contemporary Philosophy* (London: Macmillan, 1920), p. 411.

26. *Ibid.*, pp. 136–37.

27. Singh, *op. cit.*, pp. 109f.

28. *Ibid.*, pp. 112f.

29. *Ibid.*, p. 113.

30. D.G. Moses, *Religious Truth and the Relation between Religions*, (Madras: CLS, 1950).

31. *Ibid.*, p. 114.

32. *Ibid.*, pp. 116–17.

33. *Ibid.*, pp. 118–19.

34. Mahatma Gandhi, *The Message of Jesus Christ*, compiled by Anand T. Hingorani (Bombay: Bharatiya Vidya Bhavan, 1963). See also Gandhi's *What Jesus Means to Me*, compiled by R.K. Prabhu (Ahmedabad: Navajivan, 1959).

35. Mahatma Gandhi, *Christian Missions: Their Place in India*, B. Kumarappa, ed. (Ahmedabad: Navajivan, 1941).

36. Gandhi, *Message*, p. 79.

37. *Ibid.*, p. 12.

38. *Ibid.*, p. 51.

39. E. Stanley Jones, *Mahatma Gandhi: An Interpretation* (London: Hodder & Stoughton, 1948).

40. *Ibid.*, pp. 80f.

41. *Ibid.*, p. 85.

42. E. Stanley Jones, *Christ of the Indian Road* (New York: Abingdon Press, 1925).

43. Bernard Lucas, *Our Task in India* (London: Macmillan, 1914).

44. See T.K. Thomas, "The Christian Task in India: An Introduction to the Thought of Bernard Lucas," *Religion and Society* XV, 3 (1968), 20–31.

45. Kaj Baago, *The Movement around Subba Rao* (Madras: CLS for CISRS, 1968).

46. J.N. Farquhar, *The Crown of Hinduism* (London: Oxford University Press, 1913). Cf. Eric J. Sharpe, *Not to Destroy But to Fulfil. The Contribution of J.N. Farquhar to Protestant Missionary Thought in India before 1914* (Lund: Gleerup, 1965).

47. J.N. Farquhar, *Modern Religious Movements in India* (New York: Macmillan, 1915).

48. *Heritage of India Series* (16 vols.; Calcutta: YMCA Literature Dept. 1915–1923).

49. A.G. Hogg, *Karma and Redemption* (Madras: CLS, 1909). Cf. Eric J. Sharpe, *The Theology of A.G. Hogg* (Madras: CLS for CISRS, 1971).

50. Hendrik Kraemer, *The Christian Message in a Non-Christian World* (New York: Harper's, 1938).

51. C.F. Andrews, *The Ideal of Indian Nationality* (Allahabad: Indian Press, 1907).

52. C.F. Andrews, *The Renaissance in India: Its Missionary Aspect (Madras: CLS, 1913)*.

53. S.K. Rudra, *Christ and Modern India* (originally an article in *The Student Movement*, January 1910).

54. S.K. Datta, *The Desire of India* (Edinburgh: Church of Scotland, Foreign Missions Committee, 1908).

55. K.T. Paul, *The British Connection with India* (London: SCM Press, 1928).

56. Paul, *op. cit.*, pp. 198f.

57. S.K. Rudra, quoted by Andrews in *The Renaissance in India*, pp. 248–51.

58. Andrews, *The Renaissance in India*, p. 174.

59. *Christian Participation in Nation–Building* (Bangalore: CISRS, 1960).

60. P. Chenchiah et al., *Rethinking Christianity in India* (Madras: A.N. Sudarisanam, 1938).

61. V. Chakkarai, *Jesus the Avatar* (Madras: CLS, 1926).

62. V. Chakkarai, *The Cross and Indian Thought* (Madras: CLS, 1932).

63. D.A. Thangasamy, *The Theology of Chenchiah* (Bangalore: CISRS, 1966).

64. P.T. Thomas, *The Theology of Chakkarai* (Bangalore: CISRS, 1968).

65. Marcus Ward, *Our Theological Task: An Introduction to the Study of Theology in India* (Madras: CLS, 1946).

66. P. Chenchiah in *The Guardian*, 1947.

67. Ward, *op. cit.*, pp. 1f.

68. *Ibid.*, pp. 2f.
69. *Rethinking Christianity in India, op. cit.*, p. 56.
70. *The Guardian*, 1950, pp. 352 ff.
71. *Ibid.*
72. P. Chenchiah in *The Guardian*, 1947, in a review and restatement of Marcus Ward's *Our Theological Task*.
73. Paul D. Devanandan, *Christian Concern in Hinduism* (Bangalore: CISRS, 1961), pp. 119–120.

Theological Construction in a Buddhist Context

The Cultural Background

In Sri Lanka (formerly Ceylon), an island republic situated off the southern tip of India, with a population of over thirteen million, the predominant position of Buddhism has always been a crucial concern of the Christian community. From the time of the introduction of Buddhism to Ceylon in the third century B.C. up to now, this little island has had a long and dominant tradition of Buddhism and Buddhist culture, which has been the fundamental basis of its national and religious heritage.

Two dominant characteristics have been evident in this Buddhist national heritage. One is the religio-national solidarity. From the very beginning Buddhism was recognized and accepted by the state as its official religion. There has been a close-knit interpenetration of religion and state, of monk and monarch, as in the West. The other characteristic is the sense of destiny and mission. The Buddhists believe that they are the "chosen people" and that Sri Lanka is the land favored by the Buddha, the land in which the *Dhamma* (Buddhist doctrine) will shine in all its glory, its light radiating throughout the world. Tradition has it that the Buddha hallowed this land by visiting it three times. Before he passed away he instructed Sakka, the chief god, to take good care of Vijaya, who was to be the founder of the Sinhalese race; it was the Enlightened One's belief that the Dhamma would be established and preserved in its pristine purity in this land for the good of the world.

However, with the advent of the colonial powers early in the sixteenth century, and the establishment of the Western hegemony over Ceylon, conditions began to change. The Portuguese (1505–1658), followed by the Dutch (1658–1796), held the coastal areas under subjection, destroyed many Buddhist temples, persecuted the monks, and converted many Buddhists to Christianity by indiscriminately baptizing them. Then the British, who had expelled the Dutch from Ceylon in 1796, conquered the central Kandyan kingdom in 1815 and became the rulers of the whole island.

As a result of the onslaught of Western culture, Buddhism began to decline, and Buddhists lost many of the privileges they had enjoyed under the native rulers. With the gaining of Ceylon's independence in 1948, however, Buddhist leaders started a movement to restore to Buddhism the pre-eminent position it had occupied in the past. The Republic of Sri Lanka, which came into being in May 1972, has given to Buddhism "the foremost place," while granting to every citizen the right to freedom of thought, conscience, and religion. Two of the dominant factors in the Buddhist resurgence are (a) the religio-national desire to reintegrate nationalism and Buddhism, and (b) the positive missionary determination to carry the light of the Dhamma to the ends of the world.

Buddhists feel that Christianity—an ally of Western culture and Western imperialism—is an obstacle to their objectives. Hence there is a psychological aversion to, and fear and suspicion of, Christianity. This attitude is reflected in the following statement from *The Betrayal of Buddhism:*

> For 23 centuries Lanka has been nourished with the quintessence of human thought, the sublime teaching of the Sumbuddha, the Supremely Enlightened One, and now the people of this Buddhist Lanka are being asked to give it up for crude teachings of the unenlightened teachers, for exploded beliefs, outworn theories and played-out philosophies. The Buddhists do not want to exchange gold for lead, or bread for filth; they want to hold fast to their compassionate, refined, and reasonable view of life, and their noble culture which is founded on the Dhamma.[1]

This report betrays an attitude of intolerance and hostility that is quite contrary to the teachings of the Compassionate One, an attitude which the Buddhists have condemned in Christian missionary activity. But it indicates the mood of the Budhhists in Sri Lanka today. Christianity is looked down upon as a foreign religion, and the

Christian movement is regarded as a remnant of the colonial era. Even dialogue between the two religions is suspect, regarded by some as a tactical move, a smoke screen, to break down the mental resistance of the Buddhists and to lure the unwary among them into the Christian fold. In the face of these charges the Christians have been inclined to stay more or less in the background and to wait with folded arms for better times.

THE CHRISTIAN ATTITUDE TOWARD BUDDHISM

The early missionaries who came to Sri Lanka believed that Christianity was the only true religion and that all other religions were not only false but also destructive to the souls of men. Buddhism was regarded as the citadel of Satan and a religion that had to be renounced because it contained errors which were diametrically opposed to the true belief in God the Creator.

At the beginning of the twentieth century, however, there was a change in the attitude toward Buddhism which was symptomatic of the changing attitude in other parts of the world. This new outlook was reflected in the book *Gautama or Jesus?* by A. Stanley Bishop, a British Methodist missionary who served in Sri Lanka. In the Introduction he says:

> The apparently wide difference between the teachings of Gautama Buddha and of Jesus Christ have led many to suppose that there is very little in common between the two systems. Some have even been entrapped into the statement that Buddhist doctrine is in direct opposition to Christianity, or vice versa, and that there is no common ground upon which the Buddhist and the Christian may meet for mutual help. It is hard for anyone who is at all conversant with Buddhism to maintain the position so often adopted—that the Christian has nothing to learn and all to teach. Neither statement is based on anything surer than ignorance. . . . These pages are written in an attempt to show that, although the Christian may receive much light and stimulus from the teaching of the Buddha, the Buddhist may receive from Christ what Gautama was never in a position to give.[2]

Another significant step foward in this new direction was taken by the late D. T. Niles. In his book *Eternal Life Now*,[3] Dr. Niles seeks to cast the Christian message in a Buddhist mold and in the Buddhist style of writing by the use of such terms as *anicca, dukkha, samsara, anatta, sila, samadhi, panna* and *arahat*. In this book we find on the one hand a statement of the truths of Buddhism within the context of Christian faith; and on the other, a statement of the Christian message in the terms and thought-forms of the Buddhists.

The conviction of the need to restate the Christian message in a Buddhist idiom grew stronger after Ceylon became independent in 1948 and after the Buddha Jayanti (the 2500th anniversary of Buddhism) in 1956. In the dynamic context of the resurgence of Buddhism, Christians are placed in a situation full of challenges and opportunities. It was partly as a response to this that the Study Centre for Religion and Society was set up in Colombo in 1953 and became a Centre for Buddhist studies in 1962. One of the major concerns of this centre is to provide facilities for a comprehensive study of Buddhism, with a view to helping the church communicate the Gospel meaningfully to the Buddhists and to enter into dialogue with them.[4] As a result of these efforts there is now emerging an indigenous expression of the Christian faith based on a theological structure oriented to the conceptual framework of Buddhism.

THE HUMAN PREDICAMENT

The Three Marks of Existence

Buddhism has analyzed the human predicament in terms of the *Tilakkhana*, or the Three Signata—anicca, dukkha and anatta. These are the three fundamental marks of all existence. The essence of the Buddha's teaching is summed up in the Tilakkhana, and this forms the conceptual framework of Buddhism. *Anicca* affirms that all conditioned things change and are in a perpetual state of flux; *anatta* affirms that nothing changes, for there is no soul or any permanent entity in man; *dukkha* affirms that conditioned nature, being transient and "soul"-less, is the source of conflict, pain, and anxiety. At first glance this Tilakkhana concept appears to conflict with Christian belief, but a closer examination will show that it offers an analysis of the human predicament which can provide a theological framework for an expression of Christian faith in the context of Buddhist thought.

The Tilakkhana concept arose, not from a theoretical interest —empirical, psychological, or biological—but from the existential concern of Prince Siddhartha, who later became the Buddha. Hence, the Buddhist analysis of the human predicament can best be understood from the existential, or experiential, point of view.

Prince Siddhartha's experience of "ontological shock"—when his eyes met with the three sights of an old man, an invalid, and a corpse, symbolizing anicca, dukkha, and anatta and signifying the possibility of nonbeing;[5] and the sight of the serene hermit, signifying the possibility of self-affirmation against nonbeing—provides a sort of paradigm for the understanding of the human predicament. This paradigmatic experience points to the ambiguous situation in which man finds himself—pulled between the two poles of self-disintegration in finitude and self-affirmation in freedom. It is this ambiguity that drives man to seek authentic being and the reality that authenticates being. It is the experience of Everyman that has found expression in modern existential writings.

Some modern writers describe the human predicament in terms of anxiety, which has three aspects that can be expressed in terms of the Three Signata. First, anxiety is the state in which a being is *aware* of the fact of anicca (the possibility of nonbeing); secondly, this awareness is due to the fact that nonbeing is part of one's own being, since man is anatta (he does not have an immortal soul); thirdly, it is an "existential awareness" in which finitude is *experienced* as one's own finitude (the experience of dukkha).[6]

The term "dukkha" is used in the ordinary as well as the wide sense. In the ordinary sense it means all mental and bodily sufferings brought about by disease, aging, loss of loved ones, disappointments, and so forth. In the wide sense it indicates the human predicament in all its aspects, comprehending the totality of existence. Dukkha is an experiential fact whose manifold meaning, such as dissatisfaction, unrest, anxiety, despair, disharmony, estrangement, and conflict, can perhaps be best expressed by the phrase "existential anxiety."

According to the Buddhist analysis of finitude, everything changes and lacks substantiality, that is, all is anicca and anatta. On this basis we must conclude that nothing in itself, nothing in conditioned existence, has the power to resist nonbeing. Hence nothing in finite existence can be the source of that which enables man to transcend nonbeing. This accounts for the anxiety about change itself, since anxiety about change is anxiety about the threat of nonbeing and of the possible loss of self that is implied by change. It reaches its most radical form in the face of the threat of death, when the loss of self-identity is anticipated.

Crucial to the Buddhist analysis of the human predicament is the doctrine of anatta. Analytically, Buddhism sees the so-called individual as a psycho-physical compound (*nama-rupa*), consisting of the five aggregates, namely, *rupa* (form), *vedana* (feelings), *sanna* (perceptions), *samskara* (ideations), and *vinnana* (thought). Each of these aspects is minutely analyzed and shown to be devoid of any soul-substance. Thus Buddhism rejects the theory that there is an immortal, immutable soul, an unchanging entity, or an undying essence. There is nothing real in man which corresponds to such words as "I," "me," "mine." These words are used in a conventional sense and do not represent any reality or fact.

It is usually assumed that on this crucial point Buddhism and Christianity are in complete opposition. But the fact is that a great deal of the anatta doctrine has biblical support. For example, although the notion of an immortal soul is deeply embedded in popular Christian thinking and has influenced theology to some extent, biblical scholarship has established quite conclusively that there is no dichotomous concept of man in the Bible, such as is found in Greek philosophy. The biblical view of man is holistic, not dualistic, and the notion of the "soul" as an immortal entity that enters the body at birth and leaves it at death is quite foreign to it. According to the Bible, man is a unity of *psyche* (soul), *soma* (body), *sarx* (flesh), *nous* (mind), and so forth. These diverse aspects, all together, constitute the whole man, and none (not even *psyche*), has the capability to separate itself from the total structure and continue to have an independent existence.

The psycho-physical unity of man (or the psychosomatic unity, according to modern medical parlance) can thus be analyzed as psyche (soul) and sarx (flesh), which bears a close resemblance to the Buddhist nama-rupa. Psyche, like nama, corresponds to the psychical aspect of man in modern science and represents the processes which come within the field of psychology. Sarx, like rupa, corresponds to physical processes with which the biologist is concerned. Just as in Buddhism man is a unity of nama-rupa, so in the Bible man is a unity of psyche-soma; just as Buddhism says that there is no soul entity within the *nama-rupa* complex, so the Bible leaves no room for a notion of an immortal soul within the psyche-sarx unity of man. Thus we could speak of a biblical doctrine of anatta.

In a sense Christianity goes beyond Buddhism in its doctrine of anatta. Buddhism, while denying the self, teaches that man, by a natural right, has the moral capacity or sufficiency to determine his own destiny and to "save" himself. In contrast, Christianity says man is nothing by himself and can do nothing by himself to earn his salvation. However, while Christianity goes further than Buddhism in denying the soul entity in man and independent self-sufficiency, it does not deny the reality of the person. It is at this point that we come to a crucial issue. How can we in one sense deny the self and in another sense affirm the self? This is a question we shall presently take up.

TILAKKHANA IN THE BIBLICAL CONTEXT

The polarity, or conflict, that lies at the core of human existence is a familiar biblical theme. One passage, of particular relevance in the context of Buddhism, is Romans 8:18–25, which depicts the human predicament. Saint Paul says here that the present condition of creation is bondage to futility, and in that condition the whole created universe groans and travails in all its parts, and we also groan inwardly. This groaning is not to be treated lightly because of the hope of redemption. "There is here no overlooking or toning down of human suffering in order to offer some more solid consolation," says Karl Barth. Saint Paul is not attempting to "redress the tribulation of the world by fixing our attention upon the compensating harmony of another world." He sees that "beneath each slight discomfort; and notably beneath the greater miseries of human life, there stands clearly visible the vast ambiguity of its finiteness."[7] The whole universe shares this finiteness. *Ktisis* and *pasa he ktisis* here mean the whole created order—man, bird, beast, trees, everything. Nothing is exempt.

In describing the human predicament Paul uses three terms: *mataiotes, pathemata,* and *phthora,* which have close approximations to the Pali terms anicca, dukkha, and anatta, respectively. The Buddhistic overtones of the Greek words are striking. By use of these terms

Paul says (1) that the whole universe is in "bondage to decay."
(*Mataiotes mataioteton* is a refrain of the "Vanity of vanities . . . all is
vanity" of Ecclesiastes. It means that all things are subject to corruption and decay. All things are perishable and hence impermanent
[anicca].) (2) The whole of creation is groaning in travail. (That is
what dukkha means.) (3) All things are subject to dissolution and
decay; the universe is in a fallen state. (Here there is an allusion to
Genesis 3:17b and 19—man is dust and to dust he must return. He is
anatta.)

Thus we could describe the human predicament in terms of the
Tilakkhana, for there is much in this Buddhist analytic which Christian theology can accept. But the difference is in the solution that the
two religions offer.

The Buddhist solution consists in the complete extinction of the
notion of the self by the eradication of its cause, *tanha* (craving, desire,
thirst for existence). Buddhism holds that this does not amount to
annihilation of the self (*uccedaditthi*), yet at the same time it affirms its
rejection of all eternalistic notions of the self (*sassataditthi*). How to
explain this baffling paradox has always been a problem for Buddhist
theologians.

The Christian solution to the problem consists in an understanding
of authentic selfhood as being constituted in a relationship signified
by the term "spirit." "Spirit" describes a relationship to another in
which the "I" and "Thou" relate in mutual co-inherence, preserving
genuine self-identity without the need to affirm a soul entity.

To be is to be related. The individual exists through his relationship with others. In stepping into a relationship with others, an
individual can reach beyond himself, and by such self-transcendence
the self can be both negated and affirmed. In this "I"–"Thou" relationship is to be found an understanding of anatta, which denies the
soul without yielding to a nihilistic view, and which affirms the
authentic self without yielding to an eternalistic view. The "I" is not
in me or in thee, but in the relationship between me and thee.
Personality is the identity of the self in the mutuality of the "I" and the
"Thou," and to lose the "I" in thee is to find myself in communion.
Because the authentic self is not found in an individual, isolated being
but in a relationship, man is really anatta, that is, a "no-self" in and by
himself. This does not amount to nihilism because the authentic self is

not denied. But this affirmation of the authentic self does not amount to eternalism either, because it is not an individual possession which makes man immortal in his own right. It is in this relationship that man can deny himself (become anatta) or lose himself; it is also in this relationship that man can find his authentic self.

The loss of individuality (anatta) that constitutes the fulfilment of personality is the essence of the experience of love, and love is the basis of the co-inhering mutuality of the "I" and the "Thou." This love was pefectly demonstrated in the incarnation, death, and resurrection of Jesus Christ, in which he gave all without reserve, making himself nothing (Phil. 2:7–8) and in which he received all without change (Phil. 2:9–11). The law of love is the law of give-and-take, where all is given without reserve and all is received without loss. In love was perfectly demonstrated in the incarnation, death, and resuralone that is capable of negating exclusive individuality and completing and fulfilling personality. Herein we find the Buddhist quest for self-negation and herein we find the answer to man's quest for self-fulfilment.

NIBBANA AND THE KINGDOM

What happens finally? What is the nature of the consummate goal? Is it extinction, absorption, or distinction? The Buddhist answer is immortalized in a famous stanza.

> Mere suffering exists, no sufferer is found;
> The deed is, but no doer of the deed is there;
> Nirvana is, but not the man that enters it;
> The Path is, but no traveller on it is seen.[8]

In this the essential principle of self-negation, or anatta, is preserved, but the dilemma of the Buddhists is to explain that this does not mean the total extinction of the self in Nibbana (emancipation, state of release). Is there a Christian insight that could satisfy the Buddhist quest for both self-negation and fulfilment, without one concept contradicting the other? Perhaps the answer could be found in a deeper understanding of love as defined above, and of the kingdom of God as the perfection of love, fellowship, and communion.

On the one hand there can be no perfect communion, union, or fellowship without the complete loss of self. As long as man has an exclusive notion of "I," "me," or "mine," he will exclude himself from fellowship. In trying to separate oneself from others and to sever all connections, a person "individualizes" himself; but in doing so he loses his real nature, which ultimately could lead to the extinction of the self. It is in this regard that Jesus says: "He that seeketh himself shall lose himself." The right direction is not separation but integration, and for perfect integration there must be a total surrender of the exclusive self, a complete losing of oneself in communion with others. This means the extinction of the exclusive self—that is, the dying-out of separate individuality—and we could therefore speak of this goal in the negative sense in which the term *Nirvana* is used. *Tanha* (craving), and the notion of I-ness which is at the basis of tanha, are conquered. To the question, then, "Who is it that enters there?" we could give the traditional Buddhist answer, "no one," for there is no individualized, self-existent, exclusive being that enters there; there is no immortal soul that inherits the kingdom. In this sense Nirvana is an aspect of the kingdom of God.

On the other hand, perfect union implies a differentiation. Pierre Teilhard de Chardin explains that principle as follows:

> In any domain—whether it be cells of a body, the members of a society or the elements of a spiritual synthesis—union differentiates. In every organized whole, the parts perfect themselves and fulfil themselves. Through neglect of this universal rule many a system of pantheism has led us astray to the cult of a great All in which individuals were supposed to be merged like a drop in the ocean or like a dissolving grain of salt. Applied to the case of the summation of consciousness, the law of union rids us of this perilous and recurrent illusion. No, following the confluent orbits of their centres, the grains of consciousness do not tend to lose their outlines and blend, but, on the contrary, to accentuate the depth and incommunicability of their egos. The more "other" they become in conjunction, the more they find themselves as "self."[9]

The more "other," the more "self." "Union differentiates." But this differentiation is not a mark of exclusive individuality. It is an identity within a totality. It is not union in the sense of absorption, but of communion. It is not identity in the sense of a persisting self-contained entity, but a recognizability in a relationship, for we become persons only in a relationship.

The kingdom of God is the perfect synthesis of the universal and the particular. Here there is no self-conscious differentiation, but God-conscious wholeness. Both the principle of self-negation, which is the Buddhist quest, and the principle of self-realization find fulfilment in the kingdom of God without one contradicting the other. In the final state, in keeping with the nirvanic principle of self-negation, we shall cease completely to be separate individuals; but we shall be fully persons in keeping with the nature of eternal life.

The transition to this new dimension which we call eternal life is not the moment of death but the moment of spiritual rebirth. What this spiritual rebirth means is expressed in 1 Peter 1: 3–5, a passage in which are enunciated three truths that are of great significance in the context of Buddhism. Spiritual rebirth, Peter says, leads to an inheritance that is "imperishable, undefiled, and unfading." These three terms are in striking contrast to the Buddhist terms anicca, dukkha, anatta. Through the resurrection of Jesus Christ these three negativities of *samsaric* existence are conquered, and their opposites are made available to those who enter into a relationship with him in faith and love.

The Relevance of the Cross

How can we explain the relevance of the death and the resurrection of Jesus Christ to our understanding of the human predicament? One of the passages that can provide a basis for such an explanation is Philippians 2: 7–11, in which Paul speaks of the *kenosis* of our Lord. Kenotic Christology has gone out of fashion in Western theology and has even been treated with contempt; it has been called the kenosis of understanding. But it has a deep significance in relation to the Tilakkhana analytic of the human predicament when it is understood, not as the emptying of the divinity of our Lord, but as the negation of the self in which the divinity of love is disclosed. The negation of the self is the affirmation of love in which the self is not lost, but transcended. J.A.T. Robinson has suggested that this is how we should interpret the kenotic theory:

> It is in Jesus, and Jesus alone, that there is nothing of self to be seen, but solely the ultimate, unconditional love of God. It is as he emptied himself utterly of himself that he became the carrier of "the name which is above

every name," the revealer of the Father's glory—for that name and that glory is simply Love. The "kenotic" theory of Christology, based on this conception of self-emptying, is, I am persuaded, the only one that offers much hope of relating at all satisfactorily the divine and the human in Christ.[10]

The essential principle of the divine kenosis, based on the conception of self-emptying, is that Christ negated himself without losing himself. By his identity with conditioned existence he negated himself; but because of his identity with the Unconditioned (God), he did not lose himself. This identity was a relationship between the conditioned and the Unconditioned. But it was unique in that it was a relationship concerning the Unconditioned identity of the conditioned and the Unconditioned. This is the principle of kenosis, which has affinities with the Buddhist doctrine of *Sunyata* (the doctrine of the void).

IDENTITY WITH THE CONDITIONED

In the three assertions in Philippians 2:7–8 concerning Christ's identification with conditioned existence, we find echoes of the Tilakkhana—dukkha, anatta, and anicca—the fundamental marks of conditional existence.

The first assertion is that Christ took upon himself the *morphe* (form, condition, nature) of a *doulos* (slave or servant). The real significance of the word "slave" lies in the suggestion it carries of the suffering servant in Isaiah 53:4–5. Christ took upon himself the suffering of the world. He took dukkha upon himself in order to redeem man from the state of dukkha. This is the truth expressed in Hebrews 2:10: "It was clearly fitting that God for whom and through whom all things exist should, in bringing many sons of glory, make the leader who delivers them perfect through suffering."

The second assertion is that Christ was born (*genomenos*=become) in the likeness (*schema*) of man and appeared in human form (morphe). The word "schema" denotes shape and appearance, as distinguished from substance (morphe). Joseph Barber Lightfoot sums up the meaning of these two words by saying that the nature (morphe) is intrinsic and essential, whereas the likeness (schema) is accidental and outward. The actual human form in which Christ appeared was secondary, but he *really* took a human nature. He became (*ginesthai*) like every man born into the world and took upon himself the real conditions to which all men are subject. There is no room here for the Docetic view that Christ's form appeared to be human, but was actually a spiritual body. The Word really became flesh. To be born in the likeness of man is to be mortal like every man, who has no immortal soul. By becoming man Christ took upon himself this human nature.

The third assertion is that Christ became obedient even unto death, the death on the cross. Death is the ultimate mark of impermanence. The important character of conditioned existence, which Christ shared with mankind by becoming a slave and a mortal man, came to a climax in his death. In the garden of Gethsemane he experienced the anxiety that comes to all men in the face of death. That anxiety was not relieved by the expectation of the resurrection, so he was greatly troubled and prayed that the cup might pass away from him. On the cross he tasted the horror of the possibility of being ultimately lost, and he cried out: "My God, my God, why hast Thou forsaken me?" He died a real death like all men. Like every mortal being he shared the nature of anicca of all things. Thus, in his kenosis Christ became *sunya* and identified Himself fully with conditioned existence, which bears the marks of dukkha, anatta, and anicca.

IDENTITY WITH THE UNCONDITIONED

Although Jesus Christ identified himself with conditioned existence, at the same time He maintained a permanent unity with the Unconditioned (God). His kenosis was also a *plerosis*. It is only he who is totally empty who can be totally full. In Christ, kenosis and plerosis, *sunnata* and *punnata* met in a unique way. In emptying himself fully, he negated negation itself and thereby conquered the negativities of existence.

There are three major antitheses in the passage under consideration which indicate the plerosis-kenosis, sunnata-punnata identity of Jesus:

1. Though he was humiliated in his suffering and took the form of a servant, he was exalted to the highest station and given a name above every other name. The word "name" implies character and status. He suffered, but in his suffering, borne for the redemption of mankind, he glorified God. Dukkha was thus transformed into a manifestation

of God's glory by his participation in the Eternal who alone is Felicity (cf. 1 Timothy 1:11 in N.E.B.).

2. Though he was born "in likeness of man," he was in the "form of God." There is no suggestion that he renounced his divine morphe. He was one with man and one with God at the same time. By his simultaneous participation in man and God, anatta was conquered in his being by being brought into participation with the Unconditioned.

3. Though he subjected himself to death and became *anicca*, so to speak, "every tongue confesses that Jesus is Lord." All the spirit-powers of the three worlds—heaven, earth, and the underworld—to whose tyranny Christ submitted himself as a slave, now acclaim him as Lord. He became Lord of the Universe. Thus anicca was conquered in his being by his participation in the Deathless (*amata*). Thus Christ negated himself without losing himself. Negation and elevation happened together in his kenosis. This was possible because in a unique sense his identity with the conditioned was an unconditioned identity.

THE UNCONDITIONED IDENTITY

Thus far we have stated that Christ identified himself with the conditioned in his kenosis and that he maintained a unity with the Unconditioned at the same time. Thus, in his kenosis there was the identity of the conditioned and the Unconditioned. But, as we have stated earlier, the doctrine of emptiness means the unconditioned identity of the conditioned and the Unconditioned. In what sense is this identity unconditioned?

In the Christological hymn we are considering, there is an implied contrast between Christ's emptying himself and not snatching at equality with God, and Adam's wilful act of grasping at equality with God. Adam's act, Everyman's act, is motivated by tanha (greed or desire or presumptuousness). But in Christ's act of emptying himself there was no trace of tanha, which binds man to conditioned existence and puts him under the power of anicca, dukkha, and anatta. Christ was sinless; hence, conditioned existence had no power over him. His identity with conditioned existence was therefore an unconditioned identity and he was thus able to negate himself without losing himself. And this is what makes it possible for mortal man to lose himself and yet find himself, by being "in Christ," by participation in him. To be in Christ means to experience a kenosis—a negation and an elevation of the self. It is the experience of the "I am undone" of Isaiah and the "I, yet not I" of Saint Paul. Self-negation and elevation is the spiritual principle behind the concepts of anatta and Nirvana. This principle is that in which is revealed, when we have brought to light the nothingness of our human selfhood, the fulness of our being, a fulness that we find in communion with the Ultimate Reality. In this fulness of being we shall cease completely to be individuals and be fully persons. Our differentiation as persons will remain without that differentiation being expressed in the exclusiveness of self-contained individuality. We shall retain personal identity within a complete harmony. The relationship in which we live on earth, the relationship of love, will be fulfilled in the kingdom of God, except that the implications of exclusiveness in that relationship will cease to have meaning. The disappearance of exclusive individuality and the ensuing bliss is an experience that can be described in terms of Nirvana; it is an experience of negation and elevation in which one loses oneself and finds oneself in communion with God.

NOTES

1. In reply to this 1956 report of the Buddhist Committee of Inquiry (Introduction, pp. iii–iv), the NCC of Ceylon, in that same year, put out a pamphlet, "Some Reflections on *The Betrayal of Buddhism.*"

2. A. Stanley Bishop, *Gautama or Jesus?* (Colombo: Kollupitiya Press, 1907), pp. 1–2.

3. D.T. Niles, *Eternal Life Now* (Colombo: Ceylon Printers, 1946). American edition published under the title *Buddhism and the Claims of Christ* (Richmond, Va.: John Knox Press, 1967).

4. A similar study center has been set up in Jaffna to serve the needs of the church in the Hindu cultural context.

5. Friedrich Nietzsche refers to these three sights in the chapter "The Preachers of Death" in *Thus Spake Zarathustra*, trans. R.J. Hollingdale (New York: Penguin Books, 1961; reprinted 1971), pp. 71–73. Paul Tillich quotes Nietzsche in this instance in *Courage to Be* (New Haven, Conn.: Yale University Press, 1952), p. 27.

6. See Paul Tillich's analysis of anxiety in *Courage to Be*, pp. 36–37.

7. Karl Barth, *The Epistle to the Romans*, 6th ed., trans. Edwyn C. Hoskyns (London: Oxford University Press, 1933), pp. 302–303.

8. *Visuddhi Magga* XVI.

9. Pierre Teilhard de Chardin, *The Phenomenon of Man* (London: Collins, 1959), p. 262.

10. John A. T. Robinson, *Honest to God* (Philadelphia: Westminster Press, 1963), p. 74.

Theologizing for Selfhood and Service

I, Moung Nau, the constant recipient of your excellent favor, approach your feet. Whereas my Lord's three have come to the country of Burma—not for the purposes of trade, but to preach the religion of Jesus Christ, the Son of the eternal God—I, having heard and understood, am, with a joyful mind, filled with love.

I believe that the divine Son, Jesus Christ, suffered death, in the place of men, to atone for their sins. Like a heavy-laden man, I feel my sins are very many. The punishment of my sins I deserve to suffer. Since it is so, do you, sirs, consider that I, taking refuge in the merits of the Lord Jesus Christ, and receiving baptism, in order to become his disciple, shall dwell one with yourselves, a band of brothers, in the happiness of heaven, and therefore grant me the ordinance of baptism? It is through the grace of Jesus Christ that you, sirs, have come by ship from one country and continent to another, and that we have met together. I pray my Lord's three that a suitable day may be appointed, and that I may receive the ordinance of baptism.

Moreover, as it is only since I have met with you, sirs, that I have known about the eternal God, I venture to pray that you will still unfold to me the religion of God, that my old disposition may be destroyed, and my new disposition improved.[1]

This letter, now exactly one hundred fifty-five years old, was written by the first Burmese convert to Christian discipleship. The letter, addressed to Adoniram Judson, the famous Baptist missionary to Burma, and his companions, may be described as the first recorded Christian writing by a Burmese in church history. This earliest confession speaks of the convert's conviction of sin, faith in Christ and the sufficiency of His atonement on the cross, the desire to be part of

53

the fellowship of believers, and his need for Christian nurture and education. It is interesting to note that within a brief letter asking for baptism, U Nau (this earliest convert) had touched on the essentials of the faith. The letter, directly translated from Burmese into English by Dr. Judson, showed how the traditional Burmese vocabulary was used by U Nau in the confession of his faith. The Buddhists speak of taking refuge in the three jewels, namely, the Buddha, the Dharma (the Word), and the Sangha (the church). U Nau significantly used the phrase "taking refuge in the merits of the Lord Jesus Christ." Regarding his request that he "may receive the ordinance of baptism," Dr. Judson added a footnote: "At the time of writing this, not having heard much of baptism, he seems to have ascribed an undue efficacy to the ordinance. He has since corrected his error; but the translator thinks it the most fair and impartial to give the letter just as it was written at first."[2]

It is understandable that the confession of the first Burmese Christian would naturally employ vocabulary and thought-forms which were meaningful to one living in a Buddhist context. It is especially interesting that Dr. Judson had no comment about the use of the traditional religious terminology as the convert spoke of "taking refuge in the merits of the Lord Jesus Christ," but dug beneath the convert's use of the term "ordinance" for baptism and indicated the necessity of correcting his misconception about the nature and character of the rite. The earlier case was the employment of vocabulary which had no consequence of substance to the confession of the faith, while the latter required the examination of thought-forms beyond the employment of vocabulary which readily communicated in a Buddhist setting. We have dwelt at the outset on this problem of confession in a specific cultural setting because on the one hand, the theological developments in the history of the church in Burma have been very much influenced by the cultural pressures of society in which the church has come into being; and on the other, by the attempts of Christians to convey the claims of Christ over against those of tradition, family, and nation.

Before proceeding further, a brief reference to the total religious heritage and setting of Burma may be in order here. The tall golden pagoda dominating the landscape at Rangoon, the capital city of Burma, provides a landmark in the religious heritage of the country.

Tradition dates the construction of this pagoda back to the sixth century B.C. At that time two traders went from Burma to India, where they met the Buddha whom they implored to grant them some means of keeping fresh in their memory, when they returned home, the teachings they had heard from him. In response the Buddha gave them some threads of his hair, four of which traditionally were enshrined within the golden temple at Rangoon. Between these early beginnings of Buddhism and the growth of the Burmese nation, some Brahminic and other influences had set in. But the year 1057 A.D. might be described as the year of reformation in Burmese Buddhist Church history, for it was then that renewed study of the Tipitakas (the Scriptures) secured royal patronage, and impurities which had crept into the teaching and practice of Buddhism were discarded. The tradition of Burmese literature had dominant religious (that is, Buddhist) leanings, and it is well to remember that the New and Old Testaments were not available in the Burmese language until 1823 and 1834, respectively.

As far as the churches of the reformation in Burma were concerned, Christian apologetics of the early period were largely influenced by the two considerations referred to earlier—namely, the need to communicate the Gospel in intelligible terms to the Buddhists, and the necessity to emphasize the distinction between the Buddhist teachings and the claims of God in Christ Jesus. There is no doubt that the life and work of missionaries, particularly Adoniram Judson, dominated whatever theological thinking there was among the indigenous Christians of the nineteenth century. "A Burman Liturgy"[3] prepared in Burmese by Dr. Judson in 1829 to assist young missionaries and for use as a guide to indigenous assistants contained homage to the Triune God; the commands of righteousness and grace; formulas of worship; a creed in twelve articles; formulas for administering baptism, the Lord's Supper, for appointing a pastor, elder or bishop, for a deacon, and for a licentiate or an itinerant preacher. The last section contained provisionary rules, especially concerning church discipline, for the guidance of indigenous pastors. An appendix of thirty precepts, constituting a digest of Christian law, also formed a part of the material of the Burman Liturgy of 1829. Anyone with a knowledge of the Buddhist liturgy cannot help but note the similarity of their introductory structures. The Buddhist liturgy begins with an homage to the Triple Gem (the Buddha, the Scriptures, and the priesthood), while the Burman Liturgy began with homage to the Triune God. As the Buddhist liturgy goes on to the recitation of the precepts, the Burman Liturgy moves to a summary of the law. The creed in twelve articles, or a summary of the doctrine, began with the nature of the only eternal God and went on immediately to the Scriptures and their teachings on the nature of man, followed by articles on the Son, Jesus Christ, and the necessity of discipleship; it ended with three articles on eschatology declaring the hope of the faithful and the judgment of unbelievers.

These articles, formulated in 1829, have remained the basic doctrinal positions of the Baptists in Burma, and if one speaks of Protestant theological developments in this country, one must necessarily take into account the 1819 confession of the first convert and the 1829 Burman Liturgy as prepared by Adoniram Judson. While there are also Anglican and Methodist churches in Burma, both in terms of numbers within the Protestant community and in production of indigenous writings on theology, the Baptist contribution in the field surely deserves special mention. Two other writings of this period, "The Golden Balance" and "The Threefold Cord,"[4] dealt respectively with Christian apologetics and Christian ethics. "The Threefold Cord" was a manual to help new Christians in their desire to grow in grace and to attain the perfect love and enjoyment of God. It dealt with the necessity of secret prayer, self-denial, and good works. Buddhism is a religion of meditation, asceticism, and good works. No wonder the manual for new Christians dwelt on the three matters which, though close to the characteristics in Buddhist practice, have basic differences in the context of Christian faith and life. While good works are antecedents to salvation according to the message of Buddha, the same are pointed out in Christian discipleship as necessary fruits of a redeemed life.

Of the two manuals, "The Golden Balance" became more widely known, and it might have also influenced the tone and manner of Christian apologetics well beyond the 1930s. It set forth the distinctions between the eternal God and Buddha, and there was no ambiguity about who was considered the more excellent God. The comparison between the two systems of law underlined the difference between a punishing system and a pardoning system. The distinguishing marks between the two orders of priesthood, as presented to the readers, left no room for doubt as to which priesthood was the more creditable. Despite the scholarly research which lay behind the evangelistic presentations in this period, the theological writings by ardent converts, some of whom had left the Buddhist priesthood for the Christian faith, were, in the eyes of later churchmen, marked more by tones of polemics than of apologetics and led to proscription of these publications by the colonial rulers who, though Christians themselves, saw the need for defusing religious strife in a country where Buddhism had remained predominant since the sixth century B.C.

Three Periods of Theological Development

It may not be out of place here to pause and reflect on the basic trends of theological development between 1819 and 1939 and from 1939 to the present. The period between 1819 and 1885 saw Burma under its Buddhist monarchs and under the authority of those who were not very aware of the influence of Christianity in other lands. The period between 1885 and 1939 saw the colonial period and the growth of nationalism of the modern type. The predominant experience of the next thirty-five years was the struggle and attainment of national independence, with new challenges to Christian thought arising out of the situation.

In one sense the problems the church had to struggle with during the days of the monarchy have continued to present basic theological issues for the church to deal with even up to the present time. The coming of Adoniram Judson and other missionaries happened around the time when the threat of British colonial expansion was growing. Five years after the baptism of the first convert, the first Anglo-Burmese war broke out, and the sufferings the Judsons had to go through were largely due to the confusion in the minds of Burmese officials concerning the difference between Christian mission and colonialism, in spite of the fact that the Christian missionaries were American and not British during those days. Christianity was not only the religion of the foreigner but it became to be understood as the religion of the *invaders*.

The theological issues were basically threefold. First, there was the matter of *communication*. The challenge was to present the Gospel in language and terms understandable to hearers out of a Buddhist cultural setting. The second issue was that of *truth*, or proclamation of the distinctions between the Gospel and the message of Buddhism. The outbreak of the three Anglo-Burmese wars between 1824 and 1885, when the British annexed the whole of Burma, created for the church the problem of *political association* which the majority of the nation readily established between Christian mission and colonialism. This third problem, however, apparently did not occupy the attention of the indigenous church till after 1885.

INTELLIGIBLE AND FAITHFUL WITNESS

The period extending from the British annexation of Burma up to the outbreak of the Second World War may be described as another stage in the development of issues for theological reflection in the Protestant church history of Burma. The concern for intelligible and faithful presentation of the Gospel continued to manifest itself in theological writings of the period. Two scholars, bearing the same name (U Tha Din) but coming from different parts of Burma, were typical of those who dominated the scene in this field. U Tha Din of Upper Burma came to be known as Mahn Tha Din (Mahn standing for Man-da-lay, the former capital and cultural center of Burma); the other, Dr. Tha Din, who came from a background of Buddhist priestly scholarship, was known as Pye Tha Din (Pye standing for the city of Prome in Lower Burma). Their discourses, debates with Buddhist monks and thinkers, and their evangelistic sermons formed the basis of the theological literature of the period, which included such works as *Comparative Study of Buddhist and Christian Scriptures* (now a standard reference work for seminary students) by Dr. Tha Din, *Treatise on the Knowledge of Religions* by U Ba Tay of Taunggyi in Eastern Burma, and the two-volume *Commentary on the Tipitakas* by U Pan Yi. There was also a version of the Holy Bible that employed in an extremely generous measure the vocabulary of the Buddhist scriptures. The names of most of the Old Testament books in this version appeared in *Pali*, which is the scriptural language of the Buddhists. Indigenous hymns of praise included unique compositions employing thought-forms and meters of traditional Burmese music.

But this second period also saw a new complication in the theological struggle of the church to find her own direction of life and mission.

The ready response to the Gospel among the tribal or ethnic groups within Burma led to the organization of the Baptist church (the predominant Protestant church in the land) along ethnic and tribal lines, even though all the groups came together annually in nationwide conventions for common assembly, devotions, and conduct of business. Hence the ethnic groups—for example, Sgaw Karens, Pwo Karens, Kachins, and Asho Chins—found themselves in separate units brought together on the basis of ethnic affinity and convenient association. The trend of colonial administrators, in their efforts to pacify and govern the country, was to adapt the existing laws, traditions, and Burmese administration of the pre-annexation period. This meant that on the one hand the country was becoming administratively more consolidated; but on the other, the separate treatment of certain ethnic communities perpetuated the psychological and cultural distances already existing between the various groups.

The organization of the predominant Baptist church along ethnic lines had two negative by-products. First, one may with some validity claim that the presentation of the Gospel to the majority population, the Burmese Buddhists, did not secure the same attention and application in the life and mission of the church as it had during the days of Adoniram Judson. Second, the struggle for the concept and practice of the selfhood of the church became a complex affair because of the need to keep intergroup relations within the church wholesome while ownership of property, production of publications, and organization followed separate ethnic lines. In the eyes of nationalists, particularly Buddhists, the church was associated with those forces which generated hindrances to the unification of the country or to the integration of ethnic and frontier communities within the mainstream of Burmese national life.

THE CHURCH'S SERVICE AND ECCLESIOLOGY

The third period, extending roughly from the outbreak of the Second World War up to the present, saw the development of a new emphasis in the life and witness of the church. The spread of the war, bringing with it the Japanese occupation of Burma, the evacuation of the Protestant missionaries, and the emphasis on nationalism, all forced the church to reexamine its comprehension and expression of the theological bases in all aspects of her thought and action. Some were old issues needing a radically new approach. Others were matters requiring deeper and further pursuit of the questions the church had struggled with in the past. Presentation of the Gospel to the Buddhists had always been a major challenge to the evangelists. The emphasis in the third period shifted from that in the first period, and apologetics became not only devoid of "polemics," but emphasized common concerns between Christians and Buddhists, whether these were directed toward the social or moral problems of the nation or of human beings in general.

Another question the church had to grapple with was that of its selfhood, particularly in the midst of political misunderstandings about the church's nature by the Buddhists within the nation. The Japanese occupation of Burma after the evacuation of the British during the Second World War aggravated the need for consideration of this ecclesiological question. Christians in Burma were asked why they continued to remain members of the church when the colonial Christian rulers had already evacuated before the advancing Japanese forces. The church faced the challenge with courage and faith. Some members were killed. The attitude of most of the Christians reflected the situation in 1820, when the early disciples had affirmed their faith in the future of the church in spite of the departure of the missionaries. At that time Judson had written:

> We expected that after being destitute of all the means of grace for some time, and after seeing their teachers driven away from the presence of their monarch in disgrace, they [the disciples] would become cold in their affections and have but little remaining zeal for a cause thus proscribed and exposed to persecuting. . . . They all, to a man, appeared immovably the same; yea, rather advanced in zeal and energy. . . . Moung Bya [one of the disciples] said: "Do stay with us a few months. [The Judsons were planning to leave Burma then.] Do stay till there are eight or ten disciples; then appoint one to be the teacher of the rest; I shall not be concerned about the event; though you should leave the country, the religion will spread of itself; the emperor himself cannot stop it."[5]

Even in those early days indigenous Christians had spoken of their faith in the continuing work of Christ's Spirit in his church once it had been established, whether the missionaries were present or absent. This question of the selfhood of the church in relation to the work of the Lord of the church, in relation to mission and to the setting in which the church was placed, came alive with renewed impact throughout the periods of Japanese occupation and the recovery of national independence.

It also brought the whole question of the relation between church and society and between Christian faith and national aspirations to the attention of Christians in a special way. Formerly many Christians might not only have acquiesced, but even basked, in the influence of colonial Christian rulers of the land. Suddenly in the resistance movement against the Japanese and in the need to reexamine their understanding of the nature and purpose of the church, Christians (particularly the young) found themselves thrown together with Buddhists to struggle with fundamental questions on religion and society. Formerly, politics was, in the minds of Christians, something which did not have anything to do with Christian faith and practice. But the war and postwar periods forced the eyes of many Christians to be opened to the necessity of searching the Scriptures anew to formulate their Christian attitudes to these pressing problems.

As indicated earlier, interfaith dialogue also took on a new emphasis, bringing Christians and Buddhists together to look at some of the fundamental human issues out of their own backgrounds of faith in mutual understanding and encounter. The papers and activities of the Commission on Buddhism of the Burma Christian Council are indicative of the new mood and approach to such interfaith encounter.[6] The holding of the Sixth Buddhist Council at Rangoon in 1954 spurred on the work of the commission.

The essentially new element in the theological reflections and articulations of the church in this third period covering three and a half decades from 1939 may rightly be identified as the *ecumenical concern*. The World Missionary Conference at Tambaram, Madras, had taken place in 1938, and the impact of the ecumenical movement had inexorably grown in the postwar period for the Christians of Burma. Due partly to the "congregational" character of the Baptist church and partly to the background work of the Student Christian Movement, a substantial proportion of those who exercised the thought and life of the church came from the laity. Dr. Hla Bu, the son of an earlier Christian apologist and professor at Burman Seminary, himself a professor of philosophy and principal of a Christian college, is a typical example of one who provided such lay leadership in Christian thought among the Protestant community. Through the Student Christian Movement a new generation of Christians, drawn from different confessional backgrounds but having gone through common experiences, had started to contribute to the formulation of policies and programs of the churches.

The Sufficiency of the Church's Lord

One cannot help feeling that in all these areas we have touched on, more systematic and sustained thinking is still needed to bring developments to effective fruition in the coming years. Three areas may be pinpointed as follows:

CHRISTIAN COMMUNICATON (its intelligibility and faithfulness). In 1963 at the time of the sesquicentennial celebrations of the arrival of Adoniram Judson in Burma, more than ten thousand participants gathered at Rangoon for a series of devotional and business meetings. While the Baptist community alone had grown to something like 400,000 souls, the Christian ratio to the total population of Burma was only approximately 3 percent. Someone said that while God should be praised for gathering into his church so many from the tribal groups in the country, the presentation of the Gospel to the majority sector of the population—the Burmese Buddhist community—still had to be followed up with renewed vigor and devotion. In a sense, the task of evangelism, as far as the mainstream of the Burmese nation is concerned, has not yet been seriously followed up by the church in spite of the labors of Adoniram Judson and some of those who followed him. It is essentially a theological task that calls for a fresh construction of the crucial insights which the scholars of comparative religion have brought to light as well as the raising and consideration of fundamental "religious" issues confronting the nation. Speaking out of a sense of solidarity as members of the same nation and world, facing the basic questions of contemporary society, can be intelligible to others; but it also means that the church will have to be more alert than ever to speak out of her faithfulness to the demands of Christ who is the Truth. The emergence of effective apologetics to the Buddhists will require a fresh study of the church's faith in the experience and setting not only of the church universal but particularly of the past century and a half of the Burmese Church.

THE CHURCH'S SELFHOOD AND SERVICE TO SOCIETY. The nature and purpose of the church, as learned from Holy Scripture as well as from the experiences of the church in Burma, still need to be expressed in terms the people of the country can understand and even appreciate. Misunderstandings of the church by the general population cannot be disposed of by only strategic Christian actions, important as they are, but by a sustained and systematic expression of the church's life and mission, which is rooted in both the Scriptures and the common history of the people.

With the establishment of a socialist state, the traditional Christian service institutions have been taken away from the churches. There is the need to restudy the character of the *diakonia* in a world where it is not enough for the church merely to provide clothes for the naked or food for the hungry, but rather to be involved in the transformation of a society which produces nakedness and hunger. That is the helpful challenge that the Burmese way to socialism is providing today to the church in her service to society. This is largely a new area for theological reflection and Christian obedience for the church in Burma, and both laity and clergy will have to be involved in this task.

A lesson may be learned from the second period previously referred to, when the voices of liberation and development were coming mainly from those outside the church in Burma. Then the church was teaching its people not to dabble in politics, and it was the politicians who were demanding national independence and searching for ways to resolve agrarian problems.

THE CHALLENGE FOR CHRISTIAN UNITY. Finally there is the danger of the challenge for Christian unity remaining shallow and "nontheological." Among Protestants in Burma the Baptists, as we have said, far outnumber the Anglicans and Methodists, and it is possible that the whole question of baptism, the ministry, and the liturgy may not be looked at in the right context, but disposed of in despair or accommodation, removed from theological depth and a willingness really to listen to one another. Much homework still remains to be done within each of the confessions—and within the country itself, instead of leaving the initiative for guidance in these matters to referees abroad. A related problem may be the predominant Baptist community's need to integrate its structure which, in the past, has emphasized ethnic distinctions.

The challenge to the church in Burma in the field of theological
construction lies in three crucial directions and each is a huge field in
itself: the communication of the message (kerygma), the expression of
the church's service (diakonia), and the reorganization of its fellowship (koinonia). All require sustained and prayerful efforts as well as
spirit-filled insights. Can the church successfully undertake these?
The promise of the Lord of the church remains:

"My grace is sufficient for thee, for my power is made perfect in
weakness."

NOTES

1. Adoniram Judson's journal entry of June 6, 1819.
2. *Ibid.*
3. An English translation was given as an appendix to Volume II of Francis
Wayland, *A Memoir of the Life and Labors of the Rev. Adoniram Judson, D.D.* (New York:
Sheldon, 1866).
4. English translations of both are reproduced in F. Wayland's study of Judson.
5. Adoniram Judson's journal entries of February 20 and 24, 1820.
6. For examples, "Toward an Understanding" (in Burmese), and a brief summary
of the commission's activities in Dr. Pe Maung Tin, "The Study of Buddhism in
Burma" *South East Asia Journal of Theology* I, 3 (1960) 60–62.

Points of Theological Friction

The particular historical and religious background of Thailand necessitates a study of the encounter between Thailand's interpretation of history and Israel's theology of history. This primary encounter between Thailand and Israel "the troubler" (1 Kings 18:17), prepares Thailand for the decisive encounter between Thailand and Christ, "the stumbling block."

THE LORD'S CONTROVERSY

> Hear the word of the Lord, O people of Israel; for the Lord has a controversy with the inhabitants of the land. There is no faithfulness or kindness, and no knowledge of God in the land; there is swearing, lying, killing, stealing and committing adultery; they break all bounds and murder follows murder. Therefore the land mourns and all who dwell in it languish. (Hos. 4:1–3)

Israel is accused. The indictment of the Lord is forcefully presented. This is the Lord's court controversy with Israel, "the fewest of all peoples" (Deut. 7:7). He who initiated the Covenant relationship with Israel and remained faithful to it, now—on the basis of that very Covenant relationship—embarks on a controversy.[1] The controversy is of a particular kind. It is a revelational, or perhaps we should say, an "antiontocratic" controversy.[2] The Prosecutor, in his person and word, rejects man's stubborn efforts (Deut. 9:6) to confine him in an ontocratic cage framed by man's own understanding of the cosmos and of his existence. From the "incomparably high" *beyond*, the Lord stages an assault upon man's ontocratic complacency with his piercing "Therefore."[3]

The Covenant is historical. So is the controversy. The Lord's antiontocratic controversy vibrates in the heart of salvation history, and from there the waves of its vibration reach out to the broad horizon of mission history, which is a charismatic history within the great and confused world history.

The Asian world has been invaded by the antiontocratic controversy of the Lord. Whenever and wherever it is caught and entangled in the controversy it is not free to evade an experience of radical discontinuity from its own traditional valuations, and thus the controversy has become the new leaven for revolutionary social change in Asia. M. M. Thomas writes: "The Asian revolution cannot be understood apart from the impact of the West on Asia. Therefore interpreting the Asian revolution means interpreting also the Western impact on Asia."[4]

I understand this to mean that behind the Asian revolution lies the Western revolution, and behind the Western revolution lies the Lord's controversy staged in the life of Israel.

In what ways has this controversy inaugurated by the Lord reached Southeast Asia? Unless the extremely rare visitors from the Christian West had more of an impact than we are aware of, it would seem that the Lord's controversy had not arrived before 1511 when the Portuguese Alphonso d'Albuquerque, conqueror of Goa, arrived at Malacca from Cochin with a fleet of eighteen vessels. Alburquerque's conquest of Malacca, on August 10, 1511, came only thirteen years after the arrival of Vasco da Gama at Calicut in the Portuguese flagship San Gabriel, and when Francis Xavier was five years old. The fleet of Albuquerque was propelled by the power of greed for the wealth of spices and carried the cross of Christ and cannon as did the San Gabriel. The breath and contents of the Lord's controversy came contained in the ugly vessels of colonial rapacity! Through the period of immense suffering under the militarily superior colonial West, the East was brought closer to the revolutionary controversy which the Lord had initiated. God's providence and human confusion! Theologically speaking, this is perhaps the most crucial event to touch the depth of Asian existence and history, introducing the ferment of disturbing theological discontinuity into the continuous ontocratic culture of the East. God's saving presence ("the right hand of God") worked upon Asia through the violent storm of man's exploitation of his neighbors ("the left hand of God")! Was the colonial penetration into Southeast Asia the "Nebuchadnezzar" whom the Lord hired to bring his controversy into Asia?[5] One must not, however, overlook the sacrifices made by both the Catholic and Protestant missionaries during this period. Whenever Christ was preached, the Lord's controversy challenged spiritual self-satisfaction and social slothfulness of the Southeast Asian nations with unavoidable persistence.

Thailand is a land of Theravada Buddhism. The Thailand Official Yearbook lists five religions (Buddhism, Islam, Christianity, Hinduism, and Sikhism) and four doctrines (Confucianism, Taoism, Shintoism, and Animism). Of the population, 93.4 percent profess Theravada Buddhism, 3.9 percent Islam, and 0.5 percent Christianity. Religious freedom, however, has been fully recognized by every constitution since the 1932 revolution.

Portuguese Dominican priests first brought Christianity to Thailand in the sixteenth century. This history of the Catholic mission in Thailand is a combination of stormy persecution and relatively precarious peace, at least in its earlier stages. By 1949 there were 52,557 baptized Catholics in the kingdom. One of the earliest Protestant missionaries to Thailand was Karl Gützlaff (1828–31), but the missionary who represented the presence of Christian witness with far wider influence and penetration after the brief stay of Gützlaff was Dr. Dan Beach Bradley (1835–93). In North Thailand, the amazing figure of Dr. Daniel McGilvary, an American Presbyterian missionary, dominated the scene (1867–1911). His imprint of energetic evangelism over half a century is still vividly felt throughout the north. Since 1840, the main force of the Protestant mission has been sent by the United Presbyterian Church in the U.S.A. Today the Church of Christ in Thailand is a body of 24,000 Christians.

The Thai people are relative latecomers to the Indo-Chinese peninsula. Long before Thailand, as we know it today, was formed, the region came under the cultural influence of India. Indian influence was already waning when, in the thirteenth century, the Mongol invasions in Asia made it possible for the Thai, who were entering the peninsula in ever-increasing numbers, to become powerful and to develop a national identity.

Coming from China into an area which was already rich in Indianized cultures, the Thai borrowed freely from their neighbors as they developed their own distinctive culture. Before coming into a position of power, the Thai were under the domination of the Khmers and living among the Mons. These two peoples were a fertile source of influence for the assimilating Thai. Through them the Thai inherited the cultural values of far-off India. The Mons and their Burmese neighbors passed on to the Thai Sinhalese Buddhism, which was to become the spiritual pillar of the Thai nation. The once-powerful maritime state of Srivijaya was already in decline in the thirteenth century, and the Thai shared responsibility with Majapahit for the dismemberment of its empire. Certainly, Thailand tasted the influence of its civilization.

But the influence of India and Ceylon on Thailand was not entirely secondhand. In the fourteenth century a prince of the Thai made a pilgrimage to Ceylon and India in search of relics. This prince was the grandson of the Thai chief who freed the Thai of Sukothai from Khmer domination by driving out the Khmer underlord and making his friend, Bang Klang Thao, the first Thai king of Sukothai. This king, who took the name Indraditya when he assumed his reign, was the father of Rama Khamhaeng, who brought Sukothai to its glory. The prince's pilgrimage to Ceylon and India took place during the reign of Rama Khamhaeng's devout son, Loe Thai, and on his return Loe Thai conferred upon him the title of Mahathera Sri Sradhara-jachulamuni Sri Ratanalankadipa Mahasami. Thus the cultural history of Thailand is a rich process of encounters and assimilation.

THE EUROPEAN IMPACT

The critical phase of Thailand's encounter with European powers took place during the reigns of the three Chakkri kings: Rama IV, (Mongkut, 1851–1868), Rama V, (Chulalongkorn, 1868–1910), and Rama VI, (Wachirawut, 1910–1925). Throughout the stormy Vasco da Gama era, Thailand had had to go through a series of difficult negotiations and make unwilling concessions; nevertheless it had achieved the singular distinction of maintaining its independence,[6] and it is the only country in Southeast Asia not colonized by the West. However, between 1851 and 1925 numerous contacts with the West, both desirable and undesirable, superficial and substantial, facilitated the advent of Western scientific ethos, political philosophy, and the "religion of Christianity" into an awakening Thailand. The impact of these Western influences upon Thailand's traditional continuity-culture set the country on the rapid course of modernization even though, by maintaining its political independence, it "missed" a heavy dose of the "unintended gifts of Western colonialism." It is a significant historic fact that the 1932 revolution from absolute monarchy to constitutional monarchy was masterminded by Nai Pridi, a doctor of law from the University of Paris, and under his initiative Thailand acquired its first constitution (June 27, 1932).[7]

THE TWO THAILANDS

Thailand had managed to run her own destiny at some distance from the full force of the violent storm stirred up by Vasco da Gama. Thus one finds a "milder" mode of transition from the traditional to the revolutional. The two mighty pillars of classic Thailand, the monarchy and Theravada Buddhism, continue to command profound respect from her people. At the same time, however, the process of modernization inspired and propelled by the "unintended gifts of Western colonialism" is actively at work. The crucial point in this connection is that this conflict between the two foci of historical forces is growing more turbulent under the shadow of the irritating presence of the antiontocratic controversy of the Lord. When "thus saith the Lord" came to Thailand, it was automatically given the status of a guest who is supposed to be sitting on a given seat in a house dominated by the sound of the "drum of immortality" beaten by the Enlightened One. The drum, however, has not been able to drown out the Lord's controversy. The Lord's controversy persists, therefore our missionary controversy continues. Theologically speaking, Thailand is caught in the cacophony of the two resounding messages. A theological understanding of this momentously significant cacophony is urgently needed in order to guide the church from its crippling minority complex to the prophetic privilege of being the minority in this land.

A closer examination of the spiritual and historical forces at work suggests that there are two Thailands within one Thailand. It is an undeniable fact that the impact of the West on Thailand has created a new Thailand. Thailand One is a Thailand of traditional values, while Thailand Two is Thailand on the way to modernization as it constantly preaches its gospel of modernization ideals.[8] The Lord's controversy is reaching Thailand One through Thailand Two, but it must be pointed out that Thailand Two is not necessarily aware of its far-reaching mission, since it is too absorbed in the process of modernization to ponder the historical process which brought it into being. On the other hand, Thailand One, the upholder of the patient eschatology, is beginning to be aware of the invasion of Israel into Thai spirituality and religiosity, and it is interested in the message of Israel even though it feels ill at ease with this strange visitor.

ENTER: A THEOLOGY OF HISTORY

Israel is at once a stumbling block and a fascination to Thailand One.[9] Why? On two accounts. First, Israel has an entirely different appreciation and interpretation of history, and this attracts the healthy curiosity of Thailand One. Second, Israel's theology of history is an intensified theology of history indeed; yet when it is compared with the theology of history which revolves around the fulfilment point of Jesus Christ, it may be called a preintensified theology of history. In this preintensified theology of history, without the name of Jesus Christ, Thailand One finds herself more relaxed and ready to participate in discussions of grave religious importance. One of the reasons why theological history in Thailand shows a state of undernourishment is that the significance of this preintensified zone was missiologically ignored and judged to be profitless. But when one tries to conceive a theology of mission in the context of the dynamic convergence of Thailand One and Thailand Two, it becomes obvious that theology in the preintensified zone leads us into the exciting ground of preparation for the Gospel. A study of Israel's relation to Thailand is a necessary step to the discussion on Christ and Thailand.[10]

HISTORY AS GOD'S EXPERIENCE

What is the decisive feature of Israel's theology of history? Israel experienced history profoundly and inimitably. The profundity and originality are, however, not due to Israel's own mental or spiritual faculty of perception and penetration into the structure and meaning of history, but derive from the profundity and originality of God's unique presence and work in the historical life of Israel. Israel was not able to speak of history without speaking of God, nor of God without speaking of history. At the critical moment of the birth of the people of Israel in the event of Exodus, Israel confessed her faith in God's presence in history as follows:

> The Lord said, "I have seen the affliction of my people who are in Egypt, and have heard their cry because of their taskmasters; I have sympathy for, I am effected by, their sufferings." (Exod. 3:7)[11]

God was affected by the harsh life that Israel was subjected to under the cruel yoke of Egypt. "What concerns the prophet," writes Rabbi Heschel, "is the human event as a divine experience. History to us is the record of human experience; to the prophet it is a record of God's experience."[12] History is the arena where God's "ultimate concern" is worked out in the entanglement with human destiny. God, who sends despair upon his people because of their stubbornness and disobedience, is the very one who most responsibly and acutely "experiences" the pain of history for his people and all humanity (Jer. 18:5–11; 31:2–3; Isa. 43:4–7; 49:15; 54:7–10). History, boldly confessed to be God's experience, is neither absurd nor blind. History is neither orphaned nor divorced from God. History, as participated in by Israel, runs on an agitated path. The possibilities of neutrality, tranquility, and apathy are denied to history, since the Lord is the creator of the events which bring about the "shaking of the foundations" of history. The mission of Israel to the world is to transmit this striking theology of history to the nations through her own historical existence.

Friction Between Thailand and Israel

In this section we shall seek to describe the current encounter of Thailand One with Israel and the theological repercussions of this encounter for Thailand Two. The gradual invasion of Israel's "history as God's experience" into Thailand One through the medium of Thailand Two awakened Thailand One to a renewed self-understanding and a zeal for its mission.

How to determine precisely the nature of Thailand One? Gunnar Myrdal writes of Southeast Asia:

> Although a few intellectuals are, or feel that they are, completely Westernized and secularized, most observe the prescribed rites of their inherited religion and are cognizant of the broad lines of its theology. They have a

knowledge of their country's history, its architectural treasures, its literature and philosophy, music, drama, and dance, and its fine crafts, all of
which have positive connotations and add to the richness of life. Their
attachment to their nation's history, religion, and culture provides more
than mere pleasure; it is a psychological necessity, the more so because of
the long subjugation of these peoples and the shocked awareness of
economic and social backwardness following upon acceptance of the modernization ideals.[13]

This analysis by Myrdal indicates that the lives of the greater portion
of the Southeast Asian peoples are, with considerable dedication,
engaged in the practice of their ancient religions. Myrdal is specifically pointing out two facts: First, inherited religion is historically
there among the Asian peoples as a revered tutor of spirituality; and
second, the "shocked awareness of economic and social backwardness" drove people to renewed commitment to their traditional religions out of "psychological necessity." The first point can be applied
to Thailand without any hesitation, while the second point may
require some adjustment to soften the intensity implied in
"psychological necessity." In my endeavors to analyze Thailand One,
I have come to accept the view that Thailand One is essentially
Buddhist Thailand. Thus the characteristics of Thailand One are
here highlighted through a study of one of the most highly treasured
traditions of Pali Buddhism.

This part of the tradition informs us of an immensely important
experience of the young prince, Gautama Siddhartha. On one of his
outings in his state carriage the young prince saw "an aged man as
bent as a roof gable, decrepit, leaning on a staff, tottering as he
walked, afflicted and long past his prime."[14] On another occasion he
saw "a sick man, suffering and very ill, fallen and weltering in his own
water, by some being lifted up, by others being dressed." On a
subsequent outing he saw the corpse in a funeral pocession. Each
encounter is followed by a conversation between his charioteer and
Gautama. The exchange after he saw the aged man went as follows.:

"That man, good charioteer, what has he done, that his hair is not like that
of other men, nor his body?"
   "He is what is called an aged man, my lord."
   "But why is he called aged?"
   "He is called aged, my lord, because he has not much longer to live."

"But then, good charioteer, am I too subject to old age, one who has not got past old age?"

At the end of these three encounters is recorded the monologue of Gautama: "Shame then verily be upon this thing called birth, since to one born decay shows itself like that, disease shows itself like that, and death shows itself like that!" On another occasion, however, he saw one "who has gone forth" from house to homeless state. Thereupon he decided to become an ascetic recluse in order to find a way of escape from decay and death.

This brief tradition tells us of the very basic issues with which the prince, the one later to become the Enlightened One, struggled. The narrative lives at the nerve center of Thai culture and personality.

A. THAI ANTIHISTORICAL EMPIRICAL REALISM:
THE CONTROVERSY OF PATHEIA WITH APATHEIA (MODERNIZATION)

The wise charioteer succinctly explains the reality of human existence—an aged man, a sick man, and a corpse. The irreversible truth about an aged man is that he has "not much longer to live," about a sick man is that he "hardly recovers from his illness"; and about a corpse is that "neither mother, nor father, nor other kinsfold will now see him, nor will he see them." This is the truth about man based on man's honest observation of the laws of nature. This truth operates in the Thai view of life with such force as to create a sense of mistrust within the culture against that which is historical and personal. The truth concerning man is this direct deduction from the laws of nature, which is more trustworthy than such ambiguous and arbitrary categories as the historical and personal.[15] The truth about man must be empirically established, yet this empirical judgment must exclude historical and personal dimensions! Is it possible to speak at all of the truth of man outside of the historical and personal implications? This is an unfamiliar and strange anthropology, especially for those who have been influenced by the Christian view of man.

This is an anthropology of *apatheia*. "The nature and destiny of man" here cannot occasion a "passionate" debate, for it is viewed in isolation from the historical and personal. The primacy of the natural over the historical and personal provides the structural foundation for

Thai apatheia-anthropology. The natural is apathetic.[16] The history-anthropology—an understanding of man which seeks to understand human existence in terms of man's deep involvement in history—cannot espouse, without causing much domestic turbulence, the apatheia-anthropology and form a new family life, and vice versa. Yet an irritating historical fact is that for the last two-hundred years the history-anthropology has lived in proximity to the apatheia-anthropology (always within her sight!) and occasionally succeeded in carrying on an uneasy and perplexing courtship. The perplexity of this situation is caused by what is happening in the present-day Thai understanding of man. Its apatheia-anthropology is no longer enjoying its traditional tranquility. The courting of history-anthropology is forcing apatheia-anthropology to reexamine the separation of the natural from the historical and personal.

History-anthropology is derived from Israel's theology of history. Israel lives in the continuous surprise of discovering God who accompanies Israel on its journey through history and who makes history purposeful for it. Israel's experience was, mysteriously, God's experience in history. Because God is present in history, history cannot become apatheia-history.

> For a long time I have held my peace,
> I have kept still and restrained myself;
> now I will cry out like a woman in travail,
> I will gasp and pant. (Isa. 42:14. Also see
>   Isa. 1:2–3; Jer. 4:1)

The opposite of apatheia-history is obviously patheia-history. Israel's patheia-history is, however, *sui generis*. It does not come under the general category of pathos. It draws its lifeblood from the theological category of pathos, the pathos of the God of Abraham, Isaac, and Jacob.[17] To reject God's patheia-history is to alienate oneself from the grace of God historically surrounding us. Rabbi Heschel says that "sin is repudiation of history."[18]

Thrown into God's patheia-history, Israel began to speak the language of *this* history. The historical pathos of God invokes the historical pathos of his people.

> Answer me, O Lord, for thy steadfast love is good;
> according to thy abundant mercy, turn to me.

> Hide not thy face from thy servant; for I am in
> distress, make haste to answer me. (Ps. 69:16–17)

This prayer is meaningful only in the context of God's patheia-history. The psalmist wants God to turn to him in a concrete historical way, since he is historically in distress. An extraordinary existential interest in history began with Israel.

Theological friction exists between apatheia-anthropology and patheia-anthropology, and between apatheia-history and patheia-history. We must now try to place the modernizing Thailand Two within the framework of this theological friction caused at the intersection of Thailand and Israel.

Theologically speaking, Thailand One is making a significant contribution by magnifying the "point of friction" and thus providing a proper theological framework in which the issue of modernization should be discussed. In this sense, Thailand One is inadvertently prophetic. Thailand Two, by showing an interest in the shaping of history inspired by the "teleology" of the modernization ideals, is also inadvertently acting theologically. Modernization implies more than change and development. It involves transformation—"the transformation of all systems by which man organizes his society, that is, his political, social, economic, intellectual, religious, and psychological systems."[19]

Both Thailand One and Two, are irreversibly entangled in the great "Asian drama" of modernization. The people of Thailand are caught up in the conflicts "between their high-pitched aspirations and the bitter experience of a harsh reality; between the desire for change and improvement, and mental reservations and inhibitions about accepting the consequences and paying the price." Living in these conflicts they are now beginning to be convinced that history "is not taken to be predetermined, but within the power of man to shape."[20] This new interpretation and awareness of history is, indeed, a "shaking of the foundations" of life in Thailand.

History is "within the power of man to shape." Christian theologians may hasten to condemn this as an unpardonable sin of human *superbia*, but when this superbia is studied in the context of history and culture in Thailand, one is led to appreciate the positive—not negative—theological implications contained in it. It indicates the emergence of an involved interest in history. Modernization, with its massive historical forces, is achieving a critical shake-up of the ontocratic Thailand, an accomplishment at which all other historical agents (the condemning theologians included!) have heretofore failed. Thus in the light of Thai culture and history, "history is within the power of man to shape"—the modernization interpretation of history—is a significant positive *theological* statement which stands at the creative borderline between apatheia-history and patheia-history, and between secular history and sacred history. Isn't it amazing that God uses superbia as the meeting point between modernization ideals and God's pathos at work in Thai history?

B. THAI ANTINOMADIC "DECAY-ONTOLOGY": THE CONTROVERSY OF
    POSSIBILITY WITH INEVITABILITY (SECULARIZATION)

The solitary reflection of the young Gautama revolves around the theme of the inevitability of the "decay of life." Thailand's indigenous ontology is fastened to the concept of decay. One cannot and must not contemplate "being" without at the same time pondering "decay." Thus when ontology and decay are closely interrelated, the Thai concept of inevitability appears. Wherever there is "being," decay will automatically and inevitably set in, and this blurs any Thai discussion on the "nature and destiny of man." It robs history of the dimension of drama and this impoverished history becomes simply "decay-history." If ontology is decay-ontology, then salvation must be freedom from "being" and emancipation from history.[21]

The nomadic mode of existence portrayed in the Bible, however, indicates—through its pregnant theological implications—the direction of emancipation into "being" and into history. The nomad wanders in history. He battles against the power of destruction rather than that of decay, since in his wandering he experiences history as a chain of unpredictable events rather than an automatic process of decay. Even in the face of the risks and precariousness which pervade life, he finds renewal of soul (Isa. 40:28–31). The secret of the biblical nomadic life lies with God. God is nomadic! The nomad wanders in history since God wanders with him in history. In the words of the hymnist: "God of the coming years, through paths unknown we follow Thee!"

The ideas of decay-ontology and "paths unknown" are mutually incompatible. There are no paths unknown for the decay-ontology; the paths have been "automatically" determined and fixed. In contrast, the Abrahamic code of existence demonstrated, in journeying the unknown paths, the unique concept of "possibility" over against "inevitability." Possibility, according to Israel's theology of history, is basically a nomadic concept. Only those who wander are privileged to experience "possibility in the desert": "Your clothing did not wear out upon you, and your foot did not swell, these forty years." (Deut. 8:4)

On this specifically biblical level, "possibility" encounters "inevitability." Theologically speaking, the opposite of the decay-ontology is the nomadic-ontology. Israel's nomadic-ontology, the theology of possibility, is at present in a relationship of creative friction with Thailand's decay-ontology, the ontology of inevitability.

We must now try to place the secularizing of Thailand within the framework of the theological friction caused at the intersection of Thailand and Israel.

It has become an accepted interpretation that the concept of secularization originated in the theology of Israel, which was able to draw a sharp line of distinction between the Creator and the creature. God alone is holy. All else can be used for man's benefit—that is, all else can be secularized. Israel's *soli deo gloria* distinction between the creator and the creature emancipated her from the profusion of false "holies" and she was chosen to give the rest of the world the first theologically structured thrust of secularization.

Obviously, the theological concept of secularization has not operated in history in its purity. *Homo aeger* degraded theologically structured secularization into secularism. Secularism ignores the demarcation line between the creator and the creature and elevates the latter to the level of the "holy." Thus it structurally conforms to the *greedy* sacralization of all. "A god is that to which we look for all good and where we resort for help in every time of need."[22]

This observation by Luther provides a relevant theological framework from within which we can examine the idolatrous spirit of secularism.

It is obvious that the "world of inevitability" hinders Israel's theological principle of secularization from exerting its influence. Secularization implies emancipation, while inevitability implies imprisonment. Emancipation here means: Man is now free to *use* for his benefit all that is within the strictly defined context of *soli deo gloria*.

Sound secularization is built on "courage to use"! The source of this courage is in a theology of "the Holy."

Secularism, on the other hand, is vocal, particularly in the busy urban life of Thailand. The conscience of Thailand One deplores the prevailing secularist *lebensgefühl*, saying that her people are forsaking the *Dhamma* of the Enlightened One. It seems, however, as though secularism—a greedy sacralization of all—is injecting the idea of "courage to use" into Thailand. Thailand One resists the injection; Thailand Two thrives on it, although in her quieter moments she monologues that the *Dhamma* of decay-ontology rules all.

A theologically significant point here is that in Thailand's cultural and spiritual context, secularism cannot be accused of being idolatrous. If secularism is something to which the people of Thailand look "for help in every time of need," it is their god. But this "god" is a smoke-word without substance for the Thai people, since they do not see this "god" under the judgement of God. To bring "god" to the judgment of God is precisely the part of the theological operation which is so immensely difficult to execute. The culture lacks the concept of *God against "god."* Secularism, therefore, is here innocently practiced, while in Christendom, which has been nourished by the awareness of God against "god," it has been accompanied by uneasiness, arguments, and perhaps guilt feelings. It shows only an imperialistic *superbia* if one hastily launches criticism of idolatry in this region of the world, particularly in "Buddha-dom."

Innocent secularism is militating against the rule of inevitability. Thus it is preparing Thailand to see Israel's theological principle of secularization. The real *possibility to use all* comes from God who is against "god." Innocent secularism through its iconoclasm of inevitability preaches an introductory message toward the faith of possibility in God.

C. THAI MONASTIC "ULTIMATE CONCERN": THE CONTROVERSY
OF DEUS ABSCONDITUS WITH RELIGIOUS DRIVE
(RESURGENCE OF THE ANCIENT FAITH)

Tradition has it that this conversation took place between the young prince and the one who "has gone forth." The recluse answers Gautama:

"I, my lord, am one who has gone forth."

"What, master, does that mean?"

"It means, my lord, being thorough in the religious life, thorough in the peaceful life, thorough in good actions, thorough in meritorious conduct, thorough in harmlessness, thorough in kindness to all creatures."

Then the lord Gautama bade his charioteer, saying: . . . I will even here cut off my hair, and don the yellow robe, and go forth from the house into the homeless state."[23]

The apatheia-anthropology and the decay-anthropology constitute the primary truth about man's existence in the psychology and spirituality of Thailand One. This primary truth evolves itself into the soteriological truth which teaches how to *escape* "apathetically" from the universal confinement of the apatheia-anthropology and from decay-anthropology by becoming "decayless." The escape—that is, the momentous transition from the *dukkha*—is outlined in transhistorical or ahistorical language:[24]

There is, O disciples, an unborn, not become, not compounded, not constructed. If there were not this unborn, not become, not compounded, not constructed, no escape could be seen from here from that which is born, become, compounded, constructed. But since there is an unborn, not become, not compounded, not constructed, so an escape is possible from what is born, become, compounded, constructed.[25]

Here is expressed, without any hint of argumentative heat, a strange marriage between "inevitability and possibility" performed within the mind of Thailand One. To put this sublime rational understanding of "being," apathetically conceived, into practice must be man's ultimate concern, his religious drive. Thailand One is thus apathetically (ahistorically) teleological![26] Step outside the dukkha of this existence! But do not take this assignment with historical zeal. Instead, use ahistorically controlled metaphysical zeal. Then one approaches "a state of everlasting radiant smiles with nobody smiling."[27] This is the nature and structure of Thailand One's ultimate concern.

Israel presents a clear theology of ultimate concern. Its charter is expressed in the well-known *Shema:*

"Hear, O Israel: The Lord our God is one Lord; and you shall love the Lord your God with all your heart, and with all your soul, and with all your might" (Deut. 6:4).[28]

Yet this ultimate concern is dependent upon God's initial ultimate concern. In the famous "eagles' wings" passage (Exod. 19:4-5), the eagles' wings (representing the saving ultimate concern of God) precede "obey my voice and keep my covenant" (Israel's ultimate concern).[29] Verse 5 is dependent upon the foregoing verse. This order runs throughout the historical confession of faith in Israel. The transition from verse 4 to verse 5 here does not correspond with the progression from "born" to "unborn," "become" to "not become." The decisive reason for this lack of correspondence is found in the secret of Israel's existence itself. She was caught by God's ultimate concern for her salvation and for the nations as unfolded in history.

> The Lord of hosts has sworn: "As I have planned, so shall it be, and as I have purposed, so shall it stand, that I will break the Assyrian in my land, and upon my mountains trample him under foot." . . . This is the purpose that is purposed concerning the whole earth; and this is the hand that is stretched out over all the nations. For the Lord of hosts has purposed, and who will annul it? (Isa. 14:24–27)

This historical God who executes his purpose on "Assyria" is a *deus absconditus* in the sense that he cannot lightly be made our object of ultimate concern. Only the "eagles' wings" bring us to the possibility at all of having our ultimate concern in God. And God works his work "strangely" (Isa. 28:21). He remains "hidden" to those who venture to domesticate him. *Deus absconditus* is a God who is free and who rejects becoming an object of man's speculation.[30] Thus God in history is not an apparent, self-evident God, but a stumbling block to man in history.

Thailand One readily understands the concept of ultimate concern. It has cherished in its heart the thought of ultimate concern toward "unborn, not become, not compounded, not constructed." It is engaged in a creative friction relationship with Israel's theology of the historically staged ultimate concern of God which evoked, in turn, Israel's ultimate concern. Here the encounter is between monastic ultimate concern and theonomously structured ultimate concern.

We must now try to place the resurgence of the ancient Theravada Buddhist faith within the framework of this theological friction caused at the intersection of Thailand and Israel.

The resurgence of the ancient faith hosted by Thailand One is, as we have noted, to a considerable degree due to the stimuli that the frequent visitor, Israel, exerted on the country's spirituality. One of the stimuli is now theologically defined as theonomously structured ultimate concern. The encounter of these two ultimate concerns opens an enormous area of serious theological implication and discussion. This area may, in general, be called "the theology of religions."

Thailand One's ultimate concern represents a sublime religious value, and it is both inspiring and impressive to see this religious ultimate concern alive—consciously or unconsciously—in the soul of this great nation. One would intuitively rebel against any condemnatory or depreciative judgment upon Thailand's ultimate concern if one appreciates its special historical context. The issue is far greater than a few words of condemnation; it is theological. Theological appreciation consists in seeing all in God's grace *and* judgment. "Viewed with the eyes of sacred history, secular history is itself always a sacred history," writes H. R. Schlette.[31] I accept this with the following interpretation: "with the eyes of sacred history" means the *repentant* eyes of sacred history, since human disobedience *within* sacred history has repeatedly frustrated God's gracious design (Deut. 9:6–7). From this involved and repentant perspective, both sacred and secular histories belong to the history which needs "repentance," and both are under the judgment of God. Sacred history is in no sense superior to secular history. The sacredness of sacred history derives only from the sacred determination of God to be present in it in a special way.

This takes us to the grave realization that our theonomously structured ultimate concern is, in history, as distorted as the monastic ultimate concern.[32] We have no grounds for boasting of our "sacredness," since we *fail* to live in the theonomously founded ultimate concern. We stand under both the grace and judgment of God (Amos 1 and 2). This grace and judgment of God, which embraces both ultimate concerns, is the real point of contact between them.

Theonomously structured ultimate concern is not by itself an immediate stumbling block to the people of monastic ultimate concern. The failure of sacred history to live in the theonomously structured ultimate concern is the stumbling block to the people of Thailand, particularly to the people of Thailand One. Thailand One demonstrates more intensive dedication to its ultimate concern than the commitment of the Christian community to its ultimate concern.

In reality, then, the theonomously structured ultimate concern presents itself to the eyes of both Thailand One and Two as feebler and poorer than their own ultimate concern, which may be named, theologically speaking, an autonomously structured ultimate concern.

The resurgence of this great ancient faith must be studied in the context of the "theology of repentance" and the grace that heals our disobedience in our failure to live out of theonomously structured ultimate concern.

Conclusion

"Good Soil" is being prepared. The invasion of Israel's theology of history into the Thai interpretation of history has presented us with a set of pregnant theological friction points. These friction points have not been brought about by the stimulation of the Chinese and Burmese views of history in Thailand. Such influence can be described simply as "interontocratic" traffic, since they do not contain the cutting edge of the Lord's controversy. Theological friction *caused by Israel* is, perhaps, the most significant event that has happened to the spiritual life of Thailand since its adoption of Theravada Buddhism centuries ago. It is not Ahab, but Elijah, who troubles Thailand.

Israel is, by providing the meeting place called "the preintensified zone of the theology of history," preparing Thailand for the coming of the true Israelite, Jesus Christ, the focal point of the intensified theology of history. In this specifically theological sense, the friction points are called "creative." They are creative because they will cultivate the soil of Thai spirituality for the realization of the "new creation" in Jesus Christ, the "intensified" Lord of history.

The first question our Lord posed to his disciples at Caesarea Philippi was: "Who do people say the Son of Man is?" To this question, Thailand today is likely to answer, "Jesus Christ is a god of the Americans." The Thai people are already vaguely aware of the profound theological connection between the friction points and Jesus Christ. In some ways these two are related and they are disturbing the Thai people. In this fertile ground of theological friction (a friction relationship is an efficient form of communication!), Jesus Christ, as the intensification of the preintensified view of history, must be presented. Jesus Christ is not *automatically* the stumbling block. The reasons why he is the stumbling block to the Jews, to the Greeks, and to the Thai differ considerably. Thailand has her own historical and theological reasons to stumble over him. The friction points caused by Israel are "good soil" (Matt. 13:8) upon which the message of the intensified theology of history, the stumbling block, can be sown. The "good soil" is now being prepared at the converging point of the great historical forces which accompanied a series of radical unprecedented experiences for Thailand. The tension-filled coexistence between the "traditional" and the "revolutional" within Thailand, the great massive waves of modernization, secularization, and the resurgence of the great ancient faith are all *purposed* by the Lord of history in his "strange work" of producing the "good soil" in Thailand.

> He purposed long ago in his sovereign will that all human history shall be consummated in Christ, that everything exists in Heaven or earth shall find its perfection and fulfillment in him. (Eph. 1:10)[33]

NOTES

1. The Hebrew word *rib*, here translated as "controversy," connotes "strife," "contention," "indictment." It is one of the crucial words (usually in verb form) which expresses the Lord's *pathos* for the salvation of his people and the world. See Isa. 27:8; 45:9; 49:25; 50:8; 57:16; Jer. 2:9; 25:31; Hos. 4:4; 12:2; Deut. 33:8; 1 Sam. 2:10.

2. "Ontocratic" (see *Christianity in World History* by Arend Th. Van Leeuwen, pp. 158-73) means a worldview in which man seeks the meaning of his life in terms of a primordial sense of the cosmic totality—suggested for instance, by cosmic mountain, cosmic tree, phallic symbolism, primordial navel, or cosmic emperor who rules the cosmos from the center of the cosmos (such as China)—which determines the cultural, religious, and political patterns of human life. The God of Israel challenges such beliefs.

3. In the literal form of the word used by the eighth-century prophets, "Therefore" leads from the diatribe to "Thus hath the Lord spoken." Cf. Gerhard von Rad, *The Message of the Prophets* (London: SCM Press, 1968), pp. 19, 65.

4. M.M. Thomas, *The Christian Response to the Asian Revolution* (London: SCM Press, 1966), p. 9.

5. In Hendrik Kraemer, *World Cultures and World Religions* (London: Lutterworth Press, 1960), the author speaks of "unintended gifts of Western 'colonialism.' " He goes on to say, "It is a rather striking peculiarity of Western colonialism that, although there are many flagrant episodes of 'naked imperialism,' it has had in various directions a stimulating influence on the East, to a quite amazing degree" (p. 67).

6. In 1888, Thailand was forced to yield to France the territory of Sip Song Chu Thai in northern Laos; and in 1893, all territory east of the Mekong. In 1904 and 1907, two Cambodian provinces were transferred to French rule, and in 1909, Britain succeeded in obtaining four of Thailand's Malay provinces. See David A. Wilson, *Politics in Thailand* (Ithaca, N.Y.: Cornell University Press, 1968), pp. 7 f.

7. Pridi's People's party at the time of its seizure of power issued a six-point program which reflected the fruits of his study in France. The items in the six-point program belong to the"unintended gifts of Western colonialism," and through them the more emphatic invasion of the *incognito* controversy of the Lord into Thailand was facilitated. The six points set forth were by no means completely foreign to the people of Thailand before 1932; but here they found articulate and "controversial" formulation in the live politics of Thailand. The six points are: (1) freedom and equality of the people in politics, law, court, and business; (2) internal peace and order; (3) economic well-being and work for all by means of economic planning; (4) equality of privileges; (5) freedom and liberty not conflicting with the foregoing; and (6) education for all. Cf. Wilson, *op. cit.*, p. 16.

8. In this connection it is important to know that the king is the head of the secular political power as well as of the religious hierarchy. In his person Thailand One and Thailand Two are united. This is a critical factor when one discusses the implications of rapid modernization on traditional life in Thailand.

9. The lecture "Christianity and Buddhism," delivered by one of the most distinguished and controversial monks in Thailand, the Venerable Bhikkhu Buddhadasa Indapanno, in January 1967, illustrates the attraction which Thailand One feels towards the thought-land of Israel.

10. I wonder if Thailand has been, in truth, responding to the Christian message itself or rather to that of Israel contained in the Christian message? Dr. Hendrik Kraemer says that today we are not in the situation of "meeting" or "encounter" in the serious sense, but only under the "foreshadowings of a still-approaching meeting, interpenetration and *Auseinandersetzung* of cultural attitudes and orientations contained in these civilizations, and of inevitable mutual religious influence and stimulus" (Kraemer, *op. cit.*, p. 14). These "foreshadowings" are noticed in the groundfloor encounter between Thailand and Israel. In this connection I refer readers to the two great books which are by a strange providence written by this famous teacher and his brilliant student—Kraemer's *The Christian Message in a Non-Christian World* (New York: Harper, 1938) and Arend Th. van Leeuwen's *Christianity in World History* (London: Edinburgh House, 1964 and New York: Scribner's, 1966). My uneasiness with the former, which gave a good shaking to the foundations of the Christian world in 1937, is that it assumes so thoroughly and so passionately the position of the *kerygmatic* biblical realism—the position of the intensified theology of history—that it tends to overlook the groundfloor encounter between the great ancient faiths and Israel, the "preintensified theology of history." The book does not have an initial part entitled "The Message of Israel in a Non-Christian World" which, it seems to me, forms one of the most important foci of theological discussion in Asia. Some twenty-six years after Tambaram, Dr. van Leeuwen named his study *Christianity in World History*, which could just as well be titled *Israel in World History*, since theological motifs of Israel play the decisive role throughout the book. In fact the New Testament motifs are over-

shadowed by the Old Testament theological insights. These two great books in their respective ways stimulated my schema of making Israel the first crucial point of reference when trying to determine Thailand's theological whereabouts.

11. Translation by Abraham J. Heschel, *The Prophets* (New York: Harper & Row, 1962), p. 57.

12. *Ibid.*, p. 172.

13. Gunnar Myrdal, *Asian Drama: An Inquiry into the Poverty of Nations*, vol. I (New York: Twentieth Century Fund, 1968), pp. 74–75.

14. Quotations from the tradition are taken from Mircea Eliade, *From Primitives to Zen* (London: Collins, 1967), pp. 471–75.

15. "A blessed resurrection is proclaimed to us—meantime we are surrounded by decay. We are called righteous—and yet sin lives in us. . . . It is in this *contradiction* that hope must prove its power." (Italics added.) Jürgen Moltmann, *Theology of Hope* (New York: Harper & Row, 1967), pp. 18. Thai realism, which operates empirically on the straight deduction from the law of nature, does not speak of a tension-filled "contradiction."

16. See my "wrath of God *vs.* Thai Theologia Gloriae," *South East Asia Journal of Theology*, V, 1 (July 1963), 21.

17. Heschel, *op. cit.*, p. 151.

18. *Ibid.*, p. 174.

19. Manfred Halpern quoted in W. E. Moore and R. M. Cook, eds., *Readings on Social Change* (Englewood Cliffs, N.J.: Prentice-Hall, 1967), p. 182.

20. Myrdal, *op. cit.*, pp. 34–35. It would be a challenging study to relate theologically, one by one, what Myrdal lists as the "modernization ideals," to the concept of history in Thailand. Cf. Myrdal, *op. cit.*, pp. 57–69.

21. A paragraph from the closing address to the eighth World Fellowship of Buddhists, delivered by the president of the Fellowship in November 1966, carries particular significance in this connection: "Perhaps the most significant achievement of all is the clarification of our basic policy by adding a new clause, which was unanimously approved by this Conference, to our Constitution, that the World Fellowship of Buddhists shall refrain from involving itself directly or indirectly in any political activity. From now on, no act is more contrary to the spirit of our Constitution than the exploitation of Buddhism for political ends. The World Fellowship of Buddhists, in all its activities, now stands squarely behind the principle of nonpolitical activity." *The World Fellowship of Buddhists, News Bulletin* III, 6 (November/December 1966), 55.

22. Martin Luther, "The Large Catechism: Exposition of the Ten Commandments —The First Commandment," in Waldo Beach and H. Richard Niebuhr, eds., *Christian Ethics* (New York: Ronald Press, 1955), p. 245.

23. Eliade, *op. cit.*, pp. 471–75.

24. *Dukkha* is usually rendered as "suffering," but this translation is inappropriate. *Du* means "difficult" and *kha* "to endure." As a feeling, therefore, dukkha means that which is difficult to endure. Further, dukkha may be used in the sense of contemptible (du) emptiness (kha). The world rests on suffering; the world, therefore, is contemptible. When dukkha (a contemptible decay existence) is mentioned, the desire to reach the dukkhaless or transdukkha state of man is implied.

25. Udana VIII, 1–3, quoted in Winston L. King, *A Thousand Lives Away* (Cambridge, Mass.: Harvard University Press, 1964), p. 30

26. The mentality of Thailand One is ordinarily described as ateleological cyclicism. This is a misconception rising from the forcing of Western categories onto the basically different cultural thought-patterns and emotions of the East. The cardinal message of Thailand One is to inspire her people to journey "from the dukkha to the dukkhaless state," said the abbot of the Buddhist Meditation Center in Chiengmai, in one of my interviews with him. Those who aspire to obtain final release from dukkha (that is, to reach Nirvana) progress teleologically on the four states of spirally ascending steps: the *Sotapanna* (Stream-Winner), the *Sakadagami* (Once-Returner), the *Anagami* (Never-Returner), and the *Arahant* (Worthy One). Yet this teleology cannot be said to be historically structured, since the sense of history in which it operates is highly metaphysical and enormously patient. "Suppose, O Monks, there was a huge rock of one solid mass, one mile long, one mile wide, one mile high, without split or flaw. And at the end of every hundred years a man should come and rub against it once with a silken cloth. Then that huge rock would wear off and disappear quicker than a world-period, i.e., *kappa.*" *Samyutta-Nikaya* (Samyutta XV, Sutta V, quoted in King, *op. cit.*, p. 93). This remarkably patient view has implications for "salvation history" when one comes to know that the way to the dukkhaless state was first preached by the first Buddha Vipassi ninety-one kappas ago! From Moses to the present day would be a period equal to just thirty rubbings.

27. Buddhadasa Indapanno, *Towards Buddha-Dhamma*, p. 48.

28. Cf. Paul Tillich, *Systematic Theology*, vol. I (Chicago: University of Chicago Press, 1951), p. 14.

29. "Certainly God is more than 'a name for that which concerns man ultimately.' Only saints are ultimately concerned with God. What concerns most of us ultimately is our ego. The biblical consciousness begins not with man's, but with *God's concern.* The supreme fact in the eyes of the prophets is the presence of God's concern for man and the absence of man's concern for God." Abraham J. Heschel, *God in Search of Man* (New York: Meridian Books, 1959), pp. 127f. In my judgment, this Jewish criticism of Tillich, stated in this concise way, pinpoints the location of the central theological issue associated with the name of Tillich.

30. Walther von Loewenich, *Luther's Theologia crucis* (Munich: Kaiser Verlag, 1954), p. 21. Loewenich makes it clear that according to Luther there is a decisive incompatibility between *deus absconditus* and all religious speculation.

31. Heinz R. Schlette, *Towards a Theology of Religions* (London: Burns & Oates, 1966), p. 71.

32. Denigrated "ultimate concern" is graphically brought home in the indulgence controversy: "Those who assert that a soul straightway flies out [of purgatory] as a coin tinkles in the collection-box, are preaching an invention of man. It is sure that when a coin tinkles, greed and avarice are increased; but the intercession of the church is in the will of God alone." Martin Luther, "Ninety-Five Theses," articles 27 and 28.

33. Translation from J.B. Phillips, *The New Testament in Modern English*, rev. ed. (New York: Macmillan, 1972).

V: INDONESIA

T. B. SIMATUPANG

Dynamics for Creative Maturity

This essay, both in its preparation and in its substance, is in many ways characteristic of the present state of theology in Indonesia.

To start with, the essay is written by a layman, a former professional military man, who never studied theology in a seminary. It was written in cooperation with a small group of theologians in Jakarta who, after finishing their basic theological education in Indonesia, went on to acquire doctorates in theology at universities in the United States, the Netherlands, or Germany. They are at present engaged in teaching theology, in writing the textbooks needed for theological education, in the administrative and theological aspects of the work of the Council of Churches in Indonesia, in translating the Bible, and in the ecumenical outreach of the churches. In addition, some have political and journalistic responsibilities. Coresponsibility of ordained and unordained members of the churches, as reflected in the preparation of this essay, is a normal feature in the life of most of the churches in Indonesia.

This brings me to some preliminary remarks about the substance of this essay. Theology is understood in this essay as the self-conscious reflective response to God's continuing action in Christ in the midst of the concrete situation of the church's life, of man, and of society. Due to the rapid pace of change in our society and the very small number of persons who have been able to respond to these changes with systematic theological reflection, most of the responses can only be traced in the actions and statements of individual Christians and churches and, since 1950, in the work of the Council of Churches in Indonesia.

In the preparation of this essay I am particularly indebted to Dr. Liem Khiem Yang and Dr. Frank L. Cooley.

87

This essay is focused mainly on the period after the turn of the century. The situation of Christianity in Indonesia prior to the twentieth century is seen here—if I may make a generalization—as consisting of protochurches, ethnically rooted, controlled by Western missionaries who were guided by a pietistic understanding of the role of Christians in society, and most of whom were working to establish *Volkskirchen* (folk-churches) among the various ethnic groups in Indonesia.

The twentieth century is seen here as the period of moving away from that situation toward the establishment of independent churches, toward a more active involvement in the life of society, toward a growing together of the various churches under the double impact of the process of nation-building on the one hand and of involvement in the worldwide ecumenical movement on the other.

It is the burden of this essay to attempt a very tentative description and evaluation, followed by a projection into the future of the response to God's action in Christ among the churches in Indonesia in the midst of the many-sided processes referred to above—processes that continue.

The Setting

Indonesia is a country consisting of three thousand inhabited islands, stretching from east to west over a distance that is longer than the distance from New York to San Francisco. More than two hundred languages are spoken, but there is one well-established national language which is an advantage not enjoyed by many newly established nations in Asia and Africa. The existence of one language as a vehicle of communication throughout the whole nation will be of increasing importance for theological construction in Indonesia. While up to now all the dissertations presented by Indonesian theologians at universities in the United States, the Netherlands, and Germany were written in English, Dutch, or German, it is anticipated that doctoral dissertations will now be increasingly written in Indonesian and presented to a theological faculty in Jakarta and to the federated faculty of the South East Asia Graduate School of Theology. We cannot expect vigorous development of theological thinking geared to relevant theological issues in the life of church and society in this nation unless there is a theological community ready to participate in that development, conducting its communication in the national language.

In a population of 132 million (1973 est.), about 80 percent are Muslim. It is generally recognized that there are more Muslims in Indonesia than in any other country of the world. On the other hand, before it was banned in March 1966, the Indonesian Communist party was the largest Communist party outside the Communist countries. At the same time, we can say that Indonesia's Protestant Christian community is perhaps the strongest in Asia and is certainly the one experiencing the fastest growth during recent years.[1] The number of Christians is estimated at 8 percent (6 percent Protestants and 2 percent Roman Catholics; other estimates go as high as 9–10 percent, with Roman Catholics at about half the Protestant strength). Hindus account for perhaps 7 percent of the population, with the remainder consisting of Buddhists, adherents of various ethnic religions, and various kinds of mystical and syncretistic sects.

It is quite clear that theology in present-day Indonesia has to be developed in a very dynamic setting, understandably characterized at various points by considerable tension. While most of the problems arising out of this situation are presented in political forms, some of them are basically theological issues, and theologians must endeavor to interpret this situation in a theological perspective. It is the situation as a whole—church, man, and society—which challenges our theological thinking, and to understand it and the thrust of its dynamic, we must turn briefly to the history of the country.

Speaking in 1969 on "The Re-emergence of Southeast Asia: An Indonesian Perspective," H.E. Soedjatmoko—the Indonesian ambassador to the United States—said:

> If we now make a cross-cut through Southeast Asian history, the picture that emerges is one that resembles a layer cake of layer upon layer of cultural-religious sediments, some of them thick in some places, while thin or entirely absent in others. . . . It would seem to me that the capacity of the peoples of Southeast Asia to digest and adapt these influences according to their own genius does represent the most striking element in this acculturation process. As a result, the cultures of Southeast Asia emerge

with an autochthony quite distinct from the sources which have helped
shape them. Viewed in this light, there are sufficient grounds to assume
that in developing their answers to the problems of the post-independence
era, and to those which accompany their transition into the twentieth
century, the nations of Southeast Asia will eventually come up with
responses, structures and institutions that are once again very much their
own, differing from those prevailing in either the liberal-capitalist or
communist models.[2]

In the Indonesian case we have as the first "layer" the Indonesian
communal structure and natural religions, which still constitute the
underlying pattern of life and thinking for most of the people. At the
beginning of the Christian era, at the same time when Roman civilization reached the shores of northern Europe and Great Britain to be
followed later on by Christianity, Indian cultural and religious influences were brought to Indonesia. For about thirteen hundred years
Hinduism, Buddhism, and Indian culture were the dominant forces
in transforming society from tribalism into kingdoms, some of which
unified the greater part of present-day Indonesia and some adjacent
areas. However, this Hindu-Buddhist "layer" is very thin or practically absent in some parts of the interior of Sumatra and in the eastern
part of Indonesia. Toward the end of the thirteenth century there
were two important events in the history of Indonesia: Islam entered
the religious-political scene, and a Chinese-Mongol fleet attempted an
invasion of East Java. Though the invasion was repelled, it constituted the beginning of a more extensive stream of Chinese migration.
Chinese cultural and political influence was not dominant at any
period in Indonesian history. Islam, however, did become the dominant religious-political force in many parts of the country, though there
was never a period in Indonesian history when the greater part of the
country was united under a Muslim sultanate. The Islamization of
Indonesia was never fully accomplished, with the double consequence that the Islamic "layer" is absent in many parts of Indonesia,
areas which later became the "base areas" for Christianity, and that in
East and Central Java the Islamic "layer" is—in many respects—a
comparatively thin crust overlaying the pre-Islamic layers. The island of Bali is a special case, because Hinduism there has succeeded to
the present day in remaining the main religion of the population.

THE EXPANSION OF THE MODERN WEST AND THE SPREAD
OF CHRISTIANITY UNTIL THE TWENTIETH CENTURY

It was in that situation when Islam was expanding but was not yet rooted in all areas of Indonesia, and when Hinduism was retreating from Java to Bali, that the double process of the expansion of the modern West and the spread of Christianity started in Indonesia with the coming of the Portuguese, followed by the Dutch, with a brief British interregnum during the Napoleonic wars.

The Portuguese came to Indonesia with theological and political understanding behind their aims of breaking the economic power of the Muslims (who controlled the trade from Indonesia to Europe), of occupying territories in the name of the king of Portugal, and of winning the population for the Roman Catholic Church. The Muslim sultan of Ternate used military power in his effort to stop both the expansion of Portuguese power and the spread of Christianity. Thousands of Christians were killed, but there were still forty thousand left when the Dutch East India Company ousted the Portuguese in 1605.

The Dutch were enemies of the Portuguese, politically, commercially, and religiously. After the Portuguese were driven out of Indonesia, the indigenous Christians changed from Roman Catholicism to the Reformed Christianity of the Dutch. It is probably impossible to trace how those first Indonesian Christians understood their conversion from their ethnic religion into Roman Catholicism, the threat of Islam, and the subsequent change into Reformed Christianity. Their role in all this was obviously a passive one. The Bible was translated by Melchior Leydekker in 1673 into Malay, the lingua franca of those days, but Indonesian Christians probably had no active role in the work of translation. That might be one of the reasons why the translation in many ways was not very successful in conveying the biblical message in Indonesian thought-forms. Dr. Th. Müller-Krüger characterizes the insignificant position of Indonesian Christians during that time by using the phrase "Church of people under age," and the whole period prior to 1800 he considers as belonging to the prehistory of the church in Indonesia.[3]

The nineteenth century showed important changes in both the political-economic field and the church. While the initiative and responsibility in all these areas remained firmly in Dutch hands, the Indonesians were no longer as passive as in the previous period.

The government of the Netherlands-Indies, which took over administration in 1815, though still responsible for the "Protestant Church in the Netherlands-Indies," followed a liberal religious policy. It was the age of the great missionary societies, with a pietistic theology, which had their home bases in Western Europe. Devoted and often gifted missionaries, such as Ludwig I. Nommensen, the "apostle to the Toba-Bataks," and Joseph Kam, the "apostle to the Moluccas," were instrumental in establishing protochurches among certain ethnic groups or, in the case of Kam, in infusing new life into old churches. Many of these missionaries came out of the pietistic atmosphere of Western Europe, and this might be the reason why the churches in Indonesia which grew out of their work do not manifest a strong confessional or denominational awareness down to the present day.[4]

What can we say about the theological response of Indonesian Christians in these protochurches among the various ethnic groups during the nineteenth century? Real theological thinking cannot be expected from this period. For one thing, the responsibility for the life of those protochurches was fully in the hands of European missionaries. There were some seminaries during the nineteenth century—the seminary in Depok (West Java) started in 1870; the STOVIL (School of Education for Indigenous Teachers) started in Ambon and Minahasa in 1885; and the seminary among the Bataks. But the graduates of these seminaries, though ordained, remained in a subordinate position, at best as assistant pastors to the European missionaries. Nevertheless, if one reads some of the Bible translations into the local languages and listens to some of the liturgies from this period, one is inclined to believe that there must have been some among the clergy who helped the missionaries translate the Bible and church liturgies into indigenous thought-forms.

Then there were some notable individuals, such as Paulus Tosari in East Java and Sadrach in Central Java.[5] Though perhaps it is better to speak of "prototheological awareness" than to use the term "theological response" in these cases, one can say that in the nineteenth century, Indonesian Christianity no longer consisted of those faceless persons of the sixteenth century. A profile, though not yet clearly discernible, was gradually emerging.

THE TWENTIETH CENTURY: ERA OF NATIONALISM, INDEPENDENT CHURCHES AND ECUMENISM

The period from the sixteenth century to the beginning of the twentieth century was the era of colonialism and missionary expansion. In both spheres Indonesians only very gradually acquired a more active role. Initiative and leadership remained almost completely in the hands of colonial administrators, military officers, and entrepreneurs on the one hand; and foreign missionaries on the other.

The turn of the century was the end of an era. The 1900s saw the emergence of nationalism, with its ambiguous relation to colonialism. Nationalism was a reaction and an opposition to colonialism. At the same time, however, nationalism continued the process of nation-building and modernization, the conditions for which had been prepared by colonialism. Nationalism sees itself as the guardian of the precolonial heritage and at the same time the herald of a new future.

The twentieth century also saw the development of independent churches. The emergence of these constituted a break with the missionary period, but they were also a continuation and—to a certain extent—the fulfilment of the missionary enterprise.[6] It also happened that the period before and after the emergence of independent churches in Indonesia coincided with the involvement of Indonesian Christians in the ecumenical movement.

In the following paragraphs we shall try to trace the theological response among Indonesian Christians to the changing situation in church and society in the twentieth century—the era of nationalism, independent churches, and ecumenism.

THE BEGINNING OF THE NATIONALIST MOVEMENT

The mood during the first decades of the twentieth century was very strongly influenced by the emergence of the nationalist movement. Starting in 1908 as a movement among students of the Medical School in Jakarta, with strong Javanese cultural overtones, it soon captured the imagination of the educated youth in all areas of Indonesia. In the process, it acquired a more political character. It was the time of youth movements related to specific ethnic groups: the Young Batak movement, the Young Minahasa movement, the Young Ambon movement, and so on. The next step was a merger of these movements into movements encompassing whole islands: the Young Sumatra movement, the Young Java movement. The year 1928 saw the emergence of an All-Indonesia Youth movement, cemented by the "Oath of the Youth," acknowledging One People, One Fatherland, One Language (Indonesian).

In the meantime this nationalist movement had become a mass movement. While the idea first captured the youth, very soon political parties with a mass following emerged. In this process, the common aim of an independent nation-state became associated in the minds of different people with various religious and social ideals. Nationalist political parties cooperated and, at the same time, competed with Islamic, Socialist, and later Communist, parties. After the Communist-inspired rebellion in 1926, it became clear that the movement had become a formidable challenge to the continuance of Netherlands colonial rule.

HOW DID CHRISTIANS RESPOND?

There were basic reasons why the protochurches in Indonesia could not respond quickly and creatively to this new development. One was that the protochurches were ethnically limited in their perspective. While the nationalist movement very soon broke out of an ethnocentric into a national perspective, the protochurches could not grow out of their "earthen vessels." In fact, down to the present this problem has not been satisfactorily solved by the churches in Indonesia. There was also the fact, previously mentioned, that the protochurches were under the leadership of the European missionaries, while the few ordained Indonesians were usually assistants to the Europeans. Another factor was the prevailing pietistic theology with its personalistic, spiritualistic, otherworldly, and futuristic understanding of Christian faith and life.[7]

The inability of the protochurches to respond to the challenges of the new era did not prevent individual members from joining the nationalist movement. The educated youth in general and, later on, the few academically trained people in the protochurches proceeded into social thinking and social involvement without being aware of the relevance of their Christian faith in these realms.

One hundred years after the pietistically oriented missionary societies started sending missionaries from Western Europe, which was then coming more and more under the grip of the modern, secular world, the protochurches in Indonesia that resulted from their efforts were beginning to face that same modernizing, secularizing world. There was a danger of permanent estrangement between the pietistically oriented and ethnically rooted protochurches under the leadership of European missionaries and the young generation of Indonesian Christians, who were increasingly attracted by a secular-oriented Indonesian nationalism with strong overtones of racial and social equality and justice. In North Sumatra and in the Minahasa there were already groups of Christians who separated themselves from missionary-controlled protochurches to form their own churches, strongly influenced by a nationalistic outlook.

INDEPENDENT CHURCHES, SOCIAL CONCERN, AND ECUMENICAL PARTICIPATION

The emergence of independent churches, starting with the Toba Batak church in 1930, constituted a significant response to the challenge of that time. Some of the missionaries helped promote this development—Dr. Hendrik Kraemer being undoubtedly the major figure among them.

The most creative—also theological—response came from laymen. The fact that there was already a generation of Indonesian Christian medical doctors and lawyers, together with a Student Christian Movement, might be one of the reasons why from that time laymen have played important roles in the life and thinking of the churches. It was then too that Indonesian Christians came in touch with ecumenical thinking, and these contacts made a deep impression. Four laymen in particular played (and one of them is still playing) important roles in the life and thinking of the churches, as well as in the life of the nation in this period. None of them wrote systematic theological treatises, but they certainly influenced the theological thinking of the churches.

First was the late Prof. Dr. T. S. G. Mulia, who studied law in Holland and wrote a notable doctoral dissertation on "Primitive Thinking in Modern Scientific Research."[8] He was at one time minister of education of the Republic of Indonesia. Dr. Mulia was

also the first chairman of the Council of Churches in Indonesia, the
founder of the Indonesian Christian University, the first Indonesian
chairman of the board of the Joint Theological Seminary in Jakarta,
and the first chairman of the Indonesian Bible Society. At the very
end of his life, in 1967, the Free University of Amsterdam awarded
him an honorary doctorate in theology. This is symptomatic of the
state of theology in Indonesia: It is more lived out and acted upon than
written about.

After attending the International Missionary Conference in
Jerusalem in 1928, Dr. Mulia sharply criticized the policies of mission
boards in an address to the Netherland Indies Mission Association
held that same year in Bandung. His main point was that missionary
policies cannot ignore the great events in history. The peoples of Asia
and Africa, he pointed out, are being drawn into the stream of a world
economy, where imperialism is facing nationalism and communism.
Christians and non-Christians alike in Indonesia are asking: Are
Christian missions only an instrument of Western expansion? Does
the missionary enterprise oppose nationalism? Are missions working
for social justice and racial equality? Why is it that as yet there are not
enough Indonesian Christians who, by their presence in the midst of
the social changes, cooperate with other Indonesians in shaping the
future? There was a strong impression among Indonesian Christian
leaders in Tapanuli, Minahasa, and the Moluccas that missions were
only serving the colonial and capitalist systems.[9]

Dr. J. Leimena, one of the founders of the Student Christian
Movement in Indonesia, attended the International Missionary Conference at Tambaram in 1938 and was a minister in most of the
cabinets after the proclamation of the republic. Several times he was
elected vice-chairman of the Council of Churches and at present is one
of its honorary presidents. He was also influential in urging the
missions and Indonesian Christians to turn their attention to social
problems, as when he wrote:

> It is the first task of the church to preach the gospel, serve the sacraments,
> etc. Yet the church is also a signpost pointing to Christ as the Judge and
> Savior of man and society. . . . The church must judge social, economic
> and public errors, and she must cooperate in the renewal of society.[10]

Amir Sjarifuddin, undoubtedly the most brilliant among the younger
generation of Indonesian Christians at that time, must also be men-

tioned. He became a Christian when he was studying law in Jakarta, and was already one of the most promising among the young leaders of the more radical wing of the nationalist movement. He was sentenced to death during the Japanese occupation, and his life was saved only because of an urgent plea by Sukarno to the Japanese military authorities. However, he remained in prison for the remainder of the Japanese occupation, and while there, led religious services for the convicts, some of whom later became Christians. After the proclamation of independence in 1945, he went straight from prison to a post in the cabinet, later became prime minister, was involved in the rebellion against the government in 1948 after he left the cabinet, and was killed with a prayer book of the SCM written by Hans Lilje in his hand, in the midst of the confusion following the Dutch attack on the republic during Christmas 1948.[11]

Sjarifuddin was the prototype of a "political Christian." Speaking about the role of missionaries in the 1930s, he said: "There is a time to come and a time to go." Of the role of Christians in Indonesia, he said: "Christians must stay side-by-side with Muslims and other nationalists in their political aspirations. They must live out of their own convictions and vision. They must not let themselves be tolerated, but must claim their legitimate place."[12]

Dr. A. M. Tambunan, though somewhat younger than Sjarifuddin and a student of law at that time, also belonged to the generation of Indonesian Christian intellectuals who were very much impressed and influenced by the first ecumenical contacts during the First All-Asian Student Conference in Tjiteureup (West Java) in 1933. Tambunan was minister of social affairs in the cabinet and one of the honorary presidents of the Council of Churches when he died in 1972.

This generation of Christian laymen, deeply involved in both the life of the nation and the life of the churches, had enormous influence on the trend of theological thinking in Indonesia, though none of them did any systematic theological writing.

THE HIGHER THEOLOGICAL SCHOOL (HTS), JAKARTA

The Higher Theological School, started in 1934 at Bogor (60 km. from Jakarta) and later moved to Jakarta, has played an important role in the life and thinking of the churches in Indonesia over the last four decades. Prior to 1934, seminaries in the Moluccas, in Minahasa, and in Tapanuli, trained students to become assistant pastors to the European missionaries. There were two theological schools in Java—one at Yogyakarta in Central Java started in 1905, and one at Malang in East Java started in 1925 and called "Bale Wijoto." Both were related to local churches, and the school at Malang, especially, under the leadership of Dr. B.M. Schuurman, made efforts to prepare the students to interpret the Gospel in the thought categories of Javanese culture.

In contrast with the previous pattern, the HTS Jakarta planned to train Indonesian pastors who would be able to serve the churches in Indonesia on a basis of equality with the European missionaries, and eventually to bear full responsibility for the leadership of the independent churches. It was the intention of the founders of the HTS (among whom Hendrik Kraemer was included), not only that the school would teach the students the theological heritage of the Western churches, but that the students would be enabled to translate the riches of the Gospel into the realities of Indonesian culture and society with their own accent. The words "theologia in loco" were later introduced by Dr. Th. Müller-Krüger to express this ideal.[13] It should be noted in this context that during the first decades, the faculty of the HTS consisted exclusively of Western theologians for the simple reason that there were no Indonesian theologians.

What has been the impact of this school on Indonesian theological thinking? Prior to the Japanese occupation in 1942, two classes —consisting of eighteen and eleven students respectively —graduated. In many ways they were the link between the period of Western tutelage and the period of complete independence in the life of the churches. This group bore the brunt of theological and administrative leadership of the churches during the Japanese occupation and during the years of turmoil following the proclamation of independence in 1945. The first two general secretaries of the Council of Churches came from this group, which also provided the pastors who organized the chaplaincies in the armed forces. Not many of them have produced extensive theological reflections, and yet the way they filled their various positions of responsibility reflected their basic theological principles, which they exercised in such areas as the independence of the church vis-à-vis secular authorities; involvement in social problems, side-by-side with the proclamation of the gospel to all people; and the furtherance of the church's ecumenicity both nationally and internationally. Upholding these principles during the turbulent years of the last three decades absorbed so much of their time and energy that none of them has done serious theological work in the sense of "theologia in loco," as the founders of the Higher Theological School had hoped.

THE JAPANESE OCCUPATION

There was hardly any written theological reflection during the Japanese occupation because most of the theological schools were closed. Yet, the experience of the churches during those years contributed much to their theological maturity. The Japanese occupation was the beginning of a new period in the life of the nation and the churches. It was the definitive end of the period—which started in the sixteenth century—of Western colonial expansion and the spread of Christianity. With the Japanese occupation, the Western dominance over Indonesia came to an end. But the church in the meantime had become strongly rooted in the nation. Historically, the church in Indonesia was planted and matured under the umbrella of Western expansion. During the Japanese occupation the churches proved able to continue their existence after that historical external umbrella was removed. In a way, the Japanese occupation prepared the churches for the next period, the period of national independence, by infusing into the minds of the leaders of the churches the hard lesson that being the church means living under God in the midst of the realities of the day without any ties, if necessary, with churches outside the country.

The realities were the presence of military aliens who tried to reeducate and mobilize the youth, who took schools away from church control, who sometimes demanded from church leaders compliance with the rites of emperor worship. On the other hand there was a growing sense of Christian solidarity and a weakening of confessional differences.

Some years after the end of the war the University of Bonn awarded an honorary doctorate to Ephorus Justin Sihombing of the Batak Church for his leadership of the church during and after the Japanese occupation. Again this is symbolic of the fact that thus far theology in Indonesia has been more acted upon and lived out than it has been embodied and developed in theological literature.

CHRISTIANS IN A COUNTRY FIGHTING FOR INDEPENDENCE

Indonesian Christians found themselves in a peculiar situation when Indonesia—predominantly Muslim—proclaimed its independence and then had to fight on and off for four years, from 1945 to 1949, against the Dutch, who had originally brought Christianity to the country. Were the Christians and the churches theologically prepared to meet this challenge? Did they reflect theologically on their task when they were thrown into this stream of history?

The fact is they had no time to reflect on their style; they just had to swim, otherwise they would have drowned. And yet, despite the fact that there was not much conscious theological reflection, it is clear that the Christian leaders, both in the church and in the society, were guided by that body of theological ideas and principles which had developed during the recent decades when, on August 17, 1945, the proclamation of independence inaugurated a new period in the life of the nation.

Under the leadership of men like Dr. Mulia, Dr. Leimena, Dr. Tambunan, and others, both lay and ordained, whose theological and political ideas had matured during the thirties, Christians concentrated their attention first on the principles which would guide the life of the new state, with the aim that religious freedom and equal rights and opportunities would be guaranteed to all citizens, irrespective of belief and race. After being satisfied on these points, the Christian Political Party—its inception probably inspired by the existence of Christian political parties in the Netherlands—issued a statement to the effect that it considered independence to be a gift of God and that all Indonesians, regardless of their religion, had the duty to defend the independence of the nation.

While theologically and politically mature leaders of Indonesian Christianity stressed the integral unitary aspect of the nation, contacts with Dutch Christians and participation in the World Conference of Christian Youth at Oslo in 1947 and the inaugural assembly of the World Council of Churches at Amsterdam in 1948 served as reminders that Indonesian Christians were at the same time part of the worldwide Christian community. In the course of the conflict between Indonesia and the Netherlands, and especially toward the attainment of a final agreement in 1949, Christians in Indonesia and in Holland had opportunities to play a conciliatory role. Dr. Leimena and the present writer were both members of the delegation which negotiated the peace with the Netherlands during the round table conference in 1949 in The Hague.

A NEW GENERATION OF THEOLOGIANS

The most important event that influenced the life and thought of the churches following the international recognition of Indonesia's independence and the consequent normalization of its relations with the outside world was the inauguration of the Council of Churches in Indonesia in May 1950. Before considering the theological thinking of the churches as reflected in the work of the council since 1950, we shall first look briefly at the development of theological education and at some of the doctoral dissertations of Indonesian theologians who, in most cases, were preparing themselves to become seminary professors.

The Higher Theological School had been reopened in 1946, and in 1954 the standard of its work was brought up to university level. There was also greater stress in the curriculum on ethics and on the study of Islam. Prof. J. Verkuyl stressed the necessity of paying more attention to ethical subjects with an eye to the role of Christians in nation-building, revolution, and development.[14]

By 1971 the number of member schools in the Association of Theological Schools in Indonesia had increased to twelve, and significant advances had been made in raising standards, improving facilities, and developing library resources.

One of the problems that had been faced by the theological schools after 1950 was the need to increase the number and ratio of Indonesian professors. While the older generation of theologians, graduated prior to the Japanese invasion, was occupied with administering the churches and the Council of Churches, a new generation of theologians had been sent to Germany, the Netherlands, and the United States for graduate study, with a view to their teaching in Indonesian theological schools upon their return. The result has been a series of doctoral dissertations prepared by relatively young and inexperienced Indonesian theologians. Some reflect, to a greater or lesser degree, theological issues faced by the churches in Indonesia; others are of a more general and universal character. The hope has been that this new generation of theologians, by using the tools of modern theological scholarship, will be able to make a significant contribution to the development of theological thought in Indonesia. Brief mention of a few of these scholars and their doctoral dissertations will indicate both the first fruits and the promise of things to come.

Dr. J. L. Ch. Abineno wrote his dissertation on "Liturgical Forms and Patterns in the Evangelical Church of Timor"[15] in 1956 at the University of Utrecht under Professor J.C. Hoekendijk. Abineno concluded that liturgy cannot be defined in purely ecclesiological terms, because liturgy originates in the gospel of the kingdom and is performed in the open theater of the world (Matt. 24:14). Liturgy should be conceived, he said, as broadly as life itself. There should be more informal and more flexible proclamation of the Gospel, breaking with the "sermonic" tradition. Dr. Abineno is on the faculty of the theological school in Jakarta, has served as a president of the Council of Churches, and is a key figure in the translation of the Bible into modern Indonesian.

When Dr. P. D. Latuihamallo wrote his dissertation at Union Theological Seminary, New York, in 1959 on "The Relation of Church and World in the Writings of Hendrik Kraemer," his adviser was Dr. John C. Bennett. Latuihamallo's study showed that church renewal is possible only if we take the world seriously and that theology is to be formulated in terms of the meeting of church and world. Dr. Latuihamallo, who has served as a president of the Council of Churches, as rector of the Higher Theological School in Jakarta, and as a member of the Indonesian parliament, continues to focus his theological study on the relation between politics and missiology in a pluralistic society such as Indonesia.

Dr. Andar M. Lumban Tobing, in his dissertation on "The Ministry in the Batak Church"[16] (Bonn University, 1957), dealt with the "folk-church" limitations as found in the Batak Christian Protestant Church (HKBP). There is a danger, he said, that in a folk-church the boundary between church and people disappears in the thinking of the members of the church, and that church is understood exclusively as a sociological entity with no particular sense of mission. Dr. Tobing maintains that the HKBP's relations with other churches, especially with churches abroad, must be looked at critically, because such relations may easily become just a form of self-assertion and self-preservation. Dr. Tobing, formerly president of Nommensen University, has been moderator of the Protestant Christian Church of Indonesia, which separated from the Batak Church in 1964.

Dr. R. Soedarmo got his doctorate in 1957 at the Free University in Amsterdam. His dissertation, "In the World but Not of the World,"[17] is mainly a historical and analytical appraisal of the thought of Friedrich Gogarten. Soedarmo very largly rejects Gogarten's views because, in his judgment, while there are many useful elements in them, Gogarten's theology is basically an accommodation of the Gospel to existentialist philosophy and to the modern worldview, and the Gospel disappears in the process. Dr. Soedarmo teaches at the Higher Theological School in Jakarta and is one of those responsible for the new Indonesian translation of the Bible.

Dr. W.B. Sidjabat wrote his dissertation on "Religious Tolerance and the Christian Faith"[18] at Princeton Theological Seminary in 1960. He concluded that religious tolerance ought to be approached from both the theological and sociophenomenological points of view, that there is a basis for religious tolerance within Christianity and Islam, and that the increasing theological interest among Muslims might bring forth some readjustment of Islamic religious structures for modern times. Dr. Sidjabat is on the faculty of the Higher Theological School in Jakarta and has served also in the Department of Study and Research of the Council of Churches.

Dr. S.A.E. Nababan, general secretary of the Council of Churches, wrote his dissertation on "Confession and Mission According to Romans 14 and 15"[19] at the University of Heidelberg in 1962. He argues that the confession of the Christ who died and rose again from the dead, who has been installed as the Lord of the living and of the dead, is the most important confession in the life of the church. Both the unity of the church and the mission of the church are based on the confession of Christ's lordship over the whole world.

Dr. Liem Khiem-yang, in his dissertation on "The Letter to Philemon in Its relation to the Thinking of the Apostle Paul"[20] (Bonn University, 1963), argues that for Paul, social structures have no ultimate significance. Basically they no longer have power over us, and therefore we are free either to live with them or to break with them. Nor can we use the terms "social conservative" or "progressive" for Paul's attitude, because his attitude is based on faith and belongs to a different category altogether. Dr. Liem teaches New Testament at the Higher Theological School in Jakarta.

Dr. Harun Hadiwijono wrote his dissertation on "Man in the Present Javanese Mysticism"[21] at the Free University in Amsterdam, 1967. He found that while Hindu-Javanese ideas still form the substratum, Javanese mysticism has been penetrated by various influences, including Christianity, modern science, and politics. He doubts that Javanese mysticism, in its present condition, will be able to survive in any meaningful way. Dr. Hadiwijono teaches at the United Theological College of Yogyakarta in Central Java, and is one of the prominent leaders of the Javanese church in that region, a church with a Reformed background.

THE SIGNIFICANCE OF THE COUNCIL OF CHURCHES
IN INDONESIA FOR THE DEVELOPMENT OF THEOLOGICAL THINKING

A consideration of the notable contribution of certain lay members of the Christian community to theological thinking in Indonesia after the 1950s should not be ignored in this survey. Since most of their thinking, however, has affected the life and thought of the churches and the nation through their association with the Council of Churches, its significance will be recorded in the context of the following paragraphs dealing with the Council of Churches in Indonesia.

The council was inaugurated in May 1950, with various streams of events and ideas converging into its life and thought from the very beginning. There was the experience of the regional councils in East Indonesia, on Java, and on Sumatra. There was the experience of participation in the ecumenical conferences at Jerusalem (1928), Tambaram (1938), Oslo (1947), and very fresh in the minds of some people during the preparatory work leading to the inauguration of the council were the impressions they brought back from Amsterdam (1948). Undoubtedly the memory of experiences during the Japanese occupation and the war for independence, and the mood of nation-building prevailing in the country, also influenced the thinking of the founders of the Council of Churches. Missionary bodies and Christian associations such as the YMCA were excluded from membership, since from the very beginning only Indonesian churches supporting the central aim—to work toward the establishment of one church in Indonesia—were eligible for membership.

From its inception the thinking of the council has been guided by its self-image as an expression of the common mission of the churches in Indonesia, as being part of the nation as well as the church for the nation, and at the same time as part of the worldwide ecumenical fellowship of churches. The council, then, has always been the meeting place between ecumenical involvement and the common engagement of the churches in the life of the nation through their common concerns for unity, mission, and service. It is in this sense that the Council of Churches has been of significance for the development of theological thinking in Indonesia and that the thinking of the council—as reflected in its statements, consultations, assemblies, and publications—can to some extent be considered representative of the trend of theological thinking among its member churches.

The late Dr. Mulia, Dr. J. Leimena, Dr. A. M. Tambunan, and the present writer, having served the council at various times as president, vice-president, or honorary president, represent the lay element in the life and thinking of the council. The Reverend W. J. Rumambi and the Reverend Simon Marantika, the first and second general secretary, are representative of the contribution of the older generation of theologians, while the present general secretary, Dr. Nababan, symbolizes the involvement of the younger generation of theologians.

The trilogy of the ecumenical movement—unity, mission, and service—has been a living reality in the life and thought of the council since it began. The unambiguous aim has been to foster the establishment of one church in Indonesia. It has been in the area of unity, however, that the council has produced the fewest results and the least creative thinking. One reason for this is that thinking on the unity of the churches has been too much oriented to discussions among confessional groups in the West, while the main problem is how to unite the various "folk-churches," with their different cultural, linguistic, and to some extent confessional, backgrounds, at a time when the different ethnic groups in Indonesia are involved together in the process of nation-building and modernization. Mission understood as the proclamation of the Gospel, so that people may come to repentance and belief, is considered by the churches to be the main aim in Indonesia, since they themselves are the products of recent missionary efforts and are reminded by everyday events that they are living among people belonging to other faiths. The rather spectacular growth of some churches during recent years has confronted the council with various kinds of challenges, some of them of a fundamental theological nature. But it has been in the field of service, conceived as involvement in loving and in serving the whole community, that the council and churches in Indonesia have been confronted with their greatest challenges. In the face of insurrections; civil wars; coup d'états involving Communists, fanatical Muslims, and local patriots; constitutional and political crises; international conflicts; mass slaughters; interreligious tensions; revolution; modernization; secularization; and development, the council and the churches have been challenged to respond in faithfulness to the Lord and in loving and serving solidarity with the people. The following paragraphs seek to distil the theological essence out of the numerous statements of the council in response to these issues.

Toward a Common Confession?

As part of the effort toward the establishment of one church in Indonesia, the Commission on Faith and Order of the Council of Churches is working on a draft for an ecumenical council for Indonesia and a draft for a common confession for the participating churches. The draft for the common confession is centered around the following themes:

(a) The doctrine of the Trinity is to be restated in the light of challenges from the Muslims, who question the trinitarian formula in the name of the Oneness of God;

(b) the matter of the church and its ecumenicity or catholicity is to be restated to stress that the churches in Indonesia are, on the one hand, the church in and for the nation; and, on the other, part of the one Holy Catholic Church;

(c) the church's view of man is to be restated, stressing man's freedom and responsibility, especially his religious freedom, in the light of the challenge from Islam and others;

(d) social responsibility is to be emphasized, particularly as it concerns nature, science, and technology, social structures, and hope and illusions in the process of development. The problems of secularization, linked to its rejection by traditional religious and cultural worldviews on the one hand, and the threat of secularism, including the Communist worldview, on the other, will have their place also. As yet the theological thinking in the commission which must undergird this tremendous task is still in a somewhat rudimentary stage.

In the statements of the council and of some member churches, and also in the confession of the Batak church, there are already elements for such a common confession. One example among many is the October 1954 statement of the Evangelical Christian Church in Minahasa, rejecting communism "because the interpretation of communism on man and history are opposed to the Bible," but stressing that "it is God's will that man achieve life, freedom, justice and peace" and "it is the duty of the church as a real sign of God's kingdom in this world to try continuously according to its own methods and principles to participate in the development of society in every field."

The confession of the Batak Protestant Christian Church, adopted in 1951, must be mentioned here, for up till now it has been the only confession formulated by any of the churches in Indonesia. [See the new English translation of the Batak confession in the Appendix of this volume.—*Ed.*] Though the immediate motivation for drafting the confession was the desire to be admitted to the Lutheran World Federation (LWF), and though the chief architect of the confession, the then Ephorus J. Sihombing, used the confessions of Western churches during his preparatory studies, the confession fulfilled a real need in the life of the Batak church. Furthermore, the confession constitutes a serious effort to express what the church believes in the context of the cultural-religious realities and challenges around it. Though it is the general consensus among informed observers that the Batak confession cannot be considered as embodying "the unaltered Augsburg Confession," which is a condition for admission to the LWF, the Batak church was accepted by the LWF on the basis of its confession. According to Dr. Andar M. Lumban Tobing, the Batak church, "although not confessionally bound, . . . is strongly influenced by Lutheran theology and pietism."[22]

"WOE TO ME IF I DO NOT PREACH THE GOSPEL"

In trying to understand the thinking of the churches in Indonesia one must keep in mind that most of them—while persuaded by their experience during the last decades that involvement in the life of the

nation is both unavoidable and necessary for the good of the
nation—still basically see the evangelistic task as the center of their
mission. This is easy to understand if we remember that these
churches grew out of the work of pietistically oriented missionary
societies during the nineteenth and twentieth centuries. Whereas,
however, the evangelistic task was formerly seen as directed to certain
ethnic groups separately, in recent years the whole of Indonesia is
seen as one field for the common calling of all churches to witness and
service, taking into account both the particular religious-cultural
background of the various ethnic groups and the common experience
of the whole nation during the struggle for freedom and during the
consequent process of nation-building, rapid social change, revolutionary fervor, modernization, secularization, urbanization, and
the beginning of industrialization.

A book edited by Dr. W. B. Sidjabat, *Our Calling Today*,[23] compris-
ing a series of studies on different aspects of this common evangelistic
task, received widespread criticism by many Muslim newspapers and
other publications as reflecting, in their judgment, a master plan for
the total evangelization of Indonesia according to a particular timeta-
ble.

In the eyes of many Muslims, this impression, though repeatedly
refuted by Christian leaders, was strengthened if not confirmed
when, during recent years, a significant number of persons both from
an ethnic religious background and from an Islamic background,
joined the churches. In fact, the churches themselves were unpre-
pared for this large influx of new members.[24] Their number has
frequently been put at 2.5 million, primarily by Muslim newspapers
and other publications, but church leaders consider a figure of about
0.5 million to be nearer the truth.

It is in this light that the tension between Muslims and Christians is
interpreted, though informed observers also stress political factors in
their analyses. The tension was manifested in mob attacks on
churches and Christian schools at various places, and in the demands
for a freezing of the religious situation between the major religions
and the limiting of missionary efforts toward people who do not yet
belong to any of the major religions. Many voices made it clear that
the traditional cooperation between the various groups in the country
could be endangered if the Christians did not immediately stop
bringing the Christian Gospel to adherents of other major religions.

It was in that situation that the General Assembly of the Council of Churches in Makassar (1967) discussed the missionary task of the churches in Indonesia, within the context of three biblical injunctions:

(1) "Woe unto me if I do not preach the Gospel"; (2) "Blessed are you when men revile you and utter all kinds of evil against you falsely on my account"; and (3) "So be wise as serpents and innocent as doves."

The general consensus was that both for the sake of the nation and for the missionary task of the churches, Christians should cooperate with all persons of goodwill to secure human rights and freedoms, including the right to propagate and change one's religion. Contacts with persons of other faiths should be carried out on the basis of "dialogue, witness and cooperation."

At the assembly, and increasingly since 1967, responsible parties in the Council of Churches have been forced, by the growing stream of professional evangelists coming to Indonesia from the conservative "evangelical" tradition in the United States, to wrestle with the deeper theological implications of the role of evangelism (and particularly demonstrative mass evangelistic campaigns) within the mission of the church.

SOCIAL THINKING OF THE CHURCHES

Since the 1940s, some years after attaining their formal independence as folk-churches with a pietistic theological background, the churches in Indonesia have been "swimming" in the maelstrom of historical changes—from the Japanese occupation, to the struggle for national independence, the various internal and external crises, up through the events following the abortive coup of September 30, 1965. Though it is a very risky undertaking, the author ventures to identify three points as being characteristic of the social thinking of the churches, as reflected in their statements and actions during these years.

The first point is that the churches have been acting under the pressure of concrete challenges, so that most of their statements are pervaded by a sense of immediacy and urgency. The option in most cases is: Swim with whatever style and strength you have at your disposal or be drowned. The second point is that there is a strong biblical element in all these statements. The writers of these state-

ments relied on biblical themes which they considered to be the most
appropriate starting points in responding to the issue at hand.
Thirdly, the impact of ecumenical thinking, from both the EACC
(now the CCA) and the WCC, is discernable in many of the statements. This ecumenical element, however, is always placed in the
context of a biblically based response to a concrete situation. When
the present writer had the opportunity to address the World Conference on Church and Society in Geneva in 1966, he made the point that
out of our involvement as churches in the life of the nation, we try to
contribute to ecumenical thinking; on the other hand, out of our
ecumenical involvement, we try to contribute to the thinking of the
nation.

Let us now consider three recurrent themes in many of the statements and actions of the churches during recent decades. They are:
(1) the theme of reconciliation; (2) involvement in politics; and
(3) hope for the future and involvement in the present.

In response to the Indonesian-Netherlands conflict over Indonesian independence, then in the various internal conflicts such as
the rebellions in the Moluccas, in Sumatra, in the Minahasa (where on
both sides Christian leaders were involved), the mutual killing after
the abortive coup of September 1965, the Indonesian confrontation
against Malaysia, and in the West Irian problem, the churches
through statements, but in some cases also through direct steps of
mediation, have always stressed their ministry of reconciliation, appealing for mutual forgiveness and mutual respect and cooperation
with regard to the future.

Indonesian Christians for the most part became involved in politics
without much prior theological reflection, and it was relatively late
that more theoretical thinking was developed with regard to Christian
responsibility in politics; to the relation between the church and
political parties, especially the Christian Political Party; and to what
the significant contribution of political thinking, based on Christian
insights, could be toward the development of political thinking in the
nation at large.

Professor O. Notohamidjojo, professor of law and rector of the
Christian university, Satya Watjana, in Salatiga (Central Java), con-
tributed to the dialogue on political thinking in his 1969 book *The
Responsibility of the Church and of Christians in the Political Field.*[25]

Starting from the concept of the kingdom of God, he argues that the state is never as immediately involved in building up the kingdom as the church is. Nevertheless, in the light of this relationship to the kingdom, he is of the opinion that the democratic forms of state can be judged more favorably than others.

Dr. A. M. Tambunan, as one of the leaders of the Christian Political Party and a member of the cabinet, wrote that no form of state can have a universal claim. Moreover, governments always consist of sinful individuals. The state has no competence in matters regarding "the salvation of the soul." It is within these limitations that Christians participate in politics, as citizens who bear responsibility for the welfare of the state in which they are placed by God.[26]

The author of the present essay wrote a brief historical survey of Christian participation in politics, particularly in the twentieth century. While recognizing the creative role of the Christian Political Party, he stresses that the church cannot be identified with any political party, for the church must guide and serve on an equal basis all Christians involved in politics, irrespective of their party allegiance. Realism and hope are seen as important elements which Christian insight can contribute to political thinking, along with respect for the dignity of the human person.[27]

There is a strong messianic element simmering in the premodern religio-cultural worldview of various ethnic groups in Indonesia. Contacts with the modern worldview, with its utopian hopes of secularized eschatology as embodied in Communist and other revolutionary doctrines, have produced an even more explosive amalgam, consisting of a mixture of indigenous messianism and the excessive hopes of modern man in the power of science and technology to bring about a total transformation of man and society. All these elements, tending toward totalitarianism and national self-righteousness, were present in the doctrine of revolution during the years of guided democracy in Indonesia.

There were those who thought it their duty to rebel against the regime; there were those who cooperated, and there were those who stood passively on the sidelines. Responsible Christians were found in each of these categories. Could a theologically argued response be developed to such a challenge? That was the question the Council of Churches had to face during those years.

Dr. J. Leimena, who was vice-premier at that time, developed the concept of parallelism in his address to the General Assembly of the Council of Churches in 1964. Because the aims of the revolution and the aims of the church can be considered to run parallel, he said, the church can participate in the revolution. The author of this essay belonged to the group in the council who tried to steer the churches away from the rocks of rebellion, conformity, and irrelevance. In his address to the consultation on "Christian Service in the Revolution" at Sukabumi in 1962, the writer stated the problem as follows: "How can we formulate the relationship between our faith as Christians on the one hand, and our thinking and activities as revolutionaries on the other, so that we remain living by 'faith' in the midst of the revolution with its hope of liberation from various kinds of oppression and exploitation, from hunger and disease and with its hope of renewal in various fields of social life and even the renewal of man himself?" And further, "Shall we view our faith starting from the revolution, or ought we, on the contrary, start from our faith, 'renew our minds,' and from that vantage point examine the revolution in order 'to prove what is that good, acceptable, and perfect will of God'?" (Rom. 12:2)

In his address to the General Assembly of the Council at Jakarta in 1964, on "The Christian Task in the Revolution," the writer argued the following points: (1) The revolution which tries to bring about a new society, a new world, even a new man, as a result of human creativity, is not identical with the Gospel of the kingdom. (2) This does not mean that the revolution is outside of God's plan, or that the revolutionary aims must be viewed as being meaningless in the light of the Gospel. Neither does it necessarily mean that the revolution must be viewed as being demonic. God is working and man is working, and man's ideals and achievements must be judged in the light of God's plan. (3) In the light of the Gospel of the kingdom, Christians must be involved in the revolution, along with persons of other faiths, positively and creatively on the one hand, supporting, and where possible, pioneering in, the struggle for justice and a fuller human life, while on the other hand critically and realistically fighting against demonic and utopian tendencies in the revolution. At that time there was a feeling among many Christians that the stress should be on the critical and realistic aspect.

Since the abortive Communist coup in 1965, the climate of thinking, feeling, and acting has been marked by a new soberness, sometimes mixed with a feeling of doubt about whether the problems of development and modernization will ever be resolved by the so-called developing nations during the lifetime of the present generation. It may be that Christian participation in the processes of modernization and development must now stress the positive and creative aspect, while maintaining the critical and realistic element.

Toward Creative Maturity

How can we describe the present state of health of Christian thought in Indonesia, and where should theological construction be moving in the days ahead?

The key concept and concern should be that of "creative maturity." We cannot deny history, and it is only by coping with the challenges of the historical period in which we are living that the heritage of the past can be transformed. It is only by an openness to the future that something new will emerge. All this will take time and will certainly not happen automatically or artificially. After all, it was only after more than a thousand years that the churches in northern Europe produced indigenous theology.

How far has the theological heritage of the missionary controlled and pietistically oriented, ethnic protochurches of the 1930s been transformed during the last decades when man and society in Indonesia passed from colonialism, through the Japanese occupation, the war for independence, and internal turbulence to the present period of development, while the churches themselves under both the pressure of events in the nation and the impact of ecumenical thinking have increasingly grown together?

The folk-churches are still a fact of life, though many of them are already growing out of their old limitations. Much more work, theological work included, must still be done to better understand how the heritage and the living reality of the folk-churches can be integrated into a fuller manifestation of the oneness of the church in Indonesia, as part of the One Body, with its members scattered over the world. This will have significance also for nation-building in the country.

The pietistic heritage is still there, but there is at the same time a deep involvement in the life of society in all aspects. It may be the

special genius of Indonesian theology to integrate more harmoniously, through a more comprehensive understanding of the mission of
the church in a pluralistic society such as Indonesia, the evangelistic
task and the call to service, and the emphasis on personal salvation and
on social renewal.

What about the future? Will the ethnic religio-cultural worldviews
be the main challenge? Will it perhaps be the Islamic understanding of
God, man, society, state, history, and religion? Or does the real
challenge lie in the emerging modern, secular, scientific outlook, with
all its blessings and dangers as manifested in the highly developed
countries?

It is quite obvious that the modern spirit is riding on the wave of the
future. But in Indonesia it is working with religio-cultural material
that is different from that with which it has been working in the West
during the last centuries. Therefore the result of this modernizing
process in Indonesia will not necessarily be similar to the presently
developed societies of the West in all aspects. The emerging modern
culture will certainly embody many characteristics of Islam, Hinduism, and various other ethnic religio-cultural outlooks; it may even
be that from area to area marked peculiarities will remain. The
problem for the Christian church in Indonesia during the next decades is to determine how it can be integrated into the emerging
modern Indonesian culture and at the same time penetrate the value
system and the political, social, economic structures with insights
that are based on the Christian faith, but acceptable to all people
because of their intrinsic truth. It will be in that fluid and dynamic
situation too that the Gospel must be proclaimed, so that people may
believe.

The question then is: How should theological construction be
moving in the days ahead in order to undergird the churches in facing
their task? The Apostle Paul spoke with power because he was
gripped by the mystery of God's act in Christ and spoke about that
mystery with an intimate knowledge of the thought-forms and the
worldviews of his contemporaries, whether they were Jews, Greeks,
or Romans. Likewise, Christians in Indonesia can speak with power
during the coming years only if they speak about the mystery of God's
act in Christ with an intimate knowledge of the ethnic religio-cultural
backgrounds; the Islamic understanding of God, man, and society;

the modern worldview; and the interplay of these factors in the dynamic process toward a modern, developed Indonesian society.

A study of theological works resulting from confrontations with ethnic religions and cultures elsewhere, a study of theological traditions of churches which have been living with Islam over the centuries, a study of the theologies developed against the background of modern thought since the time of the Reformation—all these will be helpful. But only a creative maturity on the part of the theological community in Indonesia—older pastors, younger theologians, and responsible laity—can provide theological construction which can undergird the life and thought of the churches in the years ahead.

NOTES

1. See the table of basic facts about the churches in Indonesia in Frank L. Cooley, *Indonesia: Church and Society* (New York: Friendship Press, 1968).

2. H.E. Soedjatmoko, "The Re-emergence of Southeast Asia: An Indonesian Perspective." Talk delivered at Dillingham Distinguished Lecture Series, at the Center for Cultural and Technical Interchange between East and West, East-West Center, Honolulu, Hawaii, May 12, 1969, pp. 6–7.

3. Th. Müller-Krüger, ed., *Indonesia Raja* (Bad Salzuflen: MBK-Verlag, 1966), p. 99.

4. Th. Müller-Krüger, *Der Protestantismus in Indonesien* (Stuttgart: Ev. Verlagswerk, 1968), p. 82.

5. Paulus Tosari, from the island of Madura, is sometimes called "the father of Javanese Christianity." He remained a faithful leader of one of the earliest Christian congregations in Modjowarno (East Java) until his death in 1882. Sadrach became very influential in Central Java. Around 1890 he had about nine thousand followers, but he was not always understood by the missionaries. He finally joined the so-called apostolic congregation. Both Tosari and Sadrach were Javanese mystics. See Müller-Krüger, *Der Protestantismus in Indonesien*, pp. 196 and 206.

6. Cf. Hendrik Kraemer, *From Missionfield to Independent Church* (London: SCM Press, 1958).

7. Cf. Frank L. Cooley's description of Moluccan Christianity, "Das Gesicht der ältesten evangelischen Kirche in Asien" in Müller-Krüger, *Indonesia Raja*, pp. 117–30.

8. Dr. Hendrik Kraemer wrote a review of Mulia's dissertation in *De Opwekker* (May 1934), and described it as "extraordinary."

9. See *De Opwekker* (November/December 1928), pp. 518–37.

10. *Ibid.* (December 1941), p. 631.

11. This is from the writer's own memory, when he was serving at that time as chief-of-staff of the combined military forces of the Republic of Indonesia.

12. See *De Opwekker* (December 1941), p. 640.

13. Th. Müller-Krüger, "Theologia in loco?" in Jan Hermelink and Hans Jochen Margull, eds., *Basileia* (Stuttgart: Evang. Missionsverlag, 1959), pp. 313–25.

14. J. Verkuyl, "Enkele opmerkingen over het onderwijs in de theologische ethiek aan de theologische opleidingen in Azië en Afrika," in *Christusprediking in de Wereld* (Kampen: J.H. Kok, 1965), pp. 210–22.

15. J.L. Ch. Abineno, *Liturgische Vormen en Patronen in de evangelische Kerk op Timor* (The Hague: Voorhoeve, 1956).

16. Andar M. Lumban Tobing, *Das Amt in der Batak-Kirche* (Wuppertal-Barmen: Rheinische Missionsgesellschaft, 1961).

17. R. Soedarmo, *In de Wereld maar niet van de Wereld* (Kampen: J.H. Kok, 1957).

18. W.B. Sidjabat, *Religious Tolerance and the Christian Faith* (Jakarta: Badan Penerbit Kristen, 1965).

19. S.A.E. Nababan, *Kyrios Bekenntnis und Mission bei Paulus; Eine exegetische Untersuchung zu Römerbrief 14 und 15* (Heidelberg: Dissertation, Bosch & Kenning, 1962).

20. Liem Khiem-yang, *Der Philemonbrief im Zusammenhang mit dem theologischen Denken des Apostels Paulus* (Bonn: Dissertation, 1964).

21. Harun Hadiwijono, *Man in the Present Javanese Mysticism* (Baarn: Bosch & Kenning, 1967).

22. "The Confession of the Batak Church," in Vilmos Vajta and Hans Weissgerber, eds., *The Church and the Confessions* (Philadelphia: Fortress Press, 1963), p. 119.

23. W.B. Sidjabat, ed., *Panggilan kita di Indonesia Dewasa ini* (Jakarta: BPK, 1964).

24. For an informative report, see the article by Tasdik, "New Congregations in Indonesia," *The South East Asia Journal of Theology* X, 4 (1969) 2–9.

25. O. Notohamidjojo, *Tanggungdjawab Geredja dan Orang Kristen dibidang Politik* (Jakarta: BPK, 1969).

26. A. M. Tambunan, *Pembinaan Tata Kehidupan Sosial dan Politik dalam Orde Baru* (Jakarta: BPK, 1968), pp. 75–105.

27. T. B. Simatupang, in W.B. Sidjabat, ed., *Partisipasi Kristen dalam Nationbuilding di Indonesia* (Jakarta: BPK, 1968), pp. 7–35.

A Gospel for the New Filipino

A responsible theology is attained mainly when the Christian faith is interpreted in conscious relationship to the fundamental problems of human life as they appear in specific forms and in particular environments, and when it is in dialogue with other faiths—religious or otherwise—which have their own ways of structuring the questions of human life and formulating their own answers to them.

What follows is no more than a modest experiment and contribution toward carrying out in fragmentary fashion this particular understanding of theological responsibility as far as the Protestant situation in the Philippines is concerned. My main proposal is that the theological task in the Philippines lies in the direction of interpreting the human meaning and social content of the Christian faith. The significance of this proposal will be seen against the background of my analysis of the Protestant situation and my interpretation of the changes in, and aspirations of, Philippine society.

The Theological Situation

The first thing that can be said about the theological situation of the major Protestant churches in the Philippines is that there are no clearly defined theological movements or theological schools of thought. The influence of evangelical orthodoxy has been basic, predominant, and enduring. But there are no great or near-great writing theologians here yet.

Most Protestant churches in the Philippines are the products of American missionary activity, and they bear the characteristic features of the traditions and cultures of the mother churches. For the

This essay was written prior to the declaration of martial law in the Philippines on September 22, 1972.

most part they have inherited the creeds or lack of creeds, the liturgical practices, the ethos of the Chrisitian life, the modes of theological thinking, and the denominational emphases and conflicts that were the traditional identifying marks of the founding churches. These elements, however, have not been clearly thought through or modified and developed in terms of their indigenous significance, nor have they been articulated in systematic fashion. While they remain inchoate and undeveloped at the intellectual level, they nevertheless operate as the characteristic elements helping to shape the identity of the churches.

Another feature of the theological situation is that most of the issues of significance have arisen directly out of, or have been closely connected with, practical concerns of the churches. One such concern has been the necessity for the churches to establish themselves institutionally and to secure their existence as Christian communities. They have seen their task mainly as evangelism, pastoral work, and church extension. Therefore, in preaching and pastoral care, the emphasis is on personal salvation and on an understanding of the person of Christ primarily as Savior. The doctrinal structure which holds these elements together is one which shows a direct correlation between man as sinner and Christ as the mediator of personal salvation.

The *personal* reality of salvation is emphasized, but it is also distorted by being understood in a fragmentary and individualistic fashion. It is fragmentary in that it involves only the soul of man and not his body, not the whole man and all his relationships. It is individualistic in that it tends to make the believer withdraw from the world and its evils, and enjoy for himself the benefits of salvation, instead of being concerned with the problems of society and being responsible for its transformation and right ordering. While the emphasis on Jesus as *Savior* is proper, it is nevertheless understood in a very narrow sense—that is, that he saves mainly from sins of misdeeds and vices and not from a perverted relationship to God, which involves not only deeds but man's total self and system of relationships to himself, society, history, and nature. Jesus Christ as *Lord*—lord of salvation; lord of creation, not only of spiritual things but also of nature and of human and world history; lord of the eschaton, not only of personal destiny but also of the fulfilment and unification of all things in him—these christological theses, as well as other equally important theological themes, remain on the fringes of active faith and are undeveloped in their theological and ethical significance.

The churches also differentiate themselves from the rest of the human community. The Christian life and the forms of church life have been built upon the presupposition of conversion. The Protestant is essentially a convert; his life is structured negatively by his separation from the world and positively by the ethical resources of his newly found faith. His face is turned toward God and his back toward the world. The measure of his unworldliness is the measure of his godliness. He cultivates inner piety, personal peace, and family devotions, undisturbed by the storms and stresses of sociopolitical realities, enduring the sufferings of temporal existence until his soul is released from his body in death and returns home to heaven where it will enjoy the good things it was deprived of during its pilgrimage on earth.

The Filipino Protestant has a strong sense of distinctness from the rest of the human community. He is different in a negative sort of way: He knows what he ought not to do. His is an ethic of personal purity, not involved in the struggles of overcoming evil in the world. He begins by not doing evil and ends up by not doing good, either. As far as responsible life in society is concerned, he is good—for nothing.

Furthermore, the Protestant Christian ordinarily understands the church as a religious community, not as a fellowship of the Word and sacraments, the worship of God, common life, and mission. It is a community of religious feelings, mutual help, and mutual concern. To be a good Christian one must be active in the internal affairs of the church, helping the pastor in his work and coming to church services and meetings regularly and supporting generously the financial responsibilities of the church. He is a good layman who is active in the church as a religious fellowship and not as a member of the people of God who must live out the Gospel in the world.

Thus, the Protestant churches have come to understand their life as something apart from and closed to the world. It is open to the world only to the extent that they have an evangelistic task to carry out in it, and this consists in no more than an invitation to the world to come to church. The functions of the minister are exclusively within and for his congregation. He preaches the Word and celebrates the sacraments within and for his congregation. He exercises pastoral care primarily over the members of his own flock. He keeps the institutional machinery of the congregation and of the denomination going, for the churches must maintain themselves institutionally against each other and against the world.

To be sure, the life of these churches, despite a predominantly antiworldly evangelicalism in faith and ethos, has not been without positive social influences upon Filipino society. This influence consists, first of all, in the various service agencies established by the churches—schools, hospitals, student centers, orphanages, and rural development projects. These agencies, however, have a fundamentally evangelistic rationale: They have been set up as instruments of evangelism and conversion, and not as expressions of the social meaning of the Gospel.

Another aspect of the social influence of these churches is the quality of leadership which many of their lay members exercise in the professions and in public service and government. The leadership, by and large, is characterized not only by competence but also by moral integrity and dedication. This quality of leadership is partly a product of the ethos of moral purity and self-differentiation from society which antiworldy evangelicalism has fostered. But for the most part, this leadership and its social influence comes from the individual initiative of Christians and not as the positive expression of the church as a fellowship commited to social responsibility and public leadership as valid and necessary expressions of the practice of the Christian faith.[1] The churches do very little actually to equip their people for life in the real world; they train their laity mainly for participation in the activities of the church. This is because the posture of the churches in relation to society is still basically one of differentiation and separation from, and not *also* of solidarity with and responsible involvement in it.

There are unmistakable signs indicating that the churches may no longer be able to enjoy the splendid isolation which enabled them to pay more or less exclusive attention to their internal life. Changes radically affecting personality structure, social relations and institutions, and cultural values and outlook are occurring in Filipino society. These changes could mean that there is taking place in Filipino life a deep-going and far-reaching search for a new self-understanding, a new social order, and a new cultural synthesis. They could be the signs that a new Filipino and a new society are in process of coming into the full light of day.

The churches will eventually discover that the way to certain survival and significant existence, and to a clearer and truer understanding of the Gospel they preach, is not in the direction of withdrawal and noninvolvement, but precisely in creative participation in these changes and the goals they seek to realize. To be sure, there are preachers and leaders in the churches who have some awareness of what is going on and who feel in their bones the pressure of social change. They desire to meet it responsibly, not merely with sermons on social issues and projects of social welfare, but with a clearer and systematic understanding of the human meaning and social content of the Gospel and its particular relevance to the problems and aspirations of Filipino society. This will involve nothing less than an interpretation of the Christian faith and a restructuring and expansion of our present theological consciousness. In the last section of this essay, some suggestions on what it might involve and how it might be done will be offered. Meanwhile, a brief interpretation of what is happening in Filipino society will illuminate the significance of the proposals for theological construction.

The Direction of Social Change

Jaime Bulatao, S.J., has described the situation of Filipino Catholicism (85 percent of the population) as "split-level Christianity." It is the artificial juxtaposition of two belief-and-behavior systems—the traditional Filipino belief system and Latin Catholicism.[2] The contemporary Filipino accepts the "rightness" of each system but is not very much bothered by the incompatibility between systems. He has learned to keep them apart, letting one or the other have full play as the occasion demands and thus unconsciously avoiding conflict. The task of overcoming the split by a more authentic and comprehensive synthesis still awaits the future.

The concept of "split-level" as a description of Filipino Catholicism may also apply to Filipino culture and society generally. O.D. Corpuz observes that Filipino culture has what he calls a "suprastructure" and an "infrastructure."[3] The suprastructure consists of values and attitudes that originated in the West and that are characteristic of modernized and developed societies. He mentions these values and attitudes as follows:

1. A confidence in the potency of the individual to solve his own problems;
2. a high respect for individual achievement;
3. stress on technical expertise and impersonal rationality in the social management of public affairs;
4. a technique of enforcing social responsibility through impersonal legal rules.

The infrastructure, on the other hand, consists of indigenous traditions and customs which are the opposite of Western and modernizing values. He lists them as:

1. A reliance upon primary groups, especially kinship groups, in the solution of the individual's problems;
2. a high respect for social status rather than achievement or merit;
3. an emphasis on primary-group interests as against the interest of the individual or of the vague national community;
4. a style of social morality based on personal, traditional, or nonlegal norms.

As would be expected, the attitudes and values of the suprastructure are dominant in the urban sectors of the society which are undergoing technological and modernizing change, while the norms and values of the indigenous culture operate mainly in the rural areas, where social change is proceeding slowly but steadily. The resistance of the traditional culture to change is still considerable, and this is true in Southern Asia generally. Observers believe, however, that this resistance will eventually weaken as the pace of social change accelerates under the tremendous pressure of progressive nationalism, economic development, technological advance, population explosion, rising expectations, and the growing impatience and restlessness of a people weary of frustrated hopes for a more just, peaceful, prosperous, and free society. Contemporary history has unleashed in the Philippines, as in other parts of the world, a developmental revolution which is radicalizing and accelerating the transition from a traditional to a modern society.

In this transition the value orientations of the Filipino are subjected to a thoroughgoing ferment. Under the pressure of change the split-levelling of culture and the coexistence of different value systems will inevitably lead to profound psychological conflict and social disorientation. The deleterious effects of value conflicts in personal and social life are becoming increasingly evident. This conflict in values means that today there are many different frames of reference for determining what is right and what is wrong, that there is no overarching standard of norms and goals of behavior widely and authoritatively accepted in Filipino society, and there is no dominant worldview by which the flux of contemporary experience may be illuminated, ordered, and rendered meaningful. The result is not only increased social pluralism but also widespread violence, moral chaos, intellectual and ideological confusion, and social disorder.

This conflict in value orientations must be resolved, and a new sociocultural synthesis must be evolved. This raises the question of which way the current ferment should be directed. Into what vision or goal should the conflict be resolved? I would judge that the ideals of the Philippine revolution, the aspirations for human freedom and dignity, for a just and peaceful social order, and the current rhetoric of modernization and development provide us with a clue as to the direction and promise of the future. The revolutionary changes that have been reshaping Filipino society are etching out on the horizon of the future the lines and hues of the "profile of the new Filipino."

Juan Salcedo, Jr., has suggested seven features which he thinks indicate the shape of the new Filipino.[4] They are: an orientation to change, a disposition to take an interest in issues beyond his immediate environment, an orientation toward the future, a belief in his ability to mold his future, a reliance on science and technology, an awareness of the dignity of man, and a recognition of his responsibility to the community. This vision is more than the creation of the objective conditions—economic, political, educational, and social—which are extremely necessary for the emergence of a new social order. It aims rather at humanizing more fully the traditional Filipino, transforming him into a new man, a new Filipino with a new self-understanding, functioning responsibly in a new nation and living meaningfully in a new society.

The Theological Task

This vision of a new Filipino and a new society provides, it seems to me, the agenda for the task of theology and the mission of the church in the Philippines today. A closer look into the requirements for making the new Filipino will reveal that the issues involved are not only economic, political, educational, and social. They are also fundamentally theological. It is required that the new Filipino should achieve mastery and control over his environment, that he appreciate and understand and apply to his advantage the relationship of man to nature presupposed or implied in modern science and technology. In theological language, he is looking for a new *cosmology*. Moreover, the new Filipino is to have a new identity, a new self-understanding, a more authentic selfhood, and a more fulfilling community life. He is asking what it means to be a person and what it means to live with other people in a modern industrial and technological society. Speaking theologically, he is in search of a new *anthropology*. Finally, the new Filipino must not be concerned with the past, but with the present and the future and with change. He is to have a new orientation to time, a new sense of the dynamism of reality, a vision of the direction and goal of history. In theological terms, he needs a new *eschatology*.

For the Christian, the questions relating to cosmology, anthropology, and eschatology are fundamentally *theological* because they cannot be raised seriously without also taking into consideration the question of God and the divine-human relationship. The questions of God and of man and the nature of their relationship in turn lead directly to the heart of the question concerning Jesus Christ, who is God with and for man, and man for God and for other men. Finally, one cannot begin answering these questions without also perceiving their implications for understanding the reality and mission of the people of God in local and universal history. But while the distinctive theological quality of these issues is to be recognized as the determinative perspective in which they are to be understood, it is rather their human meaning—their capacity to illuminate the human situation, reveal the truth about man, dignify his existence with freedom and meaning, and enhance his future with humanizing possibilities —which must be emphasized and developed persuasively. It is the human meaning and social content of Christian faith which requires systematic and adequate exposition; such an exposition can only be true and adequate by being no less theological.

In this essay we can only sketch three aspects of the Gospel and indicate briefly their significance for the three requirements of the new Filipino described above. They are: (1) the Gospel as liberation, (2) the Gospel as a summons to responsibility, and (3) the Gospel as a horizon of hope. The choice of these meanings of the Gospel and the urgent need for stressing them at this time will become evident in the discussion. In treating them, however, we will confine ourselves to showing their significance as theological perspective; the limits of this essay do not allow us to develop the practical implications.

The Need for the Gospel

Independence having been restored to him, the Filipino is struggling hard to make political freedom and economic sufficiency real and meaningful in his personal and national life. But he has now also realized that he must win liberation from a system of spiritual bondage that consists in a cyclic understanding of time, a sacral view of the world, and a kinship structure of social relationships. Deliverance from this bondage is equally necessary, if not more fundamental, because it has to do with the reconception of his value-system and thus with the creation of one of the conditions of modernization necessary for the emergence of the new Filipino.

The typical Filipino pictures the movement of his life and of the world process in terms of what he calls the *gulong ng palad* (the wheel of fortune), which rolls on inevitably with its ups and downs but leads nowhere. Moreover, he attributes this movement to the gods and spirits which dominate his universe and directly affect the fortunes of his life—his health, his livelihood, his safety, his personal relationships. The events of his personal life and of history happen with a fateful inevitability beyond his power to alter. The past, as the deposit of experience, is the dominant category for interpreting the future, and the future does not bring anything essentially different from the past. The new is not expected. The present must be accepted for what it is: to be endured with patience if it brings difficulties, to be enjoyed or celebrated with abandon (the *fiesta* spirit) if it is the occasion for happiness, and to leave it to the gods or to chance or to the indefinite future if it brings about a situation he feels he cannot control. Thus, for the typical Filipino, the cyclic view of time has veiled the future as a horizon of infinite possibilities. It has bred in him a combination of the attitudes of fatalism, escapism, and improvidence, which together have crippled his ability to alter the existing state of things by personal initiative, rational planning, and purposive activity.[5] Changing reality by creative effort is not yet an article of his credo.

This optimistic resignation to the order of things as they are is further strengthened by the Filipino's sacral view of his natural surroundings and the customs of society. His relation to gods, spirits, and ancestors inhabiting his universe and controlling the events and activities of his life is basically one of fear. His poverty, ignorance, misery, and degradation have ingrained in him the feeling that the universe is fundamentally hostile and inimical to his interests. It is this fear and this experience of hostility which he seeks to neutralize by turning to the observance of religious rituals, ceremonies, and taboos with great cost in time, money, and energy, and by the wearing of talismans, amulets, and *anting-antings* with religious discipline. These rituals give him a feeling of superiority and mastery over the hostile and inimical forces of nature. They strengthen his sense of security, which is necessary for coping with life. They provide a kind of control on society and safeguard its resources. They symbolize his place in the scheme of things and supply him with explanations for the unknown and the inexplicable. But the net effect of all this is to blind him to reality with magic and superstition, to bind him to the repressive authority of tradition and custom, and to chain him helplessly to the overwhelming forces of his natural environment. This stifles his intellectual curiosity, prevents him from acquiring the scientific knowledge and technical skills which would enable him to master his environment, impedes the growth of productivity and economic progress. It is clear that nature must be swept clean of its spirits and demons, and the world disenchanted and secularized. The Filipino must learn to "subdue the earth" and assume responsibility for his world. In short, he must come of age.

In addition to the cycle of time and a sacral world, the Filipino is also seeking liberation from the stifling effect of a kinship structure of social relations. There are at least two problems in this connection. The first is that the Filipino is born in a large family group which consists of three segments: the nuclear family; the kinship family, composed of many relatives on both sides of the parents; and the ritual family, made up by the *compadrino* system. Within this large family group are roles, statuses, duties, privileges, and obligations which are more or less clearly defined. The member is duty-bound to honor them, and this is not always easy. His social world is structured by those who are in his kinship group and those who are not, and he literally never gets out of his kinship group. His primary and immediate loyalty is to this group. His personality and his individual welfare are subordinated to the interests and goals of the group. He feels obligated to employ a relative even when that person is not qualified. A great deal of nepotism, graft, and corruption in public and business life has been traced to this factor. An apparent lack of civic consciousness and concern for the national interest are also partly due to narrow family and kinship loyalties.

A second set of problems arises from the fact that the Filipino's approach to wider social relations is modeled on that of traditional family relations. The relations in the family are, of course, highly personalized, close-knit, and intimate. Every member is fully accepted, protected, and supported. The Filipino seeks social acceptance—a value he prizes very highly—through a system of personalized methods, involving *pakikisama*, euphemisms, the use of go-betweens, and so on.[6] In this the Filipino seeks to transform nonfamily relations into the pattern of family relations. Because the Filipino prizes "smooth interpersonal relations," he is willing to sacrifice other values such as clarity in communication, honesty in expressing feeling or opinion, and the pursuit of definite results or achievement. The Filipino has a "low threshold to criticism" and a "fragile sense of personal worth."[7] He is thus vulnerable to negative comments from others and is driven to great lengths to protect his self-esteem. He has difficulty separating ideas from personal feelings, and he often confuses criticism of the former with the latter. He attempts to personalize that which would better remain impersonal, such as legal procedures, objective norms, bureaucratic operations, administrative standards, and institutional structures. The result is often disastrous. To live effectively in a modernizing society, it is obvious that the Filipino must learn to operate not only through personal relations but also through impersonal structures, and incor-

porate into his norms objective standards of efficiency and competence. He must learn to rationalize his activity to achieve maximum
results with a minimum of effort and cost.

The Gospel as Liberation

How does the Gospel liberate the Filipino from cyclic time, a sacral
universe, and a kinship structure of social relations? In posing the
question this way, we are deliberately attempting to make the Gospel
speak to the situation of the Filipino. In this effort it may be that only
some aspects of the Gospel will be emphasized and developed. Thus,
direct and concrete relevance may be achieved at the expense of
comprehensive interpretation. This, it seems, is the only way we can
use theology responsibly in our specific context. We will begin by
dealing with the first two problems and reserve the problem of
liberation from kinship structure for the next section of this essay.
Our exposition will be limited to elaborating a theological perspective
without developing the practical implications.

The Gospel is God's "good news" to man in Jesus Christ. It is the
establishment of a divine-human relationship in and after the pattern
of Jesus Christ, in and through whom God comes as man to be with
and for man, and man comes to be with God and other men. The
essence of this relationship is that of a *covenant* in which man comes
into fellowship with God under his fatherly gracious rule. "I will be
your God and you shall be my people" (Jer. 7:23; Ezek. 36:28).
Through Jesus Christ and in the Holy Spirit man becomes the son of
God and will call on him, crying "Abba! Father" (Gal. 4:4–6). The
covenant relationship was inaugurated in the calling of Israel, established in the event of Jesus Christ, and will be consummated in the
kingdom of God beyond history (Rev. 21:3, 7). While the execution of
the covenant relationship is accomplished through the history of the
election of Israel and of the man Jesus of Nazareth and his historical
body, the church, it is on behalf of and for the sake of all people that it
is accomplished at all. The purpose of God in Christ is to unite all
things in him—things in heaven and things on earth (Eph. 1: 9–10).

The covenant relation is good news because it is a saving relation.
The meaning of salvation in the covenant, on the basis of biblical
evidence, is rich and varied.[8] One of its meanings is in the sense of

liberation, of making free, of deliverance. The constitutive events of the history of the covenant relation in the Bible have this basic liberating quality. But what is man delivered from in the covenant relation? And for what? In the context of war, it means deliverance from and security against the enemy and the oppressor, and victory in battle. In community life, it signifies deliverance from structures of cruelty and injustice, and the building up of a society of *shalom*. [9] In the life in the world, it means deliverance from the wrath of God, from sin, from condemnation by the law, and from death and the devil. It is freedom in Christ to love God and neighbor.

In the covenant relation man is also delivered from the worship of false gods and their images and from a sacral understanding of the world as dominated by religious powers which do not possess true divinity. The liberation from paganism is a theme that runs through the whole history of the covenant in the Bible, and it is one aspect of the Gospel that seems extremely relevant to the Filipino.

When Abraham "strayed" (Gen. 20: 13; cf. Deut. 26:5) from his father's house in Mesopotamia, he was doing something difficult but decisively important: He was seeking liberation from the primal ties of family, kindred, and country (Gen. 12: 1–4) in order to found a new nation in a new land for a new purpose in world history. In abandoning his father's house, Abraham was making a radical break with the culture of his father and the religious ethos which informed it. This culture and its religious basis were incompatible with the covenant relationship with God and with man which was to be inaugurated precisely with his departure from Haran. The covenant literally began with the abandonment of the gods and goddesses and the sacral culture they dominated.

The Exodus from Egypt and the covenant-making at Sinai mark the historical beginning of Israel as a *people* of the covenant. The deliverance that constitutes the significance of this complex of founding events was more than liberation from the bondage of slavery and suffering; it was fundamentally a liberation from the pagan culture of Egypt, which owed a great deal of its repressiveness precisely to its sacral nature. A characteristic feature of Egyptian culture was the according of official status to religion. This gave the already autocratic Egyptian state a sacral legitimation and authority. The Pharaoh ruled as a god, and was at the same time a priest of the cult. The result was an oppressive rule from which the Israelites cried out for deliverance.

The unique character of the covenant God, which sets him off in a different light from the many gods of the nations, is to be seen in the Exodus and Sinai events. Of the many gods in the universe, he alone "heard" the cry of the Israelites for deliverance, he alone "saw" and "knew" their condition, and he alone acted to deliver them out of their bondage and suffering (Exod. 2:23–25). He is the only God whose sole interest is in man, who enters into intimate relation with him, breaks the powers that oppress him, and delivers him into the kind of freedom which would release his creative powers and make him a fit partner in the covenant enterprise. He is the God of persons (of the fathers Abraham, Isaac, and Jacob) and of a people, and eventually of all peoples, not of cosmic places and natural functions. His sphere of activity is in human lives and human history, not in the vitalities and recurrences of nature. He is the God of freedom, who delivers man from political and religious bondage. "I am the Lord your God who brought you out of the land of Egypt, out of the house of bondage" (Exod. 20:2). He is a jealous God; he has taken over the powers and functions of the false gods and goddesses, and his people, therefore, are not to have any other gods but him. His people are delivered from the wearisome bother of having to deal with many gods: They have to do only with him, the one true God. The world of his people is thus secularized—cleared of all sacral powers and authorities. He demythologizes all worship of him: he will not tolerate any representation of him in images and symbols made by man. But he would be with his people in the presence of his Word, which has power to organize and move human relations according to his will. And his will is the protection of human life, the honoring of human dignity, the promotion of justice and peace, and the increase of human freedom. His will is the will of love: the love of God and the love of persons. To do his will and to remain faithful to him in the covenant were the primary responsibilities of his people.

These insights into the character of the covenant God and the nature of the covenant relation represent the fundamental break of biblical faith with the essence of paganism and the culture it rears up. As the people of the covenant began to settle in Canaan, they had to be won again and again, refined and deepened in the struggle against the Canaanite religion and against Baal and the fertility cults. But the struggle is far from complete and finished. In the Old Testament it is yet to reach its peak in the prophets, particularly in Deutero-Isaiah, who attains a faith in God as the creator of heaven and earth and the Lord of universal history with whom none can compare, as well as the Lord and Redeemer of Israel (Isa. 40:28–31; 44:67; 40:21–24). But with the settling of Israel in the promised land, the struggle moves to a slightly different level. It is against Israel herself, against her faithlessness in seeking after other gods, against religious fetishism, and the worship of idols made of wood and stone by men. But the essential meaning of the struggle is the same: It is to win faith in the one true God who is deliverer, Lord, and creator; it is to desacralize the world so that it will remain as God's creation given over to man for his dominion and responsibility; it is to deliver man from false authorities so that he may become and remain a free and responsible partner of the covenant enterprise.

When we come to the New Testament, the struggle is taken up anew, looking forward to its final conclusion in God's victory in the establishment of his kingdom when God is in all and through all and above all, and when all domination, authority, and power are abolished (1 Cor. 15:24). This time the struggle is against the law of Israel functioning as a religious authority over men and against the "elemental spirits of the universe" in Greek and Roman religion functioning as the "guardians and trustees" of man, thus continuing the subjection of man to legal, religious, and metaphysical bondage (Gal. 3: 23–24; 4: 1–4). The Gospel is: "God sent forth his Son, born of woman, born under the law, to redeem those who were under the law, so that we might receive adoption as sons" (Gal. 4:4–5). The Gospels present Jesus as engaged in victorious conflict with unclean and demonic spirits and all that cripples man. Paul sees the death and resurrection of Jesus as God's struggle with, and glorious triumph over, the cosmic powers: "He disarmed the principalities and powers and made a public example of them, triumphing over them in him" (Col. 2:15; cf. Eph. 1:20–21). The resurrection of Jesus is, at the same time, his exaltation to his lordship: "All authority in heaven and on earth has been given to me" (Matt. 28:18; cf. Phil. 2:9–11). In a pagan world, the Christian has to confess: " 'An idol has no real existence,'

and that 'there is no God but one.' For although there may be so-called
gods in heaven or on earth—as indeed there are many 'gods' and many
'lords'—yet for us there is one God, the Father, from whom are all
things and for whom we exist, and one Lord, Jesus Christ, through
whom are all things and through whom we exist" (1 Cor. 8:4–6). The
simple confession that Jesus Christ is Lord clears the world of all false
gods and liberates reality from false authorities! Through the resurrection of Jesus, God secularizes all of reality and places it under the
dominion of only one Lord.

The Gospel liberates from a sacral universe. It also liberates from a
cyclic view of time. The key to this power of the Gospel is again to be
found in the formative events of the covenant relation and its fulfilment in the event of Jesus Christ. When God inaugurates the covenant with Abraham—with a man, in his personal life and history—he
calls him to step out of his natural moorings in family, tribe, and
country. In personal life, blood and soil are man's immediate ties to
unchanging Mother Nature. Moreover, his relationships to tribe and
land are usually hallowed by the unquestioned authority of custom
and tradition, which are the bearers of the power of the past. Further,
the authority of tradition is ordinarily reinforced by the sanctions and
rewards of religion, and this is a force of conservatism and continuity
and stability in society. Thus, as long as man is a prisoner of his ties to
blood and soil, he remains chained to the past. His future is completely determined by the past. The time of his life becomes a cycle of
repetition of the past. It is not broken by the coming of the new. The
first step toward liberation from cyclic time is to cut the ties of blood
and soil. It is the step that puts one on the road toward independence
and freedom!

The word to leave tribe and country is followed by a word of
promise. Abraham was to go into a land he did not know, but which
would be shown to him. He was to have an heir and become a great
nation, and he and his descendants were to be a means of blessing to
all the families of the earth. In the Exodus, departure from the "house
of bondage" is based on the promise of deliverance into a "good and
broad land" (Exod. 3:8). In the preaching of Jesus, the call to repentance and faith—breaking with the past and reaching out into the
future—is made on the promise that the coming reign of God is at
hand (Mark 1: 14–15). The word of promise breaks the cycle of time in
a threefold way. First, it contradicts the past by revealing (to it)

something new which has not yet happened. The word of promise is always a judgment on the poverty of the past in the light of the possiblities of the future. Second, promise opens up the future and shapes it with a definite content whose terms can be grasped in anticipation. Promise reveals the future as a definite possibility awaiting realization, something new which the past does not have because it has not yet happened. The future then becomes more important and challenging than the past, and calls forth the daring and creativity of human freedom. Finally, promise creates a time space between past and present on one hand, and the future and its fulfilment on the other. This time-space *between* promise and fulfilment, between the present sinking into the past and the coming future constituting the present, is the time of opportunity, the time of creative effort, the time of changing the status quo and remolding it into the possibilities of the future, the time of translating a dream into reality. Into this time space are released the possibilities of the future that must be grasped by faith and turned into reality by hard work. Promise, therefore, besides breaking the cycle of time, creates two important attitudes that enables one to live in the time space which it opens up. It creates faith, which repents of the past and hopes in the future; it creates a sense of responsibility in the present, which drives one to do the hard work by which reality is changed! Time now moves, not only from past and present into the future, but also in reverse: the future comes to constitute the present and to fill the past with new meaning. Time ceases being cyclic, and becomes historical, as well as eschatological.

Still we have left out one decisive factor in breaking the tyranny of cyclic time. That is the factor of human decision—the decision to depart and to be on the way into the coming future. The departure from Haran into the unknown land of the future has to be made and executed by Abraham himself. The Exodus from Egypt into the wilderness, beyond which lies the land of promise, must be actually undertaken by the people themselves under the leadership of Moses. The possibility of a new beginning in personal life and in social history arises when an intolerable contradiction between the present and the future is perceived. New epochs in history become possible when history itself is experienced as critical. It becomes critical when the present and the future come into conflict and when there is no clue from the past to illuminate the way to the future. But the new comes

into being in history by way of human decision, through man acting
individually and corporately. To be in history is to be on the way
toward the future and the end. Historical time moves toward the
future through the projection of human purposes, through meaningful activity, through the occurrence of historic events, and through
the acquisition of memory and the wisdom of experience for dealing
responsibly with the present and for anticipating and planning for the
future. Life in the purposive movement of time is history.

It is at this critical point of decision against the past and in view of
the open future that God comes to be with man, not behind him, but
in front of him, so that he is always ahead, calling man to come out of
the past and leading him into the promise of the future. He leads
Abraham out of Ur (Gen. 15:7) and the Israelites out of Egypt (Exod.
20:2) into the land of promise. He delivers men from the dominion of
darkness and transfers them to the kingdom of his beloved son in
whom there is redemption and forgiveness of sins (Col. 1: 13-14). He
makes his leading and accompanying known by word and deed,
through prophet and historical event and personal life. He travels
with man in history "not only on moonlit nights, but also on the
nights without moonlight, and on winter days too."[10] He does not
stay behind but accompanies. There is always more of him to come:
He is, he was, and he is to come (Rev. 1:4). So, as man goes on the way
with God walking before him (Gen. 17:1), human history thus becomes covenant history, a history of God with man and of man with
God. This is what has become of human history in Jesus Christ, the
God-Man. But with him, covenant history is moving to its real future,
which is the coming of the kingdom of God. In Jesus Christ, covenant
history has taken on eschatological dimensions.

If the new Filipino is seeking deliverance from the past and freedom
for the future; if he is seeking liberation from the gods and spirits, and
freedom to change the world; then the Christian Gospel is indeed
"good news" for him. It is the Gospel for the new Filipino.

THE GOSPEL AS A SUMMONS TO RESPONSIBILITY

The Gospel delivers man from being a slave of the gods and cosmic
powers, from sin, from the law, from the devil, and from death, and
reconciles him to God in Christ, restoring to him the freedom and

responsibilities of sonship. Being a son of the Father in Christ through the Spirit is both a gift of grace to be received gratefully and joyfully, and a relation to be lived out responsibly in the world. To receive the freedom of sonship is to exercise it. To enter the covenant is to keep it and carry on the responsibilities of being a partner in it. The freedom of sonship is exercised properly when it is used creatively to fulfil the responsibilities that it entails. Among the many responsibilities constituted in the relation of sonship, there are two which we will consider briefly. The first is the responsibility of developing and caring for the earth, or nature; the other is the responsibility of transforming and humanizing society. Both tasks are extremely urgent in the Philippines. Again, however, all we can do here is provide some theological perspective without developing the practical implications.

One of the meanings of man being made in the image of God in Christ is that man is responsible for exercising dominion over the earth, or nature, which is also a part of God's creation.[11] In the story of creation in Genesis 1, man is told by God to "subdue" and to "have dominion . . . over all the earth" and "over every living thing that moves upon it" (Gen. 1:26–28). The story makes it clear that this is a matter of privilege—a matter of blessing—entailing responsibilities. As God is the creator and lord of all his creation—including man—so he calls on man to be his representative on earth and to exercise lordship in his name over what is below man. Thus, man may *reflect* God in that he has a dominion over which he exercises freedom and creativity according to his measure.

Nature is man's dominion (cf. Ps. 8). The gods and spirits and cosmic powers which have reigned in it are usurpers. They have to be driven away so that nature, cleared of their alien presence, may be restored to its true proportions as a creation of God and as the rightful domain of man as a son and a steward of God. In contrast to the Greek view—as expressed in the myth of Prometheus, who had to steal fire from the gods in order to have the authority and power to conquer nature—the biblical view pictures God as *giving* to man this authority and power. Man is given the privilege to develop with his creative freedom and intelligence the means whereby he may "subdue" nature, and develop and care for it. Man's commission to be the subduer and tiller and keeper of nature is part of the meaning of creation as good. It is one of the means by which man fulfils his destiny as a mirror reflecting the sovereignty of God over his creation.

Man's calling to dominate nature has to be seen in the context of the ambiguous relation between man and nature. [12] On the one hand there are those factors which clearly indicate that man is subject to the powers of nature. Man is first of all a part of nature (Gen. 2:7; 1 Cor. 15:47). In the story of creation in Genesis 1, man appears as the crown of a series of activities proceeding from lower to higher realities.

Moreover, man is nurtured by nature (Gen. 1:29; 2:15–16). Without nature man cannot exist at all. This truth and its implications for nature conservation has tremendous relevance in the Philippines where there is almost a wanton destruction of many forest and animal preserves for commercial purposes. But besides providing man with a habitat and material for food, nature also nurtures other aspects of his life by offering him aesthetic delight, meditation (cf. Ps. 104), companionship (especially of the animals), consolation, and inspiration (poets and painters).

Further, man is threatened and challenged by nature. The Filipino is quite aware of this truth. A great deal of his profound feeling that the universe is hostile comes from his experience of nature's terrors that come in the forms of typhoons, floods, droughts, earthquakes, volcanic eruptions, famine, and disease. These forces have made him fearful, instead of challenging him to develop ways and means by which he can avoid the dangers of some or resist others. The history of civilization, however, indicates that the threat of nature has played no small part in compelling man to control and humanize it.

This last point leads us to consider those elements which indicate that man transcends nature and which provide him with the means whereby he exercises dominion over it. The biblical view of man is quite clear about man's distinction from the rest of creation. Of all the creatures, he alone is given the vocation to reflect God's sovereignty through his dominion over nature. For in man, self-consciousness, rationality, moral sense, creative freedom, and all the ingredients of personalness have made their appearance in reality. In man, nature has ceased to act merely naturally and spontaneously and unconsciously, and has begun to act freely and intelligently and responsibly. Man therefore is no longer bound to act merely naturally. He is no longer satisfied with nature in its rawness. He must re-create nature in order that it might become the work not only of God's hand but also of his hand. He must know nature by observing it, probing into its secrets, interrogating and investigating it. For only when he knows how and under what conditions nature behaves, will he learn to work not only with it but also upon it, and thus control and reshape it.

The amazing fact is that nature, of which man is a part, responds to human scientific investigation and technical control. The unconscious ends of nature are now subject to man's conscious planning and guidance and transformation. This is the great turn in the history of evolution: Man who is the product of nature's evolution now has the knowledge, the power, and the technique to guide not only nature's, but his own evolution—that is, if he does not first destroy himself and incinerate the earth, and if he has the ability to make his scientific knowledge and technical skill serve higher ends than themselves.

There is no doubt that man's destiny to dominate the earth is being increasingly fulfilled by means of human science and technology. The Filipino will certainly avail himself of this means. Speaking theologically, there ought to be no contradiction between Christian faith and science and technology, although the historical connection is indirect. Christian faith clears nature of its sacral qualities, and commissions man to know and master it through his creative intelligence and freedom. Man is a fellow-worker with God in the ongoing creative process. From this viewpoint, the Christian faith provides a theological perspective for the new Filipino's desire to master his environment through the use of science and technology.

But the perspective must be more than merely supportive; it must also be critical. For technology is not an end in itself. It asks for goals which can endow it with meaning and direct its processes. Moreover, man's destiny is not simply to control nature. He also has a responsibility to develop himself. What he does with nature affects his own self considerably—for ill or for good. For through man's interacting with nature, human culture develops. And because human culture is of man and for man, its meaning lies in man and his growth toward greater humanity. In this connection, it is necessary to ask whether the kind, aims, and consequences of the technical domination which man exercises over nature does honor to man's relation to God as a son and a steward of God and a fellow-worker in the creative process, and thus helps build up a culture and a society which are truly human.

This brings us to the question of man's responsibility for transforming and humanizing society. This is a broad subject, but our comments will be limited by the need to speak a theological word to the new Filipino's desire to be liberated from a structure of social relations dominated by kinship and personalistic patterns. We saw earlier how this structure has prevented the Filipino from taking an interest in issues beyond his immediate environment and recognizing his responsibility to the wider community. To be sure, restructuring Filipino society on lines broader than those made possible in kinship and personalistic systems is not the only social problem in the Philippines. There are also the pressing problems of securing peace and order; achieving economic development, social justice, integrity and statesmanship in public office; improving the quality of life for the masses so that they will have more food, better shelter, healthier bodies, quicker minds, and become more responsible citizens and better persons. We cannot of course tackle these problems here. The problem of the structure of kinship is, nevertheless, at the base of Filipino society. Any change at this point will have far-reaching consequences, and our remarks aim at providing a theological perspective.

The point to be emphasized is simply that the task of creating and altering society—and by society is meant the structures by which man organizes his common life, together with the cultural values and goals which inform and guide his activity and give a sense of coherence and continuity to his community life—is a responsibility given to man.

Man is God's creaturely "counterpart," a being with a capacity for selfhood, exercising relative autonomy and creative rationality in dependence upon God (or against him) and in interdependence with his fellow human beings and with nature (or in alienation from them). It is persons which constitute human society. Since man is his counterpart, God freely and graciously addresses him in word and deed and in the person and work of Jesus Christ, thereby creating a situation in which man has to answer God in faith, commitment, and responsibility (or to say no to him). Thus, man is called to enter the covenant relation in which he is not only confirmed and redeemed in his selfhood, but is enlisted to become a partner with God, not only in the creative enterprise but also, and more importantly, in the ministry of reconciling people to God and to one another and in transforming society to make it a truly human community. Man's sense of community is not exhausted by his relations to subhuman nature and to human society and culture. It reaches out toward the future and toward God. This reaching-out beyond the past and the present and beyond the given forms of nature and society at any time is the condition for man's freedom and courage to say "No" to the present forms of society and to change it.

In the Sermon on the Mount (Matt. 5–7), Jesus demonstrates that the forms of society are variable and subject to change or modification when, in the light of his vision of a new order of things in the kingdom of God, he sweeps aside the foundations of Jewish society with his "But I say unto you . . . " (Matt. 5:21–48). The source of his sovereign freedom and courage is an insight into the character of the living God who himself comes into his reign and whose reign must become effective in human affairs. God comes "in power" precisely in society and in history.

In the light of his encounter with God's royal authority, Jesus announces that the absolute authority of the old order is broken, that man is delivered from the support and shackles of the old social institutions, and that he must now opt for a new life and a new set of relations in the new society which now replaces the old (Matt. 6–7). The message of Jesus is that the reign of God in human affairs shakes the foundations of social existence loose and opens them up for restructuring along lines in which man becomes a responsible person and a neighbor to, and a brother of, all men.

The contemporary Filipino has the opportunity of being a social innovator by adopting changes that would fundamentally alter the kinship structure which dominates his society. This opportunity is made possible by the rising revolutionary ferment created by the impact of modernizing values and movements, such as urbanization, industrialization, rationalization, social differentiation, and the division of labor (in Emile Durkeim's sense).[13] In a situation of ferment, not only are old forms and structures shaken loose and again rendered malleable and open to change, but new beginnings, new goals, and new structures become available to man's creative grasp. He is given the opportunity to remake history and to refashion society. Thus, under the challenge of urbanization, for example, the Filipino need not be limited to the primary, or organic, forms of relationships which are dominant in kinship, tribal, and peasant settings. He can learn to treat objects with less sentimental ritual and personal attachment, and simply appreciate their matter-of-fact usefulness. He can develop functional attitudes by which he can treat a salesgirl, a government clerk, and the mailman in terms of the services they render. By doing so, he does not depersonalize them, because he meets them at the point at which they project themselves as humanly significant, that is, rendering service that they consider important and which, in fact, is very welcome. Reducing their significance to something less would, of course, depersonalize them. But he should not feel under obligation to personalize his relationship to them, since to do so in this limited context would introduce elements of impertinence and artificiality. The point is that the new Filipino can learn to distinguish a variety of human relations and be able to operate effectively in all without reducing or transforming the one to the other.

Similarly, in an industrializing society there is need for the production and distribution of more goods and services. Achieving these goals often depends, not only on savings and investment, but on hard work, efficient organization, and effective management. Thus, performance becomes evaluated in terms of competence and achievement rather than ascribed status. The application of impersonal criteria on a universalistic scale is necessary to rationalize activity and to be able to cope with the demands of more complex and larger operations. This is true in public administration and statecraft as well as in industry. The new Filipino must therefore learn to deal with social reality not only through personal but also impersonal means. We cannot multiply these examples without making this essay too long. The point to be stressed is simply that the Filipino need not be a helpless victim trapped in his society and history. It is his responsibility to alter his society and make it more truly human. For the Filipino, like every other person, is not only made by history but is a maker of history.

THE GOSPEL AS THE HORIZON OF HOPE

So far we have described the new Filipino as the *telos* of social change in the Philippines. He is the new man of the future. But there are impediments to his coming into the full light of day. We have sought to relate the meaning of the Gospel to the coming of the new Filipino by presenting it as a perspective and a motivation for (a) his liberation from the shackles of cyclic time, a sacral world, and a kinship society, and (2) his call to accept the responsibility of mastering and developing his share of the earth and changing his society as requisite conditions for his full emergence in the future. The question that must now be raised is what more does the Gospel offer that can provide a perspective capable of illuminating the Philippine horizon with hope, so that the revolutionary changes now occurring may be further motivated, refined, and directed along lines which help firm up the human shape of the new Filipino.

Hope is indispensable to both liberation and responsibility. Without hope, liberation has no motivation by which it can be moved and no direction in which it can be led. Without hope, responsibility is deprived of the vision of fulfilment by which it is driven to strive, to endure, to create, and achieve. By the same token, both liberation and responsibility are indispensable to hope. Liberation is the power of hope to abrogate the past, contradict the present, and open up the future as an horizon of freedom and possibility. Responsibility is the courage of hope to grasp the future in the opportunities of the present and in the light of the wisdom of the past; it is through responsibility that hope risks the realization or the failure of the future. Responsibility, in short, is the creative power of hope.

The Gospel can be a horizon of hope for the coming new Filipino. By horizon is meant the range of vision in which the human shape of the new Filipino can be perceived. By hope is meant the possibility that the new Filipino will, in fact, appear. More pointedly, the Gospel has the power to form the new Filipino and help bring about his arrival. These are big claims, and we can only sketch out briefly and tentatively our reasons for making them.

First the reader should be reminded that, theologically speaking, the Gospel, as liberation and responsibility, already helps create the conditions and the process for the coming of the new Filipino. But the Gospel as hope is, of course, something more than these.

The Gospel is the proclamation of Jesus that the time has come, the kingdom of God is upon men, that they must therefore repent and believe (Mark 1:14–15). The reign of God—that is God *himself* reigning in and through Jesus—is proclaimed in the New Testament as the hope of Israel, of the church, and of all mankind. There are no separate hopes and different futures for Israel, the church, and mankind, for in God's eternal purpose for his kingdom, all three will be one in Christ (Eph. 1:10; Rev. 21; cf. Romans 9–11). Now, this one hope from the future has drawn close to men in Jesus Christ. Its coming is the dawn of a new age, creating a permanent crisis in history and compelling men to turn away from the past, to abandon the old order in repentance, and to be drawn by faith into the new age.

Jesus, in unfolding the content of hope in the reign of God, points to its power to heal the lives of people. When John the Baptist sent two of his disciples to inquire of him whether he was in fact "he who is to come," or whether (John) should look for another, Jesus' reply was: "Go and tell John what you have seen and heard: the blind receive their sight, the lame walk, lepers are cleansed, the deaf hear, the dead are raised up, and the poor have good news preached to them" (Luke 7:19–22). When Jesus pictures what will happen at the last judgment when the shepherd separates the sheep from the goats, the criterion of judgment is the service rendered to Christ and the "least" of his brethren (Matt. 25:40, 45). Christ identifies himself with the "least," and whatever is done to them is done to him. The services to be rendered consist of feeding the hungry, giving drink to the thirsty, welcoming the stranger, clothing the naked, visiting the sick and the prisoner (Matt. 25:31–48).

All this simply means that when God exercises his kingly rule, its effect on human society and history is the removal of poverty, injustice, and oppression; the wiping away of disease, ignorance, and superstition; and the coming of the joy of human freedom and the loving rule of the heavenly Father. The kingdom of God delivers man from what makes him less than human, restores him to his dignity, and places him in a climate of liberty in an environment of love and a network of fulfiling relationships. It thus enables man to enjoy and live his humanity as a true son of God should.

It would be a mistake to interpret all this as pertaining only to social welfare work, philanthrophy, social action, and the setting-up of signs of the Christian presence in the world—although all this is important and necessary, and there ought to be more of it in the Philippines and elsewhere. Rather, the kingdom of God has to do with "the glorious *liberty* of the children of God" (Rom. 8:21) and the coming of the new heaven and the new earth which is "the home of *justice*" (2 Peter 3:13). The final home of man is a *city*, the Holy City, where God and men dwell together, where tears have been wiped out, and there is no more death or mourning and crying and pain, for the old order has passed away (Rev. 21:3–4).

In other words, it is in its social content and in its power to heal human lives and to renew society and redirect world history toward the attainment of mankind's liberty and maturity, that the kingdom of God *is* the horizon of hope. It is in these dimensions that it joins with social change in the Philippines in her groaning effort to bring forth the new Filipino. From this perspective the attempts at social reform, no matter how feeble, receive a messianic significance; the efforts to etch out on the horizon the human shape of the new Filipino are given messianic encouragement. These efforts and their goals must be constantly judged and refined in the light of the human meaning and social content of the Gospel as the horizon from which they take on the dimension of hope.

But the hope of the kingdom of God is not born in human history, not even in Filipino history, without committed struggle, patient suffering, and vicarious sacrifice. As Paul portrays it, the whole of creation as well as the first fruits of the Spirit—that is, the church—inwardly groan in travail together while waiting patiently for the fulfilment of this hope (Rom. 8:22–25). The messianic ministry of Jesus, precisely because it heralded the dawning of the new age and, consequently, the passing away of the old order, aroused violent resistance from those who wanted to preserve the status quo. This led inevitably to the crucifixion of Jesus at the hands of the guardians of "the Establishment." The crucifixion of Jesus is that point in the depths of history when the old and the new came into mortal conflict on behalf of mankind and God's purpose for it. Nothing less than the glory of God and the future of mankind were at stake in that titanic struggle.

The outcome of the struggle is what the resurrection of Jesus is all about. For the resurrection is the "hinge" on which the future destiny of mankind turns, the victory of the Crucified One over the powers of the old order in world history. By this victory, world history itself is redirected to its final goal in the kingdom of God, for through it, God vindicates the messianic ministry and vicarious death of Jesus. In other words, the resurrection reveals that it is the power of the reign of God which has been at work all the while in the ministry and death of Jesus. Thus, the human meaning and social content of the messianic ministry and death of Jesus are *confirmed* by the resurrection as organic elements of the new age. The future belongs to them. They share in the power of the resurrection, and wherever and whenever they occur they are to be perceived as demonstrations of the lordship of the risen Christ in world history. From this perspective, it can be asserted that to the extent that the *telos* of social change in the Philippines is the formation of the new Filipino in the image of freedom, justice, and maturity, and the creation of a new order in society that reflects this image, it should be taken up in faith into the whole movement of world history toward its future in the kingdom of God. The extent to which it is not done indicates what must be the task of prophetic criticism and missionary participation in social change, in order to bring it into the horizon of Christian hope. In either case, the church cannot stand aloof!

NOTES

1. Cf. Gerald H. Anderson, ed., *Christ and Crisis in Southeast Asia* (New York: Friendship Press, 1968), p. 153; and Peter G. Gowing, *Islands Under the Cross* (Manila: National Council of Churches in the Philippines, 1967), pp. 191–92.

2. Jaime Bulatao, S.J., *Split-Level Christianity* (Quezon City: Ateneo de Manila University, 1966). Cf. Robert B. Fox, "The Pre-Historic Foundations of Philippine Culture," *Solidarity* (Manila), III, 2 (1968) 69–93; Raul S. Manglapus, "Philippine Culture and Modernization," in Robert N. Bellah, ed., *Religion and Progress in Modern Asia* (New York: The Free Press, 1965), pp. 30–42; and Horacio de la Costa, S.J., *The Background of Nationalism* (Manila: Solidaridad Publishing House, 1965).

3. O. D. Corpuz, *The Philippines* (Englewood Cliffs, N. J.: Prentice-Hall, 1965), p. 87; cf. Bulatao, *Split-Level Christianity*, p. 10.

4. Juan Salcedo, Jr., "The Profile of the New Filipino," *The Manila Times*, February 27, 1968, p. 7-A.

5. Raul S. Manglapus writes: "It is not optimism that governs the mind and the heart [of the Filipino]; it is the *'gulong ng palad'*—the wheel of fortune—and the *'bahala*

na'—let the gods take care of all things. Four hundred years of Euro-Asian fusion have failed to snap open this cycle. Are times good today? Relax and enjoy it; tomorrow things will be bad again. Are times bad today? No use to try and improve them; tomorrow will certainly be better. There is no escape from this cycle except in indulgence at appointed times of the year when the improvidence of centuries is given full and dramatic play. Now, no one must touch this cycle, for while it started as a philosophy, it is now known as tradition, and while a philosophy may be disputed, tradition is sacred and must not be disturbed," in *Revolt Against Tradition* (Manila: n.p., 1964), p. 96.

6. Frank Lynch, S.J., "Social Acceptance," in *Four Readings on Philippine Values* (Quezon City: Institute of Philippine Culture, Ateneo de Manila University, 1964), pp. 1–21. George M. Guthrie describes what is involved in *pakikisama*, or getting along together: "*Pakikisama* takes many forms, which may involve extravagant praise of another, the use of metaphorical language rather than frank terms, not showing one's own negative feelings or depressed spirits, smiling when things go wrong, and above all, never expressing anger or losing one's temper. Avoiding stressful situations can be made easier by keeping things vague and by letting ambiguities stand. One makes commitments with the implicit understanding that either party to the agreement may seek to have matters changed if circumstances change. The common element in many activities is the desire to maintain good feelings and non-stressful relationships. It should be added that this is difficult in a society where competition for status and drive for power are also very strong," in "Philippine Temperament," in George M. Guthrie, ed., *Six Perspectives on the Philippines* (Manila: Bookmark, 1968), pp. 63–64.

7. Lynch, "Social Acceptance," p. 12; cf. Guthrie, "Philippine Temperament," p. 63.

8. See T. Paul Verghese, "Salvation: The Meanings of a Biblical Word," *International Review of Mission* LVII, 228 (October 1968), 399–416.

9. J.C. Hoekendijk, "Notes on the Meaning of Mission (-ary)," in Thomas Wieser, ed., *Planning for Mission* (London: Epworth Press, 1966), pp. 43–44. Cf. *The Church for Others* (Geneva: World Council of Churches, 1967), pp. 14–15.

10. Martin Buber, *The Prophetic Faith* (New York: Macmillan, 1949), p. 35.

11. The word "nature" is used to indicate the whole of nonhuman reality, or as Genesis 1 puts it: the earth and the fish of the sea, the birds of the air and every living thing that moves upon the earth, which are a part of God's creation, and therefore dependent upon him. The word in its Latin and Greek meanings denotes a substance centered in itself and immanent in origin and growth. This sense of the word obviously does not express the meaning of dependence upon God as creator. Cf. "God in Nature and History," *New Directions in Faith and Order*. Faith and Order Papers, no. 50, (Geneva: World Council of Churches, 1968), p. 14.

12. I have drawn freely from the WCC document, "God in Nature and History," in developing this point.

13. For a brilliant description of the challenge of modernizing trends on the kinship system in Filipino society, see Ruben Santos-Cuyugan, "Socio-Cultural Change and the Filipino Family," in Espiritu and Hunt, eds., *Social Foundations of Community Development* (Manila: Garcia Publishing House, 1964), pp. 363–74.

Theology of the Incarnation

The Chaotic but Hopeful Present

In no epoch in the whole history of China has there been so much concentration of power, energy, and resources in this small island of 13,808 square miles as there is today. The reputed five thousand years of history have converged, by curious twists and turns of history, in present-day Taiwan. The China that could boast—for example —when conquered militarily by Mongols in the thirteenth century or invaded religiously by Buddhism in the sixth century, of overcoming foreign elements by absorption and transformation, belongs to the past. Instead, what we have today in Taiwan is a vast nation condensed to a most rigid cell and then stretched to its utmost limits under the heavy pressures of its own heritage and the merciless onslaughts of modernization. One notable consequence is that the old and the new, unable to reach a golden mean, vie with each other for dominance. This takes place at practically every level and in every aspect of the national life.

Here is something important which should command our attention. Christianity has often been blamed for not being able to adjust itself to Chinese culture and become part of the Chinese ethos. Unlike Buddhism it has maintained its distinctness as an imported religion that has never lost its foreignness.[1] On the surface the fault seems to lie entirely with Christianity, and the Chinese elite, both within and without the church, tend to align themselves with criticism of Christianity as a religion strange to the Chinese people.

At a deeper level, however, an unprejudiced observer cannot fail to observe that Christianity invaded China just at the time when the old was losing ground but the new was not yet born. The vacuum thus created made China lose her ability to assimilate and transform foreign elements, whether religious in particular or cultural in general. When China was in this way incapacitated, Christianity entered. It is really questionable whether the missionaries and the Chinese Christians realized the tremendous agony caused by this incapacitation, because for the last hundred years the Christian church in China has shown little appreciation of the cultural gap that accompanied the birth of modern China. The church's energy and effort were directed towards individual Chinese, treating them as if their cultural heritage and historical inevitability mattered little. The result was that the power of reconciliation, which constitutes the core of the Christian gospel, did not extend beyond individual converts to the history and culture of which they were a part. Organizationally, Christianity became indigenized in that national ecclesiastical bodies were formed and a considerable number of churches built in Chinese style. But a theology of history and culture that takes into full consideration the particular historical and cultural contexts of China did not come into being. The Gospel did not truly become incarnate because the Christian presence in China had failed to bring both judgment and forgiveness, death and resurrection, to the culture of China.

The lesson of history is hard to learn, but the enlightened section of the Chinese Christians in Taiwan seems determined to learn it and learn it well. To the eye of a shrewd observer, a curious turn of the tide is now taking place. The situation, according to my analysis, is something like this. The modernization which the "Christian" West brought to the East has been successfully taking root in Taiwan. When I say "modernization," I do not mean only the physical and material aspects of it. More importantly, the people on Taiwan today are adjusting themselves, consciously or unconsciously, to the new outlook on life and on the world which accompanies scientific and technological advancement. Modernization has become a fact of life and is accepted as a norm of judgment. In this stream of cultural change towards science and technology, accommodation has to be found for the traditional spiritual values which constitute the Chinese as Chinese. This is the so-called revival of Chinese culture basically geared to orthodox Confucianism.

A hundred years ago the missionary church in China had to face the chasm that divided the disintegrating Chinese culture and the invading Western culture. Today the good intentions of Taiwan's cultured

Chinese, both inside and outside the church, to learn the lesson of history will falter and waver. The Christian church is currently witnessing a cultural crisis caused by the conflict between the triumphant and self-asserting power of modernization, and the apologetic, defensive, and yet militant, guardians of traditional religious, cultural, and ethical values. The former is forward-looking and thus futuristic, whereas the latter is backward-looking and nostalgic. The former is scientific, logical, and calculating to the point of cold-bloodedness, while the latter is intuitive and evangelistic, appealing to emotion rather than to reason. The birth of a new era is imminent, and there is no question as to which side victory belongs. As a new day struggles to break, chaos and hope are mingled together in the present. Culturally, the present for Taiwan is synonymous with chaos and hope. And it is the supreme task of the church at this critical juncture to be the apostle of hope. Here and now the church is given another golden opportunity to bring the power of reconciliation to bear on individuals in the context of cultural upheavals. Unfortunately, most signs indicate that the church, both in its thinking and practice, tends to fall back on that which is old, to side with that which is past, to associate with the revival of that which is dead and buried. Perhaps the church does this out of a sense of guilt, trying to make up for its rejection of Chinese culture by consummating a marriage with it. But the end result will be far from satisfactory. The church will certainly be even more conscience-stricken fifty years hence for smothering hopes that are a vital part of the present chaos.

TWO MARRIAGE PROPOSALS AND THE SEARCH FOR IDENTITY

Marriage between Chinese culture and Christianity cannot be contracted too easily. Therefore, one cannot help despairing when one hears of a marriage proposal from the side of Chinese culture suggested almost too readily. For example, Chang Chi-yun, president of the Chinese Cultural College, proposes that "the moral teachings of Confucius can very well be supplemented and fulfilled by the spirituality of Christ." Then his wishful thinking carries him a little too far when he adds: "In fact, Confucius himself anticipated such a fulfilment when he remarked: 'If a man embraces the law of Heaven in the morning, then he may die the same evening without regret.' "[2] I cannot honestly, by any stretch of imagination, see a direct relation of anticipation and fulfilment between this particular saying of Confucius, uttered in a particular situation, and the message proclaimed by Christ. But it seems to me that the following questions are the most crucial ones to be asked by anyone attempting this line of approach: Are the teachings of Confucius, and for that matter those of Mencius or Sun-tze, directly applicable to the Chinese living under the blessings of modern science and technology? What modifications and transformations should they undergo before they may become relevant to the contemporary Chinese? Any attempt to amalgamate Chinese thought with Christianity, without settling these questions first, does justice neither to Christianity nor to Chinese culture. The following observation made by a contemporary Chinese analytical philosopher is very much to the point. He says: "The process of modernization for Chinese culture is a complicated one. On the one hand, in its struggle it has to discard, painful though this may be, some cultural obstacles blocking modernization. On the other hand, Chinese culture should re-adjust its function before it can observe new cultural elements. . . . As has been repeatedly stressed, the consciousness of Chinese culture is characterized by respect for the old, resistance to change, a despising of what is foreign, and self-sufficiency. For Chinese culture to become modernized, these concepts have to be abandoned. It has to strive for the new, to accept changes, to understand what is happening outside, and to be aware of insufficiency and be willing to learn from others."[3] Candidness of this kind represents the self-criticism going on among a small group of Chinese intellectuals on Taiwan today. In such self-criticism is hope for Chinese culture. For the Christian church to be ignorant of or to ignore such signs of hope, is for it to become disincarnated and disindigenized.

Another marriage proposal between Christianity and Chinese culture comes from Dr. Lien-hwa Chou, professor of New Testament Studies at the Southern Baptist Seminary in Taipei. The tentative nature of his attempt, inviting others to join in discussion, is expressed in a series of articles, "Preface to Establishing Chinese Theological Thought."[4] It is, to be sure, no more than a preface, but in it Dr. Chou already shows what he means by Chinese theological thought. Chinese theological thought he loosely defines as "understanding the universal Savior from the viewpoint of the Chinese."[5] A definition as is well known, delimits the connotation and the denotation of the subject under discussion. In defining his effort, however, Dr. Chou nowhere clarifies either the connotation or the denotation of the term "the Chinese." By "the Chinese" does he mean the contemporary or the ancient Chinese? The Chinese in the Republic of China or those on the mainland or the Chinese in diaspora? This is not a hair-splitting question. He himself stresses the national character of theology when he says: "Is there a Chinese theological thought and a foreign one? Yes, of course. Theology has national characteristics. . . . The Germans have their own way of thinking, and so do the Americans."[6] Precisely. But does not one have to go on and ask: German theology of which period or which century? There is still no tradition of theological thinking in China, yet it is certainly important to ask the question: For whom, and according to whom, is Chinese theological thought to be established? The answer given to this question will characterize one's theological formation. Unfortunately, Dr. Chou has not taken this into serious consideration.

Another of his statements seems to clarify his meaning somewhat. In order to avoid any misunderstanding that Chinese theological thought may result in changing Christ, he declares emphatically that his effort is "to meditate upon Christ by a Chinese way of thinking, to introduce Christ to our own people in the Chinese language."[7] But surely he must know that the content of thought, and language as the vehicle by which thought is expressed, undergoes transformation from one period to another. One of the greatest contributions made by the historical-critical method is in the area of texts of different religions and cultures. A wealth of meaning has been, and is still being, uncovered by the application of such methods. Both thought and language have history with regard to origin and development. The question that must be asked, is then: By what norm of thought and form of language does Dr. Chou plan to introduce Christ to the Chinese people on Taiwan? Again, there is no methodological stipulation directed to the question.

It is in the actual course of developing his thesis that he answers indirectly the questions raised above. He concentrates his effort on finding "points of contact" between Christianity and the religious beliefs supposed to be contained in ancient Chinese writings. As is to be expected, he finds in the concept of "heaven"

personal qualities which correspond to the concept of God in the
Christian Bible. Leaving aside the problem of whether he correctly
interprets the passages taken from the writings of ancient China, one
is not entirely clear as to what he wants to prove by this. His
conclusion is somewhat melodramatic, for he happily concludes that
"looked upon sympathetically, Christianity not only does not contradict Chinese culture, but it possesses many points which correspond with it. These corresponding points tell us that the God in our
ancient writings is the same God who manifests Himself in the Old
Testament as Yahweh."[8] This is too loaded a statement to be acceptable at face value. It suggests a marriage proposal through a middle-
man rather than through mutual understanding and wholehearted
consent.

It is a backward-looking and retrospective attitude such as this that
always makes well-meaning attempts to bring Christianity and
Chinese culture into the same orbit of existence and to adopt comparative methods that lead to uncritical accommodation of one with the
other. In the process, the question of whether the content of thought
found in the ancient writings is still applicable to present modes of
thinking is set aside. Often it is adoption of outdated thoughts into
Christianity. Willy-nilly, the church comes to associate itself with the
conservative forces at work in Taiwan society that resist progress and
modernization. When the disintegration of traditional values and
ideas is fast becoming more and more real to the cultured Chinese,
how could a Chinese theological system appeal to them if it allies itself
uncritically with outmoded thought-forms and contents?

All this points up the problem of the church's self-identity in
Taiwan. The two marriage proposals discussed above are typical of
the effort to solve the problem culturally and not theologically. It has
to be remembered that the search for Asian theology is the search for
the identity of the Christian church in this essentially non-Christian
world. It is a redefinition and re-explanation of the meaning of the
message of Jesus Christ in the cultural context of Asia today. Therefore a strongly conservative stance that is retrospective in both outlook and method does not aid the church in this task of finding
self-identity. A careful analysis of the conservative trend reveals that
its present is the acceptance of the accumulated past. There is no
forward movement, no fresh revelation of God's will through confrontation of the Scriptures with new contexts. It is a protective shell

that admits no interference of history and culture from outside. It is like a water pipeline running underground, completely insulated from the earth around it. The Association for Theological Education in Taiwan, formed in 1958, is predominantly conservative, trying to express the identity of the church in the cultural context of Taiwan by resorting to confessionalism, which rose from completely different cultural contexts. The statement of faith, adopted by the association in 1960 as the basis of fellowship and cooperation, is indicative of this fact. It includes, among other things, articles concerning the divine inspiration and consequent authority of the whole canonical Scriptures, eternal life for the saved, and eternal punishment for the condemned.[9]

In contrast, there is a new trend toward rethinking most seriously the meaning of the Gospel in the present context of Taiwan. This trend is essentially forward-looking and dynamic in its understanding of God's dealing with the world. It throbs with eschatological urgency in pointing to the future. In it creative restlessness is called forth as Christians are challenged by the message of the Gospel in the context in which they live. This partly explains why the church in Taiwan has had no time for theological system building, for indulging in metaphysical speculation about the nature of God and the person of Jesus Christ. For the first eighty years of its life, that is, since 1865 when the Gospel first reached this little island, the church had only one concern—namely, the effort to reach as many islanders as possible. At the end of the Second World War, during which the church had to undergo much tribulation, it thought it could sit back and philosophize and theologize about the content of its faith; but the extraordinary forces of cultural and social and political changes engulfed the church, along with the rest of the island and Asia, too. The church had to look for the meaning of her existence in this new revolutionary world, and the chief prophetic voice that awakened the rank and file Christians in Taiwan to the awareness of the demands and possibilities of the new day was that of Dr. C.H. Hwang. By no means a systematic thinker, Dr. Hwang combines in himself fine theological acumen and charismatic drive. In deep earnestness, he asks Christians in Asia: "Are we, in fact, being forcibly confronted by Christ's revolution through the world revolutionary events of our day? Has not the groaning of the whole creation to do with the inward groaning of the first fruits of the Spirit?"[10] Then what is the question which the community of the first fruits has to ask in these extraordinary and trying times? According to Dr. Hwang, it is this: "How is the common mission of God's people to be translated into concrete action in today's Asia?"[11] This is indeed the central question which has occupied the students of theology in Taiwan for the last decade. No direction has been clearly indicated. But it is this most urgent theological theme, rising out of the missionary nature and task of the church, that constitutes the main thrust of theological endeavor. Shall we call this "situational" or "contextual" theology? Again, in the words of C.H. Hwang: "Faithfulness to the Text (Jesus Christ as witnessed in the Bible) does not mean that we should be slavishly bound by past formulations of it, nor that we need to escape from our context, but rather that we should be renewed by the living Text, through a renewed understanding of the written texts, so that we in turn may be instrumental for its creative relevance to the contemporary text."[12] This is a somewhat complicated statement, but the intention of the author is clear. Faithfulness to Jesus Christ in the texts of the Scriptures demands from us ever-fresh interpretation and appropriation in such a way that he becomes the challenging force, to contemporary men and women, for repentance. The whole exercise is the response to God from the depths of our being, involvement in the revolutionary forces at work today, and refusal to be shackled by physical and spiritual pasts which have become obsolete for today and detrimental to new adventures tomorrow. He voices his concern that if we Christians in Asia refuse to meet Christ "outside the camp" where he was crucified, "we shall become a ghetto, irrelevant and unrelated to Asia today and tomorrow, and we shall eventually become a museum piece, a relic left over from the colonial era!"[13] This is a trumpet call to action in response to the new day which God has ushered in in Asia. How is such a passionate cry to be translated into theological formulations? This is what the theology of the incarnation attempts to do.

The Theology of the Incarnation— Perspective of the Present

The foregoing discussion prescribes for us the perspective from which theologizing should begin. What is this perspective? Needless to say, the present constitutes the perspective for the theology of the incarnation. The present is neither the past nor the future; it is the consummation of the past and the threshold to the future. In itself it has no breadth—it does not even possess the dimension of a mathematical point. Essentially it is a perspective—a perspective through which the past is evaluated and the future anticipated. It underlies and gives support to each and every moment in the ongoing stream of history. Man is bound to such a present. This characterizes his nature as God's creation. It follows that the assertion that man can transcend the present in order to scan the past and predict the future is a false presupposition, contradictory to the nature of man. In fact, there is no such transcendence, for "you are dust, and to dust you shall return" (Gen. 3:19). Any interpretation of the past and any prediction of the future on the presupposition of transcendence are destined to end in either self-deception or naive optimism. Herein is dormant the temptation to sin. What man is tempted to do, according to Reinhold Niebuhr, is to "pretend that he is not limited." Furthermore, he "assumes that he can gradually transcend finite limitations until his mind becomes identical with universal mind. All of his intellectual and cultural pursuits, therefore, become infected with the sin of pride."[14] Thus, the message of the Christian Bible is not emancipation from limitation and finiteness, but from the sin of pride.

To transcend the present is a feat not to be lightly attempted. It would result in the denial of one's own nature. Like the story of the Fall in Genesis, the wisdom of Zen Buddhism partly consists in the realization of this essential nature of man as a limited being. But unlike the Christian Bible, it teaches the transcendence of the present in terms of the transcendence of self. One transcends the present only insofar as one transcends one's self. When one succeeds in transcending one's self, one becomes a nonhistorical being. In such a state interpretation of the past becomes superfluous and prediction of the future appears meaningless. One has to be content with the enunciation of cryptic words symbolical of the blissful state of nonbeing. Paradoxically, to Zen Buddhism this is being. For the theology of the incarnation, however, the recovery of the meaning of being is possible only in the discovery of being in the affirmation of the present through Jesus Christ.

Methodologically, this observation has important bearings upon our endeavor to search for a new direction for Asian theology. The church in Asia tends to fall back on the past largely because it is not able to cope with the mysterious character of the present. The past provides comfortable terms of reference whenever the church is challenged into taking its own theological and ethical stand. Furthermore, the church is fond of indulging in speculation about the future which never threatens it with existential decision. Future is synonymous with illusion when it provides the church with a framework which does not hold for the present. In all its efforts the present is brushed aside in order for the past to be transplanted to the future. Is this not what the incarnation is not? Would not this lead to the rejection of Jesus Christ as the Lord here and now? Is not the denial of the present typical of mystical religion? Thus, the theology anchored in the present as the perspective giving meaning to the past and holding up hope for the future is the theology of the incarnation—the theology which reckons with the immediate presence of the Eternal One in the midst of the temporal and transient.

The incarnation is this present. It is the present, not as a principle to follow, but as perspective—that is, as dynamic force giving birth to new moments in the midst of the old. As such it is an event, or the event, in that something happens when it interferes with the mundane. The incarnation is not an isolated phenomenon. It is always on the move, giving one new moment after another. It is eternally present with the world, but not the eternal present. Through the incarnation thus eternally present as the powerful creative force, the past is translated to the future, darkness yields to glory, despair gives way to hope, and death is conquered. That which is done is not undone, but is transformed into that which participates in the fulness of time. Viewed under the perspective of the incarnation, the past is never simply past and the future is not simply not yet. When the past and the future are brought into the focus of the incarnation which is eternally present, an incarnational event comes into being. It is the task of the theology of the incarnation to investigate how my past and our past, my future and our future, become, when invaded by the incarnation, incarnational events. In this way, theology ceases to be confined to the domain traditionally called "church." It is, in essence, the theology which deals with what takes place between God and man, namely, incarnational events, in particular historical and cultural contexts, and, in this case, in Taiwan.[15]

The theology of the incarnation does not begin with either God or man. It begins with God-man. Here is the central mystery of the Christian faith that distinguishes it from any other faiths and beliefs. What takes place in God-man is neither humanization of God nor divinization of man; it is not God meeting man halfway or man meeting God halfway. What comes into being is what Paul calls a "new creature" (2 Cor. 5:17; Gal. 6:15). The new creature, in contrast with the old creature, partakes of the quality that is immune from decay and falsity. In this the provincial and provisional character of religion is overcome. It is the acceptance of what is deep in the human by the Deep in God. It follows that theology ceases to be a mere explanation of the contents of the Christian faith for the edification of the Christian community. Because the Christian church in Asia has tried to do just that, it retreats into a self-defined domain called "religion," and thus unwittingly joins ranks with other religions. The theology of the incarnation has to break this self-imposed restriction that deprives the Christian faith of its universal as well as particular character.

The theology of the incarnation is thus the conversation between the deep and the Deep, the interaction between truths scattered in God's creation and the Truth revealed in Jesus Christ. It is the arena where the strayed truths in human history and culture are once again united with the Truth which is in Jesus Christ. It recognizes on the one hand the manifestations of the Truth in varied forms and ways in different cultural settings. At the same time it is critical of distorted expressions and interpretations that are given to manifestations of the Truth in different cultural contexts, the so-called Christian culture not excepted. The implications of such a theological effort are far-reaching. Mission can no longer consist in "Christianizing" culture—which was a wrong step taken by the Emperor Constantine and mistakenly followed by the church in the establishment of Christendom—but in working towards the emergence of incarnational events in the meeting of the Truth and truths. The ultimate goal of theology, then, is to bring into light, in the course of the explanation of the Christian faith in a particular cultural context, how the creative power of God's saving love is at work even in the darkest corner of the world. This has little to do with a search for "points of contact" between Christianity and non-Christian faiths and beliefs, for it extends beyond what is specifically designated as religion to the embodiment of God's creative act in a particular cultural context. It is by no means accidental that the Israelite theologians had no alternative but to set the peculiar problems regarding their own nation in the context of the whole creation. Is it not true to say that the creation story was written from the perspective of the ever-present reality of God's redeeming love? Is it therefore a matter for surprise when John begins his Gospel in a way that is strongly reminiscent of the first chapter of Genesis? Incarnational events are creational events. The incarnation embodied in Jesus Christ pertains to the whole cosmos as well as to each individual person.

Applied to Taiwan, the theology of the incarnation has the primary task of interpreting the current strifes and aspirations inherent in contemporary cultural upheavals in terms of Jesus Christ. Here temptation to build a theological system has to be avoided at any cost. We do not approach the current situation with theological principles laid down in advance. The days of system-building are gone. A systematic scheme, such as dividing revelation into general and special revelation, has done more harm than good as far as the problem of the relationship between the Christian faith and non-Christian faiths is concerned. The theology of the incarnation which purports to find incarnational events in a particular historical and cultural context makes such distinction obsolete. An ontological understanding of God in terms of the trinitarian formula which originated in the Latin and Greek churches has baffled the Chinese audience. Such an ontological scheme has to be replaced by an existential dynamic that creates and re-creates man and the world with the divine love and compassion. Furthermore, the conception of the church as the communion of saints, which often restricts rather than expands the sphere of Christian influence, has to yield to the missionary nature and task of the church as the embodiment of *missio Dei*.

Since the incarnation is always a movement, theology must of necessity be on the move. From the present, theology moves forward to the future, and not backward into the past, in search of the meaning that transcends and gives meaning to life. Here the theology of the incarnation is profoundly related to ethical problems. Ethics in this context includes both its narrow sense of morality and a wider sense of the ordering of human life in accordance with the ordering of creation. Ethics thus consists of the ethical ordering of both the whole cosmos and of man. The traditional Chinese ethical system represented by the Confucianist school has succeeded in reducing the ethical ordering of the whole cosmos to human relationships. This is one of the main reasons why the Chinese find it difficult, conceptually and practically, to adjust themselves to the modern era which has rediscovered tremendous possibilities arising out of relocating man's place in the whole of the cosmos. In fact, a creative insight was at work in the person of Sun Yat-sen, the founder of the Republic of China, when he advocated the ideal of "The unity of the world and of mankind." He was strongly influenced by Christianity, and his was an effort which could be interpreted as projecting into the Chinese mentality the Christian hope of the kingdom of God. Politically, this was an endeavor to relocate the place of a new China in the fast modernizing world. Unfortunately, his effort was hampered by the narrow ethical norm of human relationships conceived by the Confucianist school. Neo-Confucianism in Taiwan may serve ideological purposes, but it has no solution to offer for reestablishing the ethical norm of human relationships in the context of the ethical norm according to which God created the world. It is the task of the theology of the incarnation to effect daily ethical decisions in accordance with the ethical decision of God revealed in creation and salvation.

In this way the theology of the incarnation does not serve as a superstructure to be imposed on the history and culture of Taiwan. It is a rational undertaking, trying to discern, analyze, and synthesize the working of God in history and culture. It begins with Jesus Christ, and from this focus it sees the creation, in all its aspects, from the perspective of the eternally present God, namely, the Word become flesh.

NOTES

1. The latest and only comprehensive study of this problem to appear in Chinese is Shih Chiang Lu's *The Origin and Cause of the Anti-Christian Movement by Chinese Officials and Gentry: 1860–1874* (Nangkang, Taipei, Taiwan: Institute of Modern History,

Academia Sinica, 1966). As the author sees it, the main reasons for opposing Christianity are the attitude of invasion taken by Christianity, the difference between Chinese social custom and Western custom, and the desire of the Chinese to protect their own dignity and interests. Although a careful study, the work does not add any new insight to the problem.

2. See the preface Chang Chi-yun wrote for Paul K.T. Sih's book, *Chinese Culture and Christianity* (Taipei: China Culture Publishing Foundation, 1957), p. 7. Sih was director of the Institute of Far Eastern Studies, Seton Hall University, South Orange, N.J.

3. Yin Hai-kwang, *Outlook on Chinese Culture*, 2 vols. (Taipei: Wen-sing Publishing House, 1966), 439ff.

4. Dr. Lien-hwa Chou's articles appeared in a 1968 series in the *Christian Tribune*, the first Christian weekly paper to gain wide recognition among the Chinese in Taiwan, as well as in Southeast Asia. It was founded in Taiwan in 1965.

5. *Christian Tribune*, June 23, 1968.

6. *Ibid.*, June 30, 1968.

7. *Ibid.*, June 23, 1968.

8. *Ibid.*, August 11, 1968.

9. Cf. Lien-min Cheng, "Planning for Joint Action in Theological Education in the Taiwan Area," *Theological Education and Ministry*. Reports from the Northeast Asia Theological Education Consultation, Seoul, Korea, November 28/December 2, 1966, pp. 264–280.

10. C.H. Hwang, "God's People in Asia Today," *South East Asia Journal of Theology* V, 2 (1963), 10. Dr. Hwang was principal of the Tainan Theological College from 1949 to 1965. He is now director of the Theological Education Fund of the WCC.

11. *Ibid.*, p. 8.

12. C.H. Hwang, "Text and Context in Theological Education," in *Theological Education and Ministry*, (Seoul, Korea: 1966), p. 223.

13. C.H. Hwang, "Into a New Era Together," *Theology and the Church* IV, 1 (1964), 5. (Publication of Tainan Theological College.)

14. Reinhold Niebuhr, *The Nature and Destiny of Man*, vol. 1 (London: Nisbet, 1949), 190ff.

15. C.H. Hwang's stress on the world-directed ministry along with the God-directed and the church-directed ministry is theologically sound. Only one has to guard against a trichotomy of what he calls the one ministry of Jesus Christ. See his article, "A Rethinking of Theological Training for the Ministry in the Younger Churches Today," *South East Asia Journal of Theology* IV, 2 (1962), 7-34.

Rough Road to Theological Maturity

While churches in other lands have hundreds or even "thousands" of years of history, the Protestant churches in Korea are only some eighty years old. Moreover, only half a century has passed since we first began to take theology seriously, leaving no time for the development of a rich theological tradition. Added to this are the facts that most of these eighty-odd years have been spent under political and cultural oppression by Japan, and that after liberation in 1945, we supposedly became independent but actually have undergone periods of great chaos. Thus, our half-century of theological activity has not been one of mature development. Indeed, our theology is impoverished.

Nevertheless, we are young, and while we have no proud tradition behind us, we do have a future that is wide open. We are devoid of Western-style tradition and theological inheritance, but our history has developed in its own peculiar fashion in spite of our impoverished theological condition. Upon this history, such as it is, we seek to build a new tomorrow. We shall therefore seek in these pages to explore theological construction in the future by reflecting on the past.

Translated by David E. Ross. The author acknowledges with appreciation the contribution of a study group organized by the Korea Christian Academy in the preparation of this essay, which was written prior to the declaration of martial law in Korea on October 17, 1972. All essays, journals, and books referred to in the text and notes, except the books by George Paik and Arthur Judson Brown, are in Korean. Their titles are given in English translation here for convenience.

Thirty Years without
Theological Activity (1885–1915)

The first resident Protestant missionaries entered Korea in 1884–85. As in the early Christian church, a period of missionary expansion was necessary before there could be concentration on theological reflection. The peculiar Korean feature of this period, however, is that it has continued too long, even—in some respects—to the present day. Missionary activity, completely devoid of theological activity, comprised the first thirty years.

There were reasons for this. First, it was a period of extreme chaos just prior to and following the fall of Korea in 1910 to Japan. Accordingly, Christians were in no position to devote leisurely creative effort to intellectual reflection on their new religion—and they lacked the cultural preparedness to do so.

A second reason was the influence of missionary policy. The early missionaries' strategy was: (1) to concentrate on women and the laboring class, (2) to lay stress on elementary education, and (3) to promote indigenous evangelistic work on the part of the Korean church.[1] Herein can be found the basic character of the Korean Protestant churches. By concentrating on women and the masses, both of whom at that time were in a deplorable condition, the churches easily achieved numerical growth. However, by the same token, the churches could not avoid becoming identified with the uneducated, powerless masses. The neglect of higher education, moreover, rendered the church ineffective in developing leadership.

The lack of an effective strategy in the theological education of church workers was a third reason. While espousing the goal of "nurturing a Korean ministry to fit the Korean Church," the practice was to provide to the Koreans who would minister to the masses the absolute minimum of training. Presbyterians in 1901 and Methodists in 1907 established seminaries, but they were little more than Bible schools which offered training courses only three months out of the year.

Still another reason was the theology of the first missionaries themselves. The man who was the executive secretary of the Board of Foreign Missions of the Presbyterian Church, U.S.A., from 1895 to 1929 described the early missionaries to Korea:

During the first twenty-five years, the average missionary was a man with a puritanical faith. Just as their New England ancestors of the previous century, these men faithfully kept the Sabbath, and regarded dancing, smoking and card playing as sin. Their theology was conservative, so they considered biblical higher criticism and liberal theology to be heretical.[2]

These four factors shaped the character of early Protestantism in Korea. Frankly speaking, the faith of the Korean churches, which became rooted among the uneducated, suffering masses, hardened into a legalistic fundamentalism. Consequently, there was little or no enthusiasm for the development of an intellectually demanding theology.

THE GERMINAL STAGE OF KOREAN THEOLOGY (1916–1927)

Although the Korean church itself was not yet prepared to engage in theological construction, theological discussion did begin on an individual basis among young men returning from study abroad. A theological consciousness was beginning to stir by the time the Korean church reached its thirtieth birthday.

Theological education had begun by 1900, but—as has been pointed out—this early period of training was merely an extension of the Bible schools started by Fundamentalist missionaries. Nevertheless, by 1910 the educational process had managed to nurture its own kind of system, and from this time on, theological studies began to be published. *World of Theology*, a quarterly issued by the Methodist Theological Seminary, was the first theological journal.[3] This magazine began publication in 1916 under the editorial direction of Yang Ju-Sam,[4] who also published an introduction to the Old and New Testaments and a series of studies on hymnody. In 1917 he published Korea's first Protestant theological essay, "The Doctrine of the Godhead in Christianity." *World of Theology* was, from its inception, a joint venture of Koreans and Western missionaries. And when Yang Ju-Sam introduced higher criticism of the Pentateuch (1916), he enjoyed an atmosphere of complete freedom.

Two years later, in 1918, the Presbyterian Theological Seminary began publication of its quarterly, *Theological Instruction*.[5] Unfortunately, however, this publication was entirely monopolized by Western missionaries until 1927, and it was not until 1928 that Korean Presbyterians began to publish their own theological studies. This reveals the extent to which the Korean Presbyterian Church was firmly controlled by missionary conservatism.

This germinal stage in Korean theology was marked by yet another incident—the appearance of a privately published journal of theological studies, an interchurch effort, unrelated to the seminary publications. This monthly magazine made its debut in 1923, under the name *New Life*, and though it lasted only two years, it represented an important step in the expression of Korean Christian thought. Both management and literary contributions were completely in the hands of Korean Christians. Editor Chon Young-T'aek and all other key staff members had received their education in Japan. Most of the articles in the magazine dealt with the relation of Christianity and culture, or with social issues.

This was a period marked by several distinctive characteristics. The first was the theological awakening within the Methodist church. Both Yang Ju-Sam and *New Life's* editor, Chon Young-T'aek, were Methodist ministers who had received their education abroad, the former in America at Vanderbilt and Yale, the latter in Japan at Aoyama Gakuin.

A second characteristic of the period was the openness and progressive thought of the theological leaders, which was largely due to the fact that the majority were Methodist. The Presbyterian church of that day was locked in the grip of the Western missionaries' conservative orthodoxy. By contrast, the forward-looking attitudes of the Methodist church enabled it to begin more rapidly to develop an indigenous theology. Yang Ju-Sam as previously mentioned, was able, without any restrictions, to introduce higher criticism, and the graduates of Japan's Aoyama Gakuin were free to criticize conservative theology from the viewpoint of contemporary problems.

The third characteristic of this period was the strong interest in Korean culture. The Korean people developed a strong national spirit through their nationwide independence movement of 1919, just nine years after the beginning of the Japanese occupation of Korea (1910-1945). Most of the contributors to *New Life* in the 1920s dealt with the issue of "Christianity and Korea."[6]

THE FLOWERING STAGE OF KOREAN THEOLOGY (1928–1939)

Half a century after Protestantism had been introduced into Korea, the church entered its third stage of development. I call this the

"flowering stage" of Korean theology. Behind this lay several con-
tributing factors. First was the stability of Korean society and culture
during this period. As conquerors, the Japanese began to develop the
pattern of their colonization of Korea, so we, the colonized, began to
settle down into a kind of quiet stability. Thus, in spite of many
restrictions, we were able to experience a growing educational and
academic maturity.

Second was the large number of students returning from theological studies abroad. The Korean churches, in their fifty years, had
managed to produce a reputable group of young men who were
attracted to the academic circles of the world, and who left Korea to
continue their studies in the United States or Japan. Consequently
there arose a large number of church leaders who were receptive to
developments in Western theology.[7] The churches had now matured
to the point where they could assume responsibility for reflection
upon their faith—with a crop of ably trained young theologians.

Among the distinguishing features of this period was the achievement of considerable freedom from the theological domination of the
early missionaries. The Presbyterian church, which had been under
the tightest control, gained its freedom in 1928, when Nam
Gung-Hyok[8] became editor-in-chief of the Presbyterian Seminary
publication *Theological Instruction*. After this, articles and studies prepared by Korean scholars began to appear regularly before Presbyterian readers.

Then also for the first time theological tradition arose as an issue,
and Korean Christians began to be burdened by controversies arising
from efforts to form and preserve such a tradition.

Two large denominations dominated the scene at this time, the
Presbyterians and the Methodists. The Methodists, with an attitude
of openness regarding the transition taking place in theology, made no
issue of commitment to its past tradition. The Presbyterians, however, engaged in limitless controversy in order to stubbornly defend
the conservative orthodoxy brought in by the early missionaries. At
the center of this struggle was Pak Hyong-Nyong.[9]

The Fundamentalist tradition in the United States vigorously de-
fended the literal interpretation of Scripture against modern science
and its offshoot, evolution. Similarly, Korean conversativism carried
as its banner the principles of biblical inerrancy and verbal inspiration
of Scripture. These two issues, central in the Presbyterian church,

were adopted as the "sole yardstick" by which to measure all other theological thinking.[10]

Two issues arose in the 1924 General Assembly of the Presbyterian Church. One involved the Reverend Kim Yong-Ju's denial of the Mosaic authorship of Genesis, and the other was an article by the Reverend Kim Ch'un-Bae to the effect that the biblical injunction "Women should be silent and should not teach" was simply the localized teaching and custom of one particular church two thousand years ago. Both men were brought to trial on charges of criticizing Scripture and adhering to liberal theology. The committee appointed to study and examine the charges, headed by Pak Hyong-Nyong, concluded that "any minister who denies the Mosaic authorship of Genesis is guilty of desecrating the inerrant and exact Scripture and should be removed from his position." Further, regarding the problem of women's privileges, the committee agreed that since women are nowhere granted any privileges of position in the church according to the Bible, to freely interpret Scripture for the sake of catering to current trends was wrong and deserving of punishment. The assembly adopted the report and condemned both men.

At the Presbyterian General Assembly the following year, the translation of the *Abingdon Bible Commentary*, edited by the Reverend Yu Hyong-Ki, arose as a controversial issue. The assembly decided not to subscribe to the work and to require those Presbyterian scholars who had worked on the translation to make a public apology.

The person largely responsible for the establishment of this kind of conservatism in Korean theology was Pak Hyong-Nyong. The publication in 1935 of his book *A Critique of Problems in Contemporary Christianity* assured him this position. A work of 847 pages, it was the first book on systematic theology by a Korean Protestant to be published in Korea. By attacking the "new theology"—Schleiermacher, Ritschl, Barth, and other modern theologians—he sought to firmly establish his own school of orthodox conservatism.

In 1939 a work in systematic theology appeared that was directly opposed to Pak's book. It was *An Outline of Christian Theology* by Chong Kyong-Ok.[11] Written against a background of Western liberal theology, especially Ritschl and Barth, it is the most significant work in the flowering stage of Korean theology—and it was the last flower of the period, because the Korean church was now entering a period of darkness. Chong Kyong-Ok has candidly summarized the major figures of the 1930s in Korean theology:

The two men who fortified the ranks of Korean conservatism were the Presbyterian Seminary's Dr. Pak Hyong-Nyong and the Methodist Seminary's Dr. Pyon Hong-Kyu. Both men held firmly to the doctrine of verbal inspiration and literal interpretation of Scripture. Dr. Pak, as a "professional Calvinist," was the spokesman for the American so-called fundamentalist school. Dr. Pyon adheared so closely to the orthodox school that he was labeled a pious intellectualist.

Among those who held to a "conservative faith and progressive theology" were Yun In-Ku of South Kyongsang Province, Kal Hong-Ki of Chosun Christian College, Kim Young-Hi of Ewha Woman's College, Song Chang-Gun of Pusan Chin and Kim Jae-Jun of Manchuria.[12]

By this time two schools of theology had begun to take form, and these two currents continue to divide theologians in Korea to the present.

THE STAGNANT STAGE OF KOREAN THEOLOGY (1940–1956)

Along with the entire nation, the Korean churches suffered a period of great upheaval after 1940, which resulted in theological stagnation. The Japanese government's suppression of Christianity began with the 1938 pronouncement that all Christians must worship at shrines. Both the Presbyterian and Methodist seminaries were forced to close their doors in 1938 and 1940, respectively. In 1940, the Second World War broke out; in 1942 all missionaries were expelled; in 1943 the Holiness, Seventh Day Adventist, and Baptist churches were disbanded; and immediately preceding the liberation of August 15, 1945, all denominations were abolished and replaced by a united body called the Japanese Christian Korean Kyodan.

The two periodicals, *World of Theology* and *Theological Instruction*, were forced to cease publication at the time the seminaries were closed. From 1942, the permit for publication of all literature related to Christianity was revoked, with only one weekly newspaper, *The Christian News*, allowed to continue. In a word, all theological activity was curtailed. Furthermore, strange demands began to be made on Christians. One such demand was contained in a document entitled "The Renewal of Christianity," which insisted that English- and

American-style Christianity be renewed by beginning again as a Japanese religion. The decree stated that "the majority of Christianity's sacred teachings and examples are spread naively as one interpretation of the Gospel, and the doctrines of eschatology, the Sabbath, the Second Coming of Christ and the Judgment, all are part of a Jewish superstitious faith." It further claimed that "all old American and British church structures will be revised. They will be put under tight control and 'Japanized.' "[13] Ultimately even the Bible and hymns were forbidden except for those passages which could be used seemingly to support the Japanese militaristic mentality. This was the chaotic scene in Korea on August 15, 1945—the day independence was declared—and which continued in the period immediately following. The churches also entered a period of confusion and factionalism, centering around two issues. One was the degradation of the churches during the latter part of the Japanese occupation, with each side placing the blame on the other. The other issue was the now open and unvarnished fighting between conservatives and liberals, which resulted in church schisms. Numerous new seminaries were founded, each espousing the position of its special faction. In short order, three seminaries were established within the Presbyterian church alone.

In the midst of this situation the tragic Korean War broke out in 1950. As Korean society became distraught, so the churches became even more disgraceful in the eyes of the world. "Orthodox faith" was the ostensible issue at stake, but ecclesiastical power politics was the real factor. Some church leaders became notorious because of their struggles over personal privileges, especially those pertaining to finances.

The Methodist church reunited in 1949. However, the Presbyterian church divided further, with the Koryo faction breaking off in 1951 and the "R.O.K." (Republic of Korea), or "Christian," Presbyterian church dividing in 1953. The period of theological stagnancy continued in this confused state until 1955.

One individual stands out as a giant in this period. Dr. Kim Jae-Jun, who might be called the leading Korean theologian, never ceased his theological endeavors even under the most trying conditions.[14] When the Presbyterian Seminary of P'yongyang was forced to close its doors in 1938, Dr. Kim left for Seoul, and in 1940

started the new "Chosun [Korea] Theological Seminary" in an effort
to preserve the work of theology in Korea. With liberation n 1945, this
seminary continued its task of theological education for church workers, and became the cradle for the present R.O.K. Presbyterian
church.

The establishment of this seminary by Korean Christians themselves was important for theological education and also because it
represented an "endowment" of the Korean people. In the words of
Dr. Kim, "The fact that the Chosun Theological Seminary has been
founded, and that the Western missionaries have all been forced to
leave this land, is not only an inevitable result of war, but also attests
to the fact that the period of missionary domination has come to an
end." The Korean church had now reached a stage where it no longer
was only one part of the work of American missionaries, but rather
where a truly autonomous history was beginning to be written.

With liberation, Dr. Kim began editing and publishing theological
studies. During 1945–49 his articles appeared in the journal *New Man*,
edited by Chon Young T'aek. Kim himself edited the journal *Soldiers
of the Cross* during the years 1950–56. Kim Jae-Jun stands alone as the
man who kept theology alive during this tragic period of stress in the
Korean church and nation.

As an Old Testament scholar specializing in the prophets, Kim is
an educator who has a keen sense of participating in history. He
believes that the otherworldly, anticultural, orthodox style of theology, which was introduced into Korea and came to be viewed as
sacred, served only to separate us from our history. Nevertheless, he
said, "Now we have received this land, this nation, as our material
with which to work. We are called by God to erect the liberating
history of Christ within the history of this nation, so that Korean
history itself may be transformed."[15] These words express clearly
this church leader's sense of history and his underlying theological
spirit. Kim Jae-Jun holds a place of strategic importance in the history
of Korean theology—he opened the door to contemporary theology.

Korean Theology Today (1957–1970s)

The cultural development of the world in the last few decades has
more than equalled the development of the past few hundred years.

The Korean nation is a part of this development, and theology is no exception. Our development has not kept pace with that of the West, but the development and change we have experienced are unprecedented.

One factor in the transition is the great number of Korean youth who have gone abroad to study since 1950. In the 1940s it was nearly impossible to study abroad; but beginning in the fifties, masses of students have gone to Europe and America for study. Among them have been many young theological students. The result is that the number of Western trained theologians has increased sharply since 1955.

A second factor is the increase in institutions of theological education. As mentioned earlier, many new denominations have arisen, each with its own educational institutions, with the result that today there are over twenty theological seminaries in Korea. Only seven or eight of these institutions, however, are of college level.[16] Nonetheless, this is a sharp increase and significant change when compared to the fact that formerly only two seminaries existed.

A further sign of development is the large-scale publication of Christian literature. Leaving aside the many translations, an average of three or four new books by Koreans are published each year. Further, each seminary publishes its own annual edition of theological studies prepared by members of its own faculty. Also attesting to this development in contemporary Korean Protestantism is the monthly magazine *Christian Thought*. Published since 1957, this interdenominational journal of theology is the most reliable organ for reflecting the situation and direction of Korean theology. Nearly all of Korea's Protestant theologians, with the exception of the most radically conservative, contribute to this journal. Through *Christian Thought* and the many other magazines and research publications, more than a hundred theological articles appear in print each year from the work of over sixty scholars.

Current theological endeavor in Korea may be divided into two streams: one following the traditions of Western theology, and the other attempting to develop a Korean theology. These may be further divided into four groups: the first stream subdivided into conservative and liberal theological perspectives, and the second into those committed to "indigenization" (or "contextualization") and "secularization."

From earliest days to the present it has been the theological traditions of the West which have formed the main currents in Korean
theology. Most Korean scholars have been imitators, re-creating what
they learned from their study in the Western academic tradition. As
suggested above, there are two factions: conservatives and liberals.
The distinction between them is that each faction follows a different
Western tradition.

The dividing lines between conservatives and liberals in Korea are
found in their views concerning the Bible and their attitudes toward
ecumenism. Conservatives view historical and critical study of the
Bible as heretical and reject the ecumenical movement. Generally
they also criticize and reject neo-orthodoxy. Among the adherents of
this faction, or school, are Pak Hyong-Nyong and his followers, one
of whom is the colorful young theologian Han Ch'ol-Ha, whose study
entitled "An Analysis of the Theological Situation of the Korean
Church" is perhaps the best statement of conservative Korean
theology.[17]

It is the progressive theologians, however, who dominate the
Korean theological scene today.[18] For the most part they are men who
were trained in the Western tradition and adhere generally to a
neo-orthodox position. Barth, Bultmann, Tillich, and Niebuhr are
the theologians whom they study and discuss the most. However,
judging by studies prepared by Korean scholars of these men and by
Korean translations of their works, there is as yet no thoroughgoing
Barthian or Bultmannian disciple among Korea's theologians.

Liberation, the taste of independence, and the Korean War all
provided us with the opportunity to reflect in a new way on the
Korean situation. A new spirit of inquiry arose among theologians
concerning Korea's distinctive characteristics and position as a nation,
and this awakening became even more evident in the early 1960s.
This newly awakened spirit could also be described—in part—as a
desire to "rest" from dependency on Western thought.

Interest in the Bible increased immediately. Interdenominational
cooperation was possible for the retranslation of the Bible, and new
Bible commentaries began to appear.

Several factors stimulated this new awareness and reflection. One
was the development of studies in Koreanology; another was the
influence of a theology of unity from the West. This theology of
unity, which cites the rapid development of modern civilization as

pointing to a theology which goes beyond the traditions of the Western church, is causing Korean theologians to turn their attention to the Korean situation itself. Consequently, a movement is beginning to take form in Korea, whereby we seek to understand the Gospel more in terms of our own situation than in terms of Western tradition—a movement in which we are struggling to create an autonomous Christianity in, and a theology for, Korea.

Here again we are divided into two groups. One is the "indigenization" group, the other the "secularization" group. Most of the members of the indigenization group have been stimulated by the renewed interest in Koreanology and attach great importance to Korea's ancient cultural traditions. They emphasize the need for Koreans to possess an awareness of who we are, as Koreans, as we seek to have an encounter with Christ. They are concerned about how the seed of the Gospel can become implanted and grow in the cultural soil of this nation. Exploring, therefore, the cultural tradition of Korea, especially the religious culture, which has molded the Korean mind, these scholars are struggling to discover a basis on which to build a Korean theology. Christianity in Korea is now beginning to develop a Korean theology because of the stimulus of this dialogue on indigenization. Several studies have been made,[19] although they have dealt for the most part only with methodology.

Leading proponents of the "secularization" group of scholars are the executive secretaries of the various Christian student movements. Directing their attention toward the social and cultural situation of Korea, along with the rapidly changing world situation, they observe and discuss the urgent task of modernization and the phenomena of technology and urbanization. Taking as their weapon today's radical theology, they aim not to be bound by archaic tradition but to struggle to attain the "new theology of the Exodus." Rather than being enslaved to the past, they attach great importance to the newly developing cultural realities. These men are theologians boldly attempting to encounter Christ within their own history and in terms of their own sociocultural context. They are encouraged by similar efforts in other settings made by the bishop of Woolwich, John A. T. Robinson; Harvey Cox; Pannenberg; and Moltmann. The truly amazing aspect of this is that the Korean church as a whole is very sympathetic with the concerns of these men, evidenced by the fact that the Korean translations of Robinson's *Honest to God* and Cox's *The*

Secular City, books which contain entirely new ideas for Korean Christians, have been best sellers. Furthermore, these Korean theologians receive much encouragement and impetus from the World Council of Churches. Among those who are active in this group, the two who lean most heavily toward activist roles are Kang Won-Yong, director of the Korea Christian Academy, and So Nam-Dong, Yonsei University professor, who is the forerunner among the radical theologians.

THE TASK OF THEOLOGY IN KOREA

If we look back at the editorial in the 1936 New Year edition of the journal *Theological Instruction*, we find the following prophetic statement:

> When Christianity entered Rome, every effort was made to consolidate its strength in order to combat heresy, paganism and persecution. The result was the formation of a religion centered about ecclesiastical authority. This was the first crisis of Christianity.
>
> At the time when this ecclesiastical religion was unable to avoid the pitfalls of the Middle Ages, Luther, Calvin et al. took the Bible and led the Church toward reformation, creating a "Bible-centered religion" in place of the ecclesiastical authority-centered religion. This was the second crisis of Christianity.
>
> This Bible-centered religion also . . . lost its vitality. . . . But how could bloodshed and injustice be allowed to remain in the world? This was a time that demanded a manifestation of great power and great acts of God, so a "Holy Spirit-centered religion" arose to replace the religion of the Book. This was the third crisis of Christianity.
>
> Who are the Christians of the Holy Spirit-centered religion? If it can be said that Christianity exalted the dynamic element in the West, it is equally true that it has made great achievements of quiet, inner power in the East. Among the peoples of the East, who will carry forth this mission? The island people are short on energy, the Chinese are covetous, and the Indians are without knowledge and therefore incapable. Our Korean people stand alone as manly, benevolent, intelligent and wise, yet without being worldly. From ancient times we have opened our spirits to God, to worship and serve Him. . . . The fruits of the success of the "Spirit-centered" religion will become manifest in this land.

These words point to both the perspective and the task of contemporary Korean theology. The timely command of God has led us to this third era—the era of the Holy Spirit. The "era of the Spirit" is the age of the new creation, the time of dynamic power. It is the era of freedom, of joy. If we direct all our attention to the tradition of the church and the literal words of Scripture we can taste neither the freedom of the Gospel nor the creativity of the new life. In this age, when religion is still enslaved to tradition and literalism and continues to bind men rather than free them, does not the scientific, technological world already rejoice in the new creation? Does not the functionally developed society already offer man dynamic freedom? If this be true, then what is the task of theology today?

First, we must meet Christ through the Holy Spirit. This is the task of *indigenization*. We must not remain indefinitely enslaved to Western traditions. To this end we must discover anew the cosmic Christ and the universality of his Gospel. The God of the Gospel, who created heaven and earth, who is the Lord of history and has redeemed all persons, cannot remain for us an unrelated, Western God. If he is the Lord of the Western church, then he must also be the Lord of Korean culture and history. He is not a "foreign God" who followed western missionaries into this country only a few years ago. He has always been present in Korea, working as the Lord of creation within our culture and history. Our task, then, is to follow the traces of his handiwork and to participate with him in his work of creation. It is for this reason that we have renewed interest in the origins and development of Korean culture. The task of indigenization is not to clothe God in Korean attire, but to render songs of praise and worship to the God who, in his providence, created all that is true and beautiful in Korean experience. We must give praise to God not only for Luther and Calvin, but also for Ui Sang and Won Hyo (Buddhist priests of the ancient Silla dynasty), and T'oe Gye and Yul Gok (renowned Korean Confucian scholars). We must praise God because before the Gospel was proclaimed in this land, we received through these men and through their religions the freedom and joy of God, and the benefits of his works of creation. Just as we saw the hand of God at work in the Renaissance, so we should see it also in our own liberation (from the Japanese in 1945), because we are attaining maturity through the historical events of our nation. Just as Christians of the West personally meet "my God" and "my Savior," so also should we meet "my God" and "my Christ." Herein is an important task of the church.

A second task is to render worship to the cosmic Christ who is at work in universal history. This involves coming to grips with *religionlessness*.[20] It is a sobering fact that 58 percent of the Korean people adhere to no particular religion. Without any religious commitment, they are living their own autonomous lives. Modern people—here, at least—are becoming more and more unconcerned with religion. What, then, is the commandment of God in Korea? Is it merely to build more churches within the narrow walls of religion? Is worship to and communication with God possible only through a sense of the religious? The dualistic view of history that divides the sacred from the secular is already meaningless. The incarnation of Christ created a kind of universal history. Christ comes as the Lord who performs his acts of creation within the total context of history. Man can meet and worship God in Christ in the church, but he can also meet and worship him in the heart of the world. The incarnate God is present among the masses in Korea who live their lives "outside the camp" of religion and the church. Today "God is my neighbor" (Rahner), and "work is a hymn about God" (Teilhard de Chardin). This God is one who speaks to us from the future, so our posture before God is not to be directed to the past with its concentration on sacrifices, nor is it to be directed to the "otherworldliness" which arises out of misdirected worship. Rather it is to be directed to the future, arising out of the secular spirit. Our posture before God must be that of research, of work, and construction.

Herein lies the new frontier of contemporary theology, and herein may be found the direction and task of Korean theology. With our eyes directed toward the fulfilment of this task, the Korean people have great expectations concerning the activist theologians engaged in industrial mission and concerning the Academy Movement of Kang Won-Yong.

The third task of Korean theology today has already been mentioned, that of discovering ways to provide a basis for nation-building and—going one step further—to formulate a "secular" theology which offers dynamic, forward-looking leadership and direction to Korean history. Just as we have no need for a metaphysical theology, so we have no need for an idealistic theology. The Korean church must become the means for the revival of the entire Korean society. Likewise, Korean theology must become the means for the renewal of the Korean church. Korean reality is no more than the reality of its society and its history. Our task is to create an environment which will guarantee the rights of people, which, in turn, will further the cause of freedom, of creativity, of joy, and thus be directed toward the future. In the midst of this reality Christ is now working. Therefore it is the task of today's theology to encounter the forces which would destroy this reality, to come face to face with social injustice and political corruption. It can be no less than a theology that provides dynamic leadership for Korean society, a theology which has set its face toward the creative activity of reconstruction.

Herein lie the tasks of contemporary theology in Korea. In order to be faithful to these tasks we must throw off the bonds, not only of Western church tradition, but also of Korea's own theological tradition. It is difficult, of course, to free oneself from tradition, but fortunately for us, we are impoverished when it comes to tradition.

To engage in the process of creating anew, one must have energy. As young churches, nothing stands in the way to hinder us. With youthful vigor we press forward with confidence in the work of creation and with hope for the future.

NOTES

1. George Paik, *The History of Protestant Missions in Korea, 1832–1910* (Pyongyang: Union Christian College Press, 1929), p. 191.

2. Arthur Judson Brown, *The Mastery of the Far East* (New York: Scribners: 1919), pp. 541 ff.

3. Beginning two years later, *World of Theology* was published bimonthly, continuing until 1940.

4. Yang Ju-Sam (1879–1950) received his B.D. (1913) from Vanderbilt University Divinity School, and Th.M. (1914) from Yale, to become Korea's first Protestant theologian.

5. The Japanese forced *Theological Instruction* to cease publication in 1938, but it was revived after liberation (1945) and is currently the oldest and most representative journal of conservative theology in Korea.

6. Representative articles were: "Christianity and the Korean People," "Christianity's Responsibility Regarding Korean Culture," "Korean Christianity's Future and Issues of Faith," and "Jesus' Teachings about Social Problems."

7. These theologians, in the 1930s, were:
Presbyterian: Nam Gung-Hyok, Paik Nak-Jun, Pak Hyong-Nyong, Lee Song-Hwi Song Ch'ang-Gun, Chae P'il-Gun, Kim Jae-Jun, Yun In-Ku, Pak Yun-Son.

Methodist: Pyon Hong-Kyu, Han Ch'i-Jin, Chong Kyong-Ok, Ryu Hyong-Ki, Kim In-Young, Kim Ch'ang-Jun, Kim Young-Ui, Lee Sang-On, Chong Il-Hyong, Kal Hong-Ki.

8. After having studied at Princeton Theological Seminary in New Jersey and Union Theological Seminary in New York, Nam Gung-Hyok returned to Korea as the first Presbyterian theologian and the first Korean professor at the Presbyterian Theological Seminary.

9. Pak Hyong-Nyong (1897–) received his education at Princeton Theological Seminary, which at that time was dominated by the Machen fundamentalist controversy. He is presently Korea's representative ultraconservative.

10. Kim Yang-Son, *History of the Korean Church in the Ten Years Since Liberation* (Seoul: n.p., 1958), p. 264 (in Korean).

11. Chong Kyong-Ok (1901–1945) graduated from Garrett Theological Seminary and became the representative Methodist theologian of Korea as well as Korea's first Barthian. His *Outline of Christian Theology* (555 pp.) has an important place among theological writings yet today.

12. Chong Kyong-Ok, in *Christian Shinmun* XX (1938).

13. *Christian News* I (1942), 5.

14. Kim Jae-Jun (1901—), studied at Aoyama Gakuin in Japan and at Princeton and Western Theological seminaries in the United States, and is the most creative theologian in Korea.

15. Kim Jae-Jun, in *Soldiers of the Cross* XXIV (1956).

16. *Liberal institutions:* The United Graduate School of Theology, Yonsei University (Interdenominational); Yonsei University Department of Theology (Interdenominational); Methodist Theological Seminary; Hankook Theological Seminary (R.O.K. Presbyterian)

Liberal-Conservative institutions: Presbyterian Theological Seminary (proecumenical)

Conservative institutions: Seoul Theological Seminary (Holiness); Presbyterian Theological Seminary (N.A.E.); Koryo Theological Seminary (Koryo Presbyterian).

17. Professor Han Ch'ol-Ha caused alarm in Korean theological circles by his criticism of neo-orthodoxy as being "relativist," in *Church and Theology* II (1967).

18. *Biblical theology:* Chon Kyong-Nyon, Kim Yong-Ok, Kim Ch'ol-Son, Mun Sang-Hi, Pak Chang-hwan, Kim Jong-Jun, Mun Ik-Hwan, Kim Ch'ang-Guk, Ahn Byong-Mu, Pak Tae-Son.

Systematic theology: So Nam-Dong, Yun Song-Bom, Pak Pong-Nang, Pak Sun-Kyong, Chi Dong-Shik, Lee Jong-Song, Ho Hyok, Pyon Son-Hwan, Pak Hyong-Kyu

Christian ethics: Hong Hyon-Sol, Hyon Young-Hak, Kang Won-Yong, Chong Ha-Un, Kim Kwan-Sok.

Church history: Lee Chang-Shik, Min Kyong-Bae, Han T'ae-Dong.

19. During the period 1962–64, twelve articles on the subject of "indigenization" were published and widely discussed in theological circles. Notable books are: Yun Song-Bom, *Christianity and Korean Thought* (1964) and Tongshik Ryu, *Christianity and the Religions of Korea* (1965).

20. See So Nam-Dong's article, "The Present Christ," *Yonsei University Journal* V (1968).

Where Theology Seeks
to Integrate Text and Context

Any discussion of theological construction in Japan—a nation of four main islands inhabited by 109 million people—must take into account that only one percent of the population is Christian (0.7 percent Protestant and 0.3 percent Catholic), while 83 percent is Buddhist and 83 percent also Shintoist (the duplicate registration of religious affiliation by 83 percent of the population reflects the loyalty problem of religions with a pantheistic background). Japan was not only non-Christian, but anti-Christian from 1614 to 1873, with a policy of national isolation from 1633 to 1854. At present it is one of the most industrialized nations in the world, with a gross national product that ranks second among the free nations.

The Development of Protestant Theology

THE PREPARATORY PERIOD, 1837–1858

The preparatory period for Protestant mission work in Japan may be traced back to the activities of the German missionary Karl Friedrich August Gützlaff (1803–1851), the American missionary Samuel Wells Williams (1812–1844), and the English missionary Bernard Jean Bettelheim (1811–1870). None of them was ever successful in

---

In the text and notes, unless otherwise indicated, books and articles by Japanese authors are written in Japanese and published in Tokyo. Their titles are given in English translation here for convenience. Exceptions are articles cited in *Japan Christian Quarterly*, *The Northeast Asia Journal of Theology*, and in Western publications. Similarly, the titles of doctoral dissertations by Japanese scholars at German universities, written in German, are given here in English translation.

getting into Japan, due to the isolationist and anti-Christian policies of the nation at that time, but each made a significant contribution to the history of Christian thought in Japan because of their pioneering work in translating the Scriptures. This is very characteristic of the Protestant as compared with Roman Catholic missionaries. Since the Jesuit Francis Xavier came to Japan at the time of the Counter Reformation (1549), Roman Catholic missionary work had shown remarkable success until the beginning of the national policy of isolation in the seventeenth century. They published catechisms and devotional works, but almost no Bible translations. It was the same situation when Catholic missionaries reopened their work in the nineteenth century. We may therefore say that it was a characteristic of Protestant missions that even in the preparatory period, they began to translate the Bible into the Japanese language. This Protestant characteristic has determined the basic features of Protestant theology in Japan, and even those who insist on their noncreedal or nonecclesiastical character, such as the Mukyokai (Non-Church) group,[1] are strongly biblical in orientation.

BEGINNING THEOLOGICAL CURRENTS, 1859–1900

Protestant missions in Japan began in 1859 with the arrival of Episcopal, Presbyterian, and Reformed missionaries. At that time Christianity was still legally prohibited. "The missionaries of the early period," says Antei Hiyane (1892–1970), "were pioneers filled with courage. They were not, however, particularly rich in their grasp of theology."[2] They were not well-trained theologians, but theology in Japan was strongly affectd by their missionary concern. Theology in Japan never sought to be theology in the sense of German *wissenschaftliche Theologie*, but aimed to be mission theology, to serve the life and mission of the church, even in highly academic ways.[3]

After the government's removal of the ban on Christianity in 1873, it was possible for the missionaries to work openly. The sphere of their work was enlarged, and three groups of Japanese Christians —the Yokohama Band,[4] the Kumamoto Band,[5] and the Sapporo Band[6]—grew out of their activities. These three groups developed into major denominations that also represented major theological currents.

With the formation of these bands, theology in Japan first began to train people for carrying out the theological task, namely, Japanese Christian nationals who gathered together quite spontaneously to confess their Christian faith. Here we may discern the early stages of another feature of theology in Japan: It was "national" but not necessarily nationalistic, at least in its basic intention. That is, Japanese theology sought to be "free" from foreign theology and independent from the state, although this was not an easy task, as we shall see later. Protestant theological construction in Japan may therefore be described as biblical, missional, national, and free in emphasis and orientation.

From the very beginning the church in Japan suffered from a discrepancy between the ecumenical ideal and the denominational reality. The first Protestant church in 1872 originated from the Yokohama Band and was called the Ecumenical Church of Christ in Japan (Nippon Kirisuto Kokai)—a product of the ecumenical ideal.[7] This developed into the United Church of Christ in Japan (Nippon Kirisuto Itchi Kyokai) in 1877 and, after the failure of a union with the Congregational churches in 1890, was organized as a denomination though still called the Church of Christ in Japan. Established on a Reformed-Presbyterian basis, this church, under the leadership of Masahisa Uemura (1857–1925), represented a kind of neo-orthodox theology.

The stream from the Kumamoto Band, on the other hand, formed the Congregational Church in Japan (Nippon Kumiai Kyokai) in 1886 and represented a liberal theological tradition under the leadership of Danjo Ebina (1857–1937). Liberal theology was introduced by the German missionaries Wilfrid Spinner (1854–1919) and Otto Schmiedel (1858–1926), who belonged to the Evangelical Missionary Society (Allgemeiner Evangelisch-Protestantischer Missionsverein), in recent years known as the German East Asia Mission. They introduced the biblical criticism of the Tübingen school to the Japanese, who had been brought up with a rather conservative understanding of the Bible learned from American missionaries of Puritan background. In 1889 the Congregational leader Hiromichi Kozaki (1856–1938) completely rejected the idea of the infallibility of the Bible and was supported in his views by Ebina and by the publication of Tsurin Kanamori's *Christianity in Japan, Present and Future* (in Japanese, 1891) and Tokio Yokoi's *Problems of Christianity in Our Country* (in Japanese, 1894).

This liberal stream developed in two directions, one in combination with nationalism and the other in combination with socialism. The problem of nationalism and Christianity had come into prominence because of the Uchimura incident, in which the young Christian teacher Kanzo Uchimura was discharged from his job because he refused to bow before the Imperial Rescript on Education in a school ceremony. This resulted in a series of debates, and many articles and books were written on the subject. Some of the liberals, such as Ebina, Kozaki, Yokoi, Miyagawa, Hiraiwa, and Harada, tried to attach themselves to nationalism by advocating a so-called Japanese theology.[8] For instance, Ebina announced that the God of the Bible was the same as the Japanese Shinto god and that Christianity was a developed form of the Japanese spirit. Beside this "Shintoistic Christianity," Zenji Iwamoto (1863–1942) and Yasu Togawa (1856–1924) advocated "Buddhist Christianity," and Kaiseki Matsumura (1859–1939) attempted a "Confucian Christianity." Apologetic motives and syncretistic dangers were both present in these efforts.

Another stream of liberalism was that which came from Unitarian-Universalism, introduced into Japan by Arthur May Knapp in 1887 (American Unitarian Association) and George L. Perin in 1890 (Universalist church). It became united with socialism. For instance, the first Socialist Democratic party in Japan was organized in May 1901, largely under the leadership of Christians from this theological tradition. A socialism study group established offices in the Unity Hall of the Unitarian Association in Tokyo, and Unitarianism was the guiding spirit of the early socialist movement. Many of them gradually left the church because they were critical of its capitalistic character and the church was critical of their Unitarianism.

From the Sapporo Band came the Non-Church Movement (Mukyokai) founded by Uchimura. Compared with the liberal school, they placed greater emphasis on the Bible and stood nearer to neo-orthodoxy. Those who followed the neo-orthodoxy of Masahisa Uemura, the Presbyterian pastor-theologian, stressed the church as a Christian community, while those who followed Uchimura stressed individualism. Interestingly, the Uemura neo-orthodox school tended to isolate themselves from society by concentrating on church development, while the Uchimura group had a keen interest in the problems of social justice.

THEOLOGY IN THE LATER MEIJI PERIOD, 1901–1912

At the beginning of the twentieth century the Japan Christian Evangelical Alliance initiated a "twentieth-century forward evangelistic movement" throughout the country. This brought about disunity between those of traditional and liberal understandings of the Gospel. Uemura, who did not necessarily support such methods of mass evangelism, expressed the opinion that if the movement were to be successful, it had to begin with a clear agreement on the nature of the Gospel—namely, that God became man and died on the cross to redeem sinners. Ebina took this as a personal challenge, and thus began the so-called Uemura–Ebina debate, lasting from 1901 to 1902, which centered on the problem of Christology. Uemura summarized the issues:

> Mr. Ebina lays stress on the current ideas of the age. He believes that Christianity in many respects is a product compounded from the idea of the period of its origin. We also recognize the historical development of Christianity, but more than that we trace it to Divine revelation. We put more stress on the work of God. Mr. Ebina does not believe in the deity of Christ; he denies him worship and says that Christianity is not centered in Christ himself. We believe in his deity. We believe that he is God made man. We believe in Christ's omnipresence and immanence. We worship him and pray to him. Mr. Ebina looks up to Christ only as a teacher. We do that, but believe him also to be Savior. Mr. Ebina emphasizes learning from Christ. We believe in him, are united to him and depend on and entrust ourselves to him in life and in death.[9]

The Japan Christian Evangelical Alliance decided to exclude those who did not believe in the deity of Christ, and Ebina was expelled at the twelfth general assembly in 1902. Later, in 1911, after the Alliance was reorganized as the Japan Federation of Christian Churches, composed of eight denominations, Ebina was accepted into this federation as a member of the Congregational church.

The Christian socialists still maintained their leadership even after the Socialist-Democratic party was ordered to disband on the same

day it was established in 1901. The shift of socialist leadership from
the Christians to the materialists began about 1903 and became very
pronounced after the Russo-Japanese War (1904–1905). During this
period Christianity grew among middle-class people, who were
helped by the development of Japanese capitalism. Thus the church
came to lose its social influence by becoming the church of the
bourgeoisie, and theology in Japan was thereby confronted with a
basic problem that continues to the present day. So far as correct
theology is concerned, the Uemura-Ebina debate indicates "theological progress." Yet in regard to the right relation between church and
society, the formation of a bourgeois church means "social retrogression."

The church's departure from socialism, moreover, prepared the
way for the growth of a serious problem for the Japanese church and
theology—namely, its accommodation to nationalism. The Russo-
Japanese War established a national consciousness in Japan. In May
1904, followers of Shinto, Buddhism, and Christianity held a great
religious meeting in Tokyo and declared the righteousness of the war.
A similar meeting was held in 1912 upon the initiative of the government, which greatly feared the revolutionary labor movement and
decided to use religion to gain control over the minds of people.
Leaders of the three major religions were invited to a meeting at the
Hall of Peers, where they presented the following statement to the
government officials:

> 1. We desire to work, in harmony with our respective doctrines, for the
> welfare of the Emperor and the moral progress of our nation.
> 2. We desire the authorities to respect religion and promote the har-
> monious relationship of politics, religion and education, utilizing them for
> the progress of our country.[10]

Christianity had now succeeded in getting public recognition as one
of the three major religions in Japan, but it was at the risk of being
used as a nationalistic tool by the government.

Japanese Protestant Christianity celebrated its fiftieth anniversary
in 1909 in a very ecumenical and international way. In 1910 Yoichi
Honda (1848–1912), leader of the Methodist church, was sent to the
World Missionary Conference at Edinburgh as an official representative of the Japanese church, and in 1911 the Japan Federation of

Christian Churches (Nippon Kirisuto Kyokai Domei) was founded. As we have seen, Protestant Christianity in Japan had an ecumenical orientation from its beginning, and the formation of the Federation of Christian Churches is further evidence of this. The movement for church unity in this period, however, cannot be explained only in terms of ecumenism, because Japanese Christianity was also increasingly motivated by nationalism. The ecumenical motive which aims at unity for mission was woven together with the nationalistic motive, which aims at unity for the nation. This tension continued right down to the formation of the United Church of Christ in Japan (Nippon Kirisuto Kyodan; abbreviated UCCJ, or Kyodan) in 1941. In this period, theology in Japan began to confront the problem of "church and state."

THEOLOGY IN THE TAISHO

AND EARLY SHOWA PERIOD, 1912–1930

Victory in World War I brought prosperity to Japan, and it is interesting to note that in just such a relaxed social atmosphere the Second Coming of Christ was stressed by some Christian leaders. In 1917 K. Uchimura began to preach the Second Coming, and in the following year the bishop of the newly established Japan Holiness church, Jyuji Nakada (1870–1939), joined by the famous evangelist Seimatsu Kimura (1874–1958), lectured on the subject. Although it did not last long, it is important to note the beginning of eschatological thinking in this movement.

Japan's economic boom was short-lived, and a postwar panic, accompanied by rice riots, took place in 1918. Inflation brought bankruptcy to one firm after another and the streets overflowed with the unemployed. Under these circumstances the Christian Socialists set to work once again after ten years of silence. Toyohiko Kagawa (1888–1960) led a strike for the rights of thirty thousand workers of the Kobe-Kawasaki Shipyard in 1921 and founded the Japan Farmer's Association the following year with his Christian friend Motojiro Sugiyama. Leaders of the Socialist People's party, the Japan Laborers' and Farmers' Party, as well as the Japan Labor Federation, were all Christians. The Japan Federation of Christian Churches was changed into the more ecumenical National Christian Council (Nippon Kirisutokyo Renmei) in 1923 and published its Social Creed, consisting of fifteen articles, in 1928. The Social Creed dealt with human rights and equality of opportunity, racial and national discrimination, marriage and chastity, the status of women, child labor and vocational guidance, Sunday as a public holiday, prostitution, labor relations, temperance, cooperatives, graduated taxes, and a world without war. In 1929 the council decided to carry out, for five years, a "Kingdom of God Movement" based on the Social Creed.[11] The leading theologian of this movement was Toyohiko Kagawa, whose theology was centered in the redemptive love of Christ on the cross which, in turn, motivates the social life of man. "Redemptive love is born when one takes the failure of another upon himself as his own failure and tries to share a part of the responsibility."[12] According to Kagawa, "Economic movements are essentially the same as the movements of love."[13] Here his image of the kingdom of God loses its eschatological perspective and is identified with cooperative societies in present history which one can establish through redeeming acts of love.

A theologian whose work stood in great contrast to Kagawa's in this period was Tokutaro Takakura (1885–1934). He wrote the first systematic statement of theology in Japanese Christian history. Baptized by Uemura, he decided to give up a promising future by leaving Tokyo Imperial University to enter the Tokyo Theological Seminary which Uemura had founded as the first seminary independently administered and financially supported by Japanese Christians. While Kagawa presupposed continuity from society to the kingdom of God, Takakura stressed discontinuity. Influenced by the Scottish theologians Forsyth, Denny, and Mosley, and by the German and Swiss theologians Althaus, Heim, von Hügel, Stange, Barth, Brunner, and Gogarten, he systematized his theological thought in *Evangelical Christianity*, which was first published in 1927 and is still widely circulated. Just as Uemura distinguished his position against Ebina, Takakura took up his position against liberal theology, which was represented in a sense by Kagawa. Liberal Christianity, says Takakura, "comes to think that the so-called Social Gospel alone is the one path Christianity must take."[14] But faith, he says, "is the crisis, the bankruptcy of self and humanity. . . . The realization of the kingdom of God is not a progressive matter, but a redemptive and creative one. . . . Here we have a battle between the kingdom of

God and history, and it is in the kingdom that the salvation of history is made certain."[15] It may be noted that the eschatological element, although different from that of the movement of the Second Coming of Christ,[16] was given a position of centrality in the theology of Takakura. He was eschatological in emphasis, while Kagawa was evolutional. The former stressed the transcendental side, the latter the immanental side. Takakura tended to be individualistic,[17] while Kagawa was more socialistic. Here theology in Japan confronted the same problem as it did at the beginning of the century, namely, the problem of theological progress and social retrogression.

THEOLOGY BEFORE AND DURING WORLD WAR II
1931–1945

The radicalization of the Student Christian Movement (SCM) seriously damaged the integrity of social-type theology. This movement was organized in July 1931 and grew out of the YMCA, which had a long history of summer conferences for students. The SCM sought to counter individualistic Christianity with a Christianity that had social and practical relevance. While it was not necessarily Marxist at the outset, in time, the leadership shifted to students who became more and more radical. They favored proletarian religion, protested against the capitalistic system and bourgeois culture, urged participation in the movement of proletarian liberation and opposition to imperialistic wars of aggression.[18] This radicalism came to a climax at the summer school of 1932, which ended in disruption and brought an end to the whole SCM movement in Japan.

The leading theologian of the SCM was Enkichi Kan (1895–1973), an Anglican influenced by the thought of Ernst Troeltsch. According to Kan, God is an immanent and dynamic "life-power,"[19] and Christianity is the expression of this "life-power" in history, which began in Jesus for the realization of the kingdom of God. The kingdom of God is the society built by men whose wills are one with God[20] and the "salvation of the individual is possible only when he finds his place in the society founded on God. He can be saved only when he takes his share in building up the God-centered society as begun by Jesus."[21] Here we see the same problem as in Kagawa. Charles H. Germany summarized his observations on the theology of social Christianity in Japan during this period as follows: "In terms of the temporal relation of the kingdom endeavor, it is clear that in Kan's mind during this period as well as in the thought of the others, the kingdom was to be realized on earth in history. The sources of the period are silent as regards eschatology in the sense of the intervention of God as the transcendent Lord of history at the end of time to bring his kingdom into reality."[22]

It is significant to trace some changes in the thought of Kan. He wrote books and articles on social Christianity until 1932; but in 1933 his articles on Brunner and Gogarten appeared, followed by several books and articles on dialectical theology, including a translation of Brunner's *God and Man* in 1934. In 1938 Kan first wrote an article on the difference between Barth and Brunner; this was followed by books in 1939 and 1942 on Barthian theology, and he has been one of the most devoted Barthians ever since. His shift from social Christianity to Barthian theology is indicative of the path followed by theology in Japan.

In 1932, when the SCM dissolved, Yoshitaka Kumano (1899–), who, in 1927, had already introduced the thought of Brunner in his book *The Original Meaning of Faith*, published *Dialectical Theology in Outline*, which was followed in 1933 by his highly regarded work *Eschatology and Philosophy of History*. Here Kumano tried to distinguish faith from worldview and to base theology on eschatological thinking, which he maintained was not properly found in liberal theology.[23] Kumano developed his thought in various books, including *Basic Problem of Christology* (1934) and *Contemporary Theology* (1936). Another leading theologian, Hidenobu Kuwada (1894–1975), also published a book on dialectical theology in 1933, a translation of Barth's *Credo* in 1936, and his *Outline of Christian Theology* in 1941, which is still widely used as a textbook in systematic theology. The journal *Theology and Church* published a special issue on "Karl Barth" in 1939 (volume III), and Katsumi Takizawa wrote *The Study of Karl Barth* (1941). Under the same impulse Takenosuke Miyamoto (1905–) published *The Basic Problem of Christian Ethics* in 1939 and *Philosophy of Religion* in 1941. *The Basic Thought of Luther as Seen in His Lectures on "Romans"* (1933), by the Lutheran theologian Shigehiko Sato (1887–1935), is important in this period, along with the complete translation of Calvin's *Institutes of the Christian Religion* between 1934 and 1939 by Masaki Nakayame (1886–1944). There was a strong feeling that theology should once again become theology of the Word of God, as it had in the Reformation.

Although dialectical theology was introduced in Japan mainly through Brunner's writings in English, interest gradually centered upon Barth, especially after the Barth-Brunner debate on natural theology in 1934, when many of Takakura's disciples joined this new trend. Not dialectical theology in general, but Barthian theology in the strict sense, gradually became dominant. This move to restore theology to the Word of God was, needless to say, theological progress, but was there not also social retrogression, especially when we think about the international situation in this period? It was in 1931 that the Manchurian War took place. The Shanghai Incident followed in 1932, and in the same year the state of Manchukuo was founded, which caused the withdrawal of Japan from the League of Nations. It was during this same time that Japanese nationalism, which resulted in World War II, began to dominate. Thus Barthian theology and nationalism flourished together in Japan and, interestingly, there was no resistance movement among Christians who held this theological position during the war.

In 1941, over thirty Protestant churches, including one-third of the Episcopal churches—thus nearly all Protestant churches in Japan—were united with the formation of the United Church of Christ in Japan (Nippon Kirisuto Kyodan). At work in this was a combination of the ecumenical motive of unity for mission (part of the tradition of Japanese Protestantism) and the nationalistic motive for unity of the nation (a response to the request of the government). Theological progress and social retrogression remained a problem.

Theological Developments after World War II[24]

A. THEOLOGY OF THE UNITED CHURCH   As we have seen, the formation of the United Church of Christ in Japan (the Kyodan) owed its glory and its shame to the mixed motives in its origins. The end of the war, therefore, was a time of challenge to its very existence. Those who were critical of its nationalistic origins seceded,[25] while others who respected its ecumenicity sought to achieve this ideal more concretely. In other words, no one was satisfied with the status quo.

At this point the supporters of the Kyodan, believing that providence was behind its founding, took up the problem of formulating a new confession of faith that would express the church's ecumenical character more precisely. Kazo Kitamori (1916–) has said, "The Kyodan's most important and difficult task has been to declare her special nature as one Church, and this lay in her work of declaring her Confession of Faith."[26] After existing for many years without a creed, the Kyodan decided in 1948 to make it clear that it stood on the Apostles' Creed. Between 1948 and 1954, when the Kyodan declared her own Confession of Faith,[27] it had to confront this "most important and difficult task" squarely. It was, so to speak, a period when ecumenical theology was in-the-making. The historical significance and particular contribution of the Kyodan's Confession of Faith to the history of the church has been discussed at length in the commentary on the confession written by Kazo Kitamori, who was the leading theologian involved in its formation.[28]

Theology in Japan, as we have noted, has always had the problem of theological progress and social retrogression. The Kyodan has tried to overcome this contradiction. In the fourth part of the preface of the Kyodan's Confession of Faith it is declared that the church commits itself to ethical activities "in works of love" with eschatological hope. Such ethical responsibility in the "time between" is expressed more concretely in the "Christian Guide for Social Action," published in 1958,[29] and in "Basic Principles of Social Action for the Kyodan," published in 1966. The document on "Basic Principles" states:

> 1. Social concern is a part of evangelical faith.
> 2. *Diakonia* is the basic attitude of all works of the church. Jesus Christ came in the form of a servant. He taught the way of service and washed the feet of his disciples. The whole life and action of a Christian cannot exist apart from service to "the poor," because "the poor" designate Jesus Christ.
> 3. Faith in Jesus Christ should be witnessed by the believer in the situation in which he is placed. Christian ethics always emerges in relation to new concrete problems. It is necessary, then, that the biblical truth be mediated with a knowledge of social science.

Moreover, the document urges mutual understanding and cooperation between the church and social welfare institutions. It encourages coordination with the latter and with other institutions that have the same purpose, according to the principle of solidarity in mission activities.

Another major problem of the Japanese church was its nationalistic tendency that followed the government's war policies. The Kyodan felt it could not proceed without making a confession of guilt in this matter. In the preface of the "Basic Principles" is the following statement:

> The United Church of Christ in Japan, which was founded during the war, bears in its own existence a sign of God's providence who forgives sin in Christ. By faith in this providence, the United Church knows about the grace which caused its existence as well as our deep sin which is included in it. The social action of our United Church starts from absolute confidence in this divine grace and through reflection on our sin that we could not socially bear witness enough to the Lordship of Christ during wartime. In this reflection we pray afresh for God's guidance in our social responsibility, that we may try to fulfil it, being strengthened by divine grace.

This was followed by the "Confession on the Responsibility of the United Church of Christ in Japan during World War II," which was published in the name of the Kyodan's moderator, the Reverend Masahisa Suzuki (1912–1969) on Easter Sunday in 1967.[30] This form and date were chosen because on the same day in 1944 the "Epistle to Christians in the Great Asian Co-Prosperity Sphere" was sent in the name of representatives of the Kyodan. The confession says:

> We are reminded of the mistakes committed in the name of the Kyodan during World War II. Therefore, we seek the mercy of our Lord and the forgiveness of our fellow men. . . . Indeed, as our nation committed errors we, as a Church, sinned with her. We neglected to perform our mission as a "watchman." Now, with deep pain in our heart, we confess this sin, seeking forgiveness of our Lord, and from the churches and our brothers and sisters of the world, and in particular of Asian countries, and from the people of our own country.

Thus the theology of the United Church is being shaped ecumenically in the "Confession of Faith," socially in the "Guide" and "Basic Principles of Social Action," and morally in the "Confession on the Responsibility During World War II."

B. VARIETIES OF THEOLOGY   As previously pointed out, theology in Japan after the 1930s, that is, after the introduction of dialectical theology, gradually became dominated by Barthian theology in the strict sense—especially after the debate on natural theology between Barth and Brunner; it remained so dominated until 1948.[31]

Eighteen volumes of Barth's works are being translated and published, in addition to a translation of his masterpiece, *Church Dogmatics*. Yoshitaka Kumano, who follows the Barthian line, has published a great deal. His *Outline of Christianity* (1947) and *Essence of Christianity* (1949) compose the basic part of his systematic work. The former, which was written during the war, deals with Christianity in history. Kumano sees Christianity as a historical religion which can be the object of any scientific research. In his book, therefore, he begins phenomenologically with Christianity as a religion, then proceeds to the problems which are particularly Christian, and finally comes to the concept of an evangelical church. In the later book he deals with the content of the faith, which Christianity as a historical religion holds as the essence of its life. These two volumes compose an argument about the essence of Christianity as seen from the outside and the inside. His basic treatment of the problem of faith and history is methodologically developed through an eschatological perspective which he had already employed in his *Eschatology and Philosophy of History* (1933). Upon this discussion about the essence of Christianity, he based his masterpiece, *Dogmatics*, a three-volume work that was published between 1954 and 1965; in it he outlined the content of the Christian faith that has developed through the historical church.

While Kumano developed his theology under Barth's inspiration, Enkichi Kan concentrated on Barth and published *The Study of Karl Barth* in 1968. A younger theologian, Keiji Ogawa (1927–), who had studied under Barth, wrote his dissertation on "The Meaning and Limits of the Kierkegaard Renaissance" (Basel, 1963), while Setsuro Osaki (1933–) wrote his doctoral dissertation at Göttingen in 1966 on "The Teaching of Predestination in Karl Barth." Yoshiki Terazono's dissertation at Bonn in 1971 was on "The Christology of Karl Barth," and Mitsumasa So-Ueda's at Göttingen in 1973 dealt with "The Anthropology of Karl Barth." Another younger theologian, Masayoshi Yoshinaga (1925–)—a disciple of E. Kan—published *Barthian Theology and its Characteristics* (1972).

In the field of biblical theology, Zenda Watanabe (1885–), a senior theologian, completed his three volumes of *The Doctrine of the Scriptures*, which consists of *The Doctrine of the Canon* (1949), *Biblical Hermeneutics* (1954), and *Bibilical Theology* (1963). Watanabe started from biblicism, but then was deeply influenced by the historical-critical approach and found a way to overcome this dilemma in Barthian theology, although he is critical of Barth's concept of canon. A woman theologian, Tamiko Okamura (1914–), who is a disciple of Watanabe, published *An Essay on Biblical Interpretation: Basic Theory of the Morphological Interpretation of the Biblical Canon* (1964). *The Ethical Thought of Dialectical Theology* (1961) and *Theology of Salvation History* (Tokyo, 1972) by Kano Yamamoto (1909–), one of Takakura's disciples, were written from a Barthian point of view, as have been his other works.

Thus Barth is still influential in postwar Japan. The situation before and after 1945 is, nevertheless, quite different. After 1945, the theology of Barth was no longer *the* theology as it was before 1945. It has become *a* theology among others. So far as *the* theology is concerned, the age of Karl Barth in Japan is over.

It was Kazo Kitamori, in his *Theology of the Pain of God*, published just after the Second World War, who showed how to read Karl Barth with a critical mind.[32] This was a significant breakthrough and marked the dawn of postwar theology—which could be called the age of recognizing varieties of theology. Kitamori's book was widely acclaimed in postwar Japan, not only because of its originality, but also because its main theme of pain *(itami)* was very familiar to people who had suffered much during and after the war.

The theology of Kitamori, who has a Lutheran background, is a *theologia crucis*, which he has expressed as the theology of the pain of God. "The straightforward theme of this book" is "God embracing completely those who should not be embraced—that is—'God in pain!'"[33] As a biblical basis for this thesis, Kitamori refers to the Hebrew word *hamah*, which means "pain," in Jeremiah 31:20 (also in Jer. 4:19; 48:36; Isa. 16:11; Ps. 55:17; 77:3), usually translated as "moan" in RSV; and "love" ("yearning" in RSV) in Isaiah 63:15. The love of God, therefore, could also mean the pain of God. "The term *hamah* implies 'pain' and 'love' interchangeably or simultaneously. God's love—which is poured out on those rebelling against him—God's pain—immediately implies his 'love' completely conquering those rebels."[34] In the pain of God the immediate love of God is mediated through a negative moment and exalted to a higher dimension. This immediate love lies in the dimension of law, while the pain of God lies in the dimension of the Gospel as the love of the cross. Modern liberalism, according to Kitamori's criticism, missed this moment of negative mediation and fell into "love monism," which is also reflected in the English and Japanese RSV, where *hamah* in Jeremiah 31:20 is translated as "yearn." Barth, on the other hand, sponsored a trinitarian view of love of God that makes God's love a reality prior to and apart from man. Namely, it is a love that transpires between Father, Son, and Holy Spirit, and is not the pain caused by God's care for the sinner, as Paul or Luther saw it.

Kitamori's criticism of Barth is developed further in his *Theology Today* (Tokyo, 1950), where he gives a critical review of the history of theology from the standpoint of the theology of the pain of God. Kitamori says that Barth made the first commandment his theological axiom, and he sees Barth's position as being merely a theology of the law which loses the content of the Gospel. The important thing is not *that* God has done (legalistic formalism), but *what* God has done (the Gospel based upon the pain of God) for us sinners. The pain of God is that kind of love which includes those who are totally against him and leads to a higher dimension of reconciliation. From this we can also understand Kitamori's role in formulating an ecumenical theology in the United Church of Christ in Japan, especially in his efforts on the Confession of Faith. The basis for an ecumenism, which tries to include totally different ecclesiastical traditions in a higher dimension, can be found only in the pain of God, for the way to true unity is nothing but a *via dolorosa*.[35]

The teaching activity of Emil Brunner in Japan in 1949 and later, from 1953 to 1955, also gave Japanese theologians a good opportunity to study Barth from other perspectives. Younger theologians such as Hideo Oki and Yoshinobu Kumazawa studied under Brunner and were challenged to read Barth with critical minds.[36] Some have found Paul Tillich, and both Reinhold and Richard Niebuhr, helpful. Others consider Bultmann, Gogarten, Ebeling, and Fuchs significant. The translation of the nine volumes of Bonhoeffer's works has been completed, and works by Thielicke, Kraemer, and Hoekendijk, as well as Pannenberg, Moltmann, Jüngel, K. Rahner, J. Metz, H. Cox, C. Michalson, the "death of God" theologians, along with J.A.T. Robinson, J. Fletcher, J. Cone, and works of biblical theologians such as von Rad, Bornkamm, Jeremias, Cullmann, and Käsemann have been translated. There is no single theologian who dominates the scene in Japan today and every theologian is, so to speak, relativized. This recognition of relativity leads to the need for mutual understanding. The age of monologue is over and the age of dialogue has begun.

C. THE AGE OF DIALOGUE   So far as apologetic theology is concerned, Masatoshi Doi (1907–), the author of *Tillich* (1960), develops his ideas in *The Theology of Meaning: An Introduction to the Theology of Mission* (1963). As director, in Kyoto, of the National Christian Council's Center for the Study of Japanese Religions, Doi also promotes dialogue with other religions. Hiroshi Shireru (1930–) compiled his Tillich study under the title *Structure of Tillich's Systematic Theology* (1971). The important factor behind dialogue is the problem of hermeneutics. Many theologians are now developing hermeneutical theology based upon the theology of Rudolf Bultmann. Hideyasu Nakagawa (1908–), who wrote *Study on the Epistle to the Hebrews* (1958), also published *Faith and History* (1967) under this impulse. Yoshio Yoshimura (1910–), the translator of Barth's *Romans*, believes that Bultmann's theology is the necessary result of the Barthian motive of *pro se*. He has written on Bultmann's demythologizing,[37] as well as *Contemporary Theology and Christian Mission in Japan* (1964).

Among theologians of the younger generation, Yoshio Noro (1925–) has published *Existentialist Theology* (1964)[38] and *Existentialist Theology and Ethics* (1970). Yoshinobu Kumazawa (1929–), who wrote his doctoral dissertation at Heidelberg in 1962 on the hermeneutics of Bultmann,[39] has published three books: *Bultmann* (1962; rev. ed. 1965), *Modern Discourse on Christianity* (1964), and *Theology and Church for Tomorrow* (1974). Akira Takamori (1928–) did his doctoral dissertation under Ebeling at Zürich in 1966 on a typological interpretation of the Old Testament.

Seiichi Yagi (1932–), who wrote *The Formation of New Testament Thought* (1963), intends to go beyond Bultmann, although he owes a great deal to him. This marks the first period of the post-Bultmannian age. While Bultmann starts from *kerygma*, Yagi asks how the kerygma came into being. Yagi uses quite an original typological approach and tries to see a form of religious existence behind each type of theological thought. Although the content of the kerygmatic ideas expressed in each type of thought can be transmitted directly, religious existence, which he thinks of as genuinely true existence, can only be transmitted and understood indirectly. Hence it is the essential task of hermeneutics to make a clear explanation of the real function of religious existence. Katsume Takizawa (1909–), who studied under Barth in the 1930s, and wrote *The Study of Karl Barth* (1941), made a careful study of Yagi's book and published his own criticism of it as a book of over 350 pages entitled *The Biblical Jesus and Modern Thought* (1965). Taking the criticism seriously, Yagi replied to Takizawa by writing another book, *Biblical Christ and Existence* (1967), and thus began the Yagi-Takizawa debate.[40] This should be seen as true dialogue, because something productive has come out of it. And it has been a dialogue between theologians in different fields, namely, the biblical and systematic fields. The main point of discussion is about Takizawa's argument concerning the double character of the *persons* of Jesus Christ. He stresses the ontological basis of human existence, which he calls the basic reality of Immanuel and which he distinguishes from the historical event of Jesus. Takizawa feels that this double character is not clearly distinguished in the thought of Yagi or Barth.

Yagi accepts Takizawa's criticism and has developed his thought to make a clear-cut distinction between the "person" of the historical Jesus and the "principle" of Christ as the reality of religious existence. Nevertheless, he does not agree with Takizawa's criticism of Bultmann and thinks that Takizawa is weak in his historical and phenomenological treatment. Takizawa wrote *Buddhism and Christianity* (Kyoto, 1964), replying to the criticism of a Buddhist scholar that a profound similarity could be found between the ontological basis of man conceived in the autonomous experience of Buddha and that of Christian faith in God. Distinguishing "principle" and "person," Yagi now thinks that the way is open for fruitful dialogue with Buddhism and other religions. The "person" of Jesus can be treated historically and phenomenologically according to strict scientific methods, because we do not need to insist upon his absoluteness in a dogmatic way. It can and should be handled in a relative way. What, then, is the essence of Christianity? It is the "principle" of religious existence, which is to be found universally in other religions also.

Turning to the dialogue of theology with culture, and especially with philosophy, the work of Seiichi Hatano (1887–1950) is particularly important. He was one of the few critics of dialectical theology during the war period. His main works, *Philosophy of Religion* (1935), *An Introduction to the Philosophy of Religion* (1940), and *Time and Eternity*,[41] are testimony to a mature theologian engaged in profound dialogue with culture. Yosuke Hamada (died 1967) wrote a large volume on *Hatano's Philosophy of Religion* (1949). Takenosuke Miyamoto (1905–), the author of *Philosophy as Symbol* (1948), *Logic of Religious Life* (1949), and *Contemporary Christian View of Man* (1958), also published *Seiichi Hatano* (1965) and *Basic Problem of Philosophy of Religion* (1968).

Hatano's successor at Kyoto University was Tetsutaro Ariga (1899–), who wrote *Symbolical Theology* (Kyoto, 1946) and *The Problem of Ontology in Christian Thought* (1969). A valuable contribution by Shishio Nakamura (1889–1953), *The Philosophical Understanding of Christianity* (1938), was reprinted in his collected works in 1968. Enkichi Kan has tried to distinguish the philosophical philosophy of the Brunnerian-type religion from the theological philosophy of the Barthian-type religion in his *Reason and Revelation: The Problem of Religion in Theology* (1953). Kazuo Muto (1913–) wrote *Philosophy of Religion* (1955), followed by *Between Theology and Philosophy of Religion* (1961). In the same field Takenosuke Miyamoto edited *The Dialogue Between Philosophy and Theology* (1967).

While former SCM leaders such as Enkichi Kan and Yoshike Shimizu (1909–), author of the two-volume work *Protestant Theology* (1961, 1963), have retreated from social problems, theologians of the post-Barthian age are getting into dialogue with modern society. Masao Takenaka (1925–) wrote *Reconciliation and Renewal in Japan*[42] and *The Community of True Humanity* (1962), and has edited a number of important volumes that deal with the problems of modern industrial workers, urbanization, and the role of the laity in modern society. Toshio Sato (1923–), who wrote *Christianity and Modern Culture* (1964), *Modern Theology* (1964), and *Christianity and Theology in Japan* (1968), recently published *Protestantism and Modern Times: An Introduction to the Theology of Culture* (1970). His concern for culture is especially remarkable in view of the negative attitude toward culture held by his father-in-law, Tokutaro Takakura. The first and most comprehensive Christian social ethics ever published in Japan is *Outline of Christian Social Ethics* (Tokyo, 1964) by Samuel H. Franklin (1902–), who taught for many years at Tokyo Union Theological

Seminary. This book, although not by a Japanese, was written through dialogue in Japan. Franklin's successor and the translator of his book, Hideo Oki (1928–), who earned his doctorate under Reinhold Niebuhr, is the author of *Ethical Thought of Puritanism* (1966), *Puritanism* (1968), *Eschatological Observations* (1969), and *Eschatology* (1972). Oki deals with social ethical problems as issues in the formation of history. Post-Barthian theologians, such as Sato and Oki, formulate their theology in terms of a theology of culture or a theology of history. Yuzaburo Morita (1930–) also focuses on existence and history in his *Modernity of Christianity: Historical Consciousness in Theological Thinking* (1972). In other words, their theology is seen in "context," whereas Barthian theology insists on the "text."

Church and Theology under the Mission of God

CRUCIAL ISSUES

Since late 1969 Japanese Christianity has been experiencing a theological earthquake, precipitated initially by a controversy over the Christian Pavilion at Expo '70. This pavilion was the first ecumenical project of the Protestant, Catholic, and Orthodox churches in Japan.[43] The Kyodan, which decided to give support to the NCC for the pavilion, had its conferences and assemblies disrupted by radicals within the church who were opposed to the pavilion. The resulting confusion gives the impression that the age of dialogue has given way to an age of confrontation.[44]

Several theological issues are involved. First is the demand for "concretization of the Confession of Faith." Behind this is the criticism that the church and theology have become empty and formal. Beginning in 1968, students at many Christian universities, including theological students, have barricaded their schools and chapels. They also barricaded some local churches to show that they were empty of meaning and had no substance at all. Students shouted that God is dead, and that Christian schools and churches have lost their meaning because they fail to embody the Gospel within the concrete situation of Japanese society. In their view, this society is capitalistic and is preparing for an imperialistic war with capitalistic America. Expo '70 was nothing but a nationalistic show by which capitalistic Japan intended to parade its prosperity. Taking part in Expo '70 by building a Christian Pavilion was not only criminal, but repeated the same crime that the churches were guilty of in World War II by compromising with the national authorities. What the Japanese church should have done in such circumstances, according to these radical critics, was to protest against the national authorities, not cooperate with them. Otherwise words of confession are dead words that have no relevance to the actual situation. Not only Expo '70 but other issues have been raised. The proposal for granting national status to the Yasukuni Shrine for the nation's war dead, and the continuation of the United States–Japan Mutual Security Pact are to be protested from the same point of view, if one would be faithful to the Confession of Faith and especially to the Confession on the Responsibility of the Kyodan during World War II. Some who hold these views have been radical enough to say that those who do not protest are no longer Christian and that the deception of such pseudo-Christianity should be exposed even if it requires violence. Here, although not always explicitly stated, is a strong legalistic understanding of the Christian faith, in contrast to *sola fide*.

On the positive side, these young people who have raised the problem of the concretization of the Confession of Faith have made a contribution. They are wrong, however, when they think of con-cretization, or embodiment, only as a fixed term based upon a particu-lar sociological, or rather ideological, analysis of the situation. They are correct in asserting that the faith should be confessed in terms of the context, but they are wrong in becoming so buried in the context that they separate it from the text itself, which has made us free. A Christian gives grateful adoration for the work of Christ who came into our sinful situation and set us free from it. This is what makes the church the church, instead of merely a phenomenological community which confesses its faith only in terms of a specific situation but has no universality. Furthermore, "confession" and "witness" should be distinguished, though not separated. Only when one is freed "from" the situation is he made free "for" the situation, to bear witness to his freedom. Confession is an act of grateful adoration to Christ and his Father, who freed us from the sinful situation, while witness is an act of man toward humanity, based upon the fact that he is set free for the situation. In other words, there should be unity in confession as confession to Christ and God, but pluralism should be permitted in witness. Otherwise, witness may fall into legalism. More precisely, a variety of witness means a variety of "methods" to realize the one "direction," which is love. So far as this variety intends to be one in the intention of love, it will not be a lazy pluralism, but a dynamic one based upon the freedom of the Gospel. This freedom, which goes beyond legalism, admits ways of Christian witness other than one's own, and makes one mature enough to enter into dialogue with the secular world in all sorts of ways. Those who supported the Christian Pavilion at Expo '70 did not do so because they found no problems in doing so. They decided to bear witness to God's love for the world in this fashion in spite of the many problems involved. The pavilion issue was, therefore, one step which showed a measure of maturity in Japanese Christianity. Scare of opposition, however, showed that it was a small step, which had to be taken with great patience.

A second theological issue of recent times has been "the split between Jesus and Christ." The first debate on Christology took place between Uemura and Ebina in 1901. A second debate involved a medical doctor, Nobuo Odagiri (1909–), a disciple of Kanzo Uchimura, and Kazo Kitamori from 1955 to 1956.[45] Odagiri, originally criticizing the Paris Basis of the YMCA, which declares "Christ as God," tried to make a clear distinction between the concept of God and the Son of God, and argued that it was not God, but the Son of God, who was crucified and died on the cross. He rejected the expression that Christ was God, but did not deny the deity of Christ. Kitamori, on the other hand, held firmly to the traditional trinitarian position and stressed that "Son of God" means essentially "Son-God," otherwise the sacrifice of God could never mean his self-sacrifice of love.

The next step in the debate was taken by Sakae Akaiwa (1903–1966), a disciple of Takakura, who became a Barthian and tried to combine Barthian theology with Marxist social theory. Later Akaiwa radically changed his position to that of Bultmann's and then went beyond Bultmann by denying the deity of Christ in his *Exodus from Christianity* (1964), which might be called a first effort at liberation theology in Japan. He held that the evils of authoritarianism, which have caused innumerable oppressions in the history of Christianity, stem from the mytho-ideological concept of Christ that has been applied to Jesus of Nazareth. It is not Christ, he said, but Jesus, who ignites the fire of humanism in us. Akaiwa tried, therefore, to go back to Jesus, the inheritor of our humanity. For Akaiwa, at the last stage of his life, Jesus became the symbol of the "human" that everyone is supposed to have, and—finally—he even declared that he was Jesus. Seiichi Yagi also has distinguished Christ from Jesus in his *Christ and Jesus* (Tokyo, 1969), according to his distinction between "principle" and "person," but his main emphasis is on Christ as the basis of religious existence, and not on the humanity of Jesus.

A young New Testament scholar, Kenzo Tagawa (1935–), who, after Akaiwa's death, became a leader in the church in the area where he was a pastor, wrote a study on the Christology of Mark. Using the hypothesis of a Jerusalem tradition and a Galilee tradition, he classifies the former in the category of establishment and the latter as antiestablishment, where Jesus, according to Tagawa, was always on the side of the people. The basic intention of Mark was to describe the human figure of Jesus as against the dogmatized Christ of Peter who represented the establishment in Jerusalem. In Tagawa's view, therefore, there was no Christology in Mark, whose main concern was to portray Jesus as he lived among the people of Galilee, which was developed to the form of the Gospel.[46]

Toshikazu Takao (1930–), one of the leaders of student movements with Tagawa, wrote *Death and Resurrection of Christian University* (1969), which denied any specific *raison d'être* for a Christian school. In his book *Basic Intention of Jesus* (1970), based on the views of Yagi and Tagawa, Takao develops the idea that Jesus was an ordinary person who inspires us to be ordinary people. He rejects all dogmatic assertions that make Jesus an extraordinary person. Giving support and encouragement to the radicals mentioned in connection with the first issue above, Takao sees Jesus as the faithful companion of the proletariat and the leader of the revolution. The establishment church is "empty" because this Jesus is not in the church, only the dogmatic Christ.

Another version of liberation theology is being developed among radical ministers mainly under Tagawa's impulse. They distinguish Paul from Jesus from an ideological point of view. While Paul had Roman citizenship and could be protected by the Roman Empire, Jesus stood outside the establishment without any protection, and was crucified by it. Paul, therefore, is not an antiestablishment person. The only thing Paul did was to carry out his religious activities within the realm of the Roman Empire and under its protection. His Christology, which became the basis of most Christological dogmas, was nothing but the product of his religious-establishment ideology. According to these radical ministers, not only Paul, but the whole development of the church within the Roman Empire that Acts describes, should be reexamined with these facts in mind. Everything which came out of the development of Christianity within this establishment—Christology as well as the atonement theory, justification by faith, the sacraments, canon, the ministerial system, and so forth—should be dealt with quite critically, so as to get rid of any elements which hinder it from being an antiestablishment, anticapitalistic, antiimperialistic movement.

While they would not admit it, both Tagawa and Takao tend toward "Jesusology" rather than "Christology." They stress the "imitation" of Jesus, but not the "adoration" of Christ. Surely the integrity of both "Jesus" and "Christ" should be recovered, but in what way? It should be deductive, not inductive. That is, it should not be from *persona* to *opera*, but from *opera* to *persona*. Only in Jesus do we find the fullness of true humanity. He stands nearer to us as a human being than anyone else; all others are prevented from coming near to another because of sin. This reality of complete humanity in Jesus, which no one else can attain, is called transcendence. His transcendence lies not in metaphysical distance, but in anthropological nearness. Because he came so near to us that not even the power of sin and death can separate us from him, he is called Christ, who redeems us from sin and sustains us at the basis of existence. Ethics (liberation *for* love) starts from the Gospel (liberation *from* sin), and imitation emerges from adoration in an eschatological tension between the "already" (basis) and the "not yet" (task). It is a natural process to fall into legalism when these two are separated and only the "not yet" motive of imitation is stressed. Recovery of integration means the recovery of the evangelical character of theology and ethics.

The third crucial issue has to do with abolishing the ministerial system. The movements described in connection with the first two issues are anti-institutional, and inevitably this leads to the issue of Christianity as an institution itself, namely, the church and its ministerial system. At least one church has already decided to abolish this system,[47] and a group of anti-Expo, anti-Security Pact clergy has been organized to abolish the system generally. Behind this drive is the positive motive of developing further the idea of the priesthood of all believers. The priesthood of all believers, however, does not mean the pastorate of all believers. There is, of course, the implied denial of the hierarchical concept of ministers in a highly institutionalized structure. The recent tendency leads to a nonministerial system and has the character of a movement. Between these two poles of "institutionalism" and "movement" there has to develop a "functional concept of the minister," which emphasizes a special role, not a special status, for the minister in the midst of the whole people of God ("to equip God's people for work in his service, to the building up of the body of Christ" [Eph. 4:12]). There also has to be a dynamic understanding of participation in the mission of God, which lies between the static dullness of a hierarchical system and the violent disruption of a revolutionary movement.

THE PROBLEM OF THEOLOGICAL RELEVANCE

All these issues are expressions of a search for relevance. Does the formal Confession of Faith have substantial relevance in the present situation? Does traditional Christology have relevance for people in modern society? Is the present ministerial system relevant for an anti-institutional movement? When we discuss relevance as a theological issue, we have to think of it in terms of relevance to the Word of God and relevance to the situation in which we live. That means there must be relevance to the text and the context.

Japanese Christianity recently experienced an unfortunate separation of the two by a one-sided concentration on the text. Now, partly as a reaction to that, we are experiencing separation again by stressing the context in a one-sided way. It is the hermeneutical task of theology in Japan to recover the organic relationship of text and context.

We know that "Jesus Christ is the same yesterday, today and forever" (Heb. 13:8). This does not mean, however, that Jesus Christ remains unchangeable in a changing situation. It is a mistake to introduce here the Greek categories of unchangeable eternity and changeable time, because the Bible tells us that the Christ event is not unchangeable metaphysical truth, but historical truth—truth for us in history. He is unchangeably the Lord in every changeable historical situation. Eternity, therefore, is not the opposite to time, as in Greek thought, but rather a historical concept that can be translated as contemporaneity (*con* plus *tempus*). Thus, our text tells us that Christ is always unchangeably with our time in the past, present, and forever as the Lord, the basis of our existence as well as the task of our life, who leads history to its end. The Christ of the text cannot be separated from the context. He who lived yesterday also lives and leads our history today, and it is our task to discover this Christ of the text in our own context. This means we are called to discover and confirm the presence of the Christ of the text in our modern world and participate in his work, being sustained by him. The hermeneutical integration of text and context should be realized by participating in the mission of God here and now, and this is the task which becomes clearer and clearer in the present situation.

TOWARD INDIGENIZED THEOLOGY

At least two basic concepts, or traditions, can be distinguished when we discuss indigenization as a theological problem.[48] One is indigenization as "planting," such as the Roman Catholic *plantatio ecclesiae;* and the other is indigenization as "participating" in the *missio Dei.* Behind the first type of indigenization as planting we find the basic structure of God-church-world. This means that God's act for the world is always mediated by the church. It can also be transcribed as meaning that God's work in non-Christian countries is mediated by so-called Christian countries; that Christianity is to be exported from Christian countries and planted in non-Christian countries. This had created many problems in the history of missions, because it has led to the mistaken thought that the so-called Christian countries are superior to non-Christian countries. The fatal flaw is the presumption that God could not work directly in non-Christian countries without being mediated by Christian countries.

The second type of indigenization as participation tries to overcome these problems. It has the structure of God-world-church. This approach recognizes that God works in non-Christian countries as he does in Christian ones. The problem (in both situations) is to find a way to participate in his work. Indigenization is the effort to find out how to participate in the mission of God—which was already at work prior to any human endeavor. It is not we, but God, who takes the initiative in mission. Our task is to join him and participate in his work that is already underway. Here is the integration of text and context that is the task of hermeneutical theology. Morevoer, indigenization as participation opens the way to secular mission. Indigenization does not mean establishing a colony of Christians in the secular or pagan world. It means identifying what God is doing in the secular world and finding out what we can do to participate in his work. We are challenged to develop a theology of urban mission, and a theology of mass-media mission—in a word, a theology of secular mission. Theology in Japan is confronted now with this challenge.[49] Ecumenism means to accept seriously the call to unite in participation in the mission of God, which leads all to final unity.[50]

NOTES

1. Founded by Kanzo Uchimura (1861–1930) [see his *A Diary of a Japanese Convert* (New York: Revell, 1895; republished in Tokyo in 1906 under the title *How I Became a Christian: Out of My Diary*)] as an independent, nontraditional group, free from foreign missionaries, based on the priesthood of all believers. In the beginning they thought theology was harmful or not important, but third-generation leaders such as Masao Sekine, Goro Mayeda, and Saburo Takahashi studied theology in Germany, and Sekine's book *Logics of Religious Revolution* (1949), has the subtitle "Theological Foundations of Mukyokai Christianity."

2. Antei Hiyane, *History of Japanese Christianity* (1949), p. 347.

3. Cf. Charles H. Germany, *Protestant Theologies in Modern Japan: A History of Dominant Theological Currents, 1920–1960* (Tokyo: IISR Press, 1965), p. 2.

4. Those who were baptized by James H. Ballagh (1832–1920) and Samuel R. Brown (1810–1880) at Yokohama from 1872.

5. Thirty-five students of the Kumamoto School of Western Learning who were taught the Bible by the school's principal, L.L. Janes (1838–1909), and who signed their names to a Prospectus of Faith on January 30, 1876 at Mt. Hanaoka near Kumamoto.

6. Those who were taught the Bible by William S. Clark (1826–1886) at the Sapporo Agricultural School and signed a Christian pledge composed by him in 1877.

7. Cf. Richard H. Drummond, *A History of Christianity in Japan* (Grand Rapids, Mich.: Eerdmans, 1971), pp. 160–62.

8. "Japanese theology" and "theology in Japan" should be sharply distinguished. The former is "nationalistic theology," as *Deutsche Christen* under Hitler's regime, while the latter is "national theology."

9. Masahisa Uemura, "Discussing the Difference," *Fukuin Shimpo*, Nr. 342, January 15, 1902; quoted in Katsuhisa Aoyoshi, *Dr. Masahisa Uemura: A Christian*

Leader (Tokyo: Kyo Bun Kwan, 1941), pp.189–90. Cf. Yoshiro Ishida, "The Uemura-Ebina Controversy of 1901–1902," *Japan Christian Quarterly* XXIX, 2 (1973), 63–69.

10. Wataru Saba, *M. Uemura and His Time*, vol. II (1938), pp. 719–20.

11. Cf. W. Axling, "The Kingdom of God Movement," *Religion in Life* I (1932), 521–29; W. Axling, "Projecting the Kingdom of God Movement," *Japan Christian Quarterly* VII, 4 (1932), 327–37; T. Kagawa, "The Policy and Programme of the Kingdom of God Movement," *Student World* XXV, 2 (1932), 132–43.

12. T. Kagawa, *The Challenge of Redemptive Love*, trans. Marion R. Draper (Nashville, Tenn.: Abingdon Press, 1940), p. 148.

13. T. Kagawa, *Love the Law of Life*, trans. J. Fullerton Gressitt (Chicago: Winston Co., 1929), p. 200.

14. Tokutaro Takakura, "Orthodoxy and the Essence of Evangelicalism" in his *Takakura Tokutaro Chosakushu*, vol. II (1964), p. 61.

15. Tokutaro Takakura, *Evangelical Christianity* (1947), pp. 40, 200.

16. Takakura believed that the rupture caused by the Second Coming of Christ would rob past history of meaning.

17. Yoshitaka Kumano on this point calls the theology of Takakura about the ecclesiastical community an "unifixed ecclesiology." Cf. Y. Kumano, *History of Japanese Christian Theological Thought* (1968), 375–426.

18. Cf. Kenji Nakahara, *History of the Student Christian Movement* (1962), p. 146.

19. Enkichi Kan, *The Changing Direction of Christianity and Its Fundamental Principle* (1930), p. 23.

20. *Ibid.*, p. 84.

21. Enkichi Kan, "Social Christianity," *Student World* XXVI (1933), 230.

22. Germany, *op. cit.*, pp. 76–77.

23. Cf. Carl Michalson, *Japanese Contributions to Christian Theology* (Philadelphia: Westminster Press, 1960), pp. 44–72.

24. Cf. James M. Phillips, "Notes for a Bibliography on Christianity in Japan since 1945," *Japan Christian Quarterly* XXXIX, 2 (1973), 108–116.

25. The Reformed Church, churches related to the Southern Baptist Convention in the United States, Holiness churches of various groups, the Salvation Army, the Anglican church and the Lutheran church seceded. Other motives for secession were those of respect for denominational traditions and the need for overseas denominational funds to rebuild the churches. About two hundred congregations withdrew from 1946 to 1950.

26. *Stimme aus der Ökumene.* Hrsg. Christian Berg (Berlin: Lettner Verlag, 1963), p. 136.

27. For text of the 1954 "Confession of Faith of the United Church of Christ in Japan," see Appendix.

28. *Commentary on the Confession of Faith* (in Japanese: Tokyo: Kyodan, 1955). Cf. Y. Kumazawa, "Confessing the Faith in Japan," *The South East Asia Journal of Theology* VIII, 1 & 2 (1966), 161–70.

29. A translation by Samuel H. Franklin was published in *The Christian Century*, November 11, 1959, pp. 1305–1306.

30. For text of the "Confession on the Responsibility of the United Church of Christ in Japan during World War II," see Appendix.

31. Carl Yasuo Furuya (1926–), a theologian of the postwar generation, still criticizes Brunner from the Barthian point of view. Cf. his "Apologetic or Kerygmatic Theology?" in *Theology Today* XVI (1959–60), 471–80.

32. Kazo Kitamori, *Theology of the Pain of God* (Tokyo, 1946; English translation Richmond, Va.: John Knox Press, 1965).

33. *Ibid.*, p. 12.

34. *Ibid.*, p. 157.

35. In the preface to the third edition of his *Theology of the Pain of God*, written in 1951, Kitamori says, "The system of the theology of the pain of God, if such exists, is the truth which 'unites the divisions.' Because the purpose of a *new* church formation was to unite the divisions, I was compelled to participate in this effort with this theology. One of the tasks of the theology of the pain of God was to suggest that such a 'unity of divisions' cannot be based on idealism" (*Pain of God*, p. 12). On Kitamori, cf. Michalson, *op. cit.*, pp. 73–99; R. Meyer, "Toward a Japanese Theology: Kitamori's Theology of the Pain of God," *Japan Christian Quarterly* XXIX (January 1963), 46–57; Keiji Ogawa, *Die Aufgabe der neueren evangelischen Theologie in Japan* (Basel: Verlag Friedrich Reinhardt, 1965).

36. Cf. H. Oki, *Brunner* (1962).

37. *Eine Japanische Stimme über die Entmythologisierung Bultmanns.* "Ergänzung zu Kerygma und Mythos IV." (Hamburg: Herbert Reich, 1959).

38. Cf. Carl Michalson's review in *The Northeast Asia Journal of Theology* 3 (September 1969), pp. 142–44.

39. See G. Bornkamm's review in his *Geschichte und Glaube*, Erster Teil (Munich: Chr. Kaiser Verlag, 1968), pp. 261–63.

40. Cf. Kenzo Tagawa, "The Yagi-Takizawa Debate," *The Northeast Asia Journal of Theology* 2 (March 1969), pp. 41–59.

41. Seiichi Hatano, *Time and Eternity* (Tokyo, 1943; English trans., Tokyo: UNESCO, 1963). Cf. Michalson, *op. cit.*, pp. 126–62, which deals with Hatano's thought in the chapter "The Maturity of Japanese Theology."

42. Masao Takenaka, *Reconciliation and Renewal in Japan* (New York: Friendship Press, 1957, rev. ed., 1967).

43. Cf. *Eyes and Hands: The Discovery of Humanity. The Christian Pavilion at Expo '70, Osaka, Japan.* Report published (in English) by the Committee for the Christian Pavilion, the Japan World Exposition (Tokyo: Enderle Shoten, 1970).

44. Cf. Special issue on "Conflicts and Confrontations in the Japanese Church," *Japan Christian Quarterly* XXXIX, 2 (1973), esp. 70–86.

45. Cf. Y. Amagai and Y. Kumazawa, "A Selected Bibliography of Christology in Japan," *The Northeast Asia Journal of Theology* 2 (March 1969), pp. 117–34, esp. pp. 124–25.

46. Kenzo Tagawa, *A Phase in the History of Primitive Christianity* (1968), based on his doctoral dissertation at Strasbourg, *Miracles et Evangile: la pensée personnelle de l'évangéliste Marc* (Paris: Presses universitaires de France, 1966).

47. Shin Morishoji church, a local congregation in Osaka, which belongs to the Japan Baptist Convention (Southern Baptist Convention in the U.S.A.).

48. Cf. the studies by Kiyoko Takeda-Cho, *Indigenization and Apostasy—The Traditional Ethos and the Protestant* (1967) and *Geneology of Apostasy: Japanese and Christianity* (1973); also the special issue on indigenization in *The Northeast Asia Journal of Theology* 3 (September 1969).

49. Cf. Y. Kumazawa, "Modern Mass Media and the Mission of God," *Confessing Christ Through Mass Communication in Changing Asia* (in English; Tokyo: EACC, 1967), pp. 6–11; and Kumazawa, *A Theologian Looks at Urban Mission* (New York: Reformed Church in America, 1969).

50. For a historical survey of ecumenism in postwar Japan, see James M. Phillips, *Ecumenicity's Unsteady Course in Modern Japan*. Oriens Studies no. 1. (Tokyo: Oriens Institute for Religious Research, 1973).

APPENDICES

APPENDIX I

COMPILED BY GERALD H. ANDERSON

Selected Creeds, Confessions, and Theological Statements of Churches in Asia

1. The Confession of Faith of the Batak Church (Indonesia), edited by Edward Nyhus and Lothar Schreiner
2. The Constitution of the Church of South India: Governing Principles
3. Proposed Constitution for the Church of Christ in South India
4. The Korean Methodist Creed
5. Theological Declaration by Christian Ministers in the Republic of Korea, 1973
6. Statement by Korean National Council of Churches, 1974
7. The Church of Christ in China: Bond of Union
8. The Christian Manifesto (of the Three-Self Movement, China)
9. Sheng Kung Hui Pastoral Letter (House of Bishops of the Anglican Church in China)
10. The United Church of Christ in Japan: Confession of Faith
11. Confession on the Responsibility of the United Church of Christ in Japan During World War II
12. Declaration of the Faith and Articles of Religion of the Philippine Independent Church.

1. The Confession of Faith of the Batak Church, Indonesia (1951)

Edited by Edward Nyhus and Lothar Schreiner

Editors' Introduction

The confession of faith of the Batak Church is the first one drawn up in an autonomous church which originated from the modern missionary movement. It was drafted and formulated by a commission of its own theologians and declared by the Synod of the Batak Church in 1951.[1]

Historically motivated by the intention of the Batak Church to join the Lutheran World Federation, the confession affirms the teaching of the Reformation against Roman Catholicism and sectarian errors as well as heathen and secularist beliefs. Referring to the three Ecumenical creeds, its 18 articles expound theology, hamartiology, ecclesiology, ethics, and eschatology. Influence of the Augsburg Confession is traceable in its ethics, and in the polemical passages ("damnamus"). The teaching on the sacraments, modeled after Luther's Smaller Catechism, has been agreed to by Reformed churchmen in Indonesia. The confession of faith does not hinder intercommunion, because it transcends the confessional positions of Western Protestantism. Significantly, the East Asia Christian Conference pointed out that "the Batak Church could equally well belong to the Presbyterian World Alliance as to the Lutheran World Federation."[2] On the doctrinal basis of this confession the way is prepared for a true ecumenical fellowship, if not union, of the churches in Indonesia.

This version of the confession of faith is based on the original Batak and offers the first complete and authentic translation in English. It has been prepared by the present editors and their former colleagues on the Theological Faculty at Nommensen University. Unfortunately, the translations that have been published in English up to this time have either not been based on the original or have not been dependable and complete. The present text is provided with explanatory footnotes, taken largely from the study in German by Lothar Schreiner cited above. Biblical quotations are from the RSV. Words in brackets are additions by the editors.

Confession of Faith of the
Protestant Christian Batak Church (H.K.B.P.)

Preface

A "Confession of Faith" is of the utmost necessity for establishing our faith and opposing heresy. In the early church there were ecumenical confessions of faith which opposed heresy. At the time of the Reformation there were creeds which opposed the doctrine of the Roman Catholic Church. So it has been that new creeds have arisen whenever heresy has appeared to trouble the church. However, in opposing new heresies, the new confessions did not forget the first confession.[3] Thus the church, in opposing heresies which arise, continuously requires new confessions. The Reformers, for example, did not only use previous confessions, because a different form was required for their situation. Therefore the church may not just doze, content with the former confessions, but rather in every age must renew and reform them.

In Germany new heresies appeared after 1933. The churches there were aroused at that time because they realized that the previous confessions were no longer adequate to oppose these heresies. Therefore they formulated a new confession called "The Barmen Declaration" (May 31, 1934). They emphasized the sovereignty of Christ alone, opposing such sovereignty of men in the matter of religion as was claimed by Hitler and his cohorts.

In Holland too an effort was made to draw up a new confession. This new confession was also based on the previous confessions but spoke with a new voice to the modern world. (Dr. H. M. Bolkestein, page 203, line 24 from the top.)[4]

Because of the pressures upon our church, our thinking must be aroused at the present time to confront the doctrines and religions around us. Until recently there were actually only two religions surrounding us, namely animism[5] and Islam. However there are now many more which have come from without as well as grown up from within.[6] We will name them individually:

1. *Roman Catholics.* Now they come again to spread their wings. Our doctrine stands in opposition to their teaching.

2. *Adventists.* They have established their seminary in Pematang Siantar. They spread their doctrine by distributing their books and by propagating their views for several evenings in a given area.

3. *Pentecostals.* Their doctrine has spread to nearly every part of our area. They stress the spirit and speaking in tongues. They pray at great length and

sing "hallelujah." Their newspaper, published in Jakarta, is entitled "Penjuluh."[7]

4. *Enthusiasts.*[8] There are many varieties of enthusiasts in our midst. Some call themselves "The Holiness Church," others "the Church of the Atonement." Some refrain from eating blood, as in Pagar Sinondi and Pematang Siantar, while others at Sionomhudon and Laeparira are followers of Sibindanamora.[9] They say that their doctrine has a biblical basis, but their interpretation is absolutely wrong because they only follow their own notions.

5. *Siradjabatak.* This group has also spread widely in many areas. They claim to be only a [secular] party or group, but it is clearly evident in their constitution that they preserve the precepts of the old animism.

6. *The Bible-Circle Group.* This group came from Balata and has spread to Siantar. It is like a woodworm in the church bringing ruin to the souls of our fellow Christians. They stress that there are many errors in the work[10] of our church which are not in accordance with the Bible. They have also moved into Tapanuli.

7. *Nationalistic Christianity.* This [movement] developed during World War II. They falsify Christian doctrine by making it conform to nationalistic aspirations.

8. *Syncretism.* Its adherents say: "All religions are good with only slight differences in value." A religion has grown up in Djakarta called "Islam–Isa," a combination of Islam, Christianity, and Judaism. They also send information about their doctrines to us. Their estimate of various religions is as follows: Their religion is the highest, like 24-carat pure gold; Christianity is 22 carats, a high religion; Judaism is 20 carats, a medium-high religion; Islam is 18 carats, medium; all other religions are 16 carats, inferior.

9. Doctrines which come from *Theosophy, Communism,* and *Capitalism.* There are indeed many teachings which come from them that can confuse faith.

10. Besides these there have arisen *groups which have separated themselves from our church,* such as Mission Batak, H.Ch.B., P.K.B and H.K.I.[11] We know that there will be others which will arise in the future, and it is to be expected that their teachings will differ from the teachings of our church.

11. *Animism* and *Islam* which surround us. Their doctrines deviate sharply from the Bible. Making the matter worse is the fact that they come to our church in another form. Remnants of animism are still deeply rooted in many members of our church, like the roots of a great tree which have penetrated into the soil where it grows.

12. One other thing is very important. Our confession must be well defined over against the *customs*[12] *and culture of our people.* We must direct more

attention, especially toward these two matters, so that they do not destroy our faith. At the present time our people urge that our customs and culture must be preserved. This is good, but although we consider it good, not all of it is in harmony with our faith; there are inherent dangers. These various religions and doctrines constitute a real danger for our church.

Because of these things which have been enumerated above, the present time requires of us: there must be in our church a "Confession of Faith" containing pure doctrine in accordance with what we have confessed from the beginning.[13] This will be a symbol and foundation for us.

Moreover, it is necessary that there be a "Confession of Faith" in our church which includes the entire basis of what we believe so that it will not be vague to others, for this is required of a Christian group which calls itself a "church." A Christian group cannot be called a "church" if it has no confession. It is therefore urgent that this confession be recorded in order that the understanding of all our church members will become clearer, thereby establishing their faith.

The necessity [for this confession] may be summarized as follows:

1. Because faith results in confession, as the Apostle Paul said to the Corinthians (2 Cor. 4:13), "I believed, and so I spoke."

2. Because the church must witness against the world, as the Apostle Peter said (1 Pet. 3:15), "Always be prepared to make a defense to anyone who calls you to account for the hope that is in you." 1 Tim. 4:6, "If you put these instructions before the brethren, you will be a good minister of Christ Jesus, nourished on the words of the faith and of the good doctrine which you have followed."

3. Because it is an illuminator which makes known what is true and what is false doctrine. 1 John 4:2, 4.

4. Because unity in the life of the church requires unity in the confession of faith. Eph. 4:5; John 17:21.

5. Because it is a valuable inheritance for future generations of the church in order that they may follow in the faith of their fathers. Deut. 6:7.

The Authority of the Confession

Only Holy Scripture has ultimate authority, for God devised or created it. But a confession of faith also has authority. To be sure, it has been formulated by men but it is firmly based on the Word of God. 2 Cor. 1:21; 2 Tim. 3:16–17.

It is proper that the members of the church be subject to this authority, but it should not be a forced subjection and it should not stifle conscience. One must be free to examine the confession. If anyone finds something which is not in accordance with the Holy Word he may convey his objections to the church leadership.

The confession of faith herein recorded is that approved by the General Synod at Sipoholon on November 28–30,1951.

CONFESSION OF FAITH OF THE H.K.B.P.

Introduction

1. This confession of faith of the H.K.B.P. is a continuation of the previously existing creeds, namely the *three* creeds which were confessed by the church fathers, which are called:

    1. The Apostles' Creed
    2. The Nicene Creed
    3. The Athanasian Creed

2. This confession of faith is the summary of what we believe and hope for in this life and in the life to come.

3. This confession of faith is the basis of the H.K.B.P. for what is to be preached, taught, and lived. Matt. 16:16.

4. This confession of faith is the basis in the H.K.B.P. for rejecting and opposing all false doctrine and heresy which is not in accordance with the Word of God.

Article 1
Concerning God

We believe and confess:

God is one, without beginning and end, almighty, unchangeable, faithful, omniscient, inscrutable, a righteous judge, of great mercy, gracious. He fills heaven and earth and is true, holy, and loving. Deut. 6:4; Exod. 3:14a; Gen. 17:1; Ps. 105:8; 1 Cor. 1:9; 2 Thess. 3:3; Luke 1:37; Rom. 11:33; Deut. 10:17; Rom. 2:11; 1 Cor. 1:30; Ps. 103:8; Ps. 24:1; Isa. 6:3; John 3:16; 1 Tim. 6:15-16.

By means of this doctrine we reject and oppose the custom of calling God "Grandfather," and the view which regards God as only gracious, as well as the conviction that blessing can come from the spirits of the ancestors, as is usual with the animist. Likewise [we reject] the choosing of fortunate days, fortune-telling, and palm-reading.

By means of this doctrine we also reject the teaching which considers God's power to be greater than his holiness and love.

Article 2
The Triune Nature of God

We believe and confess:

Our God is one, and also triune, namely, God the Father, God the Son, and God the Holy Spirit. John 5:19; 14:11; 1:1; 15:26; 2 Cor. 13:13; Matt. 28:19.

The Father has eternally begotten His Son of His own being, that is, just as the Father has no beginning and no end, so also the Son. Likewise the Holy Spirit, who proceeds from the Father and the Son, has no beginning and no end. John 15:26.

By means of this doctrine we oppose and reject the conception which states that God is only One (Maha Esa),[14] with understanding that the Son and the Spirit are considered subordinate to the Father.

We also oppose the doctrine which states that the persons of the Trinity are God the Father; His Son, the Lord Jesus Christ; and the *Mother*, the Holy Spirit.[15]

Article 3
The Special Acts of the Triune God

We believe and confess:

A. God the Father creates, preserves, and rules all things visible and invisible.

By means of this doctrine we reject and oppose the doctrine of fatalism (predestination, fate, alloted destiny).[16]

B. God the Son, who became man, was born of the Virgin Mary, conceived by the Holy Spirit, and is called Lord Jesus. Two natures are found in Him, namely, the divine and human, inseparable in one person. Jesus Christ is true God but also true man. He suffered in agony at the time of the rule of Pilate, was crucified and died in order to deliver us from sin, from death, and from the power of the devil. He became the perfect sacrifice to make reconciliation with God because of all the sins of mankind. He was buried, descended into hell, rose again on the third day, ascended into heaven to sit at the right hand of God Jehovah, His Father, Who has glory forever. He is in heaven interceding for us, ruling everything, until He will come again to the earth to judge the quick and the dead. Matt. 28:18; Eph. 1:20–22; Eph. 1:7; John 3:16; Heb. 9:14; Phil. 2:9–11.

By means of this doctrine we reject and oppose:

1. The Roman Catholic doctrine which teaches that Mary, the mother of the Lord Jesus or, as they call her, "saint," can pray for us to God.

2. The Roman Catholic doctrine which teaches that "a priest can sacrifice Christ in the mass."

3. The false Roman Catholic doctrine that the pope in Rome is the Vicar of Christ on earth. Matt. 23:8–10.

4. The human view which equates the Lord Jesus with the prophets who are in this world.[17]

C. God the Holy Spirit calls and teaches the church and preserves it in faith and holiness in the Gospel for the glory of God.[18] Rom. 8:14–17; 1 Cor. 3:16. (Compare the explanation of the Third Article.)[19]

By means of this doctrine we oppose and reject the doctrine which states that the Holy Spirit can descend on man through his own efforts, not necessarily through the Gospel.

Likewise we oppose and reject the doctrine which states that the Holy Spirit can descend only through ecstasy[20] and speaking in tongues.

Likewise we reject and oppose the doctrine which states that it is not necessary to be treated medically but that it is enough only to pray to the Holy Spirit; as well as the false prophecies in the name of the Holy Spirit; and the dissolute and immoderate fellowship which they claim has been filled by the Holy Spirit.

We oppose and reject all these doctrines because they *falsely rely on the name of the Holy Spirit.*

Article 4
The Word of God

We believe and confess:

The words written in the Bible, namely, in the Old and New Testaments, are truly the words of God. "For Prophecy came not in old times by the will of man, but men moved by the Holy Spirit spoke from God" (2 Pet. 1:21). "All scripture is inspired by God and profitable for teaching, for reproof, for correction, and for training in righteousness, that the man of God may be complete, equipped for every good work" (2 Tim. 3:16–17).

By means of this doctrine we emphasize that the Holy Scripture is completely sufficient to reveal God's being and His will, and it is sufficiently taught in the Holy Scripture what man is to believe as a means to eternal life. Rev. 22:18–19.

The Holy Scripture alone is the beginning and the conclusion of all thought, knowledge, and work in the church and in the person of the believers.

By means of this doctrine we oppose and reject any learning and wisdom of man that diverges from the Word of God. Prov. 3:5; Ps. 111:10.

Article 5
The Origin of Sin

The devil is the source of sin and he desires that all men become sinners who turn away from God. John 8:44; Gen. 3:1–7; Rev. 20:10.

Thus, although the first persons (Adam and Eve) were good and able to act according to God's will, they nevertheless, because of the seduction of the devil, transgressed the commandment which God had given them and turned away from God. "Sin is transgression." 1 John 3:4; James 1:15.

Article 6
Original Sin[21]

We believe and confess:

Since Adam and Eve fell into sin, sin has passed on to all their descendants. Therefore all men are born in sin and sin enslaves them so that they transgress God's commandments. Sin brings judgment and eternal death. Ps. 51:7; 58:4; Gen. 8:21; Rom. 5:12; Rom. 3:12, 23; Titus 3:5; John 3:5; John 6:63.

By means of this doctrine we oppose and reject the view that children born into this world have not yet sinned. Likewise the view diverging from the Word of God which says that man is led to commit sin only because he is urged on by poverty, penury, or misery, and that such [transgressions] need not be considered sin.

Likewise we reject the doctrine which states that the heart of man is like blank paper on which nothing has yet been written.

Article 7
Salvation from Sin

We believe and confess:

"Salvation from sin cannot be gained by means of good works," or through one's own strength, but only by the grace of God through the redemption of Jesus Christ. It is received by faith which is wrought by the Holy Spirit, so that one appropriates the forgiveness of sin which Jesus Christ has provided through his death. Such faith is reckoned by God as righteousness before Him.[22] John 3:16; 2 Cor. 8:9; Acts 4:12.

Article 8
The Church

A. We believe and confess:

The church is the gathering of those who believe in Jesus Christ, who are called, gathered, sanctified, and preserved by God through the Holy Spirit.[23] 1 Cor. 1:2; 1 Pet. 2:9; Eph. 1:22 1 Cor. 3.

By means of this doctrine we oppose and reject:

1. A church (a certain group) established by men *of their own will*,

which for this reason separates itself from our church and not because there has been any doctrine in our church contrary to the Word of God;

2. The conception which states that only the authority of the leaders, the assemblies, and the rights of the members govern the church: for only Christ has authority in the church and only that order which is according to His Word is to be followed. It is not *Democracy* which rules the church, but *"Christocracy"*;

3. The conception which states that our church should be a *"state-church,"* for the duty of the state is different from the ministry of the church;

4. The conception which states that the church is a gathering based upon and bound to *custom;*[24] as well as the false opinion that the life of the church depends only upon organization.

B. We believe and confess:

The church is holy. The church is called holy, not because of the holiness of its members but because of the *holiness of Christ,* its head. Thus the church becomes holy because Christ has sanctified it and God reckons them as saints. Because of the holiness of the church it is called a holy people, a temple of the Holy Spirit, a habitation of God. 1 Pet. 2:9; Eph. 2:22; Rev. 1:6; Eph. 3:21; 1 Cor. 3:16.

By means of this doctrine we oppose and reject the doctrine which states that holiness can be gained through one's own efforts; likewise [we reject] the despair and separatism caused by the continuing presence of church members who are seen to commit sin.[25]

C. We believe and confess:

The church is universal. The universal church is the gathering of all saints who are partakers in the Lord Jesus Christ and His gifts—the gospel, the Holy Spirit, faith, love, and hope. They are from every country, people, tribe, race, and language, although their ceremonies and forms differ. Rev. 7:9.

By means of this doctrine we oppose and reject the interpretation which considers the church to be a religion of one people,[26] and those who think that churches have no relationship with one another.

D. We believe and confess:

There is *one* church. This is based on Ephesians 4:4; 1 Corinthians 12:20. "For there is *one* body, that is the church, and even though there are many members there is but one body." Because it is spiritual unity, the unity of the church which is expressed here is different from secular unity, usually asserted by men. John 17:20–21.

By means of this doctrine we oppose and reject any separations that are based only on external forms and not on the doctrine of faith.

E. Signs of the true church.
We believe and confess that the signs of the true church are:
   a. the pure preaching of the gospel;
   b. the proper administration of the two sacraments as instituted by the Lord Jesus;
   c. the exercise of church discipline in order to prevent sin.

Article 9
Those Who Minister in the Church

We believe and confess:
All Christians are called to be Christ's witnesses. In order to carry out the work in the church, God has called through the church those who minister according to the threefold office of Christ—prophet, priest, and king. These ought to be observed in the church. 1 Cor. 12:28.
The offices of the ministry are:
1. Preaching of the gospel to the members of the church and those who are not yet members;
2. Administering of the two sacraments, namely, Holy Baptism and Holy Communion;
3. Pastoral care of the members of the church;
4. Preserving pure doctrine through the exercise of spiritual discipline, together with opposition to false doctrine;
5. Doing works of mercy (diakonia).
For this work there are appointed in the church apostles, prophets, evangelists, pastors, and teachers, Eph. 4:11, and deacons, Acts 6.

By means of this doctrine we oppose and reject the conception of those who, on the basis of their own opinion and not because of anything done contrary to the office, reject and deny the office of the ministry.

By means of this doctrine we also oppose and reject anyone in the church who arises to preach, teach, and administer the sacraments without being installed by the church to the office of ministering in the church.

Article 10
The Sacraments

We believe and confess:
There are only two sacraments commanded by the Lord Jesus which we should administer, Holy Baptism and Holy Communion. The Lord Jesus has instituted them for His church in order to grant through visible signs His

invisible grace, namely, forgiveness of sins, salvation, life, and bliss, which are to be appropriated by faith. Matt. 28:19; Mark 16:15–16; Matt. 26; Mark 14; Luke 22; 2 Cor. 11.

By means of this doctrine we oppose and reject the Roman Catholic doctrine which states that there are seven sacraments.

A. Holy Baptism
We believe and confess:
Holy Baptism is a means of God's grace toward men, for through baptism the believer obtains forgiveness of sin, second birth, deliverance from death and the devil, and everlasting bliss.[27]

By means of this doctrine we confess that children also should be baptized, since by this means they will be brought into the company of those for whom Christ has given Himself. This is also in accordance with Jesus' acceptance of children. Mark 10:14; Luke 18:16.

When baptizing it is not necessary to immerse into water. Acts 2:41; 10:48; 16:33; Rom. 6:4; 1 Cor. 10:1–4; Titus 3:5; Heb. 11:29; 1 Pet. 3:21.

B. Holy Communion
We believe and confess:
Holy Communion is the eating of the bread as a means of mediating the body of our Lord Jesus Christ, and the drinking of the wine as a means of mediating the blood of our Lord Jesus Christ, whereby we obtain forgiveness of sins, life, and bliss. 1 Cor. 11:17–34; Matt. 26; Mark 14; Luke 22.

By means of this doctrine we oppose and reject the doctrine which states that only the bread without the wine should be given to the members of the church, for the Lord Jesus Himself, when he instituted the Lord's Supper, spoke the words, "Drink of it, all of you." The early church also acted in accordance with this, 1 Cor. 11:24–25. The mass is not based on the Word of God (that is, when it says that our Lord is sacrificed each time in the mass). Therefore we definitely reject it.

Article 11
Church Order

We confess:
There must be a church order which is based upon the Word of God,[28] for it is an instrument which regulates the life of the church and gives it peace. 1 Cor. 14:33. Likewise the church festivals are to be celebrated, namely, the festivals of the birth, death, resurrection, and ascension of the Lord Jesus, and the feast of Pentecost. But it must be distinctly remembered that the faithful observance of all these cannot bring us the benefit of the forgiveness of sin.

Article 12
Concerning Government

We confess:

The government which has authority comes from God;[29] that is, a government which opposes evil and administers justice, which helps the believers to live in peace and tranquillity, according to what is written in Romans 13 and 1 Timothy 2:2. Nevertheless one should also remember what is written in Acts 5:29: "We ought to obey God rather than man."

By means of this doctrine we confess that the church ought to pray for the government that it may walk in righteousness. However, the church should also let its voice be heard by the government.

By means of this doctrine we oppose and reject the conception that *"the state is a religious state,"* for the state remains the state and the church remains the church. Matt. 22:21b.

When it is necessary to go to court in order to seek justice, a Christian is permitted to take an oath. The same may be done at the time of induction into an office or position.

Article 13
Sunday

We keep Sunday holy:

It is *"The Lord's Day"* (the first day of creation by God), the day of the resurrection of the Lord Jesus, and the day of the outpouring of the Holy Spirit, which has been celebrated by Christians from the beginning of the church. Because we are Christians we do not return to the Jewish Sabbath.

By means of this doctrine we oppose and reject the doctrine of the Sabbatarians who say that Saturday is the Sabbath to be kept holy.

Article 14
Concerning Food

We believe and confess:

Everything created by God is good, and nothing is prohibited which is received with thanksgiving, for it is sanctified by the Word of God and by prayer.[30]

Man does not become holy by observing prohibitions concerning foods, for faith receives holiness from God. Man does not become holy by observing food regulations. This is the reason the Apostle Paul opposed the Jewish laws concerning food. The gospel must not be pushed into the background by prohibitions resulting from Moslem laws or other traditions. Matt. 15; Rom. 14; Col. 2; Acts 15; 1 Tim. 4:4–5.

By means of this doctrine we oppose and reject the doctrine of those who teach these things.

Article 15
Faith and Good Works

We believe and confess:

Good works must be the fruit of faith. He errs who hopes to obtain righteousness, life, comfort, and bliss by doing good works. The Lord Jesus alone can forgive sins and reconcile man with God.

We must keep the ten commandments. However, man lives by faith and not only by doing good works. The Holy Spirit moves men to do good works. (If not moved by the Spirit, good works become sin.)[31] John 5:15–16; Eph. 2:8; Rom. 5:1.

Article 16
Remembrance of the Dead

We believe and confess:

"It is appointed for men to die once, and after that comes judgment." Heb. 9:27. They will rest from their labors.[32] Rev. 14:13. Jesus Christ is the Lord of the quick and the dead. So in remembering the dead we remember our own passing and strengthen our hope in the fellowship of those who believe in God, thereby establishing our hearts in this life of struggle.

By means of this doctrine we oppose and reject the teaching of animism which states that the souls of the dead have a relationship with the living, as well as the doctrine which teaches that the souls of the deceased remain in the grave. We also oppose and reject the Roman Catholic doctrine which teaches that there is a purgatory through which the dead must pass for the purification of their souls before they can enter into life; furthermore, that a mass may be said for the dead and that the dead may be prayed for in order that they may more quickly be released from purgatory. We also reject prayers to the souls of the deceased saints, and the expectation that the power and holiness of the dead may pass over from their tombs, clothes, belongings or bones (mementos, relics).

Article 17
Concerning the Angels

We believe and confess:

The angels were created by God to serve Him; they are ministering spirits "sent forth to serve, for the sake of those who are to obtain salvation." Heb. 1:14.

Article 18
The Last Judgment

We believe and confess:

The Lord Jesus Christ will come on the Last Day to awaken the dead. John 5:28; 1 Thess. 4:16; Matt. 24:3; Luke 21:28; Rev. 20:11–15. He will judge all men. Matt. 25; 1 Cor. 15:52; 2 Cor. 5:10. Then he will call the believers to inherit everlasting life. Matt. 25:34. But the unbelievers will go into everlasting torment. Matt. 25. The portion of the believers with God is sure throughout eternity.

By means of this doctrine we oppose and reject the doctrine which states:

a. the time of Christ's second coming may be calculated by men;

b. after death there is still a period of grace.

We strongly emphasize that His coming will be unexpected. Thess. 5:2; Matt. 24:42, 44, 50; Luke 12:35–36. Therefore we should always be ready, as He reminded us. Luke 12:35–36.

NOTES

1. For an historical account of the rise and development of Christianity among the Batak in North Sumatra, Indonesia, see Paul B. Pedersen, *Batak Blood and Protestant Soul* (Grand Rapids, Mich.: Eerdmans, 1970). See also the authoritative presentation by Theodor Müller-Krüger in *Der Protestantismus in Indonesian: Geschichte und Gestalt* (Stuttgart: Evang. Verlagswerk, 1968), pp. 250–87. For a detailed account of the origin, structure, and importance of the Batak Confession see Lothar Schreiner, *Das Bekenntnis der Batak-Kirche* (Munich: Chr. Kaiser Verlag, 1966).

2. The context of the statement reads, "There are those churches which are not the result of the work of any particular denomination in the West. The confessional position of these churches will be acceptable to more than one confessional family. For instance, the Batak Church could equally well belong to the Presbyterian World Alliance as to the Lutheran World Federation. Membership in more than one confessional family for such churches will be useful as pointing to the fact that it is not all that simple to fix denominational labels with their Western connotation on the churches in Asia. It is this same fact that is illustrated by the refusal of most of the churches in Indonesia to belong to any World Confessional Organization." *The Christian Community within the Human Community, Containing Statements from the Bangkok Assembly of the E.A.C.C.* (February–March 1964). Minutes, part 2, p. 80.

3. Refers presumably to the Kyrios confession in the New Testament.

4. H.M. Bolkestein, *Asas-asas Hukum Geredja* (Bandung: 1951). The fundamental principles of Church-law, where the author refers to a Dutch document "Fundamenten en Perspectieven van Belijden" (1949).

5. The original "hasipelebeguon" is a composite structure, commonly used in the Batak language for "heathenism" and "heathendom" as an institutional religion shaping

all aspects of life as well as extant pagan beliefs of individual Christians. As worship of spirits is the chief aspect of heathenism as a tribal religion, the word "animism" seems to convey best what is meant here and in the other places of the text where the word "hasipelebeguon" is used with some hesitation, since it refers to a theory of primal religion that is not upheld any more. See also E. Nyhus, "The Encounter of Christianity and Animism Among the Toba Bataks of North Sumatra," *The South East Asia Journal of Theology* X, 2 & 3 (1968/1969), 33–52.

6. From within the church.

7. "The Torch."

8. The original "tonditondion" means people who bear the spirit and are possessed by it, predominantly, though not universally, used in a pejorative sense.

9. The title of the Batak prophet Iskandar Samosir, who during the forties of this century encouraged the people to renounce and distribute their belongings and possessions. His teaching is a syncretism of Christian and traditional Batak beliefs.

10. The original here may also be rendered "life and work."

11. H.Ch.B. (Huria Christen Batak/Christian Batak Church); P.K.B. (Punguan Kristen Batak/Batak Christian Assembly); H.K.I. (Huria Kristen Indonesia/Indonesian Christian Church). Of these schismatic groups the H.K.I., by far the largest, has recently joined the Council of Churches in Indonesia (D.G.I.) and is entering fellowship with the H.K.B.P. For details, see Pederson, *op. cit.*, pp. 149ff.

12. The original "adat" is of Arab origin and the common word in the Indonesian archipelago for customary law and the whole order of life and beliefs. For an investigation into the encounter of the Adat and the Gospel, see Lothar Schreiner, *Adat und Evangelium* (Gütersloh:Gerd Mohn, 1972).

13. Refers to the members of the Batak Church.

14. "Maha Esa," Indonesian, literally "The High One," expresses the oneness of God. The clause refers to the Islamic understanding of God.

15. The clause refers to an Islamic misunderstanding of the Trinity.

16. The original words here are "takdir," i.e., predestination in Islamic teaching; "sibaran," i.e., prenatally destined fate; and "bagian," i.e., alloted part in life. The last two refer to traditional Batak beliefs.

17. Refers to the Islamic interpretation of Jesus Christ.

18. Literally, "in the gospel" does not make good sense. In the Indonesian version it has been translated "through the gospel," which presumably conveys the intended meaning.

19. The third article of the Apostles' Creed, here referring to Luther's Smaller Catechism.

20. The original word "siarsiaran" is used for the descent of the ancestral spirit upon the medium-person capable of enacting the shamanism in the Batak ancestor worship. Here it refers more particularly to Pentecostal groups.

21. The original "dosa na tinean" means "inherited sin" or "Erbsünde."

22. Rom. 4:5.

23. Compare the explanation of the third article of the Apostles' Creed in Luther's Smaller Catechism.

24. The original word here, "par-adat-on," is a composite of "adat," explained in note 12 above.

25. Unbelief and a separatist mentality, produced by a deficient understanding of sanctification.

26. The emphasis here is on "people"; the original comes close to meaning a national religion.

27. Compare in the fourth chapter of Luther's Smaller Catechism the question about the use and purpose of baptism.

28. The church must necessarily have a church order. The clause does not refer to the order of Christian worship and to liturgy. There is no hint at "reformed deprecation of ceremony" here, as J. Ellwanger assumed ("The Batak Protestant Christian Church," *Concordia Theological Monthly* XXX, 1 (1959), 15). Article 11 is directed against the environment of the Batak Church with its different religious beliefs.

29. Rom. 13:1.

30. 1 Tim. 4:4–5

31. The reference here ought to be to John 15:5; compare *Confessio Augustana* article 20.

32. Heb. 4:10.

2. The Constitution of the Church of South India (1947)

Governing Principles

The Faith of the Church—The Church of South India accepts the Holy Scriptures of the Old and New Testaments as containing all things necessary to salvation and as the supreme and decisive standard of faith; and acknowledges that the Church must always be ready to correct and reform itself in accordance with the teaching of those Scriptures as the Holy Spirit shall reveal it.

It also accepts the Apostles' Creed and the Creed commonly called the Nicene, as witnessing to and safeguarding that faith; and it thankfully acknowledges that same faith to be continuously confirmed by the Holy Spirit in the experience of the Church of Christ.

Thus it believes in God, the Father, the Creator of all things, by whose love we are preserved;

It believes in Jesus Christ, the incarnate Son of God and Redeemer of the world, in whom alone we are saved by grace, being justified from our sins by faith in Him;

It believes in the Holy Spirit, by whom we are sanctified and built up in Christ and in the fellowship of His Body;

And in this faith it worships the Father, Son and Holy Spirit, one God in Trinity and Trinity in Unity.

The Church of South India is competent to issue supplementary statements concerning the faith for the guidance of its teachers and the edification of the faithful, provided that such statements are not contrary to the truths of our religion revealed in the Holy Scriptures.

The Sacraments in the Church—The Church of South India believes that the Sacraments of Baptism and the Supper of the Lord are means of grace through which God works in us, and that while the mercy of God to all mankind cannot be limited there is in the teaching of Christ the plain command that men should follow His appointed way of salvation by a definite act of reception into the family of God and by continued acts of fellowship with Him in that family, and that this teaching is made explicit in the two Sacraments which He has given us. In every communion the true Celebrant is Christ alone, who continues in the Church today that which He began in the upper room. In the visible Church, the celebration of the Lord's Supper is an act of the Church, the company of believers redeemed by Christ, who act as the local manifestation of the whole Church of Christ in heaven and on earth. It has in experience been found best that one minister should lead the worship of the Church, and pronounce the words of consecration in the service of Holy Communion. From very early times it has been the custom of the Church that those only should exercise this function who have received full and solemn commission from the Church to do so; this commission has ordinarily been given by the laying on of hands in ordination.

The only indispensable conditions for the ministration of the grace of God in the Church are the unchangeable promise of God Himself and the gathering together of God's elect people in the power of the Holy Ghost. God is a God of order; it has been His good pleasure to use the visible Church and its regularly constituted ministries as the normal means of the operation of His Spirit. But it is not open to any to limit the operation of the grace of God to any particular channel, or to deny the reality of His grace when it is visibly manifest in the lives of Churches and individuals.

In the Church of South India the Sacraments will be observed with unfailing use of Christ's words of institution and of the elements ordained by Him.

The Ministry in the Church—The Church of South India believes that the ministry is a gift of God through Christ to His Church, which he has given for the perfecting of the life and service of all its members. All members of the Church has equally access to God. All, according to their measure, share in the heavenly High Priesthood of the risen and ascended Christ from which alone the Church derives its character as a royal priesthood. All alike are called to continue upon earth the priestly work of Christ by showing forth in life and word the glory of the redeeming power of God in Him. No individual and no one order in the Church can claim exclusive possession of this heavenly priesthood.

But in the Church there has at all times been a special ministry, to which men have been called by God and set apart in the Church. Those who are ordained to the ministry of the Word and Sacraments can exercise their offices only in and for the Church, through the power of Christ the one High Priest.

The vocation of the ordained ministry is to bring sinners to repentance, and to lead God's people in worship, prayer, and praise, and through pastoral ministrations, the preaching of the Gospel and the administration of the Sacraments (all these being made effective through faith) to assist men to receive the saving and sanctifying benefits of Christ and to fit them for service. The Church of South India believes that in ordination, God, in answer to the prayers of His Church, bestows on and assures to those whom He has called and His Church has accepted for any particular form of the ministry a commission for it and the grace appropriate to it.

Necessary Elements in the Life of the Church of South India—The Church of South India recognizes that episcopal, presbyteral, and congregational elements must all have their place in its order of life, and that the episcopate, the presbyterate, and the congregation of the faithful should all in their several spheres have responsibility and exercise authority in the life and work of the Church, in its governance and administration, in its evangelistic and pastoral work, in its discipline, and in its worship.

The Congregation in the Church of South India—The Church of South India accepts the principle that as the Church of a whole region, being in fellowship with other regional Churches, is ideally the embodiment of the Church Universal in that region, and as similarly the Church of a diocese as a living part of a regional Church is the Church Universal expressing its one life in that diocese, so also in the purpose of God every local group of the faithful, organized for Christian life and worship as a congregation or pastorate within the fellowship of the diocese, represents in that place the same one, holy, catholic and apostolic Church.

Subject to the provisions of this Constitution, and to such general regulations thereunder as may be issued in any matter by the Synod of the Church or by a Diocesan Council, every congregation of the Church shall, with its pastor, be responsible for watching over its members, for keeping its life and doctrine pure, for ordering its worship, and for the proclaiming of the Gospel to those outside the Church; and every pastorate shall have general administrative authority within its area, shall have certain responsibilities in Church discipline, and shall have an opportunity of expressing its judgment both as to the appointment of its pastor and the selection of candidates for ordination from that pastorate.

The Presbyterate in the Church of South India—The Church of South India believes that presbyters are specially called and commissioned by God to be dispensers of His Word and Sacraments, to declare His message of pardon to penitent sinners, to build up the members of the Church in their most holy faith, and, through the councils of the Church and otherwise, to share with the bishops and lay members in its government and in the administration of its dicipline.

It is a rule of order in the Church of South India that the celebration of the Holy Communion shall be entrusted only to those who have by ordination received authority thereto. But it is desired that, with the ordained presbyter, there be present to assist him in the administration of the Lord's Supper others appointed by the Church for this purpose.

The Episcopate in the Church of South India—The Church of South India accepts and will maintain the historic episcopate in a constitutional form. But this acceptance does not commit it to any particular interpretation of episcopacy or to any particular view or belief concerning orders of the ministry, and it will not require the acceptance of any such particular interpretation or view as a necessary qualification for its ministry.

Whatever differing interpretations there may be, however, the Church of South India agrees that, as Episcopacy has been accepted in the Church from early times, it may in this sense fitly be called historic, and that it is needed for the shepherding and extension of the Church in South India. Any additional interpretations, though held by individuals, are not binding on the Church of South India.

The meaning in which the Church of South India thus officially accepts a historic and constitutional episcopacy is that in it:

(i) the bishops shall perform their functions in accordance with the customs of the Church, those functions being named and defined in the later chapters of this Constitution;

(ii) the bishops shall be elected, both the diocese concerned in each particular case and the authorities of the Church of South India as a whole having an effective voice in their appointment;

(iii) continuity with the historic episcopate will be effectively maintained, it being understood that, as stated above, no particular interpretation of the historic episcopate as that is accepted in the Church of South India is thereby implied or shall be demanded from any minister or member of the Church; and

(iv) every ordination of presbyters shall be performed by the laying on of hands by the bishops and presbyters, and all consecrations of bishops shall be performed by the laying on of hands at least of three bishops. The Church of South India believes that in all ordinations and consecrations the true Ordainer and Consecrator is God, who in response to the prayers of His Church, and through the words and acts of its representatives, commissions and empowers for the office and work to which they are called the persons whom it has selected.

In the service of consecration of a bishop in the Church of South India, the person to be consecrated shall be solemnly presented to the bishop presiding at the consecration by three presbyters of the diocese to which he is to be appointed, and these three presbyters shall join with the bishops in the laying on of hands. If, however, the Diocesan Council concerned specially so determine, hands shall be laid on by the bishops only.

In making the provision for episcopal ordination and consecration, the Church of South India declares that it is its intention and determination in this manner to secure the unification of the ministry, but that this does not involve any judgment upon the validity or regularity of any other form of the ministry, and the fact that other Churches do not follow the rule of episcopal ordination will not in itself preclude it from holding relations of communion and fellowship with them.

The Worship of the Church of South India—The Church of South India will aim at conserving for the common benefit whatever of good has been gained in the separate history of those churches from which it has been formed, and therefore in its public worship will retain for its congregations freedom either to use historic forms or not to do so as may best conduce to edification and to the worship of God in spirit and in truth.

No forms of worship which before the union have been in use in any of the uniting Churches shall be forbidden in the Church of South India, nor shall any wonted forms be changed or new forms introduced into the worship of any congregation without the agreement of the pastor and the congregation arrived at in accordance with the conditions laid down in Chapter X of this Constitution.

Subject to these conditions, and to the provisions of this Constitution and any special regulations which may hereafter be issued by the Synod under the Constitution with regard to the services of ordination and consecration and the essential elements or central parts of other services, especially those of Baptism, Holy Communion and Marriage, every pastor and congregation shall have freedom to determine the forms of their public worship.

Unity in Ministry and Life within the Church of South India—Every presbyter of the Church of South India may minister and celebrate the Holy Communion in any church of the united Church, and is eligible to be appointed to any charge therein, subject only to the subsequent provisions of this section.

The Church of South India recognizes that the act of union has initiated a process of growing together into one life and of advance towards complete spiritual unity. One essential condition of the attainment of such complete unity is that all the members of the Church should be willing and able to receive communion equally in all of its churches, and it is the resolve of the Church of South India to do all in its power to that end.

But it is convinced that this can only take place on the basis of freedom of opinion on debatable matters and respect for even large differences of opinion and practice, and it believes that this freedom and mutual respect can be safeguarded not by the framing of detailed regulations but by assurances given and received in a spirit of confidence and love.

The Church of South India therefore pledges itself that it will at all times be careful not to allow any over-riding of conscience either by Church authorities or by majorities, and will not in any of its administrative acts knowingly transgress the long-established traditions of any of the Churches from which it has been formed. Neither forms of worship or ritual, nor a ministry, to which they have not been accustomed, or to which they conscientiously object, will be imposed upon any congregation; and no arrangements with regard to these matters will knowingly be made, either generally or in particular cases, which would either offend the conscientious convictions of persons directly concerned, or which would hinder the development of complete unity within the Church or imperil its progress towards union with other Churches.

The Relations of the Church of South India with Other Churches—The Church of South India desires to be permanently in full communion and fellowship with all the Churches with which its constituent groups have had such communion and fellowship.

Any communicant member of any Church with which the Church of South India has relations of fellowship shall be at liberty to partake of the Holy Communion in any church of the Church of South India, and any minister of such a Church shall be free as a visitor to minister or celebrate the Holy Communion in any church of the Church of South India, if he is invited to do so.

The Church of South India will also gladly accept invitations to send delegates as visitors to the assemblies or other representative bodies of the Churches through whose labours its constituent groups have come into being, and will seek, by inter-change of visiting delegates or such other means as may be available, to promote and maintain brotherly relations with other Churches in India, Burma and Ceylon and to work towards a wider union of Churches in those countries.

The Relations of the Ministers and Members of the Church of South India with Other Churches—None of the ministers or members of the Church of South India shall because of the union forego any rights with regard to inter-communion and inter-celebration which they possessed before the union.

Every minister of the Church of South India who was ordained outside its area shall be at liberty to retain the ecclesiastical status (e.g., connection with a home presbytery or conference) which he had before the union in the Church in which he was ordained, subject to such arrangements between the Church of South India and any of the Churches concerned as may be found necessary, and provided that he shall not by any such arrangement be released from the obligations of his position as minister of the Church of South India.

Every minister of the Church of South India shall be at liberty to exercise any ministry in a Church outside its area which he was entitled to exercise before the union, provided that that Church permit him to do so.

Every minister of the Church of South India shall be at liberty to minister and to celebrate the Holy Communion in any church of a Church with which any of the uniting Churches have enjoyed relations of fellowship, if he is invited to do so.

In all these, as in other matters, the Church of South India desires to avoid on the one hand any encouragement of licence or condonation of breaches of Church comity and fellowship, and on the other hand any unchristian rigidity in its regulations or in their application; and in all its actions it will seek the preservation of unity within, the attainment of wider union, and the avoidance of immediate contests on particular cases.

3. Proposed Constitution for the Church of Christ in South India[1]

THE FAITH OF THE CHURCH

1. The Scriptures

This Church receives and holds the canonical Scriptures of the Old and New Testaments as the inspired record and testimony of God's revelation of himself to mankind, through which he speaks his word to us. The centre of the witness of Scripture is the incarnate Word, Jesus Christ. He speaks to us in them and gives us his Spirit, by whose illumination we receive them as the Word of God.

This Church holds and confesses that the Scriptures contain all things necessary to salvation and are the supreme and decisive standard of faith to which all teaching in the Church and all creeds and confessions are subordinate. It acknowledges that it must always be ready to correct and reform its life as the Holy Spirit continues to interpret the Scriptures to the Church.

2. Creeds and Confessions

This Church accepts and acknowledges the Apostles' Creed and the Nicene Creed as a true response and witness to the Word of God and as safeguards to the faith of the Church.

It recognises the Athanasian Creed as giving a true exposition of the Trinitarian faith.

It recognises the confessions of the Reformation as valuable for interpreting the teaching of Scriptures on the salvation of man, especially on his being justified in Christ by grace through faith alone.

It also acknowledges its responsibility to confess its faith in the context in which God places it and under the guidance of the Holy Spirit, always conscious of the fact that all creeds and confessions are subordinate to the authority of the Scriptures.

3. Faith in God

We believe in God the Father through Jesus Christ.

God has revealed himself to us fully and finally in Jesus Christ as one, holy,

---

1. (Madras: Published for the CSI—Lutheran Inter-Church Commission by the CLS, 1970), pp. 1–8. Prepared by an Inter-Church Commission representing the Andhra Evangelical Lutheran Church, the Arcot Lutheran Church, the South Andhra Lutheran Church, the India Evangelical Lutheran Church, the Tamil Evangelical Lutheran Church, and the Church of South India.

loving, and almighty Father. Nevertheless he has not left himself without witness to all men, for he has been and is ceaselessly at work in creation, history, culture, religion, and in the conscience of men. Through Christ we are enabled to recognise the work of God.

We call him "Father" because in Christ he has revealed himself to us as Father. We believe that we are God's children through faith in Christ the Son of God. We declare that God is love, and that love was manifested by the Father in sending his Son and is declared to us in the Gospel of Christ crucified.

This God in whom we believe is the one Almighty Creator and Sustainer of all things. He is the same God as he who called Israel out of Egypt, who revealed himself to them in acts of deliverance and who spoke to them through their prophets. God has revealed himself finally and fully to us in Christ.

God, who has created all things through Christ, has acted in Christ to redeem the fallen creation from the bondage of sin, corruption, and death. By his work in Christ he has made his Church to be the first fruit of a new creation which waits with longing for the glorious liberty of the children of God.

We believe in Jesus Christ our Saviour as Lord and God.

Our knowledge of God in Jesus Christ is not a message about God by someone other than God: we believe that God himself, the eternal Son of the Father, became man in Jesus Christ to deliver mankind from the power of Satan, and to bring him under his own kingly rule. He who knows Christ knows the Father. Christ has accomplished for us what God alone can do. He has accomplished it by becoming true man for us, tempted in all points as we are. He has redeemed us from sin by his atoning death and resurrection. He ever lives with us and in us, and our life is in him. In him alone we are justified by grace through faith. In him, who has overcome all things that separate man from God and man from man, we are reconciled to God and to one another and belong together as members of one Body.

We believe that he is the eternal Word of God, who gives life and light to men, and we have known this life and light in our experience. Therefore we are called to proclaim him as the Saviour of the world, and to announce to every one that he shall come to judge the living and the dead.

We believe in God the Holy Spirit as the Lord, the Giver of Life.

The Spirit of God, who spoke and acted in the prophets and saints of the old Testament, was given in the fullness of power to the first disciples after the completion of Christ's earthly ministry. He is the "Paraclete" whom Christ promised, the Spirit of the Father and of the Son. His indwelling is none other than the presence of God himself.

The same Holy Spirit sends Christ's disciples out into the world to bear witness to him, convicts the world of sin, and empowers the Church to be the instrument of forgiveness. The Spirit goes before the Church in its mission, giving to men, who are by nature enemies of God and blind to his truth, the gift of faith in Jesus Christ, bringing them to repentance and shedding abroad in their hearts the love of God. Through his Word and Sacraments he calls, gathers, enlightens, and sanctifies the whole Christian Church on earth, preserves us in one true faith, unites us in his fellowship, interprets Christ to us, and gives us the assurance that we are the children of God and heirs of his kingdom. The Holy Spirit is thus the foretaste and the guarantee of God's new creation.

We believe in the Triune God.

We know God by revelation and the experience of Christian faith as the Triune God. We bow before this mystery and worship one God, eternally Father, Son, and Holy Spirit, living and reigning in perfect unity.

4. The Church

The Church is the people chosen and called by God to belong to him through faith and baptism, to confess Jesus Christ as Lord and Saviour and to make disciples of all nations. They have been united with Christ the risen and ascended Lord and continue their fellowship with him and with one another through the Word of God, the Lord's Supper and the common life of prayer, mutual love, and service. The Church's life is sustained by the continued presence of the risen Lord through the Holy Spirit.

The Church as the Body of Christ has a God-given unity because there is one Lord, one faith, one baptism, and one hope of our calling; and since it is called to manifest this unity to the world and in order to manifest this unity to the world, it is necessary to agree about the true preaching of the Word of God, the right administration of the Sacraments and an accepted ordering of the essentials of the common life of the Church in love. However, it is not necessary that traditions, rites, ceremonies, and the details of Church order and organization should be everywhere alike.

The Church is holy because it belongs to God who is holy and who has granted to its members forgiveness of sins and the Holy Spirit, and has chosen them for fellowship with himself. They are, therefore, all called to holiness of life.

The Church is catholic because it is called to be the place in which all men of every kind are to find their true home both as the first fruit of the new creation in which all things are to be summed up in Christ, and as the body which teaches the fullness of God's truth.

The Church is apostolic because it is called to continue the mission of Christ committed to the apostles and is entrusted with the same Gospel which they proclaimed.

We confess that the Church which is called by God to be one, holy, catholic, and apostolic, is at the same time sinful and disobedient, contradicting in its life the calling of God. But he who called us is faithful and we

believe that he who has begun a good work in us continues it through the Holy
Spirit and will bring it to completion at the day of Jesus Christ.

5. The Ministry

The whole Church is called and commissioned by God through Christ to
fulfil his ministry in the world. Jesus Christ himself is our great High Priest,
and the Church, his body, is to continue his ministry and all who are baptised
are called to a "royal priesthood." He is the Good Shepherd and all members
of his Church are called to seek the lost and to lead them into the way of
salvation. He is the son of man who came to serve, and the whole Church is
called to serve the world for his sake.

Within this ministry of the whole people of God, from the beginning Christ
has given to his Church the ministry in the special sense of persons set apart to
preach the Gospel and to administer the Sacraments. They are called upon to
proclaim God's word to all men, to declare his forgiveness to penitent sinners,
to gather together and shepherd his flock, and to feed them with the bread of
life.

In this special ministry those who have been duly called are set apart by the
rite of ordination for a variety of functions. In ordination God through his
Church commissions, authorises, and empowers for the specific ministry to
which they are called the persons whom the Church believes he has chosen.
This commission is given that, in accordance with the mind of Christ, the
minister may give himself in humble service. All ministers, whatever their
particular function, are ordained to the one ministry of reconciliation to God
through Jesus Christ.

The authorisation of this special ministry lies in this ordination and not in a
person's worthiness. Normally this authorisation is transmitted by those who
have already received authority in the Church. But there are times when the
regular transmission of authority becomes impossible if the faithful preaching
of the Gospel is to continue. Therefore, the presence or absence of an
unbroken transmission of ministerial authority cannot of itself determine the
relation of churches to one another.

6. The Sacraments

This Church believes and confesses that the Sacraments of Baptism and the
Lord's Supper were ordained by Christ as visible means of grace through
which we are incorporated into and built up in the fellowship of the Body of
Christ. In them the Word of God is operative through the material elements
and outward actions, through which God bestows his grace in Christ unto
forgiveness of sins and a life of fellowship with him.

In the Sacrament of Baptism God adopts us as his children, granting us through faith the benefits of Christ's redemptive work and newness of life. Since Baptism is first and foremost an act of God, the Church holds that infants also should be baptised, and thus brought within God's covenant of grace. It is the responsibility of the Church, and especially of Christian parents, to ensure that those baptised as infants are given the necessary nurture, and the opportunity to grow up into the fullness of the faith and to make their own public profession of faith and obedience. However, since baptism does not depend primarily on our faith or our response, but on the promises and faithfulness of God, the Church confesses one baptism which is not to be repeated.

In the Sacrament of the Lord's Supper, Christ, who is really present, gives us his Body and his Blood to eat and drink in the bread and wine according to his Words at the Last Supper "This is my body. . . . This is my blood. . . . Do this in remembrance of me." The manner of Christ's presence is a mystery which our minds cannot comprehend, but which we joyfully confess and in which we glory. The cup of blessing which we bless is a participation in the blood of Christ. The bread which we break is a participation in the body of Christ. In this sacrament we commemorate with thanksgiving and proclaim the once-for-all events of his sacrificial death and resurrection by which he redeemed the world, we know and confess the presence of the Risen Lord with us, and we look forward in hope to his coming again in glory. While all who participate in the Sacrament receive the body and blood of Christ, to those who receive this gift of himself in repentance and faith he grants forgiveness of sins, life, salvation, and the power to be his witnesses to the world, and calls upon them to pledge themselves to renewed life of holiness and fellowship with one another. But those who participate without repentance and faith receive the Sacrament to their own judgment. In the Lord's Supper Christ is present both as Redeemer and as Judge.

7. The Church's Hope[2]

Because God who created all things in Christ has promised through his prophets and apostles that he will bring all things to their consummation in Christ; because he has given us the first fruit of this consummation in the resurrection of Jesus from the dead; and because he has given us his Holy

---

2. Section 7 was drafted by a subcommittee in Septebmer 1969 at the request of the Churches, wehreas Sections 1–6 were drafted in 1952, discussed by the Churches in 1962–1968 and revised by the Inter-Church Commission in 1969 in the light of the official opinions of the Churches.

Spirit as the guarantee of our inheritance; therefore we look forward with a hope which is both eager and patient. We wait for and pray for the coming again in glory of our Lord Jesus Christ to reign with his people over all things. We do not know the time of his coming, but we know that his coming is sure. Thus we hope and believe both that he will overcome our own death and give to us a life of perfect fellowship with him and with all his people, and that he will consummate his whole work of creation.

Having this hope for all men and for all things, we nevertheless confess that Christ's coming to this world will be the coming of its Judge. We may reject the gift of fellowship with Christ and go into the darkness of eternal death. The way into eternal life is narrow. Much of the achievement of men and nations will prove to be stubble which will be burned up so that the gold and precious stones may remain. Even now his judgments are at work in history; he puts down the mighty and raises the meek.

Because God is both Judge and Saviour, we know that the form of this world is passing away and that God is going to transform all things. Therefore we do not accept this world as it is, but we are set free from it in order to be servants and witnesses of God's purpose to transform it. This service is a service of love and compassion through which Christ's love flows out into the world. It is concerned both to help the individual and to transform the structures by which the dignity of the human person is to be safeguarded. It is likewise a service of hope, because we believe that God who raised up Jesus from the dead can raise up all that we do for his sake for truth, freedom, justice, and peace in this world to have a place in his eternal kingdom. Therefore we are assured that our labour in the Lord is not in vain.

4. The Korean Methodist Creed

(Adopted by the Korean Methodist Church in 1930)

We believe in the one God, maker and ruler of all things, Father of all men, the source of all goodness and beauty, all truth and love.

We believe in Jesus Christ, God manifest in the flesh, our teacher, example, and Redeemer, the Savior of the world.

We believe in the Holy Spirit, God present with us for guidance, for comfort, and for strength.

We believe in the forgiveness of sins, in the life of love and prayer, and in grace equal to every need.

We believe in the Word of God contained in the Old and New Testaments as the sufficient rule both of faith and of practice.

We believe in the Church as the fellowship for worship and for service of all who are united to the living Lord.

We believe in the kingdom of God as the divine rule in human society, and in the brotherhood of man under the fatherhood of God.

We believe in the final triumph of righteousness, and in the life everlasting.

5. Theological Declaration by Christian Ministers in the Republic of Korea, 1973

We make this declaration in the name of the Christian community in South Korea. However, under the present circumstances, in which one man controls all the powers of the three branches of government and uses military arms and the intelligence network to oppress the people, we hesitate to reveal those who signed this document. We must fight and struggle in the underground until our victory is achieved.

The historical situation of the Korean people has been very grave since last October. President Park's consolidation of power has had certain demonic consequences for the life of the Korean nation and people.

The Christian community, as an integral part of the Korean people, now stands up and speaks out on the present situation, compelled by the divine mandates of the Messianic Kingdom.

Since World War II, our people have gone through trials and sufferings, of social chaos, economic deprivation, and especially the tragic Korean War and the resulting political dictatorships. It has been an ardent aspiration of our people that a new and humane community might be restored to their lives. However, the hopes of the people for such a restoration of humane community has been cruelly crushed by President Park in his absolutization of dictatorship and ruthless political repression. This is done in the name of the so-called October Revitalization, a set of false promises which is only the sinister plan of some evil men.

We Christians are compelled to speak out and take accompanying actions on the following grounds:

1) We are under God's command that we should be faithful to his Word in concrete historical situations. It is not a sense of triumphant victory that moves us today; rather it is a sense of confession of our sins before God; and yet we are commanded by God to speak the truth and act in the present situation in Korea.

2) The people in Korea are looking up to Christians and urging us to take action in the present grim situation. It is not because we deserve to represent them. We have often fallen short of their deeper expectations, and yet we are urged and encouraged to move on this course of action, not because we envision ourselves as the representatives of our people, but because we are moved by their agony to call upon God for their deliverance from evil days.

3) We stand in a historical tradition of such struggles for liberation as the independence movement by Christians against Japanese colonialism. We realize that our Christian community has often lacked the courage to take a decisive stand, and that the theological outlook of the official bodies of our Christian churches has been too pietistic to take up revolutionary roles. However, we do not feel disheartened by the weakness of some of our brothers; rather we are determined to seek our theological convictions from the historical traditions of our church.

The firm foundation of our words and deeds is our faith in God the Lord of history, in Jesus the proclaimer of the Messianic Kingdom, and in the Spirit who moves vigorously among the people. We believe that God is the ultimate vindicator of the oppressed, the weak, and the poor; he judges the evil forces in history. We believe that Jesus the Messiah proclaimed the coming of the Messianic Kingdom, to be subversive to the evil powers, and that his Messianic Kingdom will be the haven of the dispossessed, the rejected, and the downtrodden. We also believe that the Spirit is working for the new creation of history and cosmos, as well as for the regeneration and sanctification of individual man.

In this grave historical situation, we as a Christian community believe:

1) that we are commanded by God to be representatives before God the Judge and Lord of History, to pray that the suffering and oppressed people may be set free.

2) that we are commanded by our Lord Jesus Christ to live among the oppressed, the poor, and the despised as he did in Judea; and that we are summoned to stand up and speak the truth to the powers that be, as he did before Pontius Pilate of the Roman Empire.

3) that we are compelled by the Spirit to participate in his transforming power and movement for the creation of a new society and history, as well as for the transformation of our character; and that this Spirit is the Spirit of Messianic Kingdom who commands us to struggle for socio-political transformation in this world.

Therefore, we express our theological convictions on the following issues:

1) The present dictatorship in Korea is destroying rule by law and persuasion; it now rules by force and threat alone. Community is being turned into jungle. Our position is that no one is above the law except God; worldly power is entrusted by God to civil authority to keep justice and order in human society. If anyone poses himself above the law and betrays the divine mandate for justice, he is in rebellion against God. Oriental tradition, too, understands that good rule is carried out through the moral persuasion and virtue of the ruler. One may conquer people by the sword; but they cannot be ruled by the sword.

2) The present regime in the Republic of Korea is destroying freedom of conscience and freedom of religious belief. There is freedom neither of expression nor of silence. There is interference by the regime in Christian churches' worship, prayer, gatherings, content of sermons, and teaching of the Bible.

The Christian Church and other religious bodies must be the defenders of conscience for the people; for destruction of conscience is a most demonic act. In defending the freedom of religious belief against interference by the regime in Korea, Christian churches are also defending freedom of conscience for all people.

3) The dictatorship in Korea is using systematic deception, manipulation, and indoctrination to control the people. The mass media have been turned into the regime's propaganda machine to tell the people half-truths and outright lies, and to control and manipulate information to deceive the people.

We believe that Christians are witnesses to truth, always struggling to break any system of deception and manipulation, for to tell the truth is the ultimate power that sets men free for God's Messianic Kingdom.

4) The dictatorship in Korea uses sinister and inhuman and at the same time ruthlessly efficient means to destroy political opponents, intellectual critics, and innocent people. The use of the Korean Central Intelligence Agency (CIA) for this purpose is somewhat similar to the evil ways of the Nazi Gestapo or the KGB of the Stalin era. People are physically and mentally tortured, intimidated and threatened, and sometimes even disappear completely. Such treatments are indeed diabolical acts against humanity.

We believe that God has created humans in body and soul. Body as well as soul will be resurrected at the day of judgment of the Messianic Kingdom. We believe especially in the sanctity of the human body; therefore any violation of it is equal to killing a man. It is a murderous act.

5) The present dictatorship is responsible for the economic system in Korea, in which the powerful dominate the poor. The people, poor urban workers and rural peasants, are victims of severe exploitation and social and economic injustice. So-called "economic development" in Korea turned out to be the conspiracy of a few rulers against the poor people, and a curse to our environment.

We as Christians must struggle to destroy this system of extreme dehumanization and injustice; for we are witnesses to the ongoing movement of the Messianic Kingdom in history, in which the poor will be enriched, the oppressed will be vindicated, and peace will be enjoyed by the people.

6) The present regimes in the South and North are using the unification talks only to preserve their own power; and they are betraying the true aspirations of the people for the unification of their land. We believe as Christians that the people deeply yearn for authentic community on the basis of true reconciliation. Without transcendence beyond the past experiences of bitter conflict and differences in ideological and politico-economic systems, and without transformation of our historical conditions of oppression, true unification cannot be realized.

A CALL FOR ACTION AND SUPPORT

1) *To the people in Korea:* Withdraw any form of recognition of the laws, orders, policies, and other political processes of dictatorship that have been wrought since October 17, 1972. Build various forms of solidarity

among the people to struggle for the restoration of democracy in South Korea.

2) *To the Christians in Korea:* As preparation for the above struggle, we Christians should renew our churches by deepening our theological thinking, by our clear stance and solidarity with the oppressed and poor, by the relevant proclamation of the gospel of the Messianic Kingdom, and by praying for our nation; and we should prepare ourselves for martyrdom, if necessary, as our forefathers did.

3) *To the Christians of the world:* Most of all we need your prayers and solidarity, and we ask you to express our common bond through actions of encouragement and support.

CONCLUSION

Jesus the Messiah, our Lord, lived and dwelt among the oppressed, poverty-stricken, and sick in Judea. He boldly stood in confrontation with Pontius Pilate, a representative of the Roman Empire, and he was crucified in the course of his witness to the truth. He has risen from the dead to release the power of transformation which sets the people free.

We resolve that we will follow the footsteps of our Lord, living among our oppressed and poor people, standing against political oppression, and participating in the transformation of history, for this is the only way to the Messianic Kingdom.

May 20, 1973

6. Statement by Korean National Council of Churches on Recent Pronouncements of Korean Government Leaders Regarding Christianity, 1974

Today when our people face many difficult domestic problems, we Christians feel a deep responsibility to overcome this difficult time of our nation, through the united effort of all our people. We believe that the recent pronouncements by Prime Minister Kim Jong Pil and other government leaders regarding the Christian Church, were clearly illegitimate and most unfortunate statements. Accordingly it is our responsibility to clarify our position, and thus we issue the following statement:

We believe that the state is a created order in human community, established by God. Under God's absolute authority, therefore, the state is commissioned a conditional authority to promote the welfare of the people, to keep peaceful order, and to realize social justice.

All powers that be are determined by God (Rom. 13:1–7). This biblical passage shows the limits of the political authority and the nature of its legitimacy. The question is whether the state authority as a servant of God promotes what is good, whether it does not hold swords in vain, and whether it shows the wrath of God to those who do real evil. Namely, the real question is whether before God the power is legitimately established, whether it is keeping peace and order for the people and promoting their welfare, whether it is protecting basic human rights and sincerely doing its best to realize social justice. Christians as citizens of this nation must fulfil their duty and responsibility to a legitimate political power that fulfills the above role.

But when the established power abandons the justice of God, goes beyond its limits, and is not faithful to the duties entrusted to it by the people, Christians as witnesses of the Word of God, must have the responsibility to criticize and rectify this power.

It is very unfortunate that the present government grossly suppresses the freedom of speech and, moreover, keeps surveillance over the preaching of sermons. This is in violation of the human rights and religious freedom that are clearly guaranteed in the Constitution. This is a clear trend toward dictatorial rule. Christians' criticism of the political power is motivated neither to protect any particular political party, nor to overthrow a regime. Our declaration is an expression of our conscience and faith before God on a spiritual, moral, and religious level, to appeal to the moral sense and conscience of the people.

There cannot be identification between loyalty to the nation and loyalty to a particular regime. The power holder should humbly realize that when any regime ignores the just law and the will of the people and is thus dictatorial, then it is true loyalty to the people and nation to resist such a regime, for the protection of the people's human rights and for the realization of social justice. When our criticism of the regime is founded upon this pure motive, this is not contrary to the principle of non-interference between church and state.

If we remember from history that the principle of separation between church and state emerged to prevent absolutization of political power due to the symbiotic mixture of political power and religious authority, and to keep the political regime from preferential treatment of one religion, then even from the viewpoint of history of political thought, there is no reason to argue that the church should say nothing, whatever the political regime may do. Religion is the nucleus and essence of culture. It is natural that religious substance is manifest in all dimensions—political, economic, and social—of national life. When a particular regime is against such a cultural essence and spiritual ethos, the religion cannot help but speak out.

Today's human being lives in a matrix of political, economic, and social organizations. There is no individual apart from this organizational system. The church is commissioned with the divine mission to save such a modern man; and therefore the church cannot divide salvation into individual and social salvations. This means that salvation today should be the "mission of God" to restore a true human being, liberating him from his predicament within evil social institutions and systems.

Social participation on this religious ground has been a great contribution to national development. This is attested to by Korean history itself. Korean churches' contribution in the Enlightenment and in creation of democratic thought, and Christian resistance against the Japanese colonial regime in the March First Independence Movement (1919) cannot be evaluated too highly. Also, we should not forget that there was a sacrificial effort of missionaries for this cause. In short, the mission of God is a cosmic and universal event that transcends national boundaries.

A Christian is a responsible citizen of a nation. But we also believe that mankind, ruled by God, is one family of brothers and sisters. On the basis of the ecumenical unity and solidarity of humanity, we reject any narrow nationalism that idolizes a nation. It is on this foundation that foreign missionaries are engaged in missionary work in Korea. We wholeheartedly invite and accept them as our brothers and sisters and as co-workers, along with their great achievements of the past. We believe that, even though they hold citizenship in other nations, they speak and make critical remarks out of pure motives, and that their acts are results of their love for our nation and our people. It is unfortunate that the Prime Minister has threatened to expel such missionaries.

The ultimate judgment is in the hands of God. A regime of a nation can pass only relative judgments within the limits defined by law. The term "relative" means that any particular regime or particular law is subject to justice, natural law, and the law of God. When a regime or any particular law does not recognize its limits, the regime easily becomes a dictatorship and the law is apt to be idolized. Moreover, when this has been done in the name of God, there has arisen dictatorial rule such as Nazism. This is a living historical lesson that we must remember.

We shall support positively a government that, following God's will, expands human rights, promotes the safety and welfare of the people, estab-lishes social justice, and contributes to world peace. But when a regime is against the will of God, does not listen to the voice of the people, and ignores the appeals of conscience and faith in order to perpetuate the power of the regime, we feel a strong responsibility before God not only to withdraw our cooperation, but to resist actively such a regime. Especially at a time when there is tension between the Christian Church and government, the Prime Minister, who does not have deep knowledge of Christianity, has overstepped himself to publicly give his own interpretation of the Bible at will, mentioning "judgment," etc. This incident gives the strong impression that he is trying to interfere with even the content of Christian faith. It was indeed also unfortu-nate, we strongly feel, that Carl McIntire, a man who is isolated from the international Christian community, and whose influence is very limited even in the U.S.A., was publicized under the auspices of the government as though he were a representative of the mainstream of Christian tradition.

In conclusion, we earnestly pray that the present government may listen conscientiously to the people and to the appeals of Christians through frank dialogues, and that it may become a government which pursues truth, justice, and peace according to the will of God.

Korean National Council of Churches
November 18, 1974

7. The Church of Christ in China
Bond of Union

Based on the principle of the freedom of formulating her own faith, the bond of union shall consist:

1. In our faith in Jesus Christ as our Redeemer and Lord on whom the Christian Church is founded; and in an earnest desire for the establishment of His Kingdom throughout the whole earth.

2. In our acceptance of the Holy Scriptures of the Old and New Testaments as the divinely inspired word of God, and the supreme authority in matters of faith and duty.

3. In our acknowledgement of the Apostles' Creed as expressing the fundamental doctrines of our common evangelical faith.

The Constitution; Article 3 —approved by the First General Assembly of the Church of Christ in China, October 1927.

8. The Christian Manifesto

"Direction of Endeavor for Chinese Christianity in the Construction of New China"

This document of May, 1950, was worked out by the founding group of the Three-Self Movement in consultation with Premier Chou En-lai. It was eventually signed by at least 400,000 Protestant Christians in a mass campaign for public endorsement of the document.

Protestant Christianity has been introduced to China for more than a hundred and forty years. During this period it has made a not unworthy contribution to Chinese society. Nevertheless, and this was most unfortunate, not long after Christianity's coming to China, imperialism started its activities here; and since the principal groups of missionaries who brought Christianity to China all came themselves from these imperialistic countries, Christianity consciously or unconsciously, directly or indirectly, became related with imperialism. Now that the Chinese revolution has achieved victory, these imperialistic countries will not rest passively content in face of this unprecedented historical fact in China. They will certainly seek to contrive by every means the destruction of what has actually been achieved; they may also make use of Christianity to forward their plot of stirring up internal dissension, and creating reactionary forces in this country. It is our purpose in publishing the following statement to heighten our vigilance against imperialism, to make known the clear political stand of Christians in New China, to hasten the building of a Chinese church whose affairs are managed by the Chinese themselves, and to indicate the responsibilities that should be taken up by Christians throughout the whole country in national reconstruction in New China. We desire to call upon all Christians in the country to exert their best efforts in putting into effect the principles herein presented.

The Task in General

Christian Churches and organizations give thoroughgoing support to the "Common Political Platform," and under the leadership of the government oppose imperialism, feudalism, and bureaucratic capitalism, and take part in the effort to build an independent, democratic, peaceable, unified, prosperous, and powerful New China.

Fundamental Aims

(1) Christian churches and organizations in China should exert their utmost efforts, and employ effective methods, to make people in the churches everywhere recognize clearly the evils that have been wrought in China by imperialism; recognize the fact that in the past imperialism has made use of Christianity; purge imperialistic influences from within Christianity itself; and be vigilant against imperialism, and especially American imperialism, in its plot to use religion in fostering the growth of reactionary forces. At the same time, the churches and organizations should call upon Christians to participate in the movement opposing war and upholding peace, and teach them thoroughly to understand and support the government's policy of agrarian reform.

(2) Christian churches and organizations in China should take effective measures to cultivate a patriotic and democratic spirit among their adherents in general, as well as a psychology of self-respect and self-reliance. The movement for autonomy, self-support, and self-propagation hitherto promoted in the Chinese church has already attained a measure of success. This

---

From *Documents of the Three-Self Movement* (New York: Far Eastern Office, National Council of Churches, 1963), pp. 19–20.

movement from now onwards should complete its tasks within the shortest possible period. At the same time, self-criticism should be advocated, all forms of Christian activity re-examined and readjusted, and thoroughgoing austerity measures adopted, so as to achieve the goals of a reformation in the church.

Concrete Methods

(1) All Christian churches and organizations in China that are still relying upon foreign personnel and financial aid should work out concrete plans to realize within the shortest possible time their objective of self-reliance and rejuvenation.

(2) From now onwards, as regards their religious work, Christian churches and organizations should lay emphasis upon a deeper understanding of the nature of Christianity itself, closer fellowship and unity among the various denominations, the cultivation of better leadership personnel, and reform in systems of church organization. As regards their more general work, they should emphasize anti-imperialistic, anti-feudalistic and anti-bureaucratic-capitalistic education, together with such forms of service to the people as productive labor, teaching them to understand the New Era, cultural and recreational activities, literacy education, medical and public health work, and care of children.

When this Manifesto was published, a covering letter signed by Bishop Kaung, T. C. Chao, Y. T. Wu, Cora Deng, Y. C. Tu, H. H. Tsui, L. M. Liu and N. S. Ai went out to Chinese Christian leaders, making some of the statements in the Manifesto more explicit. The Church must support the Common Platform, accept the leadership of the Government and work harmoniously with it. It must come to a clear understanding of the way American imperialism has used the church, and eradicate all the results of that imperialism. As a principle it must use no foreign funds and no foreign personnel, and on these two points it must consult with the Government. During the period of Land Reform all church activities except routine Sunday services, prayer-meetings, etc., should cease.

9. Sheng Kung Hui Pastoral Letter

The House of Bishops of the Sheng Kung Hui [Anglican Church in China] could not accept the Manifesto–later they all did–and so as an alternative statement issued the Pastoral Letter given herewith.

We, the members of the Standing Committee and the House of Bishops at the joint meeting in Shanghai on July 5, 1950, send to you, our fellow-members in the Lord in the whole nation, our greetings and respects!

At this joint meeting we have discussed in detail the problems of the Church in relation to this new era. Herewith are the important results of our discussions.

1. We consider that the Church not only cannot compromise with imperialism, feudalism, or bureaucratic capitalism, but also that these are fundamentally against the faith of the Church. Therefore we oppose them. Christianity has always recognized that to welcome and cooperate with the powerful and the rich and to oppress the masses is against the spirit of Christ. Christ himself never compromised with the powerful and the rich; records of such lessons by the Apostles are numerous in the Bible.

2. Christianity believes that God is Lord of all the Universe. The purpose of God's love of the world in sending his son to be born as man is to give freedom to the oppressed. Therefore we feel deeply fortunate to have the national liberation and heartily support the Common Platform (provisional national constitution) with its guarantee of freedom of religious belief.

3. In self-government, self-support, and self-propagation our Church has made some achievements. Hereafter we determine to co-operate with all the members of the Church to reach the goal of self-reliance in the shortest possible time.

4. In the midst of the Church there are indeed a few corrupt members not following the purpose of the Church and against the Christ. Their personal and individual behavior cannot represent the whole Church and their sins are condemned by the Church. Therefore we should hereafter endeavour to inoculate the spirit of Holiness and Universality into the Church.

5. Hereafter our Church should on the one hand positively promote spiritual life and religious education, so as to enable us all to have the Christlike personality and family, and on the other hand pay attention to productive labor and social service.

6. Christ is the King of Peace! Our Church has been promoting peace and we oppose all the cruel and human killing weapons.

Documents of the Three-Self Movement, pp. 21–22

Finally we must strengthen our Church; we must prepare ourselves to overcome difficulties. We have recommended that all the members of our Church in China during the coming year have a few minutes'intercession before our noonday meal. Thus we shall be reminded of our united mission and burden at mealtimes. For the concrete work of our Church and the deeper understanding of our faith by our Church members, we are preparing a number of Church Handbooks to be distributed later.

Signed by
The Standing Committee of the General Synod
July 5th, 1950.   and The House of Bishops

10. The United Church of Christ in Japan Confession of Faith

(Official Translation)

We believe and confess that:

The Old and New Testaments, inspired of God, testify to Christ, reveal the truth of the Gospel, and are the sole canon upon which the Church should depend. By the Holy Spirit the Holy Bible is the Word of God which gives us full knowledge of God and salvation, and is the unerring standard of faith and life.

The One God, revealed by the Lord Jesus Christ, and testified to in the Holy Scriptures, being Father, Son and Holy Spirit, is the triune God. The Son, for the salvation of us sinners, became man, was crucified, offered Himself to God as the perfect sacrifice once for all, and became our redemption.

God chooses us by His grace, and by faith in Christ alone He forgives our sins and justifies us. In this unchangeable grace the Holy Spirit accomplishes His work by sanctifying us and causing us to bear fruits of righteousness.

The Church is the Body of Christ the Lord, and is the congregation of those who are called by grace. The Church observes public worship, preaches the Gospel aright, administers the sacraments of Baptism and the Lord's Supper, and being diligent in works of love, waits in hope for the coming again of the Lord.

Thus we believe, and with the saints in all ages we confess the Apostles' Creed:

I believe in God the Father Almighty, Maker of heaven and earth; and in Jesus Christ his only Son our Lord; who was conceived by the Holy Spirit, born of the Virgin Mary, suffered under Pontius Pilate, was crucified, dead, and buried; He descended into hell; the third day He arose again from the dead; He ascended into heaven, and sitteth on the right hand of God the Father Almighty; from thence He shall come to judge the quick and the dead. I believe in the Holy Spirit; the holy catholic Church; the communion of saints; the forgiveness of sins; the resurrection of the body; and the life everlasting. Amen.

Enacted October 28, 1954

11. Confession on the Responsibility of the United Church of Christ in Japan During World War II

The 25th Anniversary of the establishment of the United Church of Christ in Japan (Kyodan) was celebrated during the 14th General Assembly of the Kyodan held in October 1966 at Osaka, Japan. Now we are faced with the serious task of building the Kyodan. In order to express our sense of responsibility which the Kyodan has toward Japan and the world, we prayerfully take as our theme: "Our Church Tomorrow."

At this time we are reminded of the mistakes committed in the name of the Kyodan during World War II. Therefore, we seek the mercy of our Lord and the forgiveness of our fellowmen.

At the time of the founding of the Kyodan the Japanese Government, then under pressure, asked that all religious bodies be brought together and that they cooperate with the national policy to bring the war to a victorious end.

Since the time that the Gospel was first presented in the early part of the Meiji Era, Japanese Christians had desired to establish one evangelical Church in Japan, by the merging of denominations. Therefore, they entered into the Union and the Kyodan was established, taking advantage of an order of the government.

Concerning this founding and the continued existence of the Kyodan, we recognize, with deep fear and gratitude, that even in our failures and errors the Providence of God, "The Lord of History," was at work.

The Church, as "the light of the world" and as "the salt of the earth," should not have aligned itself with the militaristic purposes of the government. Rather, on the basis of our love for her and by the standard of our Christian conscience, we should have more correctly criticized the policies of our motherland. However, we made a statement at home and abroad in the name of the Kyodan that we approved of and supported the war, and we prayed for victory.

Indeed, as our nation committed errors we, as a Church, sinned with her. We neglected to perform our mission as a "watchman." Now, with deep pain in our heart, we confess this sin, seeking the forgiveness of our Lord, and from the churches and our brothers and sisters of the world, and in particular of Asian countries, and from the people of our own country.

More than 20 years have passed since the war, and we are filled with anxiety, for our motherland seems unable to decide the course that we should follow; we are concerned lest she move in an undesirable direction due to the many pressures of today's turbulent problems. At this moment, so that the Kyodan can correctly accomplish its mission in Japan and the world, we seek God's help and guidance. In this way we look forward to tomorrow with humble determination.

Masahisa Suzuki
Moderator
United Church of Christ in Japan

Easter Sunday
March 26, 1967

12. Declaration of the Faith and Articles of Religion of the Philippine Independent Church

We, the Bishops, Priests and lay members, delegates to the General Assembly of the Philippine Independent Church (Iglesia Filipina Independiente), held in the City of Manila on the 5th day of August, A.D. 1947, do reiterate our Faith and publicly declare that

WE BELIEVE IN

1. *The Holy Trinity:*
    One God, true and living, of infinite power, wisdom and goodness; the Maker and Preserver of all things visible and invisible. And that in the unity of this Godhead there be three Persons, of one substance, power and eternity—the Father who is made of none, neither created nor begotten; the

Son who is of the Father alone, not made nor created, but begotten; the Holy Ghost who is of the Father and the Son, neither made, nor created, nor begotten, but proceeding.

2. *Jesus Christ, the Only-Begotten Son of God:*
Jesus Christ, the only-begotten Son of God, the second Person of the Trinity, very and eternal God, of one substance with the Father, took man's nature in the womb of the Blessed Virgin, after she had conceived by the Holy Ghost. He suffered under Pontius Pilate, was crucified, died and was buried. He descended into hell. The third day He rose again from the dead, He ascended into Heaven, and sitteth at the right hand of God the Father Almighty: from thence He shall come to judge the living and the dead.

3. *The Holy Ghost:*
The Holy Ghost, the Lord, and the Giver of life, Who proceedeth from the Father and the Son: Who with the Father and the Son together we worship and glorify.

4. *One Catholic and Apostolic Church:*
The Church, Holy, Catholic and Apostolic, which is the Body of Christ, founded by Christ for the redemption and sanctification of mankind, and to which Church He gave power and authority to preach His Gospel to the whole world under the guidance of His Holy Spirit.

WE HOLD TO THE FOLLOWING ARTICLES
OF RELIGION TAUGHT BY THIS CHURCH

1. *Salvation:*
Salvation is obtained only through a vital faith in Jesus Christ, the Son of God, as Lord and Saviour. This faith should manifest itself in good works.

2. *Holy Scriptures:*
The Holy Scriptures contain all things necessary to salvation and nothing which cannot be proved thereby should be required to be believed.

3. *The Creeds:*
The Articles of the Christian Faith as contained in the ancient Creeds known as the Apostles' and Nicene Creeds are to be taught by this Church and accepted by the faithful.

4. *The Sacraments:*
The Sacraments are outward and visible signs of our faith and a means whereby God manifests His goodwill towards us and confers grace upon us.

Two Sacraments, Baptism and Holy Communion commonly called the Mass, ordained by Christ Himself, are held to be generally necessary to salvation.

Baptism is necessary for salvation. It signifies and confers grace, cleansing from original sin as well as actual sin previously committed; makes us children of God and heirs of everlasting life. It effects our entrance into the Church of God. It is administered with water in the Name of the Father, the Son, and the Holy Ghost.

Confirmation, whereby, through the imposition of the Bishop's hands, anointing and prayer, baptized Christians are strengthened by the gifts of the Holy Spirit and confirmed in the Faith.

Penance, the confession of sins as commanded by Jesus Christ.

The Holy Eucharist, the sacrament of the Body and Blood of Christ, taken and received by the faithful for the strengthening and refreshing of their bodies and souls.

Holy Unction, whereby the sick, especially one in danger of death, is anointed with oil with prayer. He receives, if necessary, remission of sins, the strengthening of his soul, and, if it be God's will, restoration to health.

Holy Orders, a sacrament by which Bishops, Priests and Deacons are ordained and receive power and authority to perform their sacred duties.

Holy Matrimony, a sacrament in which a man and a woman are joined together in the holy estate of matrimony.

5. *The Holy Eucharist:*

The Holy Eucharist, commonly called the Mass, is the central act of Christian worship. It is the sacrament of our redemption by Christ's death. Those who partake of it receive the Body and Blood of Christ. All who purpose to make their communion should diligently try and examine themselves before they presume to eat of that Bread and drink of that Cup. For as the benefit is great, if with a true penitent heart and lively faith a man receive that Holy Sacrament, so is the danger great if he receive the same unworthily.

The Mass is to be said in the official language of the Church in such a way that it can be heard by the worshipers.

The authorized Order for the celebration of the Mass is that set forth in the Filipino Missal or Book of Divine Office adopted by this Church.

6. *Sacred Ministry:*

From Apostolic times there have been three Orders of Ministers in the Church of God: Bishops, Priests and Deacons. These Orders are to be reverently esteemed and continued in this Church. And no man is to be accepted as a lawful Bishop, Priest, or Deacon in this Church, or permitted to execute any functions pertaining to these Orders, except he be called, tried, examined, and admitted thereunto according to the Canons of this Church, and in accordance with the Order prescribed by this Church for Making, Ordaining and Consecrating Bishops, Priests, and Deacons, or has had Episcopal Consecration or Ordination.

7.   *Celibacy of the Clergy:*

Bishops, Priests, and Deacons are not commanded by God's law to marry or to abstain from marriage, therefore they are permitted to marry at their own discretion, as they shall judge the same to serve better to godliness.

8.   *Church Buildings:*

Churches for the worship of God are to be erected and separated from all unhallowed, worldly, and common uses, that men may reverence the Majesty of God and show forth greater devotion and humility in His service.

9.   *The Altar:*

The altar is the most sacred part of the Church because there Jesus is sacramentally present. It symbolizes Mount Calvary, and, therefore, if images of Saints are used for adornment, care is to be exercised that such ornaments may not distract the minds of the worshipers from the Person of Jesus Christ.

10. *Worship, Rites, and Ceremonies:*

Only such Orders of Service as have been authorized by this Church shall be used in Public Worship; provided, however, that the Diocesan Bishop or the Supreme Council of Bishops may authorize Orders of Service for special occasions.

11.   *Language of Public Service:*

All public services shall be conducted in the official language of the Church, or in any other language the Supreme Council of Bishops may prescribe.

12.   *Purity of Life:*

Holiness, altruism, obedience to God's Commandments, and a zeal for His honor and glory are incumbent upon the Clergy and Laity alike, therefore all should be trained in a clean and disciplined life, not neglecting prayer, study, and the exercise of moral discipline.

13.   *Knowledge:*

All truth is of God, therefore, the Church should promote sound knowledge and good learning. No books except those detrimental to good morals are to be prohibited.

14. *The Blessed Virgin:*

The Virgin Mary was chosen by God to be the Mother of Jesus Christ. As Jesus Christ is truly God and Mary is the Mother of Jesus Christ, she is the Mother of God in His human generation. She whom God honored is to be honored above all.

15. *The Saints:*

Persons universally recognized for their holiness of life, loyalty, and courage, especially the Blessed Virgin and the New Testament Saints, are to be held in reverent remembrance. Veneration of Saints is not contrary to God's commandments as revealed in the Scriptures; but their deification is condemned by the Church as a monstrous blasphemy. Veneration of the Saints must not obscure the duty of the faithful to direct approach to God through Jesus Christ. Honor rendered the Saints must in no wise detract from the honor due the Three Persons of the Holy Trinity.

16. *Miracles:*

Holy Scriptures teach us that events take place in the natural world, but out of its established order, which are possible only through the intervention of divine power, like the Incarnation of Jesus Christ. So-called miracles, based not on well-authenticated facts but on merely fantastic rumors are repudiated. Belief in unsubstantiated miracles leads to pagan fanaticism and is to be condemned as destructive to the true faith.

17. *Attitude Towards the Roman Church:*

When this Church withdrew from the Roman Catholic Church, it repudiated the authority of the Pope and such doctrines, customs, and practices as were inconsistent with the Word of God, sound learning, and a good conscience. It had no intention of departing from Catholic doctrine, practice, and discipline as set forth by the Councils of the undivided Church. Such departures as occurred were due to the exigencies of the times, and are to be corrected by official action as opportunity affords, so that this Church may be brought into the stream of historic Christianity and be universally acknowledged as a true branch of the Catholic Church.

18. *Attitude Towards Other Churches:*

Opportunity is to be sought for closer cooperation with other branches of the Catholic Church, and cordial relations maintained with all who acknowledge Jesus Christ as Lord and Saviour.

19. *Church and State:*

This Church is politically independent of the State, and the State of the Church. The Church does not ally itself with any particular school of political thought or with any political party. Its members are politically free and are urged to be exemplary citizens and to use their influence for the prosperity and welfare of the State.

20.   *Doctrine and Constitutional Rules of the*
      Church and the Fundamental Epistles:

The Doctrine and Constitutional Rules of the Philippine Independent Church, adopted on October 28th, 1903, and subsequently amended, and the Fundamental Epistles of the Philippine Independent Church, are henceforth not to be held as binding either upon the Clergy or Laity of this Church in matters of Doctrine, Discipline, or Order, wherein they differ in substance from the Declaration of Faith or the Articles of Religion contained herein. They are to be valued as historical documents promulgated by the Founders of this Church when they were seeking to interpret the Catholic Faith in a manner understood by the people. Under the inspiration of the Holy Spirit the Church has sought to eradicate such errors of judgment and doctrine as crept into its life and official documents in times past.

21. *Additions, Amendments, Repeal:*

The Declaration of Faith shall not be altered, amended, or repealed. However, the Articles of Religion may be amended, repealed, or added to by an absolute majority of the delegates to the General Assembly having the right to vote. Such action before it becomes binding upon the Church must be ratified by the Supreme Council of Bishops and approved by the Supreme Bishop.

APPENDIX II

A SELECTED BIBLIOGRAPHY
IN WESTERN LANGUAGES

Compiled by
Gerald H. Anderson, Mariano C. Apilado, and Douglas J. Elwood

Prepared with the assistance of grants from the Theological Education Fund and the Foundation for Theological Education in Southeast Asia. Mr. Paul A. Byrnes, Periodicals Librarian at the Missionary Research Library, New York City, and Mrs. Evelyn Kimbrough, Nashville, rendered valuable assistance to the compilers.

ABBREVIATIONS

AF	*Asia Focus*
BTF	*Bangalore Theological Forum*
CC	*Church and Community*
CCA	Christian Conference of Asia
CF	*Ching Feng*
ChC	*Christian Century*
CISRS	Christian Institute for the Study of Religion and Society
CLS	Christian Literature Society
EACC	East Asia Christian Conference
EMM	*Evangelisches Missions Magazin*
EMZ	*Evangelische Missions-Zeitschrift*
ER	*Ecumenical Review*
ICHR	*Indian Church History Review*
IES	*Indian Ecclesiastical Studies*
IJT	*Indian Journal of Theology*
IRM	*International Review of Mission*
JCQ	*The Japan Christian Quarterly*
JES	*Journal of Ecumenical Studies*
JR	*Japanese Religions*
LW	*Lutheran World*
NB	*New Blackfriars*
NEAJT	*Northeast Asia Journal of Theology*
NCCR	*National Christian Council Review*
NZM	*Neue Zeitschrift für Missionswissenschaft*
OB	*Occasional Bulletin* from the Missionary Research Library
PA	*Practical Anthropology*
PPF	*Philippine Priests' Forum*
PS	*Philippine Studies*
PSB	*Princeton Seminary Bulletin*
RL	*Religion in Life*
RS	*Religion and Society*
SA	*Social Action*

SEAJT   *South East Asia Journal of Theology*
SJ   *Silliman Journal*
SJT   *Scottish Journal of Theology*
SW   *Student World*
TAN   *Teaching All Nations*
TC   *Theology and the Church*
TS   *Theologische Stimmen aus Asien, Afrika und Lateinamerika.* Edited by Hans-Werner Gensichen, Gerhard Rosenkranz, and Georg F. Vicedom. Munich: Chr. Kaiser Verlag, vol. I, 1965; vol. II, 1967; vol. III, 1968. English tr. of vol. III, *Christ and the Younger Churches* (London: SPCK, 1972).
TT   *Theology Today*
TTCA   *Trinity Theological College Annual*
USQR   *Union Seminary Quarterly Review*
UTC   United Theological College
UTS   Union Theological Seminary
WCC   World Council of Churches
ZMR   *Zeitschrift für Missionswissenschaft und Religionswissenschaft*

I. *Bibliographies*

Anderson, Gerald H., ed. *Christianity in Southeast Asia: A Bibliographical Guide.* New York: Missionary Research Library, 1966.
Includes Ceylon and Taiwan.

"Annotated List of Periodicals Concerned with the Vocation, Role and Function of Christianity in Africa, Asia and Latin America," *Exchange* (Leiden), no. 1 (1972), pp. 1–24.

Baago, Kaj. *Library of Indian Christian Theology: A Bibliography.* Madras; CLS, 1969.
Includes most of what Indians have produced in Christian theology, but suffers from the absence of important Western contributions to the indigenization of Indian theology.

Balchand, Asandas. *The Salvific Value of Non-Christian Religions According to Asian Christian Theologians Writing in Asian-Published Theological Journals, 1965–1970.* Manila; East Asian Pastoral Institute, 1973. Also in *TAN*, X, 1 & 2 (1973) 10–37, 115–52.
A bibliographical study by an Asian Jesuit on what Asians are saying in Asian-published journals.

Chao, Jonathan Tien-en. "Chinese Theological Development: A Selected Bibliography," *Reformed Bulletin of Missions* (Philadelphia), III, 5 (1968).

Henkel, Willi. "Theologische Zeitschriften in Afrika, Asien und Australien," *NZM*, XXVIII, 2 (1972), 139–43.

Ikado, Fujio and McGovern, James R. *A Bibliography of Christianity in Japan, Protestantism in English Sources, 1859–1959.* Tokyo: International Christian University, 1966.

Kumazawa, Yoshinobu and Amagai, Yukimaro. "A Selected Bibliography of Christology in Japan," *NEAJT*, no. 2 (1969), 117–34.

MacInnis, Donald E. "Selected Bibliography of Books, Pamphlets, Articles, Dissertations, Study Packets, and Translated Materials on the Christian Church in People's Republic of China: 1958–1968; and Related Material from Church Periodicals, Reports, Books and Other Sources," *OB*, XX, 5 (1969).

Phillips, James M. "Notes for a Bibliography on Christianity in Japan since 1945," *JCQ*, XXXIX, 2 (1973), 108–16.

―――. "Biblical Studies in Japan, 1945–1974," *Japan Missionary Bulletin*, XXVIII, 9 & 10 (1974), pp. 549–59, 617–24.

Rhee, Jong Sung. "Writings on Christology in Korea," *NEAJT*, no. 2 (March 1969), 111–16.

Thomson, Alan. "Theological Publications in Indonesia: A Bibliography," *SEAJT*, XV, 1 (1973), 113–16.

Yanagita, Tomonobu. *Japan Christian Literature Review.* Sendai: Seisho Tosho Kankokai, 1958. Supplement, 1960.
"A comprehensive subject listing of Protestant and Catholic books."

II. Journals

Al-Basheer. Bulletin of Christian Institutes of Islamic Studies. Henry Martyn Institute, P.O. Box 153, Hyderabad, A.P., India. Quarterly.

Al-Mushir (The Counselor). Theological Journal of the Christian Study Centre, 128 Saifullah Lodhi Road, Rawalpindi, Pakistan. Quarterly.

Asia Focus. CCA. 480 Lorong 2, Toa Payoh, Singapore 12. (Successor to *Church and Society.*) Quarterly.

Bangalore Theological Forum. United Theological College, 17 Miller's Road, Bangalore 6, South India. Semi-annually.

Boletin Eclesiastico de Filipinas. Official Interdiocesan Organ (English). Fathers' Residence, University of Santo Tomas, Manila, Philippines. Monthly.

The Bulletin. Christian Institute for Ethnic Studies in Asia, P.O. Box 3167, Manila, Philippines. Occasional.

China Notes. East Asia Department, Division of Overseas Ministries, NCC-USA, 475 Riverside Drive, N.Y., N.Y. 10027. Quarterly.

Ching Feng. Quarterly Notes on Christianity and Chinese Religion and Culture. Christian Study Centre on Chinese Religion and Culture, Tao Fong Shan, Shatin, New Territories, Hong Kong. Quarterly.

Church and Community. United Church of Christ in the Philippines, P.O. Box 718, Manila, Philippines. Bimonthly.

Church and Society. EACC. Bangalore, India. (Had eleven issues from September, 1960 to September, 1967, before it was superseded by *Asia Focus.*)

Clergy Monthly. Catholic Press, Ranchi (Bihar), India. Monthly.

Dialogue. Study Centre for Religion and Society, 490/5 Havelock Road, Colombo 6, Sri Lanka. Thrice annually.

Exchange. Bulletin of Third World Christian Literature. Interuniversity Institute for Missiological and Ecumenical Research, Boerhaavelaan 43, Leiden, Netherlands. Three or four issues annually.

Indian Church History Review. The Church History Association of India. Wesley Press, Post Box no. 37, Mysore City, India. Semi-annually.

Indian Ecclesiastical Studies. Pharmaram, Bangalore 29, South India. Quarterly.

Indian Journal of Theology. Bishop's College, 224 Acharya Jagadish Bose Road, Calcutta 700 017, India. Quarterly.

Japan Christian Quarterly. Fellowship of Christian Missionaries, Box 5030, Tokyo International, Tokyo, Japan. Quarterly.

Japan Missionary Bulletin. Oriens Institute for Religious Research, 28-5 Matsubara, 2 chome, Setagayaku, Tokyo, 156 Japan. Eleven issues annually.

Japanese Religions. NCC Center for the Study of Japanese Religions, School of Theology, Doshisha University, Kyoto, Japan. Quarterly.

Jeevadhara. Theology Centre, Alleppey, Kerala, India. Bimonthly.

Korea Religions. Institute for Ecumenical and Inter-Religious Studies, International P.O. Box 3251, Seoul, Korea. Occasionally.

Logos. A Journal of Christian Thinking in Asia. Aquinas University College, Colombo 8, Sri Lanka. Quarterly.

National Christian Council Review. The Wesley Press, P.O. Box 37, Mysore City, India. Monthly.

Northeast Asia Journal of Theology. Northeast Asia Association of Theological Schools, c/o Japan Lutheran Theological College, 3-10-20, Osawa, Mitaka-shi, Tokyo 181, Japan. Semi-annually.

Philippine Priests' Forum. P.O. Box 1525, Manila, Philippines. Quarterly.

Philippine Studies. Ateneo de Manila University, P.O. Box 154, Manila, Philippines. Quarterly.

Philippiniana Sacra. Fathers' Residence, University of Santo Tomas, Manila, Philippines. Thrice annually.

Quest. A Forum for Reflection in Sri Lanka. Aquinas University College, Colombo 8, Sri Lanka. Monthly.

Religion and Society. Christian Institute for the Study of Religion and Society, 17 Miller's Road, Box 604, Bangalore 560006, India. Quarterly.

Religious and Social Issues. Bulletin of the Christian Institute for the Study of Religion and Society. Ashram, Chunnakam, Sri Lanka. Semi-annually.

Silliman Journal. Silliman University, Dumaguete City, Philippines. Quarterly.

South East Asia Journal of Theology. Association of Theological Schools in South East Asia, P.O. Box 841, Manila, Philippines. Semi-annually.

Teaching All Nations. East Asian Pastoral Institute, P.O. Box 1815, Manila, Philippines. Quarterly.

Theology and the Church. Tainan Theological College and Taiwan Theological College, 115 Tung Men Road, Tainan, Taiwan. Quarterly.

III. *General*

Anderson, Gerald H., ed. *Christ and Crisis in Southeast Asia*. New York: Friendship Press, 1968.
>   Critically examines the historical life situations of the churches. Statistics and bibliography.

————, ed. *Sermons to Men of Other Faiths and Traditions*. Nashville: Abingdon Press, 1966.
>   Includes sermons by four Asian theologians: Tetsutaro Ariga, David G. Moses, D.T. Niles, and Paul Verghese.

Balasuriya, Tissa. *Development of the Poor Through the Civilizing of the Rich*. Christchurch, New Zealand: NCC, 1972.
>   Fr. Balasuriya of Sri Lanka (Ceylon) presents the situation and thinking of

people in the "Third World," as he sees them, in relation to current "aid" programs.

Beeby, H.D. "Living Theology in Today's Northeast Asia," *NEAJT*, no. 7. (1971), 55–65.
   Introducing the theme at the Second Study Conference of the NEAATS, meeting at Seoul, Korea, May 3–4, 1971.

Boivin, Marcel. "Theology and Developing Countries," *NB*, LI, 602 (1970), 328–35.

Caspersz, Paul. "The Role of the Church in Asia," *NB*, LI, 596 (1970), 17–29.
   A Jesuit in Sri Lanka urges adaptation, but warns of the dangers.

Chatterji, Saral K., ed. *The Asian Meaning of Modernization.* Delhi: ISPCK, 1972.

Cho, Kiyoko Takeda "The Ideological Spectrum in Asia," pp. 79–90 in *Man in Community. Christian Concern for the Human in Changing Society.* Edited by Egbert de Vries. New York: Association Press, 1966.

Christian Conference of Asia. See: East Asia Christian Conference.

"Christ the Light of the World and Our Unity, Witness and Service: An Asian Symposium," *SEAJT*, I, 2 (1959), 52–64.
   A document resulting from group discussions among Asian Protestant theological teachers in July–August, 1959, prior to the WCC Assembly on the same theme.

Clasper, Paul D. "Asian Voices and Theological Study," *SEAJT*, VI, 2 (1964), 39–45.
   The Asian voices to be listened to are those of the Hindu priest, the Buddhist friend, the secularist, and the Asian Christian, especially that of the responsible churchman.

Corwin, Charles. *East to Eden? Religion and the Dynamics of Social Change.* Grand Rapids, Mich.: Eerdmans, 1972.
   Asks and answers the question: "What is it about Christianity that, when accepted by any people, stimulates radical social transformation?" Examines the historical record of China, India, and Japan.

Cuttat, Jacques Albert. *Asiatische Gottheit–Christlicher Gott. Die Spiritualität der beiden Hemisphären.* Einsiedeln: Johannes Verlag, 1971.

Dumoulin, Henrich. *Christlicher Dialog mit Asien.* (Theologische Fragen heute, 14.) Munich: Max Hueber Verlag, 1970.

East Asia Christian Conference (EACC; name changed in 1973 to Christian Conference of Asia). *Asian Conference on Church and Society,* Seoul, 1967.
   Reports and addresses from EACC meeting at Seoul, October 1967, on the theme "Modernization of Asian Societies."

———. *Asians and Blacks: Theological Challenges.* Bangkok, 1973.
   Cook Memorial Lectures in Asia for 1972, by Choan-seng Song and Gayraud Wilmore.

———. *Bangkok '68. "In Christ All Things Hold Together."* Statements and Findings of the Fourth Assembly of the EACC, Bangkok, 1968.

———. *The Biblical Basis of Men-Women Cooperation in Society.* A Bible study guide prepared by Yoshinobu Kumazawa. Tokyo, 1966.

———. *Buddhist-Christian Encounter.* Edited by U Kyaw Than. Rangoon, 1961.

———. *The Christian Community Within the Human Community.* 2 vols. Statements and Papers of the EACC Assembly at Bangkok in 1964.

———. "Christian Encounter with Men of Other Beliefs." Statement from an EACC Assembly Commission, Bangkok, 1964. *ER*, XVI, 4 (1964), 451–55.

———. *Christian Service in the Revolution.* Report of the consultation sponsored by the EACC Committee on Inter-Church Aid and on Church and Society, 1963, in Sukabumi, Indonesia.

———. *The Christian Witness in Changing Asia.* Special issue of *SEAJT*, VIII, 3 (1967). The fourth series of John R. Mott Memorial Lectures, by Joan Metge, Harry Sawyer, T.B. Simatupang, Joseph J. Spae, Lukas Vischer, and W.A. Visser 't Hooft.

———. *Christian Witness in Contemporary Ceylon.* Jaffna Report. Colombo, Ceylon, 1961. Report of the EACC working conference held at Jaffna, April 1961.

———. *Christ's Ministry and Ours.* Singapore, 1962. The 1961 John R. Mott Memorial Lectures given in Bangkok by Alfred Carleton, Masao Takenaka, and U Kyaw Than.

———. *Church's Witness in Relation to Religion and Society, International Affairs, Religious Liberty.* Bangkok, 1964. "Program for 1964–68"; being a statement of the priorities for the quadrennium.

———. *The Common Evangelistic Task of the Churches in East Asia.* Papers and Minutes of the EACC Assembly at Prapat, Indonesia, March 17–26, 1957.

———. *Common Worship and the Renewal of the Church in Asia.* Singapore, 1962. A study document prepared by the EACC assembly at Bangalore, November 1961; superseded later by the East Asia section of the 1963 Faith and Order Reports.

———. "The Concern for Dialogue in Asia," *IRM*, LIX, 236 (1970), 427–29. An EACC statement drawn up in July 1970 after widespread discussion and reflection.

———. "The Confessing Church in Asia and Its Theological Task," *IRM*, LV, 218 (1966), 199–204. Section III of "Statements Issued by a Consultation on Confessional Families and the Churches in Asia," EACC meeting at Kandy, Ceylon, December 1965.

———. *Confessing the Faith in Asia Today.* Statement issued by the consultation convened by the EACC and held in Hong Kong, October 26–November 3, 1966. A major document of historic significance from the first Asian Faith and Order consultation. See also the preparatory study papers on "Confessing the Faith in Asia Today," in *SEAJT*, VIII, 1–2 (1966).

———. *Confessional Families and the Churches in Asia.* Report from a consultation convened by the EACC at Kandy, Ceylon, 1965.

Emphasizes autonomy for the churches in Asia; distinguishes between a confessing theology and a confessional theology. See especially "Questions Relative to the Confessing Church in Asia and the Theological Task."

——. *A Decisive Hour for the Christian Mission.* Edited by Norman Goodall. London: SCM Press, 1960.
The inaugural series of John R. Mott Memorial Lectures, given at the Kuala Lumpur assembly of the EACC in 1959; by Norman Goodall, Lesslie Newbigin, W.A. Visser 't Hooft, and D.T. Niles.

——. *EACC Hymnal.* Edited by D.T. Niles, 1963.
One-third of the hymns are compositions of Asians.

——. *God's People in Asian Industrial Society.* The report of the EACC on Christians in industry and lay training. Edited by Robert M. Fukada, Kyoto, 1967.

——. *Ideas and Services.* A Report of the EACC, 1957–67, by the General Secretary, D.T. Niles. Christchurch, New Zealand, 1968.
Brief but extremely important document on the history and directions of the EACC.

——. *Living With Questions.* Edited by Soritua A.E. Nababan. Jakarta, 1964.
Bible study lessons first used during the Asian Christian Youth Assembly at Dumaguete City, Philippines, December 24, 1964–January 8, 1965.

——. *Men and Women in Home, Church and Community in Asia.* Papers and Statements of an Asian Consultation on "The Christian Home in Changing Society." Rangoon, 1963.

——. *New Forms of Christian Service and Participation.* Edited by Alan Brash, 1962.
An annotated report of four consultations in Asia.

——. *New Songs of Asian Cities.* Edited by I-To Loh. Tainan and Tokyo, 1972.
Songs which are mainly explicit expressions of Christian faith in the urban context in Asia. Forty-nine songs of Asian origin; thirteen non-Asian.

——. *One People, One Mission.* Edited by John R. Fleming. Singapore, 1963.
Addresses, reports, and reflections on the "Situation Conferences" held in 1963 to consider the mission and unity of the church.

——. *Presenting the Christian Message in Buddhist Lands.* Report of consultation held at Kandy, November 3–10, 1953. Geneva: WCC, 1955.

——. *Proclaiming Christ in Asia.* Edited by U Kyaw Than. Rangoon, 1962.
Statement on the work and witness of the EACC.

——. "The Purpose of Dialogue. Findings of Inter-Faith Dialogue Consultation," *AF*, IV, 1 (1969), 60–69.

——. *Religion, State and Ideologies in East Asia.* Edited by M.M. Thomas and M. Abel. Bangalore: EACC Committee on Church and Society, 1965.
A country-by-country study of the situation.

——. *Structures for a Missionary Congregation. The Shape of the Church in Asia Today.* Edited by John R. Fleming and Ken Wright. Singapore, 1964.

———. *Theology in Action*. Edited by Oh Jae Shik and John England. Tokyo, 1972.
Report of the EACC-sponsored "Workshop on Theology in Action" (Manila, 1972); includes essays by Kosuke Koyama, Edicio de la Torre, C.G. Arevalo, and Peter Latuihamallo.

———. *Theology in Action, No. 2*. Edited by John England. Singapore, 1974.

———. *This We Believe. Asian Churches Confess Their Faith*. Edited by John R. Fleming. Singapore, 1968.
A "Study Edition" of the report from the Hong Kong, 1966, Faith and Order consultation on "Confessing the Faith in Asia Today."

———. *Witnesses Together*. Edited by U Kyaw Than. Rangoon, 1959.
The official report of the inaugural assembly of the EACC at Kuala Lumpur, Malaya, May 14–24, 1959.

"East Asia Theological Commission on Worship," (Faith and Order Report), *SEAJT*, IV, 4 (1963), 26–41.
The East Asia section of the 1963 Faith and Order Reports, later published by SCM Press, London; concerned particularly with the indigenization of Christian worship in Asia.

Elwood, Douglas J., ed. *What Asian Christians Are Thinking. Readings from Asian Theologians*. Manila: New Day Publishers, 1976.

Fleming, John R. "Confessions, Confessionalism and the Confessing Church in Asia Today," *SEAJT*, VIII, 1–2 (1966), 7–19.
Background to the Hong Kong Faith and Order consultation on "Confessing the Faith in Asia Today."

———. "The Evangelistic Situation and the Confessing Church in Asia Today," *SEAJT*, VIII, 4 (1967), 29–33.

———, ed. *Some Asian Orders of Worship*. Singapore: *SEAJT*, 1966.
With little that is distinctively "Asian," this modest effort reflects the strong Western influence in Asian worship.

Gensichen, Hans-Werner. " 'Einheimische' Theologie und ökumenische Verantwortung," *TS*, I, 15–31.

———, Rosenkranz, Gerhard, and Vicedom, Georg F., eds. *Theologische Stimmen aus Asien, Afrika und Lateinamerika*. 3 vols. Munich: Chr. Kaiser Verlag, 1965–68. (Abbreviation: *TS*.) Vol. I; "Das Problem einer 'einheimischen' Theologie," 1965; Vol. II: "Beiträge zur biblischen Theologie," 1967; Vol. III: "Beiträge zur systematischen Theologie," 1968.

Gracias, Valerian Cardinal. "Christianity and Asian Cultures," *TAN*, VIII, 3 (1971), 3–29.
The president of the Episcopal Conference of India shows how Christian influence has played a part in the rise and growth of national movements in Asia.

Hallencreutz, Carl F. *Kraemer towards Tambaram. A Study in Hendrik Kraemer's Missionary Approach*. (Studia Missionalia Upsaliensia, VII.) Lund: Gleerup, 1966.
Important for an understanding of the earlier challenge to which the emerging "Christian theology of Asian religions" is a response.

Hargreaves, Cecil. *Asian Christian Thinking: Studies in a Metaphor and Its Message.* Delhi: ISPCK, 1972.
A survey of Christian life and thought in Asia, illustrated from contemporary writers.

Harms, Hans Heinrich. *Bekenntniss und Kircheneinheit bei den jungen Kirchen.* Berlin: Lettner-Verlag, 1952.

Heim, Kenneth E. "A Theological Orientation to the Problems of Indigenization," *NEAJT*, no. 3 (1969), 127–41.

Heinrichs, Maurus. *Katholische Theologie und asiatisches Denken.* Mainz: Matthias-Grünewald-Verlag, 1963. French tr., *Théologie Catholique et Pensée Asiatique.* Tournai: Casterman, 1965.

———. "Cultural Perspectives in Presenting the Faith," *TAN*, IV, 2 (1967), 144–61.
Part I of a paper on the theme, "True and False Adaptation of the Christian Message." One of the very best treatments of this subject.

———. "An Attempt at a Systematic Theology Along Eastern Lines of Thought," *TAN*, IV, 3 (1967), 327–39.
Part II of the previous paper. Emphasizes that theologizing in Asia must begin with the doctrine of man.

Henkel, Willi. "Das Echo einheimischer Theologen auf das II. Vatikanische Konzil in afrikanischen und asiatischen Zeitschriften," *NZM*, XXVIII, 2 (1972), 95–107.

Holth, Sverre. "Towards an Indigenous Theology," *CF*, XI, 4 (1968), 5–26.
Starts "with the fundamental facts of the Asian interpretation of existence and the universe."

Howell, Barbara and Leon. *Southeast Asians Speak Out: Hope and Despair in Many Lands.* New York: Friendship Press, 1975.

King, Winston L. *Buddhism and Christianity: Some Bridges of Understanding.* Philadelphia: Westminster Press, 1962.
A contribution to the theology of dialogue. See review by E. D. Mendis, *IES*, IX, 4 (1970), 231–39.

Knight, George F. "From Hebrew to Chinese," *SEAJT*, III, 4 (1962), 51–54.
"It may well be that the East has been chosen to formulate a Christology that will meet the needs not just of the East, but of the West as well."

Koyama, Kosuke. *Five Minute Theology.* Singapore: SPCK Bookstore, 1972.
"A collection of short theological stories written for Asian theological students . . . to initiate discussion." Samples: "Beauty Salon Jesus," "Do As a Buddhist Does," "Helicopter History," and "Theology in South East Asia."

———. *Pilgrim or Tourist?* Singapore: CCA, 1974.
A collection of fifty short theological meditations. This is an enlarged edition of *Five Minute Theology.*

———. *Theology in Contact.* Madras: CLS, 1975.
Six meditations in contact with the Asian context.

———. "Appetiser and Main Course," *Frontier* (London), XII, 3 (1969), 193–96.

A Japanese theologian who taught theology in Thailand and then became director of the ATSSEA and dean of the SEA Graduate School of Theology, based in Singapore, sees Western theology in South East Asia as a mere "appetizer" to the "main course"—theology which accommodates Christ to South East Asians.

———. "Christian Presence in the Light of Our Theme 'In Him All Things Hold Together,' " *SEAJT*, X, 1 (1968), 12–22.

———. "Christianity Suffers from 'Teacher Complex,' " pp. 70–75 in *Mission Trends No. 2*. Edited by Gerald H. Anderson and Thomas F. Stransky. New York: Paulist Press; and Grand Rapids, Mich.: Eerdmans, 1975.

———. "God Is Disturbed," *Frontier*, VII, 2 (1964), 107–10.

———. " 'Gun' and 'Ointment' in Asia," pp. 43–55 in *The Future of the Christian World Mission*. Edited by William J. Danker and Wi Jo Kang. Grand Rapids, Mich.: Eerdmans, 1971.

———. " 'Imitatio Christi' in Luther's Theology of Faith," *IJT*, XII, 2 (1963), 59–65.

———. "The Mad Man Sits Down," *SEAJT*, XIV, 2 (1973), 3–12.

———. "Missiology in South East Asia," *SEAJT*, X, 2 & 3 (1968/1969), 3–8.

———. " 'Not By Bread Alone': How Does Jesus Free and Unite Us?" *ER*, XXVII, 3 (1975), 201–11.

———. "Theological Statement," *IRM*, LXII, 246 (1973), 224–25.
At the Bangkok 1972 conference on "Salvation Today."

———. "Theology in the Time of Acute Complexity in History," *SEAJT*, XII, 2 (1971), 5–9.
The revolutionary ferment in Asia today offers the greatest single challenge to Asian theologians to root the Gospel in their own cultural milieu.

Kraemer, Hendrik. *Uit de Nalatenschap van Dr. H. Kraemer*. Edited by B.J. Brouwer, E. Jansen Schoonhoven, and S.C. Graaf van Randwijck. Kampen: Kok, 1970.
See especially Kraemer's "Het Evangelie in Asie," pp. 40–46; and "De Theologische Problematiek der Jonge Kerken," pp. 47–69.

———. "The Encounter Between East and West in the Civilization of Our Time," pp. 92–107 in *The Ecumenical Era in Church and Society*. Edited by Edward J. Jurji. New York: Macmillan, 1959.

———. "Kort Apercu van Schuurman's Javaanse Geloofsleer," pp. 201–210 in *Over Alle Bergen . . . B.M. Schuurman*. The Hague: Dammen, 1951.
A study of the effort of a Dutch missionary who went to Java in 1922 to develop a Christian theology with Javanese cultural categories.

Manikam, Rajah B., ed. *Christianity and the Asian Revolution*. New York: Friendship Press, 1954.
Dated, but still useful symposium.

Meyer, Heinrich. *Bekenntnisbindung und Bekenntnisbildung in jungen Kirchen*. Gütersloh: Bertelsmann, 1953.

Miller, Randolph C. "Some Asian Contributions to Christian Education," *SEAJT*, XII (1970), 3–13.

Summary, with reflections, on some thirty-one papers prepared by Asian Christian educators at the Ninth Theological Study Institute, Singapore, summer of 1970.

Minz, Nirmal. "Theologies of Dialoque—A Critique," *RS*, XIV, 2 (1967), 7–20.

Discusses the approaches of Devanandan, Niles, Panikkar, and others.

Missionary Service in Asia Today. A Report on a Consultation Held by the Asia Methodist Advisory Committee, Feb. 18–23, 1971, in cooperation with the EACC. Hong Kong: Chinese Christian Literature Council, 1971.

Includes the address of Emerito P. Nacpil in which he said, "The most *missionary* service a missionary under the present system can do today in Asia is to go home!"

Mooneyham, W. Stanley, ed. *Christ Seeks Asia*. Official Reference Volume, Papers and Reports, Asia-South Pacific Congress on Evangelism, Singapore 1968. Hong Kong: Rock House Publishers, 1969.

Sponsored by the Billy Graham Evangelistic Association as a regional follow-up to the 1966 Berlin World Congress on Evangelism, attended by 1,100 conservative evangelicals. See review article by Gerald H. Anderson in *Encounter*, XXXII, 2 (1971), 156–58.

Müller-Krüger, Theodor. "Theologia in loco? Erwägungen zur theologischen Ausbildung in Indonesien," pp. 313–25 in *Basileia, Walter Freytag zum 60. Geburtstag*. Edited by Jan Hermelink and Hans Jochen Margull. Stuttgart: Evangelischer Missionsverlag, 1959.

———. "The Cultural Orientation of Theological Education," *SEAJT*, VI, 3 (1965), 59–73.

"Our attempt is to emancipate Asian and African theological education from its Western bonds . . . in order to release it for its own encounters."

Nakamura, Hajime. *Ways of Thinking of Eastern Peoples: India, China, Tibet, Japan*. Rev. English tr. edited by Philip P. Wiener. Honolulu: East-West Center Press, 1964. This is the basic book on the subject.

NEAJT. No. 3 (1969).

Special issue on "Toward a Theology of Indigenization," with articles by Sung Bum Yun, Yoshio Noro, Kazoh Kitamori, Pong Nang Park, and Kano Yamamoto.

———. No. 7 (1971).

Special issue on "Living Theology in Today's Northeast Asia," including articles by Yong Ok Kim, Nobuo Kobashi, Chung Choon Kim, and Takeshi Takasaki.

Needham, Joseph. "Christianity and the Asian Cultures," *Theology* (London), LXV, 503, (1962), 180–88.

Neuner, Joseph, ed. *Christian Revelation and World Religions*. London: Burns & Oates,

1967. These papers were first published in a special number of *IES*, IV, 3–4 (1965). Extremely important papers by Hans Küng, Piet Fransen, Joseph Masson, and Raymond Panikkar, from a conference at Bombay in 1964.

Nicholls, Bruce. "Toward an Asian Theology of Mission," *Evangelical Missions Quarterly*, VI, 2 (1970), 65–78.
Appeals for an Asian confession of the Gospel and for a more serious involvement in dialogue, while maintaining an infallibility theory of the Christian scriptures.

Ohm, Thomas. *Asia Looks at Western Christianity*. New York: Herder and Herder, 1959. English tr. by Irene Marinoff of *Asiens Kritik am Abendländischen Christentum*. Munich; Kösel Verlag, 1948.

———. *Die Christliche Theologie in asiatischer Sicht*. Münster: Aschendorffsche Verlag, 1949.

Oosthuizen, G.C. *Theological Battleground in Asia and Africa*. London: Hurst; and New York: Humanities Press, 1972.
Devotes three-fourths of its discussion to issues and theological currents of Protestantism in Asia. A revision of the author's influential dissertation-book, *Theological Discussions and Confessional Developments in the Churches of Asia and Africa* (Franeker: Wever, 1958).

Panikkar, Raymond. "The Church and the World Religions," *RS*, XIV, 2 (1967), 59–63.
"There is no such thing as 'non-Christian religions' . . . Any man who lives his own religion adheres, even if he does not know it, to Christ."

———. "Indirect Methods in the Missionary Apostolate: Some Theological Reflections," *IJT*, XIX, 3 & 4 (1970), 111–13.
Argues against "indirect methods" aimed at conversion, as contrary to the spirit of the Gospel.

Parrinder, Geoffrey. *The Christian Debate: Light from the East*. London: Victor Gollancz, 1964.
Suggests that Christianity can be universal only if it can be recognized that it is Asian and if it can also assimilate Oriental religions.

Rayan, Samuel. "Mission After Vatican II: Problems and Positions," *IRM*, LIX, 236 (1970), 414–26.
An Indian Jesuit theologian uses the work of Vatican II for a challenging new missiological approach.

Reichelt, Karl L. *Meditation and Piety in the Far East*. New York: Harpers, 1954.

Rogers, C. Murray. "Worship and Contemporary Asian Man," *RS*, XVI, 2 (1969), 51–63.

Rosin, H.H. "Theologia in loco en in oecumenisch verband," *Wereld en Zending*, I, 1 (1972), 31–43.

Rossman, Vern. "The Breaking in of the Future: The Problem of Indigenization and Cultural Synthesis," *IRM*, LII, 206 (1963), 129–43.

In the same issue M.M. Thomas wrote a comment, "Indigenization and the Renaissance of Traditional Cultures," pp. 191–94.

Samartha, Stanley J. " . . . And Ideologies," *ER*, XXIV, 4 (1972), 479–86.

————. "Christian Study Centres and Asian Churches," *IRM*, 234 (1970), 173–79.

————. "Dialogue as a Continuing Christian Concern," *ER*, XXIII, 2 (1971), 129–42. Reprinted in *Mission Trends No. 1*. Edited by Gerald H. Anderson and Thomas F. Stransky. New York: Paulist Press; and Grand Rapids, Mich.: Eerdmans, 1974.

————. "Dialogue: Significant Issues in the Continuing Debate," *ER*, XXIV, 3 (1972), 327–40.

————. "Mission and Movements of Innovation," *Missiology* (Pasadena), III, 2 (1975), 143–54. "The name of 'Christ' biblically and theologically cannot be restricted to the historical figure of Jesus of Nazareth."

————. "*More* than an Encounter of Commitments," *IRM*, LIX, 236 (1970), 392–403. An interpretation of the Ajaltoun Consultation on "Dialogue between Men of Living Faiths."

————. "The Progress and Promise of Inter-religious Dialogue," *JES*, IX, 3 (1972), 463–74.

————. "The Quest for Salvation and the Dialogue Between Religions," *IRM*, LVII, 228 (1968), 424–32.

————. "Religious Pluralism and the Quest for Human Community," pp. 129–48 in *No Man is Alien. Essays on the Unity of Mankind*. Edited by J. Robert Nelson. Leiden: Brill, 1971.

————. "The WCC and Men of Other Faiths and Ideologies," *ER*, XXII, 3 (1970), 191–98.

————, ed. *Dialogue Between Men of Living Faiths*. Geneva: WCC, 1971. Papers presented at a consulation held at Ajaltoun, Lebanon, March 1970.

————, ed. *Living Faiths and the Ecumenical Movement*. Geneva: WCC, 1971. See especially the chronology and bibliography for the study on "The Word of God and the Living Faiths of Men," pp. 165–82. Dr. Samartha, an Indian theologian, is an associate secretary in the Department on Studies in Mission and Evangelism, WCC.

————, ed. *Living Faiths and Ultimate Goals. Salvation and World Religions*. Maryknoll, N.Y.: Orbis Books, 1975. Persons of differing religious and ideological persuasions writing on "What is the ultimate goal of human life?"

Scherer, James A. *Mission and Unity in Lutheranism*. Philadelphia: Fortress Press, 1969. Includes important treatment of confession and ecumenicity in Asia. Bibliography.

————. "The Confessions of the Younger Church with Particular Reference to the

Problem of Christian Unity in Asia," pp. 148–61 in *The Church and the Confessions*. Edited by Vilmos Vajta and Hans Weissgerber. Philadelphia: Fortress Press, 1963.
Discusses the role of confessions and doctrine in the life of Lutheran churches in Asia.

Schilling, S. Paul. "Emerging Ecumenical Theology in South East Asia," *SEAJT*, XII (1971), 65–73.

———. "Living Theology in Southeast Asia," *RL*, XXXIX, 3 (1970), 334–45.
Examines the thought of "three alert theologians of Southeast Asia": Emerito P. Nacpil, Kosuke Koyama, and Choan-seng Song.

Schultz, Hans Jürgen, ed. *Tendenzen der Theologie im 20 Jahrhundert. Eine Geschichte in Porträts*. Stuttgart: Kreuz-Verlag, 1966.
Includes essays on the theology of two Asian Christian theologians: D.T. Niles (by John R. Fleming, pp. 543–48), and Paul Devanandan (by M.M. Thomas; pp. 466–69).

Sovik, Arne, ed. "Confessions and Churches. An Afro-Asian Symposium," *LW*, V, 4 (1959), 363–74.
Opinions on Lutheranism and the missionary movement by younger church leaders.

Takenaka, Masao, ed. *Christian Art in Asia*. Tokyo: Kyo Bun Kwan with CCA, 1975.
Indigenous Christian art by 108 Asian artists from 18 countries, with interpretation and bibliography by the editor.

To, Thi Anh. *Eastern and Western Cultural Values. Conflict or Harmony?* Manila: East Asian Pastoral Institute, 1975.
Dr. To, a South Vietnamese woman, seeks to bridge the gap between East and West, by helping each to understand the thought, the values, the philosophy of the other.

Veitch, J.A. "Is An Asian Theology Possible?" *SJT*, XXVIII, 1 (1975), 27–43.

Visser 't Hooft, W. A. "Accommodation—True and False," *SEAJT*, VIII, 3 (1967), 5–18. Also published in *Japan Missionary Bulletin*, XXII (1968), 30–36.
One of the John R. Mott Memorial Lectures at the EACC Faith and Order Conference in Hong Kong, 1966. Agrees with M.M. Thomas, as against Arend Th. van Leeuwen, concerning the interaction of traditional and modern factors, making accommodation always a dynamic task.

———. "Asian Churches," *ER*, II, 3 (1950), 229–40.

———. "Asian Issues in the Ecumenical Setting," pp. 59–71, and "The Significance of the Asian Churches in the Ecumenical Movement," pp. 46–58 in *A Decisive Hour for the Christian Mission*. Edited by Norman Goodall. London: SCM Press, 1960.
John R. Mott Memorial Lectures at the EACC Assembly in Kuala Lumpur in 1959.

Weber, Hans-Ruedi. *Asia and the Ecumenical Movement, 1895–1961*. London: SCM Press, 1966.
Defines and discusses the Asian element and experience in the ecumenical movement; full bibliography. A basic study.

Williams, Daniel Day. "The Advancement of Theological Education in Asia," *SEAJT*, XII, 1 (1970), 52–64.

IV. Burma

Chain, Anna May. "Entmythologisierung und Birma," *TS*, II, 70–79.

Clasper, Paul D. "Buddhism and Christianity in the Light of God's Revelation in Christ," *SEAJT*, III, 1 (1961), 8–18. Also in *RS*, VII, 4 (1961), 28–37.
Moves beyond mere comparison to the concern for how Buddhism can be seen as an authentic human response to divine revelation.

————. "The Buddhist-Christian Encounter in Burma," *OB*, X, 4 (1959), 1–10.

Hmyin, U Ba. "Each in His Own Native Tongue," *Church and Society* (EACC), no. 4 (1962), 35–38.
Part of a sermon delivered at the opening service of the WCC Third Assembly in New Delhi, 1961.

Huang, Hsing-peng. "Power and Justice," *SEAJT*, VII, 4 (1966), 58–65.

Kio, Stephen Hre. "The Doctrine of the Last Things," *SEAJT*, VII, 4 (1966), 58–65.

SEAJT. "Special Burma Issue," VII, 4 (1966).

Shearburn, V.G. "Spirituality: Buddhist and Christian," *SEAJT*, VII, 4 (1966), 6–14.

Than, U Kyaw. "Man in Buddhism and Christianity," *SEAJT*, III, (1961), 19–24.

————. "The Christian Laity in Asia," *SEAJT*, III, 3 (1962), 49–59.

————. "Unity," *SEAJT*, III, 2 (1961), 22–26.

Tin, Pe Maung. "Certain Factors in the Buddhist-Christian Encounter," *SEAJT*, III, 2 (1961), 27–33.

————. "The Study of Buddhism in Burma," *SEAJT*, I, 3 (1960), 60–62.

Wah, Thramu Eh. "The Word of God," *SEAJT*, VII, 4 (1966), 15–21.

Yin, Daw Myat. "The Doctrine of the Lord's Supper," *SEAJT*, VII, 4 (1966), 37–48.

V. China, Hong Kong, and Taiwan

Baker, Gilbert. "The Hand of God in Chinese Religious Experience," *CF*, IX, 3 (1966), 24–35.

Beeby, H.D. "Incarnating the Gospel—An Old Testament Approach," *TC*, VI, 1 & 2 (1966), 4–12.
"Our need to reincarnate the gospel in the 'flesh' of 20th-century Taiwan . . . requires a borrowing of elements similar in character to Israel's borrowing three millenia earlier."

Berndt, Manfred. "Servanthood Among Para-Christian and Non-Christian Religions in Hong Kong," *CF*, XIV, 4 (1971), 157–82.

Brandauer, Frederick P. "Selected Works of Lao She and Mao Tun and Their Relevance for Christian Theology," *CF*, XI, 2 (1968), 24–43.
A discussion of the writings of the two leading novelists in modern China.

Bush, Richard C. *Religion in Communist China*. Nashville, Tenn. Abingdon Press, 1971.
  By the former director of Tao Fong Shan, Hong Kong, the book includes a
  discussion of Christianity in China.

———. "Communication in Context," *CF*, IX, 1 (1965), 9–18.
  Effective Christian communication depends on how much Christians are willing to accept the fact that cultural values are powerful factors in Asian religions.

———. "Incarnating the Gospel in Chinese Tradition," *TC*, VII, 4 (1968), 29–46.

Chao, Andrew. "A New Catechism for Taiwan," *TAN*, VI, 1 (1969), 80–89.
  Intended for adults, to replace the official Shanghai Catechism in use since 1924;
  Chinese classics and proverbs are cited in suitable places throughout the new
  text.

———. "The New Chinese Catechism: An Experiment in Bringing the Message of the
  Gospel to Our People," *TAN*, VIII, 4 (1971), 10–24.
  Describes the new Catholic catechism for Chinese adults, published in an
  experimental edition.

Chao, Jonathan Tien-en. "Some Ideas on the Direction of Chinese Theological Development," *OB*, XX, 6 (1969), 1–14.
  With five pages of bibliography.

Chao, T.C. "Revelation," pp. 24–62 in *The Authority of the Faith* (Tambaram Madras
  Series, Vol. I). London: Oxford University Press, 1939.
  An early indication of Asian resistance and reaction to the Barth–Kraemer
  views. See the article below by Ng, Lee-ming on Chao's thought.

Chen, David S.C. "The Church in the Secularized World," *NEAJT*, no. 4 (1969),
  21–34.
  Appreciates the Biblical bases of the adulthood of the world and the nonreli-
  gious interpretation of the Christian Gospel.

———. "The Task of Theological Education in Northeast Asia Today: Viewed from a
  Theological Angle," *NEAJT*, no. 7 (1971), 17–8.

Chow, Lien-hwa. "The Minister as Theologian," *SEAJT*, III, 4 (1962), 16–24.
  By a professor at the Baptist Theological College, Taipei; makes the point that
  indigenization must be accomplished collectively.

Coe, Shoki. (See also C.H. Hwang.) "Text and Context," *NEAJT*, no. 1 (1968),
  126–31.
  Keynote address at the formation of the Northeast Asia Association of Theological Schools.

Eilert, Haakan. *Boundlessness. Studies in Karl Ludwig Reichelt's Missionary Thinking with
  Special Regard to the Buddhist-Christian Encounter*. (Series Studio Missionalia XXIV,
  Uppsala, Sweden.) Aarhus, Denmark: Forlaget Aros, 1974.

Elwood, Douglas J. "Christian Theology in an Asian Setting: The Gospel and Chinese
  Intellectual Culture," *SEAJT*, XVI, 2, (1975).

The Faith of the Catholic Church ("The Chinese Catechism"). Taipei: Catholic Book
  Center, 1972.

First edition in English of the new catechism for Chinese Catholic adults.

Fang, Mark Che-yong. "The Catholic Church in China: Present Situation and Future Prospects," pp. 55–77 in *Re-thinking the Church's Mission*. Edited by Karl Rahner. New York: Paulist Press, 1966.

————. "The Church as a Living Community in the New Testament," *TAN*, VII, 2 (1970), 127–39.
A position paper at the Pastoral Workshop in Tainan, held in 1969, on the theme "Indigenization—the Church as Living Community."

Feng, Shang-li. "The Chinese Church and Chinese Culture," *CF*, XI, 2 (1968), 5–19.
Concerned with points of conflict and harmony between Christianity and Chinese religions; a "hidden monotheism" is discerned in ancient Chinese thought.

————. "The Contours of a Chinese Theology," *CF*, XIII, 1 (1970), 16.
Briefly suggests a blending of Christian and Confucian thought and ethics.

Hsiao, Ching-fen. "Some Issues Raised by the Polemical Writings of Buddhists and Christians Against Each Other in Taiwan," *SEAJT*, XI (1969), 52–63.

Hu, Chung-yuan. "Why Did the Word Have to Become Flesh?" *SEAJT*, VI, 3 (1965), 9–14.

Huang, Chu-yih. "The Christian Understanding of History," *TC*, I, 1 (1957), 110–58.

Hwang, C.H. (See also Shoki Coe.) *Joint Action for Mission in Formosa. A Call for Advance into a New Era*. (C.W.M.E. Research Pamphlets, no. 15.) Geneva: WCC; and New York: Friendship Press, 1968.

————. "Come, Creator Spirit! For the Calling of the Churches Together," *ER*, XVI, 5 (1964), 485–99.

————. "Confessing the Faith in Asia," *SEAJT*, VIII, 1 & 2 (1966), 65–86.

————. "Conversion in the Perspective of Three Generations," *ER*, XIX, 3 (1967), 285–90.

————. "God's People in Asia Today," *SEAJT*, V, 2 (1963), 5–17.
Discusses the relevance of "Christ's revolution" to Asia's social, political, and religious revolutionary ferment today.

————. "The Life and Mission of the Church in the World," *SEAJT*, VI, 2 (1964), 11–38.
Address at the World Institute on Christian Education, Queen's University, Belfast, Ireland, July 1962.

————. "A Rethinking of Theological Training for the Ministry in the Younger Churches Today," *SEAJT*, IV, 2 (1962), 7–34.
A perceptive analysis of the problem of imported patterns of Christian ministry in Asia, and the theological and sociocultural reasons why the Asian churches must be free of these patterns.

Jones, Francis P. "Theological Thinking in the Chinese Protestant Church Under Communism," *RL*, XXXII, 4 (1963), 534–46.

———, ed. *Documents of the Three-Self Movement. Source Materials for the Study of the Protestant Church in Communist China.* New York: NCC, 1963.
> Basic materials on the China Christian Three-Self patriotic movement which undertook overall authority of Protestant churches in China after 1949.

Kraemers, R.P. "Changing Chinese Identity: From Cultural Totality to Nation Among Nations," *SEAJT*, I, 4 (1960), 31–43.

———. "Relevant Theology," *SEAJT*, I, 2 (1959), 45–49.

Lai, En-tse. "The Task of a Church Historian in Formosa: Church History as a History of Encounter," *SEAJT*, III, 4 (1962), 42–50.

Lee, Peter K.H. "A Christian Attitude toward Traditional Chinese Culture," *CF* XVII, 4 (1974), 171–80.

———. "Editorial: Is the Stage Set for Chinese Theology?" *CF*, XVIII, 1 (1975), 3–6.

———. "Indigenous Theology—Over-Cropped Land or Underdeveloped Field?" *CF*, XVII, 1 (1974), 5–17.

Lin, Timothy Tian-min. "The Concept of Man in Confucianism and Christianity," *NEAJT*, no. 14 (March 1975), 20–24.

———. "The Confucian Concept of *Jen* and the Christian Concept of Love," *CF*, XV, 3 (1972), 162–72.

———. "Confucian Filial Piety and Christian Faith," *JCQ*, XXXVII, 4 (1971), 203–15.

Lin, Yu-tang. *From Pagan to Christian.* New York: World Publishing Co., 1959.
> Attempts to understand Christianity in the light of Confucian, Taoist, and Buddhist philosophies.

Lutheran World Federation and Pro Mundi Vita. *Theological Implications of the New China.* Geneva and Brussels: LWF/PMV, 1974.
> Papers presented at the ecumenical seminar held in Bastad, Sweden, Jan. 29 to Feb. 2, 1974. Includes essays by C.T. Hu, Julia Ching, Winfried Glüer, C.S. Song, Donald E. MacInnis, Joseph Spae, Richard Madsen, and others.

———. *Christian Faith and the Chinese Experience.* Geneva and Brussels: LWF/PMV, 1974.
> Papers and reports from an ecumenical colloquium held in Louvain, Belgium, September 9 to 14, 1974. See especially the report of Workshop II on "Faith and Ideology in the Context of the New China"; reprinted in *CF*, XVII, 4 (1974), 181–88.

MacInnis, Donald E. *Religious Policy and Practice in Communist China. A Documentary History.* New York: Macmillan; and London: Hodder and Stoughton, 1972.
> While not focused on Christian theological construction, it contains all the significant documentary materials on religion in mainland China that have appeared since 1949.

Miao, Chester S., ed. *Christian Voices in China*. New York: Friendship Press, 1948. Dated but still useful, includes essays by T.C. Chao and Y.T. Wu.

Ng, Lee-ming. "A Bibliography of T.C. Chao and Y.T. Wu," *CF*, XVI, 3 & 4 (1973), 166–77.

———. "Dialogue—A Reappraisal of Priorities," *CF*, XIV, 3 (1971), 89–91. Reflects some reservations concerning the stance that dialogue requires of the Christian.

———. "An Evaluation of T.C. Chao's Thought," *CF*, XIV, 1 & 2 (1971), 5–59. Chao was one of the first presidents of the WCC.

———. "A Study of Y.T. Wu," *CF*, XV, 1 (1972), 5–54. A controversial leader of the Three-Self Movement.

———. "Wang Ming-tao: An Evaluation of His Thought and Action," *CF*, XVI, 2 (1973), 51–80. A popular preacher, writer, and opponent of the Three-Self Movement.

Pan, James Ying-kau. "Dialogue—Some Reflections," *CF*, XIV, 3 (1971), 77–88. A minister of the Chinese Methodist church responds positively to the WCC studies on "Dialogue with Men of Other Faiths," pointing up the "latent Christ" theme for Asians.

———. "Myths and Demythologizing—New Myths or Old?" *SEAJT*, II, 3 (1961), 31–38.

Pro Mundi Vita. *China and the Churches in the Making of One World. (PMV-Bulletin*, no. 55). Brussels: PMV, 1975.

———. *The Louvain Consultation on China: Essential Documents. (PMV-Bulletin*, no. 54). Brussels: PMV, 1975. Gives introductory addresses, workshop reports, and appendix, from ecumenical colloquium held in Louvain, September 1974. See Lutheran World Federation/Pro Mundi Vita volumes listed above.

Smith, Carl T. "Radical Theology and the Confucian Tradition," *CF*, X, 4 (1967), 20–33. "The formulation of humanism within the Chinese tradition provides one perspective by which to view the Christian humanism of radical theology."

Song, Choan-seng. "An Analysis of Contemporary Chinese Culture and Its Implications for the Task of Theology," *SEAJT*, IV, 4 (1963), 9–25. German tr. "Die zeitgenössische chinesische Kultur und ihre Bedeutung für die Aufgabe der Theologie," *TS*, I, 52–72. Dr. Song opts for a process of "incarnating" the Gospel in Asian cultures, since "indigenization" leads to abuse when understood superficially.

———. "The Christian Ministry and Theological Education," *SEAJT*, VII, 1 (1965), 73–78.

———. "The Christological Reality of the Event of Faith," *NEAJT*, no. 2 (1969), 61–69.

———. "Confessing the Faith in Today's World," *SEAJT*, VIII, 1 & 2 (1966), 95–107. Also revised and enlarged version in *TC*, VI, 1 & 2 (1966), 13–34.

———. "Culture and Incarnation," *PA*, XI, 3 (1964), 138–41.

———. "Development: Christian Dilemma and Responsibility," *NEAJT*, no. 9 (1972), 53–64.

———. "Election for Mission," *SEAJT*, XIII, 2 (1972), 40–48.

———. "Hope in Christ—Its Authentification in Asia," *IRM*, LXIV, 253 (1975), 4–12.

———. "Man and the Redemption of the World," *SEAJT*, II, 4 (1961), 63–73.

———. "New China and Salvation History—A Methodological Enquiry," *SEAJT*, XV, 2 (1974), 52–67.

———. "The Obedience of Theology in Asia," *SEAJT*, II, 2 (1960), 7–15.

———. "The Possibility of an Analogical Discourse on God," *SEAJT*, VII, 2 (1965), 55–76.

———. "The Role of Christology in the Christian Encounter with Eastern Religions," *SEAJT*, V, 3 (1964), 13–31. German tr. "Die Bedeutung der Christologie in der christlichen Begegnung mit dem östlichen Religionen," *TS*, III, 86–111.

———. "Theological Education and Diversified Ministries," *IRM*, LVI, 222 (1967), 167–72

———. "Theological Education—A Search for a New Breakthrough," *SEAJT*, IX, 4 (1968), 5–16; also in *NEAJT*, no. 1 (1968), 22–35.

———. "Theologia Viatorum," *SEAJT*, VII, 1 (1965), 115–28.
A "theology of the way" is one that is flexible and mobile in terms of method, without compromising the absolute nature of the *kerygma*.

———. "Whither Protestantism in Asia Today?" *SEAJT*, XI, (Spring 1970), 66–76.
Raises the question, "Is Protestantism in Asia open and ready for re-formation?"

———. "The Witness to Christ in the World of Religions and Cultures," *SEAJT*, II, 3 (1961), 20–25.

Thomas, M.M. "K.H. Ting's Theology of Society," *Church and Society* (EACC), no. 1 (September 1960), 32–36.

Thomson, Alan. "Christianity and Imperialism: The Chinese Example," *SEAJT*, XIII, 1 (1971), 89–101.
Are missionaries imperialistic? In terms of imperialistic ends, no. As regards means, admittedly yes, at times.

Thornberry, Mike. "The Encounter of Christianity and Confucianism: How Modern Confucianism Views the Encounter," *SEAJT*, X, 1 (1968), 47–62.

Ting, K.H. "Christian Theism," *SW*, LI, 4 (1958), 373–88.
An address by the president of Nanking Theological Seminary to the student body on June 12, 1957.

———. "The Church's Mission in the Secular Movements of the People," *Church and Society* (EACC), no. 4 (March, 1962), 56–58.

——. "The Task of the Church in Asia," *SW*, XLII, 3 (1949), 235–48.

Ting, Simon. "Rufus Jones and Lao Tzu," *CF*, VIII, 3 & 4 (1964), 31–56.
Comparative study of Eastern and Western types of mysticism.

Wang, Hsien-chih. "Evangelism in Taiwan Today: Obstacles and Opportunities," *CF*, XVIII, 1 (1975), 49–56.

Wu, John C. H. *Chinese Humanism and Christian Spirituality*. Edited by Paul K. T. Sih. Jamaica, N.Y.: St. John's University Press, 1965.
Includes useful chapters such as: "Christianity, the Only Synthesis Really Possible Between East and West"; "Technology and Christian Culture: An Oriental View"; "St. Therese and Lao Tzu: A Study in Comparative Mysticism"; and "Water and Wine: Chinese Ethics and Christian Faith."

Yeow, Choo Lak. "Philosophy and Theology," *SEAJT*, IX, 4 (1968), 68–71, and X, 1 (1968), 34–38.

Zia, N. Z. *Christianity and Chinese Thinking*. Singapore: Chinese Christian Literature Council for the ATSSEA, n.d.

——. "The Common Ground of the Three Chinese Religions," *CF*, IX, 2 (1966), 17–34.
Sees the concepts of the "Mean" and "Mutuality" as the common ground in terms of which Chinese Christian theology should be written.

VI. India

Abhishiktananda, Swami. *The Church in India*. Madras: CLS, 1969.
An essay in Christian self-criticism, by a French Catholic monk.

Amaladoss, M. A. "Towards an Indian Christian Spirituality," *RS*, XVI, 2 (1969), 6–25.
A Jesuit proposing an Indian Christian spirituality along the lines of "Christian renunciation," "Divine indwelling," and "Christian Yoga."

Appasamy, A. J. *The Gospel and India's Heritage*. London: SPCK, 1942.
Jesus's teaching, described on the background of Hindu teaching on the same.

——. *My Theological Quest*. Bangalore: CISRS, 1964. German tr. "Erwägungen zu einer indischen Theologie," *TS*, I, 83–98.

——. "Christian Theology in India," *IRM*, XXXVIII, 150 (1949), 149–55.

——. "Christological Reconstruction and Ramanuja's Philosophy," *IRM*, XLI, 162 (1952), 170–76.

——. "Warum 'indische' Theologie?" *NZM*, VI, 3 (1964), 343–59.

Arapura, J. G. "The Effects of Colonialism upon the Asian Understanding of Man," pp. 109–28 in *No Man Is Alien*. Edited by J. Robert Nelson. Leiden: Brill, 1971.

Ariarajah, S. Wesley. "Chenchiah's Christology," *BTF*, II, 1 (1968), 47–61.

Asirvatham, Eddy. *Christianity in the Indian Crucible*. 2nd rev. ed. Calcutta: YMCA, 1957.
The three chapters especially significant are (V) "Rethinking Christian Theol-

ogy in India"; (VI), "An Indigenous Christianity"; and (VII), "Indigenous Evangelism." Substantial bibliography.

——. *The Evolution of My Social Thinking.* (Indian Christian Thought Series, no. 10.) Madras, CLS, 1970.

Athyal, Saphir P. "Israel Amid the Nations: A Confrontation of Faiths," *RS*, XIV, 1 (1967), 21–30.

Baago, Kaj. *The Movement Around Subba Rao.* Madras: CLS, 1968.

——. *Pioneers of Indigenous Christianity.* (Confessing the Faith in India, no. 4.) Madras: CLS–CISRS, 1969.
     Studies early attempts at indigenous theological construction in India.

——. "The Post-Colonial Crisis of Missions," *IRM*, LV, 219 (1966), 322–32 and LVI, 221 (1967), 99–103.
     See comments on Baago's views by Ian H. Douglas and John B. Carman in *IRM*, LV, 220 (1966), 483–89; and by M.M. Thomas in *RS*, XVIII, 1 (1971), 64–70.

——. "Ram Mohan Roy's Christology—An Early Attempt at Demythologization," *BTF*, I, 1 (1967), 30–42.

Bergquist, J. A. "Baptism in the Context of Christian Mission," *IJT*, XVI, 3 (1967), 180–86.

Blanchard M. "Christianity as Fulfillment and Anti-Thesis," *IJT*, XVII, 1 (1968), 5–20.

Boyd, Robin H. S. *An Introduction to Indian Christian Theology.* Madras: CLS, 1969.
     Identifies the emergence of a genuinely Indian theology and examines the development of that theology, from De Nobili to Devanandan. Extensive bibliography.

——. *India and the Latin Captivity of the Church: The Cultural Context of the Gospel.* London: Cambridge University Press, 1974.
     Suggests that the Western church can learn from the Eastern, and must do so if it is to liberate its theological language from the traditional forms which now impede it.

——, ed. *Manilal C. Parekh and Dhanjibhai Fakirbhai.* (Library of Indian Christian Theology, no. 2.) Madras: CLS for UTC, 1974.
     Presents the work of two outstanding twentieth-century Christian theologians who were converts from Jainism and Hinduism.

——. "Indian Christian Thinking in Relation to Christ," *SJT*, XIX, 4 (1966), 446–56.

——. "An Outline of Gujarati Theological Literature," *IJT*, XII, 2 & 3 (1963). Also reprinted as an occasional Bulletin of the Theological Education Fund.
     Since 1961 Dr. Boyd has taught at the Gujarat United School of Theology, Ahmedabad, Gujarat.

——. "Some Indian Christian Interpretations of the Resurrection," *IJT*, XVII, 1 (1968), 49–61.
     Covers the interpretations of three important Indian Christian theologians: Chenchiah, Surjit Singh, and Chakkarai.

————. "The Theological Basis of the Teachings of the Lord's Supper in the North Indian Plan," *IJT*, XI, 2 (1962), 47–53.

Defends the statement on the Lord's Supper in the Plan of Church Union for North India and Pakistan, against the charges that it is "ultra-Catholic" and inconsistent with Protestant teaching and practice.

Braybrooke, Marcus. *The Undiscovered Christ: A Review of Recent Developments in the Christian Approach to the Hindu.* (Inter-religious Dialogue Series, no. 5.) Madras: CLS-CISRS, 1973.

Bürkle, Horst, ed. *Dialog mit dem Osten. Radhakrishnans neuhinduistische Botschaft im Lichte christlicher Weltsendung.* Stuttgart: Evang. Verlagswerk 1965.

Discusses Radhakrishnan's thought and suggests modifications in contemporary Christian mission theology.

————, ed. *Indische Beiträge zur Theologie der Gegenwart.* Stuttgart: Evang. Verlagswerk, 1966. English ed., *Indian Voices in Today's Theological Debate.* Lucknow: Lucknow Publishing House, 1972.

Important essays by R.H.S. Boyd, Surjit Singh, John G. Arapura, J.R. Chandran, Herbert Jai Singh, Richard W. Taylor, Klaus Klostermaier, and others.

Camps, Arnulf. "The Person and Function of Christ in Hinduism and in Hindu–Christian Theology," *Bulletin Secretariatus pro non-Christianis* (Città del Vaticano), no. 18, 1971, pp. 199–211.

————. "A Survey of Non-Western Christian Theology with Special Reference to India," *Bulletin Secretariatus pro non-Christianis*, no. 14, 1970, pp. 67–76.

Cenkner, William. "The Emergence of an Indian Christian Theology," *ZMR*, LVII, 2 (1973), 81–98.

Well-documented survey.

Chakkarai, V. *The Gospel and Indian Heritage.* New York: Macmillan, 1942.

————. "The Destiny of Man and Interpretation of History," *Madras University Journal*, XXIX, 1 (1957), 1–58.

Chandran, J. Russell. "The Christian Approach to Non-Christian Religions," pp. 185–209 in *Christianity and the Asian Revolution.* Edited by Rajah B. Manikam. New York: Friendship Press, 1954.

Dr. Chandran is principal of United Theological College, Bangalore.

————. "The Authority of the Bible for Christian Social Action," *RS*, XXI, 1 (1974), 18–35.

————. "Baptism—A Scandal or a Challenge?" *RS*, XIX, 1 (1972), 51–58.

————. "The Church in and Against Its Cultural Environment," *IRM*, XLI, 163 (1952), 257–72.

————. "Concern for Man in the Ecumenical Renewal," *RS*, XV, 1 (1968), 32–38.

————. "Confessing the Faith in Asia Today," *SEAJT*, XVIII, 1 & 2 (1966), 91–94.

————. "The Problem of Indigenization of Christian Theology in Asia," *SW*, LI, 4

(1958), 334–42. German tr. "Das Problem der 'Heimischmachung' christlicher Theologie in Asien," *TS*, I, 73–82.

———. "The Theological Task in the Indian Church," *USQR*, XX, 3 (1965), 247–59. German tr. "Die Theologische Aufgabe der indischen Kirche," pp. 152–66 in *Indische Beiträge zur Theologie der Gegenwart*. Edited by Horst Bürkle. Stuttgart: Evang. Verlagswerk, 1966.

———. "Where Other Religions Dominate," pp. 215–30 in *Christian Social Ethics in a Changing World*. Edited by John C. Bennett. New York: Association Press; and London: SCM Press, 1966.

Chatterji, Saral K. "Towards a Revolutionary Transformation of Society," *RS*, XIV, 4 (1967), 15–25, and *AF*, IV, 1 (1969), 1–12.

———, ed. *The Asian Meaning of Modernization*. Delhi: ISPCK, 1972.

———, ed. *The Legalisation of Abortion*. Madras: CLS, 1971.

Chetthimattam, John Britto. *Patterns of Indian Thought*. Maryknoll, N.Y.: Orbis Books, 1971.

———, ed. *Unique and Universal: Fundamental Problems of an Indian Theology*. Bangalore: Centre for the Study of World Religions, Dharmaram College, 1972.
      Essays resulting from a seminar of younger Indian theologians.

———. "Concept of Love in Catholic Thought," *RS*, X, 1 (1963), 21–36.

———. "An Epistemological Critique of Our Knowledge of Christ," *IJT*, XVIII, 1 (1969), 7–13.

———. "The Scope and Conditions of a Hindu-Christian Dialogue," pp. 156–78 in *The Pastoral Mission of the Church* (Concilium, vol. 3). Edited by Karl Rahner. Glen Rock, New Jersey: Paulist Press, 1965. Also in *IES*, (1964), 280–302.
      By an Indian Carmelite theologian.

"Christian Faith in the Contemporary Indian Context," *RS*, XIII, 3 (1966), 56–61.
      The findings of an NCC Consultation on "The Mission of the Church in Contemporary India."

"Christian Understanding of and Concern for Development," *RS*, XVII, 2 (1970), 4–8.
      Statement on the theology of development prepared by the All-India Christian Consultation on Development, New Delhi, February 1970.

Coaldrake, Frank. "The Concept of Man in Indian Thought," *RS*, X, 3 (1963), 14–19.

Cole, T.F. "The Expression of Alienation in Indigenous Indian Theology," *TC*, IX, 4 (1971), 20–40.

The C.S.I.—Lutheran Theological Conversations, 1948–1959. Madras: CLS, 1964.
      A selection of the papers read together with the "Agreed Statements" and appendices.

Das, R.C. *Convictions of an Indian Disciple*. (Indian Christian Thought Series, no. 6.) Bangalore: CISRS, 1966.
      By an evangelist and ashram leader who appreciates the values and deeper meanings of the sacrificial system of Hinduism.

David, P. *The Contemporary Debate on God*. Madras: CLS, 1969.
Part One deals with the historical setting and discusses the contemporary debate, and Part Two develops the "prophetic interpretation" of the "reality and life of God."

———. "The Meaning of God for Modern Man," *IJT*, XXI, 1 & 2 (1972), 1–8.

Deshphande, P.Y. "Genesis: A Hindu Reflection on the Bible," *Journal of Ecumenical Studies*, VIII, 3 (1971), 575–80.
By a Hindu student of the Hebrew-Christian Scriptures.

De Smet, R.V. "Affinities Between Guru Nanak and Jesus Christ," *IES*, VIII, 4 (1969), 260–68.

———. "Categories of Indian Philosophy and Communication of the Gospel," *RS*, X, 3 (1963), 20–26.

———. "Materials for an Indian Christology," *RS*, XII, 4 (1965), 6–15.
Attempts to translate basic New Testament concepts into Hindu terms, but suffers from a traditionalistic interpretation of those concepts.

Devadutt, V.E. "What Is an Indigenous Theology? With Special Reference to India," *ER*, II, 1 (1949), 40–51.

Devanandan, Paul D. *Christian Concern in Hinduism*. Bangalore: CISRS, 1961.
Examines the intrinsic values in Hinduism which must be preserved even after one has embraced the Christian faith.

———. *The Gospel and the Hindu Intellectual*. Bangalore; CISRS, 1959.

———. *The Gospel and Renascent Hinduism*. London: SCM Press, 1959.

———. *I Will Lift Up Mine Eyes Unto the Hills. Sermons and Bible Studies*. Edited by S.J. Samartha and Nalini Devanandan. Bangalore: CISRS, 1963.

———. *Preparation for Dialogue. A Collection of Essays on Hinduism and Christianity in New India*. Edited by Nalini Devanandan and M.M. Thomas. Bangalore: CISRS, 1964.

———. "Called to Witness," *ER*, XIV, 2 (1962), 154–63.

———. "The Christian Attitude and Approach to Non-Christian Religions," *IRM*, XLI, 162 (1952), 177–84.

———. "The Christian Message in Relation to the Cultural Heritage of India," *ER*, II, 3 (1950), 241–49.

———. "The Nature of Ultimate Truth: The Christian Understanding," *RS*, IX, 3 (1962), 7–13.

———. "The Relevance of the Christian Hope to Our Time," *ER*, V, 3 (1952), 253–60.

———. "Renascent Religions and Religion," pp. 148–76 in *The Ecumenical Era in Church and Society*. Edited by E.J. Jurji. New York: Macmillan, 1959.

———. "The Resurgence of Non-Christian Religions," pp. 148–57 in *The Theology of the Christian Mission*. Edited by Gerald H. Anderson. New York: McGraw-Hill, 1961.
"Is the preaching of the Gospel directed to the total annihilation of all other religions than Christianity?"

————. "Whither Theology in Christian India?" *IRM*, XXXIII, 2 (1944), 121–27.

Devanesan, Chandran D. S. and Abel, M. "The Powers of Government and the Claims of Human Freedom," pp. 197–212 in *Responsible Government in a Revolutionary Age*. Edited by Z.K. Matthews. New York: Association Press, 1966.

Dhavamony, Mariasusai, ed. *Evangelization, Dialogue and Development*. (Documenta Missionalia, 5.) Rome: Pont. Univ. Gregoriana, 1972.

Dockhorn, Kurt. "Christus im Hinduismus in der Sicht der neueren indischen Theologie," *EMZ*, XXX, 2 (1973), 57–74. English tr. in *RS*, XXI, 4 (1974), 39–57.

Dupuis, J. "The Presence of Christ in Hinduism," *Clergy Monthly*, XXXIV, 4 (1970), 141–48.

> Fr. Dupuis, who teaches at St. Mary's Theological College in Darjeeling, here clarifies the theological issue involved in affirming that Christ is present to the Hindu who is sincere in his practice of Hinduism.

Duraisingh, C. "The Meaning of God in Process Perspective," *IJT*, XXXI, 1 & 2 (1972), 92–106.

Estborn, Sigfried. *Luther-Lutheranism in the Indian Church*. (Gurukul Notes, no. 5) Madras: Diocesan Press, 1961.

> Some essays on Luther and Lutheran confessions and their relation to Indian Christianity.

————. *The Religion of Tagore in the Light of the Gospel*. Madras: CLS, 1949.

————. *The Teaching of Krishna in the Light of the Gospel, and Other Essays*. (Gurukul Notes, no. 4) Madras: Diocesan Press, 1961.

Fakirbhai, Dhanjibhai. *Khristopanishad (Christ-Upanishad)*. (Indian Christian Thought Series, no. 3) Bangalore: CISRS, 1965.

————. *The Philosophy of Love*. Delhi: ISPCK, 1966.

> An exposition of love as the inner life of the Trinity, the essence of the incarnation.

Fallon, P. "A Critical Evaluation of the Hindu Interpretation of Christ," *IJT*, XVIII, 1 (1969), 81–87.

> Views the many *avatars* in Hinduism as prefiguring the one great incarnation of God in Christ.

————. "The Cosmic Christ and the Asian Revolution," *IJT*, XV, 4 (1966), 150–53.

Forman, Charles W. "Freedom of Conversion: The Issue in India," *IRM*, XLV, 178 (1956), 180–93.

Gensichen, Hans-Werner. "Auf dem Wege zu einer indischen Theologie," *Neue Zeitschrift für systematische Theologie*, I (1959), 326–49.

George, Munduvel V. "Existentialism and Its Message to Indian Thought Pattern," *IJT*, XI, 2 (1962), 68–74.

> "Many of the points on which Kierkegaard attacked the Hegelian system of rational philosophy may be applied in evaluating the Hindu mode of speculation."

————, ed. *New Life in an Old Church: A Symposium.* Calcutta: The Syrian Orthodox Church, 1963.

    Essays on the being, belief, and the task of the Syrian Orthodox Church in contemporary India.

George, Poikail J. "Some Theological Reflections on the Chinese Revolution," *RS,* XVI, 4 (1969), 70–81.

    An Indian scholar reflecting on the possibility of a Chinese-style revolution in India.

Griffiths, Bede. *Christ in India, Essays Towards a Hindu-Christian Dialogue.* New York: Scribners, 1966. British edition under the title *Christian Ashram.* London: Darton, Longman & Todd, 1966.

    The author argues that "certain aspects of the Gospel can only be brought to light through contact with the Eastern mind."

Gurukul Theological Research Group. *A Christian Theological Approach to Hinduism.* Madras: CLS, 1956.

    A critical study of the theologies of A.J. Appasamy, P. Chenchiah, and V. Chakkarai, by the Gurukul Theological Faculty.

————. *The Gospel for India.* Madras: Diocesan Press, 1963.

Hogg, Alfred George. *The Christian Message to the Hindu.* London: SCM Press, 1947.

    In response and reaction to Kraemer, Hogg insists that God does reveal himself to the devout faith of the non-Christian, and that what is unique in the Gospel is not the occurrence of revelation, but its content.

————. *Karma and Redemption. An Essay Toward the Interpretation of Hinduism and the Re-Statement of Christianity.* With an introduction by Eric C. Sharpe. Madras: CLS, 1970.

    Important reprint, first published in 1909. Its influence is attested to by the fact that significant modifications have taken place in the doctrine of Karma along the lines Hogg suggested; also in the Christian theology of religion to which he pointed.

Hummel, Reinhart. "Die Identitätskrise der indischen Kirche," *EMZ,* XXIX, 4 (1972), 161–81.

Immanuel, Rajappan D. *The Influence of Hinduism on Indian Christians.* Jabalpur: Leonard Theological College, 1950.

Indian Journal of Theology, XXV, 3 & 4 (1976).

    Special 25th annversary issue of *IJT* that surveys trends in Indian theological thinking over the past 25 years.

"Indian Understandings of Jesus Christ," special issue of *RS,* XI, 3 (1964).

Irudayaraj, X. "An Attempt at an Indian Christology," *IES,* IX (1971), 125–31.

————. "From the 'Fulfilment-View' to the 'Sacramental Approach,' " *Jeevadhara,* I, 3 (1971), 200–11.

Itty, C.I. "Dynamics of a Pluralistic Society: The Indian Experience," pp. 308–29 in *Man and Community.* Edited by Egbert de Vries. New York: Association Press, 1966.

Jai Singh, Herbert. *My Neighbors: Men of Different Faiths.* Bangalore: CISRS, 1966.

———. "Christian Conversion in a Hindu Context," *ER*, XIX, 3 (1967), 302–306.

———. "Christian Presence Amid Men of Other Faiths: Deenabandhu C.F. Andrews," *SW*, LVIII, 3 (1965), 275–83.

———. "Existentialism, Hindu Insights and the Gospel of Christ," *RS*, XII, 4 (1965), 26–33.
     The author's conclusion: "Whether the Ultimate Resource is personal or impersonal is a matter of little concern to the Christian Gospel."

———. "Rethinking Church in India," *RS*, X, 4 (1963), 9–15.
     Considers, and rejects, the option of a "Churchless Christianity."

———, ed. *Inter-Religious Dialogue.* (Devanandan Memorial volume, no. 3.) Bangalore: CISRS, 1967.
     Essays by S.J. Samartha, Lynn de Silva, Surjit Singh, Paul Verghese, M.M. Thomas, and others.

James, Emmanuel E. "Bonhoeffer, Radhakrishnan and Modern Secularism," *IJT*, XIX, 3 & 4 (1970), 127–44.

Jesudasan, I. "Gandhian Perspectives on Missiology," *ICHR*, IV, 1 (1970), 45–72.
     Gandhi's opposition to conversion in favor of dialogue, examined by an Indian Jesuit.

Jesudason, S. *Unique Christ and Indigenous Christianity.* (Indian Christian Thought Series, no. 4) Bangalore: CISRS, 1966.
     A plea for indigenization by a recognized Indian leader, which suffers from an overstress on the externals.

———. "Interpreting the Christian Doctrine of Creation in India," *IJT*, XXI, 1 (1963), 11–16.

John, George M. *Youth Christian Council of Action, 1938–1954.* Madras: CLS, 1972.
     The start of the social theology of M.M. Thomas, E.V. Mathew, A.K. Thampy, J.R. Chandran, and others.

John, Mathew P. "The Idea of Grace in Christianity and Hinduism," *IJT*, XIX, 2 (1970), 59–73.

———. "The Religion of C.F. Andrews," *ICHR*, IV, 2 (1970), 147–61.

———. "The Use of the Bible by Indian Christian Theologians," *IJT*, XIV, 2 (1965), 43–51. German tr. "Der Gebrauch der Bibel durch indische christliche Theologen," *TS*, II, 97–108.

Klostermaier, Klaus. *Hindu and Christian in Vrindaban.* London: SCM Press, 1969, American edition, *In the Paradise of Krishna.* Philadelphia; Westminster Press, 1969.
     The author, who taught philosophy at the Vaishnava Theological College in Vrindaban, says, "Christ does not come to India as a stranger; he comes into his own. Christ comes to India not from Europe, but directly from the Father."

———. *Kristvidya: A Sketch of an Indian Christology.* (Indian Christian Thought Series, no. 2.) Bangalore: CISRS, 1967. German tr. "Kristividya: Versuch einer indischen Christologie," *Kairos* (Salzburg), IX (1967), 2–21.

————. "Indian Christian Theology," *Clergy Review* (London), LIV, 3 (1969), 175–98.

Kumaresan, J. "Man's Nature and Destiny: A Christian Theological Approach," *IJT*, X, 4 (1961), 167–71.

Kurien, C. T. "Economics, Philosophy and Theology," *RS*, XI,4 (1964), 18–23.

Lesser, R. H. "Towards an Indian-Christian Theology," *IES*, IX, 4 (1970), 222–30.
A review of Robin Boyd, *An Introduction to Indian Christian Theology* (Madras: CLS, 1969).

Luke, P. Y. and Carman, John B. *Village Christians and Hindu Culture*. London: Lutterworth Press, 1968.
Raises theological questions.

Lyon, David and Manuel, Albert, eds. *Renewal for Mission*. 2nd rev. ed. Madras: CLS, 1968.
Included are essays on "Indigenisation" by D.G. Moses, "The Struggle for Human Dignity as a Preparation for the Gospel" by M.M. Thomas, and "A Christian Approach to Men of Other Faiths," by T.K. Thomas.

McGlashan, Robin. "Conversion—A Comparative Study," *RS*, XIII, 4 (1966), 5–21.

Mathai, P.S. (Nathan, P.S.). *A Christian Approach to the Bhagavadgita*. Calcutta: YMCA, 1956.
Appreciates the spiritual value of the Gita, but concludes with a firm commitment to the biblical faith.

Mathew, E. V. *The Secular Witness of E.V. Mathew*. Introduction by J.R. Chandran. (Confessing the Faith in India, no. 8.) Madras: CLS, 1972.

Mathew, K.C. "A Glimpse of the Atonement." *IJT*, XVII, 1 (1968), 1–4.
Stresses the note of self-sacrifice in the atoning work of Christ.

————. "The Remembrance of Me," *IJT*, XIII, 4 (1964), 130–34.

————. "The Sacrament of Infant Baptism," *IJT*, XI, 4 (1962), 143–49.

Mathias, T.A. "The Living God," *IJT*, XVIII, 4 (1969), 246–58.
A response to the "Death of God Theology," by an Indian Jesuit.

Matthew, Anjilvel V. *The Message of the Rshis. Studies in the Upanishads from the Standpoint of a Christian Reader*. (Indian Christian Thought Series, no. 6.) Bangalore: CISRS, 1967.

Melzer, Frisco. "Dem Hinduismus begegnen," *EMZ*, XXIII, 3 (1966), 157–69.

Minz, Nirmal. *Mahatma Gandhi and Hindu-Christian Dialogue*. Madras; CLS, 1970.

————. "Theologies of Dialogue-Critique," *RS*, XIV, 2 (1967), 7–20.

Moffitt, John. *Journey to Gorakhpur. An Encounter with Christ Beyond Christianity*. New York: Holt, Rinehart and Winston, 1972.
The writer was a member of a Hindu monastic order for twenty-five years before turning to Catholicism.

————. "Christianity Confronts Hinduism," *Theological Studies*, XX, 2 (1969), 207–24.
Emphasizes the need for "dehellenization" of Christian theology.

Moses, David G. *Religious Truth and the Relation Between Religions*. Madras: CLS, 1950.

The author was principal of Hislop College, Nagpur; chairman of the EACC, and a president of the WCC.

------. "Christianity and the Non-Christian Religions," *IRM*, XLIII (1954), 146–54.

------. "The Identity of the Indian Church," pp. 209–218 in *The Indian Church: Identity and Fulfillment*. Edited by Mathai Zachariah. Madras: CLS, 1971.

------. "India," pp. 227–44 in *Prospects of Christianity Throughout the World*. Edited by M. Searle Bates and Wilhelm Pauck. New York: Scribner's, 1964.

------. "To the Hindu: 'The Costliness of Salvation,' " pp. 65–73 in *Sermons to Men of Other Faiths and Traditions*. Edited by Gerald H. Anderson, Nashville, Tenn.: Abingdon Press, 1966.

Muliyil, F. "The Interpretation of the Fourth Gospel," *IJT*, VIII, 1 (1959), 1–9.

------. "The Parable of History," *RS*, XIV, 1 (1967), 14–20.

Neuner, Josef. "Auf dem Wege zu einer indischen Theologie," *ZMR*, XLVII, 1 (1963), 1–15.

------. "The Place of World Religions in Theology," pp. 55–75 in *The Church as Sign*. Edited by William J. Richardson. Maryknoll, N.Y.: Maryknoll Publications, 1968.
    Discusses the implications of the Vatican II documents for the development of an indigenous theology in India.

------, ed. *Hinduismus und Christentum. Eine Einführung*. Vienna: Herder, 1962.

Newbigin, Lesslie. *Christ Our Eternal Contemporary*. Madras: CLS, 1968.
    Meditations given at the Christian Medical College, Vellore.

------. *A Faith for This One World?* New York: Harper's, 1961.
    In lectures at Harvard University the former CSI Bishop in Madras studies the claim of Christianity to be the faith for our world in light of the arguments of men such as Radhakrishnan, Toynbee, and Hocking.

------. *The Finality of Christ*. London: SCM Press, and Richmond, Va.: John Knox Press, 1969.

------. *Honest Religion for Secular Man*. London: SCM Press, 1966.

------. *Trinitarian Faith and Today's Mission*. Richmond, Va.: John Knox Press, 1964.

------. "Conversion," *RS*, XIII, 4 (1966), 30–42.

O'Connor, Daniel. *The Contribution of C.F. Andrews*. (Confessing the Faith in India Series, no. 10.) Madras: CLS-CISRS, 1974.

Panikkar, Raimundo. *Kerygma und Indien, Zur heilsgeschichtlichen Problematik der christlichen Begegnung mit Indien*. Hamburg: Reich-Evang. Verlag, 1967.
    Born of a Hindu father and a Catholic mother, Fr. Panikkar writes as one who is in dialogue with himself.

------. *Kultmysterium in Hinduismus und Christentum*. Freiburg: Alber, 1964.

------. *Offenbarung und Verkündigung. Indische Briefe*. (Schriften zum Weltgespräch 2. Bd.) Fribourg: Herder, 1967.

——. *Patriotismo y Cristiandad*. Madrid: Rialp, 1961.

——. *Religionen und die Religion*. Munich: Hueber, 1965.

——. *The Trinity and the Religious Experience of Man*. Maryknoll, N.Y.: Orbis Books and London: Darton, Longman & Todd, 1973. First published as *The Trinity and World Religions*. Madras: CLS for CISRS, 1970.
Deals with forms of spirituality, the Trinity, and Theandrism.

——. *The Unknown Christ of Hinduism*. London: Darton, Longman & Todd, 1964.
The author says, "There is a living presence of Christ in Hinduism." He maintains that "Christ is not only the ontological goal of Hinduism but also its true inspirer, and his grace is the leading though hidden force pushing it towards its full disclosure." He speaks of Hinduism as both "a vestibule of Christianity" and "a kind of Christianity in potency." See Dankfried Reetz, "Raymond Panikkar's Theology of Religions," *RS*, XV, 3 (1968), 32–54.

——. *Die vielen Götter und der eine Herr*. Weilheim: Barth, 1963.

——. *Worship and Secular Man*. Maryknoll, N.Y.: Orbis Books, and London: Darton, Longman & Todd, 1973.

——. "Advaita and Bhakti: Love and Identity in a Hindu-Christian Dialogue," *JES*, VII, 2 (1970), 299–309.

——. "Confrontation Between Hinduism and Christ," *Logos*, X, 2 (1969), 43–51.

——. "Faith—A Constitutive Dimension of Man," *JES*, VIII, 2 (1971), 223–54.

——. "Faith and Belief: A Multireligious Experience," *Anglican Theological Review*, LIII, 4 (1971), 219–37.

——. "The God of Silence," *IJT*, XXI, 1 & 2 (1972), 116–24.

——. "The Internal Dialogue—The Insufficiency of the So-Called Phenomenological 'Epoche' in the Religious Encounter," *RS*, XV, 3 (1968), 55–66.

——. "Rules of the Game in the Religious Encounter," *AF*, V, 3 (1970), 223–27.
States eight "rules" based on the principle that religious dialogue itself is fundamentally "a religious act, in which the vitality of religion manifests itself."

——. "Toward an Ecumenical Theandric Spirituality," *JES*, V, 3 (1968), 507–34.
A Trinitarian approach to ecumenism.

Paradkar, Balwant A.M. *The Theology of Nehemiah Goreh*. (Confessing the Faith in India Series, no. 3.) Madras: CLS–CISRS, 1969.

——. "The Christian Encounter With Men of Other Faiths," *RS*, XIV, 2 (1967), 21–37.

——. "A Fragment on Albert Schweitzer's Inter-Religious Encounter," *RS*, XIII, 2 (1966), 34–48.

——. "Hindu Interpretation of Christ from Vivekananda to Radhakrishnan," *IJT*, XVIII, 1 (1969), 65–80.

——. "The Meaning of the Resurrection," *IJT*, XVII, 2 (1968), 62–70.
Views the resurrection faith of the New Testament as symbolizing the Chris-

tian evaluation of the bodily and the material, so as to provide the directive for social concern.

Pathrapankal, J. M. "Faith and Conversion: A Study in the Context of the Covenantal Significance of Baptism," *IJT*, XVI, 3 (1967), 166–79.
  The author is on the staff of Dharmaram College, Bangalore.

———. "The Problem of 'History' in the Gospels in the Light of the Vatican's Constitution on 'Divine Revelation,' " *IJT*, XVI, 1 & 2 (1967), 86–105.

Premasagar, Peddi V. "Crisis for Salvation Theology," *IRM*, LXI, 241 (1972), 61–66.
  Questions the doctrine of salvation as an "exclusive deliverance theology" favoring some over others and justifying privileged position.

Presenting Christ to India Today. Madras: CLS, 1965.
  Three addresses and a sermon delivered to the Synod of the Church of South India, January 1956, by P. D. Devanandan, A. E. Inbanathan, A. J. Appasamy, and J. E. L. Newbigin.

Quaas, Martin. "The Theological Significance of Western Culture in India," *RS*, XIV, 3 (1967), 60–70.

Radhakrishan, John. "Selfhood of the Church and Its Identity," *New World Outlook*, XXXII, 8 (1972), 31–35.
  "What is needed is an affirmation of secular holiness," the principal of Leonard Theological College in Jabalpur reminds us.

Rao, K. L. S. "A Hindu View of Jesus Christ," *Harvard Divinity Bulletin*, XXVII, 3 (1963), 1–12.

Rao, Mark Sunder. *Ananyatva, Realisation of Christian Non-Duality*. (Indian Christian Thought Series, no. 2) Bangalore: CISRS, 1964. Part of this in German tr. in *TS*, III, 122–39.
  The author, a research associate of the CISRS in Bangalore, has been engaged in a lifelong effort to reconcile the major insights of Christianity with the values inherent in Hindu religious traditions.

———. *Concerning Indian Christianity*. New Delhi: YMCA Publishing House, 1973.
  Suggests that the task of synthesis between Eastern and Western cultures involves a creative role which can best be played by intellectual Indian Christians.

———. "Christa Darsana: A Christian Vision of Reality," *RS*, XIV, 4 (1967), 6–14.
  "Christa Darsana" embraces the two mainstreams of the Indian religious mind—the Eastern and the Western—and therefore offers a clue to an emerging Indian Christian theology.

———. "The Knowledge of Ultimate Truth: A Christian Approach," *RS*, IX, 3 (1962), 41–49.

Rayan, Samuel. "An Indian Christology: A Discussion of Method," *Jeevadhara*, I, 3 (1971), 212–27.

———. "Evangelization and Development," pp. 87–105 in *Mission Trends No. 2*. Edited by Gerald H. Anderson and Thomas F. Stransky. New York: Paulist Press; and Grand Rapids, Mich.: Eerdmans, 1975.

Rajarigam, D. "Theological Content in the Tamil Christian Poetical Works," *IJT*, XI, 4 (1962), 130–34, and XII, 1 (1963), 3–5.

Rethinking Christianity in India. Madras: CLS, 1938; 2nd ed., 1939.

By a group of unorthodox but highly stimulating thinkers, including Chenchiah and Chakkarai, who published this famous book on the eve of the IMC world conference at Tambaram, Madras, as an Indian reply to Hendrik Kraemer's Barthian position in *The Christian Message in a Non-Christian World.*

Rogers, C. Murray. "Worship and Contemporary Asian Man—Some Reflections," *RS*, XVI, 2 (1969), 51–63.

Rouner, Leroy S. "Individualism, Communalism, and Existentialism," *RS*, XII, 4 (1965), 16–25.

——. "The Place of Provincialism in Theology," *Christianity and Crisis*, XXVI, 1 (1966), 4–7.

Relevance requires restating the universal Gospel in provincial terms with special reference to India where the author taught philosophy of religion at United Theological College, Bangalore.

——. "Re-thinking the Christian Mission in India Today," *RL*, XXXV, 4 (1966), 530–45.

Ruthnaswamy, Mariadas. *India After God.* Ranchi: Catholic Press, 1965.

Thesis: The search for God in Indian religions finds fulfillment in Christ.

Ryerson, Charles. "A Theological Approach to the Renascence," *RS*, XII, 2 (1965), 60–83.

The author has lived and worked in Tamilnad as a participant observer of the Tamil cultural renaissance, seeking the meaning of Christian presence in that Indian subculture.

Sadiq, Emmanuel. "Man in Society According to Islam, With a Christian Evaluation," *IJT*, X, 4 (1961), 159–66.

Sadiq, John W. "Interfaith Dialogue and Communication of the Gospel," *RS*, XII, 1 (1965), 5–13.

By the former Bishop of Nagpur.

Samartha, Stanley J. *Hindus vor dem universalen Christus, Beiträge zu einer Christologie in Indien.* Stuttgart: Evang. Verlagswerk, 1970.

German tr. of *The Hindu Response to the Unbound Christ.* (Inter-religious Dialogue Series, no. 6.) Madras: CLS-CISRS., 1974.

——. *Introduction to Radhakrishnan; The Man and His Thought.* New York: Association Press, 1964.

A critical biography of an outstanding Hindu philosopher and student of the Christian religion.

——. "Major Issues in the Hindu-Christian Dialogue in India Today," pp. 145–69 in *Inter-Religious Dialogue.* Edited by Herbert Jai Singh. Bangalore: CISRS, 1967.

Sambayya, Emani. *Faith and Conduct: An Introduction to Moral Theology.* Madras: CLS, 1965.

Emphasis is on the issues of personal ethics.

———. "Christian Spirituality," *IJT*, XIX, 2 (1970), 53–58.
> The author was on the teaching staff of Bishop's College, Calcutta, and was principal from 1958 to 1968.

Samuel, V.C. "The Manhood of Jesus Christ in the Tradition of the Syrian Orthodox Church," *BTF*, II, 2 (1968), 15–30.

Scott, David C. "The Household of God in the Indian Context," *RS*, XVII, 1 (1970), 22–36.

Sharpe, Eric J. *Not to Destroy But to Fulfil: The Contribution of J.N. Farquhar to Protestant Missionary Thought in India Before 1914.* (Studia Missionalia Upsaliensia, V.) Lund: Gleerup, 1965.
> Reviewing this book, M.M. Thomas said, "No one who wants to build up a proper theology of religion or mission today in India, or elsewhere, can ignore this book." *RS*, XXI, 2 (1965), 67.

———. *The Theology of A.G. Hogg.* (Confessing the Faith in India Series, no. 7). Madras: CLS-CISRS, 1971.

Singh, Surjit. *Christology and Personality.* Philadelphia: Westminster Press, 1961. Originally published under title *Preface to Personality. Christology in Relation to Radhakrishnan's Philosophy.* Madras: CLS, 1952.
> Claims that the core of the Christian message to the Hindu is the gaining of a unique personality as contrasted to the loss of one's being in the nothingness of Nirvana.

———. *Communism, Christianity and Democracy.* Richmond, Va.: John Knox Press, 1965.
> Discusses their interrelationship in a polarized and pluralized society.

Subbamma, B.V. *Christ Confronts India. Indigenous Expression of Christianity.* Madras: Diocesan Press. 1973.
> Suggests functional Christian substitutes for Hindu rites and practices.

Tamilnad Christian Council. *A Christian Theological Approach to Hinduism.* Madras: CLS, 1956.

Taylor, Richard W. *The Contribution of E. Stanley Jones.* (Confessing the Faith in India Series, no. 9.) Madras CLS-CISRS, 1973.

———. *The Interpretation of Jesus in Indian Painting.* (Confessing the Faith in India Series, no. 11.) Madras: CLS-CISRS, 1975.

———. "Missionary Societies and the Development of Other Forms of Associations in India," pp. 189–206 in *Voluntary Associations.* Edited by D.B. Robertson. Richmond, Va.: John Knox Press, 1966.

———. "On Acknowledging the Lordship of Jesus Christ Without Shifting Tents," *RS* XIX, 1 (1972), 59–68.
> Must all those who acknowledge Christ as Lord "formally leave the community of their birth and formally join the Christian community?"

Thangasamy, D.A. *The Theology of Chenchiah with Selections from His Writings.* (Confessing the Faith in India Series, no. 1.) Bangalore: CISRS, 1966.

Chenchiah was a leading spokesman of the "Rethinking Group" in India in the late 1930s.

———. "The Process of Conversion," *IJT*, XVI, 3 (1967), 204–10.

———. "The Rationale and the Meaning of Christian Mission," *RS*, XV, 4 (1968), 42–52.
Applies to the Indian scene the broader understanding of the Church's mission as the "responsibility for the total welfare of the people of the world."

———. "Some Trends in Recent Theological Thinking in Madras City," *ICHR*, III, 1 (1969), 55–74.
Discusses the emergence of the "Rethinking Group" of Indian Christian laymen in the 1930s and '40s; though overwhelmed by the forces of orthodoxy at the time, they now brighten the horizon once again.

———. "Views of Some Christian Thinkers in India on Conversion and Baptism," *RS*, XIX, 1 (1972), 37–50.

"The Theology of Hindu-Christian Dialogue," *RS*, XVI, 2 (1969), 69–88.
Report of a consultation at Bombay, January 1969. See "Dialogue as a Concern of Christian Theology" section.

Thomas M.M. *The Acknowledged Christ of the Indian Renaissance.* London: SCM Press; and (Confessing the Faith in India Series, no. 5.) Madras: CLS-CISRS, 1969.
By the director of the CISRS at Bangalore, who is chairman of the WCC Central Committee. The book deals with issues posed by the neo-Hindu leaders as they grapple with the person of Jesus Christ and the historical phenomenon of Christianity.

———. *The Christian Response to the Asian Revolution.* London: SCM Press, 1966.
A profound and provocative book in which the author asks, "Can we speak of the relevance of the Asian revolution itself as a preparation for the gospel?"

———. *Man and the Universe of Faiths.* (Inter-religious Dialogue Series, no. 7.) Bangalore: CISRS, 1975.

———. *The Realization of the Cross.* Madras: CLS, 1972.
A collection of unusual meditations that also tell the story of a man's struggle in search of meaning.

———. *Salvation and Humanisation. Some Crucial Issues of the Theology of Mission in Contemporary India.* Madras: CLS, 1971.
Takes up the debate on mission from Section II of the Uppsala Assembly and the subsequent polemical position of Peter Beyerhaus. See the review by Lesslie Newbigin in *RS*, XVIII, 1 (1971), 71–80, and the exchange which followed between Thomas and Newbigin in *AF*, VII, 4 (1972), 72–79.

———. "Awakened Peoples, Developing Nations, and the Dynamics of World Politics," pp. 27–46 in *Responsible Government in a Revolutionary Age.* Edited by Z.K. Matthews. New York: Association Press, 1966.

———. "Basic Approaches to Power: Gandhiji, Andrews, and King," *RS*, XVII, 3 (1969), 15–25.
Examines certain theological dimensions of the ethic of nonviolence, and shows the relevance of interfaith dialogue in deepening these dimensions.

———. "The Christian Basis of Inter-Faith Dialogue" (editorial), *RS*, XII, 1 (1965), 1–8.

———. "Christian Confession in the Asian Revolution," pp. 159–70 in *The Sufficiency of God. Essays on the Ecumenical Hope in Honor of W. A. Visser 't Hooft*. Edited by Robert C. Mackie and Charles C. West. Philadelphia: Westminster Press, 1963.

———. "A Christian View of Society," *RS*, VII, 3 & 4 (1960), 51–69.

———. "Christianity and World History," *ER*, XVI, 5 (1964), 546–52, and *RS*, XIV, 1 (1967), 31–36.
A significant response to the challenge of Van Leeuwen's controversial study, *Christianity in World History*.

———. "Christ's Promises within the Revolution: The Meaning of Evangelism and Service in the Post War World," *RS*, VIII, 1 (1961), 15–25.

———. "The Ecumenical Movement and Christian Social Thought in India," *IJT*, X, 2 (1961), 64–71.

———. "Faith and Ideology" (editorial), *RS*, XIV, 4 (1967), 1–6.

———. "The Gospel and History in India," *RS*, XII, 4 (1965), 34–43.

———. "The Gospel and the Problem of the Indigenous Church," *SW*, XLV, 3 (1952), 233–39.

———. "The Gospel and the Quest of Modern Asia," *USQR*, XXII, 3 (1967), 229–41.

———. "India," *RL*, XXXVII, 2 (1968), 203–17.
Part of a *Religion in Life* symposium on "Current Theology Around the World."

———. "Indigenization and the Renaissance of Traditional Cultures," *IRM*, LII, 206 (1963), 191–94.

———. "The Meaning of Death and Dying" (editorial), *RS*, XVIII, 2 (1971), 1–11.
Theological reflections on the theme.

———. "The Meaning of Salvation Today—A Personal Statement," *IRM*, LXII, 246 (1973), 158–69.
Opening address at the Bangkok conference, December 1972, on "Salvation Today."

———. "Modernisation of Traditional Societies and the Struggle for New Cultural Ethos," *ER*, XVIII, 4 (1966), 426–39.
"My thesis is that the spiritual dimensions of the contemporary awakening of the peoples of Asia and Africa, stimulated by the Western impact, and their search for a new humanism provide a starting point for the process of building indigenous cultural foundations for modernisation."

———. "The Pattern of Christian Spirituality," *RS*, XVI, 2 (1969), 64–68.
Concludes that Christian attempts to enter the world of Hindu mysticism must be accompanied by efforts to redefine it in the light of Christ.

———. "Patterns of Modern Man's Search for Salvation," *RS*, XI, 2 (1964), 8–15.

———. "Paul Devanandan," pp. 466–69 in *Tendenzen der Theologie im 20. Jahrhundert: Eine Geschichte in Porträts*. Edited by Hans Jürgen Schultz. Stuttgart: Kreuz-Verlag, 1966.

————. "Peace and Radical Social Changes," *RS*, XV, 2 (1968); 15–24.

————. "The Post-Colonial Crisis in Mission—A Comment," *RS*, XVIII, 1 (1971), 64–70.

    A response to an earlier article by Kaj Baago, "The Post-Colonial Crisis of Missions," *IRM*, LV, 219 (1966), 322–32 and LVI, 221 (1967), 30–42.

————. "Revolutionary Ferment and the Church," *AF*, IV, 1 (1969), 54–65.

————. "Salvation and Humanisation: A Crucial Issue in the Theology of Mission for India," *IRM*, LX, 237 (1971), 25–38.

————. "Significance of Marxist and Barthian Insights for a Theology of Religion," *RS*, XXI, 4 (1974), 58–66.

————. "The Significance of the Thought of Paul D. Devanandan for a Theology of Dialogue," pp. 1–37 in *Inter-Religious Dialogue*. (Devanandan Memorial Volume, no. 3.) Edited by Herbert Jai Singh. Bangalore: CISRS, 1967.

————. "Some Crucial Issues in Christian Social Ethics Today," *SA*, XXXIII, 5 (1967), 5–15.

————. "Some Notes on a Christian Interpretation of Nationalism in Asia," *SEAJT*, II, 2 (1960), 16–26.

————. "Theology of Salvation Today," *RS*, XV, 4 (1968), 1–4.

————. "Towards an Indian Understanding of Jesus Christ," pp. 17–28 in *The Indian Church: Identity and Fulfilment*. Edited by Mathai Zachariah. Madras: CLS, 1971.

————. "Understanding the Tides of History," *SEAJT*, V, 4 (1964), 21–31.

————. "Universalism and the Unchanging Core of the Christian Dogma," *RS*, XIV, 2 (1967), 48–59.

    Settles for a Christian universalism which can "justify demythologization in every situation without losing its kerygmatic character."

————. "Uppsala 1968 and the Contemporary Theological Situation," *SJT*, XXIII, 1 (1970), 41–50.

———— and Devanandan, Paul D. *Christian Participation in Nation Building*. Bangalore: CISRS, 1960.

Thomas, P. T. *The Theology of Chakkarai, with Selections from His Writings*. (Confessing the Faith in India Series, no. 2.) Bangalore: CISRS, 1968.

    A sympathetic but critical study of the theological development of an influential Indian theologian.

Thomas, T. K. *The Witness of S.K. George*. (Confessing the Faith in India Series, no. 6.) Madras: CLS-CISRS, 1970.

    One of the most controversial figures in the development of Christian witness in India.

————. "The Christian Task in India: An Introduction to the Thought of Bernard Lucas," *RS*, XV, 3 (1968), 20–31.

————. "Confessing Christ: My No—His Yes," *IRM*, LXIV, 253 (1975), 20–24.

————. "Dialogue as Presence," *RS*, XIV, 2 (1967), 38–47.

Discusses the meaning of the concept of "Christian Presence" in the Indian context.

Thomas, V.P. "Indian Christian Approaches to the Knowledge of Christ," *IJT*, XVIII, 1 (1969), 88–99.

Discusses the Christology of Appasamy, Chakkarai, and Chenchiah, who belong to the "Rethinking Group" that tried to understand the Christian faith from inside Hinduism.

——. "Salvation: The Meanings of a Biblical Word," *IRM*, LVII, 228 (1968), 399–416.

Valles, C.G. "Pastoral Approaches and Dialogue Methods—Towards a Hindu–Christian Theology," *Clergy Monthly*, XXXII, 3 (1968), 116–20.

Fr. Valles says, "The Christian faith shall not be fully understood until it is expressed in all the philosophies and religious systems of the world."

Venugopal, C.T. *Witness to Christ*. (Indian Christian Thought Series, no. 12.) Madras: CLS, 1972.

Verghese, T. Paul. *The Freedom of Man*. Philadelphia: Westminster Press, 1972.

The problem of freedom *vs* authority. Proposes a revision of Christian thought, starting with Gregorian rather than Augustinian categories. An enlarged Indian edition entitled *Freedom and Authority* (Madras: CLS, 1974), adds three new chapters, setting the volume in the context of Indian life and thought.

——. *The Joy of Freedom: Eastern Worship and Modern Man*. London: Lutterworth Press, 1967.

——. "Christ and All Men," pp. 159–64 in *Living Faiths and the Ecumenical Movement*. Edited by S.J. Samartha. Geneva: WCC, 1971.

A former associate general secretary of the WCC, Fr. Verghese is now a bishop of the Syrian Orthodox Church of the East and is known as Metropolitan Paul Gregorios. He continues as principal of the Syrian Orthodox Seminary in Kottayam, South India.

——. "The Crisis in Theological Education—The Need for New Perspectives," *IJT*, XX, 4 (1971), 189–97.

——. "The Cultivation of the Christian Life," *SEAJT*, V, 4 (1964), 37–52.

The first section represents an extremely negative view of the Christian mission, placing it in opposition to the Christian life.

——. "Dialogue with Secularism," pp. 225–37 in *Inter-Religious Dialogue*. (Devanandan Memorial Volume, no. 3.) Edited by Herbert Jai Singh. Bangalore: CISRS, 1967.

——. "The Finality of Jesus Christ in the Age of Universal History," *ER*, XV, 1 (1962), 12–25.

——. "Humanization as a World Problem," *Study Encounter* (Geneva), V, 1 (1969), 3–16; German tr. in *Okumenische Rundschau*, XVIII, 2 (1969), 193–210.

——. "Mastery and Mystery," *RS*, XXI, 4 (1974), 29–38.

——. " 'On Choosing the Good Portion'—A Sermon to the Western Church Activist from an Eastern Orthodox Perspective," pp. 163–69 in *Sermons to Men of Other Faiths and Traditions*. Edited by Gerald H. Anderson. Nashville, Tenn.: Abingdon Press, 1966.

———. "On God's Death," *IJT*, XVII, 4 (1968), 151–61.
A critique of deficiencies in Western theology and a call for appreciation of the Eastern tradition.

———. "A Sacramental Humanism," *ChC*, LXXXVII, 38 (September 23, 1970), 1118–19.
"The basic mistake of Western mission is not so much cultural aggression as missionary colonialism. . . . So now I say, 'The mission of the church is the greatest enemy of the gospel.' "

———. "Secular Society or Pluralistic Community?" pp. 359–82 in *Man in Community*. Edited by Egbert de Vries. New York: Association Press, 1966.

———. "Some Perspectives of Christian Spirituality: An Eastern Orthodox View," *RS*, XVI, 2 (1969), 29–35.

———. "The Spiritual Foundations of Christian Service," *RS*, XV, 1 (1968), 39–45.
Finds the basis of Christian service in a eucharistic theology which sees the creation in the perspective of the incarnation.

———. "The Theology of Development: Can It Lead Us Astray?" *IJT*, XIX, 3 & 4 (1970), 99–110.
Warns against the danger of "immanentizing the gospel."

Wagner, Herwig. *Erstgestalten einer einheimischen Theologie in Südindien*. Munich: Chr. Kaiser Verlag, 1963.
"Ein Kapitel indischer Theologiegeschichte als kritischer Beitrag zur Definition von 'einheimischer Theologie.' " Well-documented study of developments toward an indigenous theology in the work of Appasamy, Chenchiah, and Chakkarai. See the review by Kaj Baago in *IRM*, LX, 218 (1966), 221–25.

Ward, Marcus. *Our Theological Task. An Introduction to the Study of Theology in India*. Mysore City: Wesley Press, 1946.
Deals with the importance and urgency of cultural orientation for theological construction in India.

Wilkinson, T.S. and Thomas, M.M., eds. *Ambedkar and the Neo-Buddhist Movement*. Madras: CLS, 1972.
Important as an example of implicit theology in this Indian Christian treatment of a different, non-Hindu/Islam, non-Christian religion.

Yesudhas, D. "Indigenization or Adaptation? A Brief Study of Roberto de Nobili's Attitude to Hinduism," *BTF*, I, 2 (1967), 39–52.

Younger, Paul. *Indian Religious Thought*. Philadelphia: Westminster Press, 1972.
Discusses basic concepts in Indian thought-patterns and views them in contrast to Western theological categories.

Zachariah, Mathai, ed. *The Indian Church: Identity and Fulfilment*. Madras: CLS, 1971.

Stimulating symposium of twenty-one essays, nearly all by Indians, including M.M. Thomas, "Towards an Indian Understanding of Jesus Christ," and D.G. Moses, "The Identity of the Indian Church."

VII. *Indonesia*

Abineno, J.L. Ch. "Church and Confession," *SEAJT*, VIII, 1 & 2 (1966) 53–64.
The author is a former rector of Sekolah Tinggi Theologia, Jakarta, and a chairman of the Indonesian Council of Churches.

———. "Patterns of Liturgy," *SEAJT*, VI, 2 (1964), 56–68.
Does not agree that indigenization is an essential element of the *kerygma*. "For us," he concludes, indigenization "is not a matter of principle, but of relevance."

———. "The State According to Romans 13," *SEAJT*, XIV, 1 (1972), 23–27.

"The Confession of Faith of the Huria Kristen Batak Protestant," pp. 119–47 in *The Church and the Confessions: The Role of the Confessions in the Life and Doctrine of the Lutheran Churches.* Edited by Vilmos Vajta and Hans Weissgerber. Philadelphia: Fortress Press, 1963.
Includes an introduction and explanation by Andar M. Lumban Tobing.

Cooley, Frank L. "Theology and Theological Education in Southeast Asia Today," *SEAJT*, XII (Spring 1971), 16–28.
Relates specifically to the situation in Indonesia, where the author served as a United Presbyterian missionary for many years.

Hadiwijono, Harun. "Theology in Asia Today," *SEAJT*, XII (Spring 1971), 10–15.

Hartoko, Dick. "The Ministry of the Word, Divine and Human," *SEAJT*, XII (Spring 1971), 69–74.
This is the pen-name of an Indonesian Jesuit priest who teaches at the Catholic University in Yogyakarta.

Ihromi. "Respect for the Integrity of Another's Religion," *SEAJT*, XIV, 2 (1973), 61–63.

Kruyt, Jan. *Het Zendingsveld Poso: Geschiedenis van een Konfrontatie.* Kampen: Kok, 1970.
The encounter of Christianity and the Toradja people of Central Celebes, leading up to the 1950s.

Latuihamallo, Peter D. "Missiology and Politics: Christian Alertness in Indonesia," *SEAJT*, X, 2 & 3 (1968–69), 99–131.
The author teaches at Sekolah Tinggi Theologia, Jakarta.

———. "The Search for Consensus Democracy in the New Nations," pp. 213–31 in *Responsible Government in a Revolutionary Age.* Edited by Z.K. Matthews. New York: Association Press, 1966.

———. "A Theological Consultation in Indonesia: A Twofold Struggle," *SEAJT*, XIII, 1 (1971), 20–24.

Lumban Tobing, Andar. *Das Amt in der Batak-Kirche.* Wuppertal-Barmen; Verlag der Rheinischen Missions-Gesellschaft, 1961.

A study of pre-Christian offices in Batak society and the forms of the Christian ministry in the Batak Church since.

———. " 'Sahala' of a Medicine Man and a Theological Graduate," *SEAJT*, IV, 3 (1963), 7–12.

A view of the "image of the ministry" in the Batak Church.

Matsuoka, Fumitaka. "An Asian Church: A Thought on the Indigenizing Process of Christianity," *SEAJT*, XIII, 2 (1972), 22–39.

By a Japanese theologian teaching at Institut Theologia, Ambon.

Pedersen, Paul B. *Batak Blood and Protestant Soul: The Development of National Churches in North Sumatra.* Grand Rapids, Mich.: Eerdmans, 1970.

A survey of the Christian movement in North Sumatra "from missionfield to independent church," emphasizing the plurality and providing primary information on some of the smaller Batak churches.

Schreiner, Lothar. *Adat und Evangelium. Zur Bedeutung der altvölkischen Lebensordnungen für Kirche und Mission unter den Batak in Nordsumatra.* (With a summary in English.) Gütersloh: Gerd Mohn, 1972.

Scholarly investigation into the relevance of tribal traditions for Christianity among the Toba Batak people in northern Sumatra.

———. *Das Bekenntnis der Batak-Kirche.* (Theologische Existenz Heute, Neue Folge Nr. 137.) Munich: Chr. Kaiser Verlag, 1966.

Definitive study of the historical background, context, and theological meaning of the Batak Confession, with a new German translation and commentary.

Sianipar, F.H. "Religion and *Adat*," *SEAJT*, XIV, 1 (1972), 28–32.

Sidjabat, Walter Bonar. *Religious Tolerance and the Christian Faith.* Jakarta: Badan Penerbit Kristen, 1965.

A doctoral dissertation at Princeton Seminary "Concerning the Concept of Divine Omnipotence in the Indonesian Constitution in the Light of Islam and Christianity."

———. "Die Forderung Gottes," *TS* II, 40–54. (German tr. of pp. 177–89 from the above book.)

Sihombing, T. "The Church in the World: An Asian View," pp. 29–42 in *The Missionary Church in East and West.* Edited by Charles C. West and David M. Paton. London: SCM Press, 1959.

The author was formerly president of Nommensen University and is presently head of the Toba Batak church.

Simatupang, T.B. "The Aftermath of Colonialism in Asia," pp. 170–82 in *Responsible Government in a Revolutionary Age.* Edited by Z.K. Matthews. New York: Association Press, 1966.

———. "The Challenge of Christian Mission in Indonesia Today," *AF*, IV, 1 (1969), 83–90.

———. "The Confessing Church in Contemporary Asia," *SEAJT*, VIII, 3 (1967), 53–70.

With special reference to Indonesia, what does it mean for Asian churches to confess Christ as Lord and Judge of history, and as Fulfilment of history?

————. "Politics in Modernization," *AF*, IV, 1 (1969), 13–22.

————. "The Situation and Challenge of the Christian Mission in Indonesia Today," *SEAJT*, X, 4 (1969), 10–27.

Soedarmo, R. "Confessing the Faith in Indonesia Today," *SEAJT*, VIII, 1 & 2 (1966), 155–59.

————. "Waarom is er zo weinig inheems Christendom in Indonesië?" pp. 198–209 in *Christusprediking in de Wereld*. Edited by J. van den Berg et al. Kampen: Kok, 1965.

Soejatno, R. Ardi. "The Church as a Dynamic Instrument," *SEAJT*, XIII, 1 (1971), 11–19.

Tasdik, Ds. *Motives for Conversion in East Java*. (An F.T.E. Research Paper.) Singapore: Foundation for Theological Education in Southeast Asia, 1970.
    A study of the movement of Muslim Javanese into the churches from 1965 to 1969.

Thomson, Alan C. "Faith and Politics: The Indonesian Contribution," *SEAJT*, XI (Spring, 1970), 1–18.

Ukur, Fridolin. "Development and Mission," *ER*, XXVI, 1 (1974), 53–59.

Van Akkeren, Philip. *Sri and Christ: A Study of the Indigenous Church in East Java*. (World Studies of Churches in Mission.) London: Lutterworth Press, 1970.
    Opts for a positive relationship between Christianity and culture in Java, symbolized by the Christ and the *Sri* (goddess of the rice).

Widjaja, Albert. "Beggarly Theology: A Search for a Perspective Toward Indigenous Theology," *SEAJT*, XIV, 2 (1973), 39–45.

VIII. *Japan*

Abe, Masao. "Man and Nature in Christianity and Buddhism," *JR*, VII, 1 (1971), 1–10.

Aikawa, Takaaki and Leavenworth, Lynn. *The Mind of Japan. A Christian Perspective*. Valley Forge, Pa.: Judson Press, 1967.
    Probes into Japan's struggle for self-identity and national integrity as she strives for technological advancement.

Arai, S. *Die Christologie des "Evangelium Vertitatis," Eine religionsgeschichtliche Untersuchung*. Leiden: Brill, 1964.

Ariga, Tetsutaro. "Christian Mission in Japan as a Theological Problem," *RL*, XXVII, 3 (1958), 372–80.

————. "Christian Tradition in a Non-Christian Land," *ER*, XII, 2 (1960), 199–205.

————. "The Japanese Church and the Ecumenical Church," *JCQ*, XXVI, 3 (1960), 151–54.

————. "Jesus of History and the Christ of Faith," pp. 157–76 in *The Theology of Emil Brunner*. Edited by Charles W. Kegley. New York: Association Press, 1962.

————. "The Problem of Indigenizaton," *JR*, III, 1 (1963), 40–45; and "Some Further Thoughts on Indigenization," *JR*, III, 4 (1963), 33–49.

————. "The Significance of World Confessionalism for the Life and Witness of the Asian Churches," *SEAJT*, VI, 3 (1965) 19–30.

————. "To the Shintoist: 'Makoto,' " pp. 103–114 in *Sermons to Men of Other Faiths and Traditions*. Edited by Gerald H. Anderson. Nashville, Tenn.: Abingdon Press, 1966.

————. "World Confessionalism: An Asian Point of View," *USQR*, XIX, 4 (1964), 311–22.

Barksdale, John O. "Christianity and Other Religions: In Search of a Heritage," *JCQ*, XXV, 2 (1969), 107–111.

Best, Ernest E. *Christian Faith and Cultural Crisis: The Japanese Case*. Leiden: Brill, 1966.
    Concentrates on the economic and political dimensions of Japanese society in relation to Protestant Christianity. Bibliography.

Beyerhaus, Peter. "Die gegenwärtige Krise von Kirche und Theologie in Japan," *EMZ*, XXIX, 1 (1972), 1–16.
    See also the ensuing response and debate between Hans Jochen Margull and Beyerhaus over the issues raised in this article: *EMZ*, XXIX, 2 (1972), 83–85.

Buri, Fritz. "The Fate of the Concept of God in the Philosophy of Religion of Keiji Nishitani," *NEAJT*, no. 8 (March 1972), 49–56.

"The Christian's Guide for Social Action," *ER*, XII, 2 (1960), 260–66.
    A statement adopted by the United Church of Christ in Japan in 1958.

Cho, Kiyoko Takeda. "The Weeds and the Wheat: An Inquiry into Indigenous Cultural Energies in Asia," *ER*, XXVIII, 3 (1975), 220–29.
    Dr. (Mrs.) Cho is dean of the graduate school at International Christian University and one of the presidents of the WCC.

Corwin, Charles. *Biblical Encounter with Japanese Culture*. Tokyo: Christian Literature Crusade, 1967.
    Thesis: Man's concepts of reality can be pieced together by examining the verbal symbol system he employs to express such reality.

Doi, Masatoshi. "Christianity and Buddhism in Encounter," *Studies in the Christian Religion* (Kyoto), XXXV, 4 (1968), 10–22.
    "A search for the true meaning of human existence is the common basis for interfaith dialogue." The author is director of the NCC Center for the Study of Japanese Religions, and editor of *JR*.

————. "Confessing the Faith in Asia Today," *JR*, IV, 4 (1966), 1–30.

————. "Dialogue Between Living Faiths in Japan," *JR*, VI, 3 (1970), 49–73; also pp. 32–46 in *Dialogue Between Men of Living Faiths*. Edited by S.J. Samartha. Geneva: WCC, 1971.

————. "Dialogue with Other Faiths: From Tambaram to Kandy," *JCQ*, XXXV, 3 (1969), 140–52.

Dialogue must be carried on in fairness and openness, "not precluding conversion but leaving it to 'God's graceful work.'"

———. "The Implications of the Ecumenical Council for Catholic-Protestant Relations in Japan," *JCQ*, XXX, 2 (1964), 100–105.

———. "Interfaith Dialogue: Methodological Reflections," *JR*, VII, 2 (1971), 1–13.

———. "A Methodological Reflection on the Theology of Mission," *JR*, IV, 3 (1966), 1–11.

———. "The Nature of Encounter Between Christianity and Other Religions as Witnessed on the Japanese Scene," pp. 168–78 in *The Theology of Christian Mission*. Edited by Gerald H. Anderson. New York: McGraw-Hill, 1961.

———. "On Interfaith Cooperation," *JR*, II, 4 (1962), 21–32.

———. "Religion and Nature," *JR*, VI, 3 (1970), 1–14.

———. "Salvation as Fulfilment," *JR*, VII, 3 (1972), 1–14.

Edwards, Clifford W., ed. *Japanese Contributions to the Study of John Wesley*. (Wesley Studies no. 3.) Macon, Ga.: Wesleyan College, 1967.
    Includes essays by Zenda Watanabe, Yoshio Noro, Yuki Kishida, Gan Sakakibara, Masanobu Fukamachi, and Hiroaki Masumoto.

Fukada, Robert M. "New Frontiers of Encounter and Witness," *IRM*, LIV, 214 (1965), 173–84.

Furuya, Y. "Apologetic or Kerygmatic Theology?" *TT*, XVI, 4 (1960), 471–80.

———. "The Influence of Barth on Present-Day Theological Thought in Japan," *JCQ*, XXX, 4 (1964), 262–67.

Germany, Charles H. *Protestant Theologies in Modern Japan: A History of Dominant Theological Currents from 1920–1960*. Tokyo: IISR, 1965.
    Competently covers the formative years of Protestant theological formation in Japan, with particular reference to its assimilation of foreign currents. Extensive bibliography.

———. "Japan," *RL*, XXXVII, 2 (1968), 197–202.
    Part of a *Religion in Life* symposium on "Current Theology Around the World." This is a chapter from Germany's book.

Günther, Heinz. "Das Problem der Eschatologie in Japan," *EMZ*, XXIII, 2 (1966), 101–20.

Hatano, Seiichi. *Time and Eternity*. Tokyo: Japanese Government Printing Bureau, 1963.
    With an introductory essay on "The Life and Thought of Dr. Seiichi Hatano," who died in 1950. Carl Michalson devotes much of chapters 4 and 5 to a discussion of Hatano in *Japanese Contributions to Christian Theology*.

Henning, Liemar. "Zur Theologie Kagawas," *EMZ*, X (1953), 129–37 and 167–75.

Hirano, Tamotsu. "The Problem of the Historical Jesus," *NEAJT*, no. 2 (1969), 1–16.

Hyers, M. Conrad. "Some Methodological Reflections on Interfaith Dialogue in Japan," *JR*, VII, 2 (1971), 14–37.

Iisaka, Yoshiaki. "Christian and Political Life in a Dynamic Asia," pp. 324–36 in *Responsible Government in a Revolutionay Age*. Edited by Z. K. Matthews. New York: Association Press, 1966.

――. "Changes in the Japanese Church's Concept of Ministry," *NEAJT*, no. 13 (September 1974), 9–22.

――. "The State and Religion in Postwar History," *Japan Interpreter*, VIII, 3 & 4 (1972), 306–20.

Ishida, Yoshiro. "Salvation, Mission and Humanization," *LW*, XVIII, 4 (1971), 370–75.

――. "The Concept of Self-Realization in the Uemura-Ebina Controversy (1901–1902)," *NEAJT*, no. 10 (March 1973), 32–50.

――. "The Theology of Kazoh Kitamori," *TTCA*, V, (1968), 18–22.
Sees "Kitamorian theology" as an indigenous theological effort offering a third alternative to both Western and exclusively nativistic theological trends in Japan.

―― "The Uemura-Ebina Controversy of 1901–1902," *JCQ*, XXXIX, 2 (1973), 63–69.

Jennings, Raymond P. *Jesus, Japan and Kanzo Uchimura*. Tokyo: Kyo Bun Kwan, 1958.
Subtitle: "A study of the view of the Church of Kanzo Uchimura and its significance for Japanese Christianity."

Kagawa, Toyohiko. *The Challenge of Redemptive Love*. Nashville, Tenn.: Abingdon Press, 1940.
One of several books by the author (1888–1960) who has been described as "one of the most outstanding Christian witnesses in Asia in modern times." See William Axling, *Kagawa* (New York: Harper's, 1932), and Charlie May Simon, *A Seed Shall Serve: The Story of Toyohiko Kagawa* (New York: Dutton, 1959).

Kishi, Chitose. "The Renewal of the Church and Theological Education," *NEAJT*, no. 1 (March 1968), 7–21.

Kitagawa, Joseph M. "Some Reflections on Theology in Japan," *Anglican Theological Review*, XLIII, 4 (1961), 375–93. German tr. in *TS*, I, 32–51.

Kitamori, Kazoh. *Theology of the Pain of God*. Richmond, Va.: John Knox Press, 1965.
The first indigenous theology from Japan to appear in an English translation; claims that theology starts from an understanding of, and revolves around, the experience of pain at its depth. The author teaches at Tokyo UTS.

――. "Christianity and Other Religions in Japan," *JCQ*, XXVI, 4 (1960), 230–38.

――. "Is 'Japanese Theology' Possible?" *NEAJT*, no. 3 (September 1969), 76–87.
With special reference to the Meiji era theologians Uemura and Uchimura, the author stresses the importance of "non-theological factors" in the indigenization of Christian theology in Japan.

――. "The Japanese Mentality and Christianity," *JCQ*, XXVI, 3 (1960), 167–74.

――. "Das Problem des Leidens in der Christologie," *TS*, III, 112–21.

Kitamori, Yoshizo. "A Theology of Dialogue," *JR*, III, 1 (1963), 1–10.

Kobayashi, Nobuo. "Living Issues of Theological Education in Northeast Asia Today," *NEAJT*, no. 7 (September 1971), 8–16.

Kohler, Hans Werner. "Theologie als Um-denken des heidnischen Denkens. Zur theologie des Schmerzes Gottes bei Kazoh Kitamori," *EMZ*, XXX, 3 (1973), 113–20.

Kumano, Yoshitaka. "A Review and Prospect of Theology in Japan," *NEAJT*, no. 4 (March 1970), 66–75.

———. "Social Christianity in Japan," *NEAJT*, no. 8 (March 1972), 1–22.

Kumazawa, Yoshinobu. "Asian Theological Reflections on Liberation," *OB*, XXIV, 4 (1974). Also in *NEAJT*, no. 14 (March 1975), 1–9.

———. "Confessing the Faith in Japan," *SEAJT*, VIII, 1 & 2 (1966), 161–70.

———. "Salvation Today: A Theological Approach," *JR*, VII, 3 (1972), 15–28. Also in *Mission Trends No. 1*, ed. Gerald H. Anderson and Thomas F. Stransky. New York: Paulist Press; and Grand Rapids, Mich.: Eerdmans, 1974, pp. 87–99.

Kurosaki, Kokichi. *One Body in Christ: The Ecclesia of the New Testament*. Kobe: Eternal Life Press, 1954.
    One of the very few theological texts in English (apart from Uchimura Kanzo's) related to Mukyokai.

Kuwada, Hidenobu. "The Problem of Faith and Culture," *SEAJT*, I, 2 (1959) 13–18.

———. "Protestant Theological Education in Japan," *IRM*, XLVI, 184 (1957), 372–79.
    Valuable observations by the longtime president of Tokyo UTS.

Lee, Robert; Howes, John F.; and Furuya, Yasuo C. "Trialogue on Christianity in Japan," *TT*, XXII, 1 (1966), 73–100.

Luz, Ulrich, "Japanese Student Revolt and Christian Faith," *JCQ*, XXXVII, 4, (1971), 203–15.

——— and Yagi, Seiichi, eds. *Gott in Japan: Anstösse zum Gespräch mit japanischen Philosophen, Theologen, Schriftstellern*. Munich: Chr. Kaiser Verlag, 1973.
    Essays representing the latest radical wing of Protestant theology in Japan.

Margull, Hans Jochen. "Zur Gegenwärtigen theologischen Arbeit in Japan," *Verkündigung und Forschung*, XIII, 2 (1968), 73–87. (Beihefte zu "Evangelische Theologie," Tübingen.)

Masuda, K. "Luther Studies in Japan," *Church History*, XXXI, 2 (1962), 227–31.

Matsumura, K. "Die Einzigartigkeit des christlichen Glaubens gegenüber anderen Religionen," *EMZ*, XXI, 3 (1964), 105–14.

Meyer, Richard. "Towards a Japanese Theology: Kitamori's Theology of the 'Pain of God,'" *JCQ*, XXIX, 1 (1963), 46–57.

Michalson, Carl. *Japanese Contributions to Christian Theology*. Philadelphia: Westminster Press, 1960. German tr. *Japanische Theologie der Gegenwart*. Gütersloh: Gerd Mohn, 1962.
    Discusses, on the basis of translations furnished by associates, the work of

Hatano, Kitamori, Kumano, and other prominent Protestant theologians. Nothing, unfortunately, on Uemura Masahisa (1858–1925) and Takakura Tokutaro (1885–1934).

Muto, Kazuo. "Kitamorian Theology," *JCQ*, XIX, 4 (1953), 321–24.
A sympathetic appraisal by one of his peers.

———. "A New Possibility for a Philosophy of Religion," *NEAJT*, nos. 5 & 6 (September 1970/March 1971), 57–70.

Nomoto, Shinya. "Renewal in the Old Testament," *NEAJT*, no. 2 (March 1969), 97–109.
By a professor at Doshisha School of Theology, Kyoto.

Norman, W.H. "Non-Church Christianity in Japan," *IRM*, XLVI, 184 (1957), 380–93.

Noro, Yoshio. "Christ and History," *NEAJT*, no. 2 (March 1969), 71–96.

———. "Ethics of Destiny," *NEAJT*, nos. 5 & 6 (September 1970/March 1971), 78–106.

———. "Transcendence and Immanence in Contemporary Theology: A Report Article," *NEAJT*, no. 3 (September 1969), 54–75.
Discussion about the ways in which Barth, Bultmann, and Tillich have been "indigenized" in Japan.

Odagaki, Masaya. "Philosophical Theology and Christianity in Japan," *NEAJT*, no. 4 (March 1970), 76–87.

Ogawa, Keiji. *Die Aufgabe der neueren evangelischen Theologie in Japan.* Basel: Verlag Friedrich Reinhardt. 1965.
To be read with Michalson's and Germany's books on the same subject.

Ohki, Hideo. "Democracy, Eschatology, and Ecstasy," *Encounter*, XXXI, 2 (1970), 106–20. Also in *NEAJT*, no. 4 (March 1970), 15–29.

———. "On the Meaning of Transcendence," *NEAJT*, no. 14 (March 1975), 10–19.

Omiya, Hiroshi. "The People of God as the People of the Word," *SEAJT*, I, 4 (1960), 9–19.

Phillips, James M. "Changing Perspectives in Church History," *NEAJT*, no. 4 (March 1970), 30–39.
Implications of the Newman-Harnack debate for East Asia.

———. "N.E.A.A.T.S. Theological Consultation on 'The Historical Jesus and the Contemporary Christ,' " *NEAJT*, no. 2 (March 1969), 141–54.

Piovesana, Gino K. *Recent Japanese Philosophical Thought, 1862–1962; A Survey.* Tokyo: Enderle, 1963.
Includes many theological concerns.

Piryns, E. *Japan en het Christendom: Naar de overstijging van een Dilemma.* 2 vols. Utrecht: Lannoo, 1971. Includes a ten-page English summary.
Stresses the need for the "japanization of Christianity," not simply by adapting to the Japanese religions, but by seeking to discover "what lives beneath them"; shows how this provides a starting point for an indigenous Japanese theology.

Powles, Cyril H. "Foreign Missionaries and Japanese Culture in the Late Nineteenth Century," *NEAJT*, no. 3 (September 1969), 14–28.
    Earlier approaches to indigenization.

Rosenkranz, Gerhard, ed. *Christus kommt nach Japan*. Bad Salzuflen: MBK Verlag, 1959.

Satake, Akira. *Die Gemeindeordnung in der Johannesapokalypse*. Neukirchen-Vluyn: Neukirchener Verlag, 1966.
    A 1962 doctoral dissertation at Heidelberg.

Sekine, Masao. "Die Geschichte der japanischen Christenheit und die Bibelwissenschaft," *EMZ*, XXVIII, 4 (1971), 145–53.

———. "Vom Verstehen der Heilsgeschichte: Das Grundproblem der alttestamentlichen Theologie," *Zeitschrift für alttestamentlichen Wissenschaft*, LXX, 2 (1963), 145–54.

Spae, Joseph J. *Christian Corridors to Japan*. 2nd rev. ed. Tokyo: Oriens Institute for Religious Research, 1967.
    A study of precatechetics for Japan in the light of social and cultural conditions. The author, now on the staff of SODEPAX in Geneva, was formerly director of the Oriens Institute.

———. *Christianity Encounters Japan*. Tokyo: Oriens Institute for Religious Research, 1968.
    Examines the sociological, psychological, and theological factors influencing the encounter.

———. *Japanese Religiosity*. Tokyo: Oriens Institute for Religious Research, 1971.
    The theological implications of the religious awareness of the Japanese to the mission of the church.

———. *Shinto Man*. Tokyo: Oriens Institute for Religious Research, 1972.
    "Some of the basic elements of Japan's religious mind, particularly those which are reflected in the Shinto tradition."

———. "A Theology in the Service of Japan" (a series of three articles), *Japan Missionary Bulletin*, XXII (1968): Part I, "Fundamental Theology as Environmental Research," 389–97; Part II, "Systematic Theology and Japan's Salvation History," 435–44; Part III, "A Moral, Pastoral, and Ecumenical Theology for Japan," 507–18.

Sugai, Taika. "A Missionary Theology of Encounter: Three Works of Dr. Joseph J. Spae," *JR*, VII, 1 (1971), 67–76.
    A Japanese critique of the first three books by Fr. Spae listed above.

Suzuki, Masahisa. "The Problem of Church Renewal in Japan Today," *NEAJT*, no. 1 (March 1968), 89–107.

Tagawa, Kenzo. *Miracles et Évangile, la pensée personnelle de l'évangéliste Marc*. Paris: Presses universitaires de France, 1966.
    A doctoral dissertation at Strasbourg.

———. "The Yagi-Takizawa Debate," *NEAJT*, no. 2 (March 1969), 41–60.

Discussion of a running debate in Japan between a theologian and a New Testament scholar over the possibility of scientific neutrality in New Testament studies.

Takahashi, Masoshi. "An Oriental's Approach to the Problem of Angelology," *Zeitschrift für die alttestamentliche Wissenschaft*, LXXVIII (1966), 343–50.

Takao, Toshikazu. "Representative Critical Approaches to the Contemporary Japanese Situation," *JCQ*, XXXIX, 2 (1973), 75–86.

A review of the writings of Seiichi Yagi, Katsumi Takizawa, and Kenzo Tagawa.

Takenaka, Masao. *Reconciliation and Renewal in Japan*. Rev. ed. New York: Friendship Press, 1967.

Particularly helpful are the sections on nationalism, a divided world, and ecumenical mission. The author teaches social ethics at Doshisha School of Theology, Kyoto.

——. "Auf dem Weg zur Wiederentdeckung des Dienstes der Kirche in einer sich andern den Welt—aus japanischer Sicht," *Zeitschrift für Theologie und Kirche* (Tübingen), LVIII, 4 (1961), 379–86.

——. "Between the Old and the New Worlds," pp. 38–56 in *Man in Community*. Edited by Egbert de Vries, New York: Association Press, 1966.

——. "Called to Service: The Service of the Church in the Changing World," *ER*, XIV, 1 (1961), 164–76.

——. "Christian Encounter with Men of Non-Christian Faiths," *Harvard Divinity Bulletin*, XXVII, 3 (1963), 13–23.

Shows how Christianity under the influence of Mahayana Buddhism has developed a more adequate theology of nature.

——. "Christians in Industry: A Reflective Report," *JCQ*, XXXII, 4 (1966), 251–60.

——. "The First Fruits in Asia: (1) Towards a New Style of Christian Life in Asia Today; (2) Towards a New Structure of the Church in Asia," *SEAJT*, III, 3 (1962), 10–39.

The EACC-sponsored J.R. Mott Lectures, Bangalore, 1961.

——. "Japan," pp. 227–44 in *The Prospects of Christianity Throughout the World*. Edited by M. Searle Bates and Wilhelm Pauck. New York: Scribner's, 1964.

——. "Joint Action for Mission," *JCQ*, XXX, 2 (1964), 140–48.

——. "A New Understanding of the World and the Need of Theological Renewal," *SEAJT*, II, 1 (1960), 12–21.

——. "Our Common Calling in One World Today," *USQR*, XVIII, 3, Part 2 (1963), 320–25.

——. "Salvation in the Japanese Context," *IRM*, LXI, 241 (1972), 79–89.

Takeuchi, Yoshinori. "Buddhism and Existentialism: The Dialogue Between Oriental and Occidental Thought," pp. 291–318 in *Religion and Culture: Essays in Honor of Paul Tillich*. New York: Harper's, 1959.

Takizawa, Katsumi. "Jesus und das asiatische Denken," *Die Zeichen der Zeit* (Berlin), XXI, 1 (1967), 16–19.

––––––. "Zen Buddhism and Christianity in Contemporary Japan," *NEAJT*, no. 4 (March 1970), 106–21.

Uoki, Tadakazu "Theological Trends in Japan Today,"*JCQ*, XVIII, 3 (1952), 209–14.
     Highly competent analysis by the late president of Doshisha University.

Waldenfels, Hans. "Uberlegungen zu einer japanischer Theologie," *ZMR*, LV, 4 (1971), 241–65.

Watanabe, Zenda. "The Lack of Cultural Consciousness and Power in the Churches of Japan," *JCQ*, XXV, 1 (1959), 48–55.

Woodard, William P. "Interfaith Communication in Japan,"*Japan Missionary Bulletin*, XIX, 1 (1965), 35–40.

Yagi, Seiichi. "Geschichte und Gegenwart der neutestamentlichen Forschung in Japan," *TS*, II, 29–39.

––––––. "The Dependence of Japanese Theology upon the Occident," *JCQ*, XXX, 4 (1964), 258–61.
     Says that Christian theological thought in Japan has come of age.

–––––– and Luz, Ulrich, eds. *Gott in Japan. Anstösse zum Gespräch mit japanischen Philosophen, Theologen, Schriftstellern.* Munich: Chr. Kaiser Verlag, 1973.

Yamamoto, Kano. "Christianity Confronts Non-Christian Religions in Japan," *NEAJT*, no. 3 (1969), 115–26.

––––––. "Theology in Japan: Main Trends of Our Time," *JCQ*, XXXII, 1 (1966), 37–47.
     Describes briefly "three generations of Japanese theologians."

Yamauchi, Ichiro. "The Teaching Ministry of Jesus Our Lord: Bible Study at the NEAATS Inaugural Assembly," *NEAJT*, no. 1 (March 1968), 103–109.

IX. *Korea*

Bieder, Werner. "How I Experienced South Korea Theologically," *NEAJT*, no. 10 (March 1973), 1–14.

Breidenstein, Gerhard. "Humanization in Korea" *NEAJT* no. 8 (March 1972) 23–42.

Conn, Harvie M. "Studies in the Theology of the Korean Presbyterian Church: An Historical Outline," *Westminster Theological Journal* (Philadelphia); XXIX, 1 (1966), 24–57; 2 (1967), 136–78; XXX, 1 (1967), 24–49; 2 (1968), 135–84.
     The only extended survey yet written in English of Korean theological trends and Presbyterian schisms (up to 1954), documented from both English and Korean sources; with frank Orthodox Presbyterian bias.

Han, Tai Dong. "Meditation Process in Cultural Interaction: A Search for a Dialogue Between Christianity and Buddhism," *NEAJT*, no. 3 (September 1969), 88–105.

Hong, Harold S.; Ji, Won Yong; and Kim, Chung Choon, eds. *Korea Struggles for Christ. Memorial Symposium for the Eightieth Anniversary of Protestantism in Korea.* Seoul: CLSK, 1966.
     Sixteen essays, all by Koreans; see "The Church and the Problem of Indigeniza-

tion" by Chung Choon Kim, and "The Role of the Christian Church in the Modernization of Korean Society" by Kyung Dong Kim.

Kang, Wi Jo. "The Nevius Methods: The Study and an Appraisal of Indigenous Mission Methods," *Concordia Theological Monthly*, XXXIV, 6 (1963), 335–42.

Kang, Won Yong. "Christian Response to the Asian Revolution," *SW*, LV, 3 (1962), 286–303.

———. "The Church and Nation-Building: An Appraisal," *SEAJT*, VI, 2 (1964), 50–55.

———. "Common Mission—Common Life," *SEAJT*, V, 2 (1963), 31–44.

Kim, Chung Choon. "The Confessing Church in Korea," *SEAJT*, VIII, 1 & 2 (1966), 183–96.

———. "Living Theology and Indigenization," *NEAJT*, no. 8 (March 1972), 68–71.

———. "Seeking Relevance in Methods of Theological Education," *NEAJT*, no. 7 (September 1971), 29–41.

Kim, Stephen. "Evangelization in the Asian Context," pp. 190–92 in *Mission Trends No. 2*. Edited by Gerald H. Anderson and Thomas F. Stransky. New York: Paulist Press and Grand Rapids, Mich.: Eerdmans, 1975.
This Korean cardinal believes "the Christian message will remain an idiom foreign to our cultural soil" unless the church recognizes and integrates the "valid spiritual values" of the cultural heritage and religions of Asia. Reprinted from *TAN*, XI, 4 (1974), 224, 254.

Lee, Jung Young. *The I: A Christian Concept of Man*. New York: Philosophical Library, 1973.
A Korean theologian applies the Yin-Yang way of thinking to the Christian understanding of man. Compare his essay, "The Yin-Yang Way of Thinking."

———. "Can God Be Change Itself?" *Journal of Ecumenical Studies* (Philadelphia), X, 4 (1973), 752–70.
The author concludes that the concept of God as "Change-itself" is more in keeping with the Judeo-Christian tradition than the more dominant Greek concept of "Being-itself." Finds support for his thesis in the ancient Chinese philosophy of *I-Ching*—the "Book of Changes."

———. "The Yin-Yang Way of Thinking: A Possible Method for Ecumenical Theology," *IRM*, LX, 239 (1971), 363–70.

Palmer, Spencer J. *Korea and Christianity: The Problem of Identification with Tradition*. Seoul: Hollym Corp. Publishers, 1967, and Seattle: University of Washington Press, 1975.
Conclusion: "Christian identification with Asian tradition *can* be a distinct advantage, and it *was* so in Korea. But cultural connection is a double-edged sword." Bibliography.

Park, Pong Bae. "Christianity in the Land of Shamanism, Buddhism and Confucianism," *SEAJT*, XIV, 1 (1972), 33–39.

Park, Pong Nang. "A Theological Approach to the Understanding of the Indigenization of Christianity," *NEAJT*, no. 3 (September 1969), 106–14.
> Represents the conservative pole in a running debate with Sung Bum Yun over the past ten years.

Pyun, Sun Hwan. "Review of Sung Bum Yun, *The Korean Theology: A Yellow Theology*," *NEAJT*, no. 10 (March 1973), 56–59.

Ryu, Tongshik. "Ch' on Do Kyo: Korea's Only Indigenous Religion," *JR*, V, 1 (1967) 58–77.

―――. "The Religions of Korea and the Personality of Koreans," pp. 148–65 in *Korea Struggles for Christ*. Edited by Harold S. Hong et al. Seoul: CLSK, 1966.

―――. "Revolution in Missions and the Mission of Revolution," *AF*, V, 3 (1970), 252–57.

Sauer, Charles A. "Is the Korean Creed Really Korean?" *Christian Advocate*, December 24, 1970, p. 16.
> Concerning the Korean Methodist Creed, which is reprinted in the Appendix of this volume. See also the article by Bishop Herbert Welch.

Suh, Nam Dong. "The Contemporaneous Christ," *NEAJT*, no. 3 (September 1969), 1–13.

―――. "The Korean Church's Understanding of the Cross as Reflected in Journal Articles," *NEAJT*, no. 13 (September 1974), 23–29.

Welch, Herbert. "The Story of a Creed," *Christian Advocate*, August 1, 1946, pp. 973–74.
> Concerning the Korean Methodist Creed, which is reprinted in the Appendix. See also the article by Charles A. Sauer.

Yun, Sung Bum. *Das Idealistisch-Gnostische im Taoismus*. Seoul: Yonsei University Press, 1968.
> The author is professor of systematic theology at the Methodist Theological Seminary in Seoul.

―――. "Der Protestantismus in Korea 1930–1955," *Theologische Zeitschrift*, XII, 1 (1956), 44–55.

―――. *Römer 7:25 und der Pneumatikos: Ein exegetisches Problem der Anthropologie des Paulus*. Seoul: Tong–A–Verlag, 1958.

―――. "A Theological Approach to the Indigenization of the Gospel," *NEAJT*, no. 3 (September 1969), 29–37.

―――. "Theology of Sincerity: An Attempt to Form a Korean Theology," *NEAJT*, nos. 5 & 6 (September 1970/March 1971), 71–77.

X. *Philippines*

Abesamis, Carlos H. "Reflections on the Task of the Asian Theologian," *PPF*, I, 2 (1969), 44–47.
> This Filipino Jesuit says that the theological task is to reflect on "the occurrences of God's revelation" in Filipino experience and history.

Arevalo, Catalino G. "Development: The Christian Vision," *PPF*, II, 4 (1970), 27–34.
By a Filipino Jesuit who is dean of the Loyola House of Studies at Ateneo de Manila University.

———. "Mission Theology for Our Times," *TAN*, VI, 3 (1969), 247–58.

———. "Notes for a Theology of Development," *PS*, XIX, 1 (1971), 65–91; also "Towards a Theology of Development," *AF*, VI, 1 & 2 (1972), 106–16.

———. "On the Theology of the Signs of the Times," *PPF*, IV, 4 (1972), 14–26.

Arichea, Daniel C., Jr. "Effective Communication of the Christian Message in the Philippines," *SJ*, XVIII, 3 (1971), 298–311.

———. "Kerygma und Kultur: Die Apostelgeschichte und die Verkündigung auf den Philippinen," *TS*, II, 55–69.

"An Asian Theology of Liberation: The Philippines," *IDOC International* (Rome and New York), No. 5 in "The Future of the Missionary Enterprise" Series, 1973.
Articles and statements from Filipinos on liberation positions, and the church under martial law.

Bonoan, Raul J., ed., *Challenges for the Filipino* (Theology Series, no. 2). Manila: Ateneo de Manila, 1971.
Lectures by Horacio de la Costa, Edicio de la Torre, and Pacifico A. Ortiz, on nationalism, Maoism, and the new Philippine Constitution.

Bulatao, Jaime. *Split-Level Christianity*. Manila: Ateneo de Manila University, 1966.
Important essay by a noted Filipino Jesuit that contributes to an understanding of the cultural context affecting Christianity in the Philippines.

Cruz, Jose A. "Confessing the Faith in Asia Today," *TAN*, IV, 1 (1967), 27–34.

Deats, Richard L. and Gorospe, Vitaliano R., eds. *The Filipino in the Seventies: An Ecumenical Perspective*. Manila: New Day Publishers, 1973.
Part IV on "The Church and Justice in the World" includes essays of specifically theological nature dealing with liberation, development, and the new morality.

De la Costa, Horacio. "Church-State Relationships: A Theological Perspective," *PPF*, II, 4 (1970), 17–26.
Concludes that the relationship is a variable and evolving one, depending on the historic moment which it is meant to serve.

———. "The Concept of Progress and Traditional Values in a Christian Society," pp. 15–29 in *Religion and Progress in Modern Asia*. Edited by Robert N. Bellah. New York: Free Press, 1965.
The author is a highly respected Filipino Jesuit, with a Ph.D. in history from Harvard.

———. "The Filipino Priest—Yesterday and Today," *PPF*, II, 2 (1970), 10–20.

De la Torre, Edicio. "The Challenge of Maoism and the Filipino Christian," pp. 16–31 in *Challenges for the Filipino*. Edited by Raul J. Bonoan. Manila: Ateneo University Press, 1971.
"To take the challenge of Maoism seriously is to take Incarnation in Philippine society seriously."

——. "Christian Participation in the Struggle for Liberation," *AF*, VII, 4 (1972), 55–60.

——. "Some Notes for a Theology of Social Reform," *PPF*, I, 3 (1969), 20–26.
This S.V.D. priest has become an articulate spokesman among the younger Filipino clergy on social issues.

Elwood, Douglas J. "Popular Filipino Concepts of Christ: Report of an Exploratory Study," *SJ*, XVIII, 2 (1971), 154–63.
Shows that many attach a disproportionate significance to the suffering and death of Christ over that of his life and thought.

——. "A Theological Approach to Some Traditional Filipino Beliefs About Man," *SEAJT*, XI, 2 (1970), 37–53.

—— and Magdamo, Patricia L. *Christ in the Philippine Context*. Manila: New Day Publishers, CLSP, 1971.
A college text which interprets the life and teachings of Jesus in relation to Philippine culture.

Gorospe, Vitaliano R. *The Filipino Search for Meaning. Moral Philosophy in a Philippine Setting*. Manila: Ateneo, 1974.

——. "Christian Koinonia and Some Philippine Cultural Forces," *SEAJT*, XI, 2 (1970), 19–36.
A Filipino Jesuit examines critically the relation of Christ to Philippine culture.

——. "Christian Renewal of Filipino Values," *PS*, XIV, 2 (1966), 191–227.

——, ed. *Responsible Parenthood in the Philippines*. Manila: Ateneo, 1970.

Jacinto, Jose S. "The Christian Faith and Philosophy," *SJ*, II, 4 (1955), 255–61.

Lagunzad, Ciriaco Ma., Jr. "Doing Theology: Challenges in Field Education," *AF*, VI, 1 & 2 (1971), 127–37.
Suggests that field education helps to make relevant a theology of "wholeness" in education.

Manaligod, Ambrosio. "Indigenization of the Church in the Philippines is Filipinization," *PPF*, III, 3 (1971), 16–26.
The author has been a leader for many years in a movement to "Filipinize" the Catholic church in the Philippines.

——. "Theological Basis of Filipinization," *PPF*, IV, 4 (1972), 32–42.

——. "Towards a Theology of the Local Church," *PPF*, II, 1 (1970), 11–22.

Mercado, Leonardo N. "Filipino Thought," *PS*, XX, 2 (1972), 207–72.
An interdisciplinary study, by a Filipino priest, using the metalinguistic approach to show the core of Filipino thought and how the core spells out logically in a system.

Montemayor, Jeremias U. *Ours to Share: An Approach to Philippine Social Problems*. Manila: Rex Book Store, 1966.
See "The Christian and the Social Problem," pp. 13–25; by an articulate Catholic layman.

Nacpil, Emerito P. *Mission and Change*. Manila: EACC, 1970.
A biblical-theological treatment of the relation of Christian mission to social change.

――――. *I. The Secular and Secularization. II. A Christian Understanding of Secularization.* (Asia Study Fellowship Series, no. 1.) Tokyo: WSCF Asia Office, 1968.

――――. "The Character of Theological Knowledge in Bultmann," pp. 142–59 in *Politics, Religion and Modern Man: Essays on Reinhold Niebuhr, Paul Tillich, and Rudolf Bultmann*. By Charles W. Kegley et al. Quezon City: University of the Philippines Press, 1969.

――――. "History and Theology Today," *SEAJT*, IV, 1 (1962), 4–14.
Locates the context of theological reflection in our experience of the "historical," in contradistinction to the "natural" and the "supranatural."

――――. "Mission and Modernization," pp. 120–30 in *The Asian Meaning of Modernization*. Edited by S.K. Chatterji. Delhi: ISPCK, 1972.

――――. "Mission but Not Missionaries," *IRM*, LX, 239 (1971), 356–62.
"I believe that the present structure of modern missions is dead. . . . The most *missionary* service a missionary under the present system can do today in Asia is to go home."

――――. "The Mission of the Laity," *AF*, IV, 3 (1969), 21–29.

――――. "Mission in Today's World," *AF*, IV, 2 (1969), 47–56.

――――. "Modernization and the Search for a New Image of Man," pp. 132–56 in *The Living God*. Edited by Dow Kirkpatrick. Nashville, Tenn.: Abingdon Press, 1971.

――――. "Religious Freedom and Proselytism in the Philippines," *SJ*, XII, 2 (1965), 184–95. German tr. in *EMZ*, XXI, 1 (1964), 79–89.

――――. "Revolution in Missions and the Mission of the Church," *AF*, V, 3 (1970), 252–57.

――――. "Theological Education in a Changing Society: Some Pointers and Implications," *SEAJT*, IX, 4 (1968), 17–35.

――――. "Theological Education in the 70's in the Philippines," *SEAJT*, XII, 1 (1971), 83–86.

Radel, Manalo. "The Theologian at Work, Philippines 1970–80's: A Suggestion," *PS*, XIX, 3 (1971), 445–55.
"Manalo Radel" is a pen-name for an anonymous theological discussion group in the Philippines concerned with renewal.

Sitoy, Valentino T. "The Encounter Between Christianity and Bukidnon Animism," *SEAJT*, X, 2 & 3 (1968/1969), 53–79.
Bukidnon is an inland province on the island of Mindanao, Phillipines.

Wideman, Bernard. "A Filipino Liberation Theology," *ChC*, XCII, 14 (April 16, 1975), 390–93.

XI. *Sri Lanka (Ceylon)*

Ambalavanar, D.J. "The Christian Understanding of Man," *Religious and Social Issues*, III, 3 & 4 (1970), 49–69.
>By a Presbyter in the Jaffna diocese of the Church of South India (Sri Lanka).

Balasuriya, Tissa. "Christian-Buddhist Dialogue in Ceylon," *Logos*, X, 1 (1969), 33–39.
>By an Oblate Father who was rector of Aquinas University College, Colombo.

————. "Christians and the Asian Revolution," *Worldmission* (New York), XXIII, 1 (1972), 48–53.

————. "Renewal of the Liturgy in Asia," *TAN*, IV, 2 (1968), 174–99.
>The theology of Christian worship in an Asian context.

Caspersz, Paul. "Ceylon and the Search for an Asianized Church," *NB*, LI, 601 (1970), 288–96.

De Kretser, Bryan. *Man in Buddhism and Christianity*. Calcutta: YMCA Publishing House, 1954.
>A doctoral dissertation at the University of Edinburgh; the author was formerly a minister of the Reformed church in Ceylon, and is now a Roman Catholic layman.

————. "Incarnational Implications," *AF*, V, 3 (1970), 228–30.
>"Clearly the time for mass conversions from these religions [of Asia] to Christianity is gone." Incarnational theology, according to the author, suggests a new direction.

De Silva, Lynn A. *Creation, Redemption and Consummation in Buddhist and Christian Thought*. Chiengmai: Thailand Theological Seminary, 1964.

————. *The Problem of the Self in Buddhism and Christianity*. Colombo: The Study Centre for Religion and Society, 1975.
>The biblical concept of the self in relation to the Buddhist doctrine of *anatta*.

————. *Reincarnation in Buddhist and Christian Thought*. Colombo: The Study Centre for Religion and Society, 1968.

————. *Why Believe in God? The Christian Answer in Relation to Buddhism*. (Dialogue Publications, no. 2.) Colombo: Study Centre, Division of Buddhist Studies, 1970.

————. "Buddhist-Christian Dialogue," pp. 170–203 in *Inter-Religious Dialogue*. (Devanandan Memorial Volume, no. 3.) Edited by Herbert Jai Singh. Bangalore: CISRS, 1967.

————. "Good News of Salvation to the Buddhists," *IRM*, LVII, 228 (1968), 448–58.

————. "Non-Christian Religions and God's Plan of Salvation," *Study Encounter* (Geneva), III, 2 (1967), 61–67.

————. "Some Issues in the Christian-Buddhist Dialogue," pp. 47–58 in *Dialogue Between Men of Living Faiths*. Edited by S.J. Samartha. Geneva: WCC, 1971.

———— and Vitanage, Gunaseela. "Die Frage nach dem historischen Jesus. Ein Briefwechsel," *TS*, II, 80–96.

Fernando, Mervyn. "God Is Not: An Eastern Viewpoint," *The Ecumenist*, IX, 1 & 2 (1971), 22–23.

A brief but important reminder of the distinction in traditional Eastern and Western theologizing, by the Catholic chaplain at the University of Colombo.

Fleming, John R. "The Theology of D.T. Niles," *TTCA*, IV (1967), 5–9. German tr. in *Tendenzen der Theologie im 20. Jahrhundert*. Edited by Hans Jürgen Schultz. Stuttgart: Kreuz-Verlag, 1966, pp. 543–48.

Jackson, Graeme. "Confessing the Faith in Ceylon," *SEAJT*, VIII, 1 & 2 (1966), 149–54.

Kulandran, Sabapathy. *Grace: A Comparative Study of the Doctrine in Christianity and Hinduism*. London: Lutterworth Press, 1964.

——. *Resurgent Religions*. London: Lutterworth Press, 1957.

——. "Non-Christian Faiths and Faith. Our Attitudes Towards Them," *RS*, V, 2 (1958), 7–21.

Neill, Stephen C. "D.T. Niles and the Future of Missions," pp. 131–42 in *Brothers of the Faith*. Nashville, Tenn.: Abingdon Press, 1960.

Niles, Daniel T. *As Seeing the Invisible. A Study of the Book of Revelation*. New York: Harper's 1961; and London: SCM Press, 1962.

——. *Buddhism and the Claims of Christ*. Richmond, Va.: John Knox Press, 1967. First published in Colombo, Sri Lanka under the title *Eternal Life Now* (1946).

——. *Living With the Gospel*. London: Lutterworth Press, 1957.

——. *The Message and Its Messengers. Missions Today and Tomorrow*. Nashville, Tenn.: Abingdon Press, 1966.

The author looks at the church and asks about its faith, its mission, its structure, and its direction for the future.

——. *The Power at Work Among Us. Meditations for Lent*. Philadelphia: Westminster Press, 1967; and London: Epworth Press, 1968.

——. *The Preacher's Calling to Be Servant*. New York: Harper's; and London: Lutterworth Press, 1959.

——. *The Preacher's Task and the Stone of Stumbling*. New York: Harper's, 1958; and London: Lutterworth Press, 1959.

The Lyman Beecher Lectures at Yale for 1957; deals with the question "What is the nature of the existence of the Christian message in a non-Christian world?"

——. *Preaching the Gospel of the Resurrection*. Philadelphia: Westminster Press, 1954; and London: Lutterworth Press, 1953.

——. *Studies in Genesis*. Philadelphia: Westminster, Press, 1958.

——. *A Testament of Faith*. Compiled by Dayalan Niles. London: Epworth Press, 1972.

An unfinished book manuscript, completed by his son and published posthumously, gives a personal restatement of faith.

————. *Upon the Earth. The Mission of God and the Missionary Enterprise of the Churches.* New York: McGraw-Hill; and London: Lutterworth Press, 1962.
>   Deals with the question: "What does it mean in theological terms and in practice in this ecumenical era for the church to discharge its mission to all the nations?"

————. *We Know in Part.* Philadelphia: Westminster Press, 1964; and London: Lutterworth Press, 1965.
>   An Asian response to Bishop Robinson's *Honest to God;* a wrestling with "radical theology."

————. *Who Is This Jesus?* Nashville, Tenn.: Abingdon Press, 1968.

————. "The Christian Claim for the Finality of Christ," pp. 13–31 in *The Finality of Christ.* Edited by Dow Kirkpatrick. Nashville, Tenn.: Abingdon, 1966.

————. "A Church and Its 'Selfhood,' " pp. 72–96 in *A Decisive Hour for the Christian Mission.* Edited by Norman Goodall. London: SCM Press, 1960.

————. "The Confessing Church and Unity," *SEAJT,* VIII, 1 & 2 (1966), 197–200.

————. "The Ecumenical Task," *SEAJT,* V, 2 (1963), 18–25.
>   Presents the ecumenical responsibility of the Asian churches under four dimensions: eschatological, ecclesiastical, Christological, and secular.

————. "The Evangelistic Situation," *USQR,* XV, 2 (1960), 111–16.

————. "Travailing for a New World," *PSB,* LXI, 2 (1968), 20–28.

————. "What Is the Church For?" *PSB,* LVIII, 3 (1965), 3–10.

Pieris, Aloysius. "The Church, the Kingdom, and Other Religions," *Dialogue,* no. 22 (1970), 3–7.
>   A Jesuit speaking on the "Sacramental Theory" of the church's relationship to other religions.

Rosa, Christie H. "The Presence of the Living God Amidst the Cultural Revolution of a People," pp. 116–31 in *The Living God.* Edited by Dow Kirkpatrick. Nashville, Tenn.: Abingdon Press: 1971.

Schrading, Paul E. "D.T. Niles: Ecumenical Evangelical," *Christian Advocate,* XV, 9 (April 29, 1971), 13–15.

Thomas, Winburn T. "D.T. Niles—An Appreciation," *OB,* XXI, 8 (1970), 1–7.
>   Includes selected bibliography of works by Dr. Niles.

"We Live by His Gifts." A Niles Memorial. Special issue of *AF,* V, 4 (1970).
>   Leaders of the churches on three continents pay tribute to Dr. and Mrs. D.T. Niles. Includes bibliography and biographical data.

XII. *Thailand*

Koyama, Kosuke. *Waterbuffalo Theology,* Maryknoll, N.Y.: Orbis Books, 1974.
>   A collection of the author's most important articles, based on his experience as a Japanese missionary teaching theology at Thailand Theological Seminary for eight years.

——. " 'Eating With' Human Brokenness, We Meet God the Paraclete," *SEAJT*, V, 5 (1964), 54–55.

——. "Strengthen the Discernment of the 'Christocentric': German Mysticism in Thailand (exemplis discimus!)" *SEAJT*, IV, 2 (1962), 52–60.

Ulliana, John. "Christianity and Buddhism in Thailand," *Logos* (Colombo, Sri Lanka), X, 2 (1969), 52–63.

Wells, Kenneth E. *Theravada Buddhism and Protestant Christianity*. Bangkok: Church of Christ in Thailand, 1963.
By a longtime Protestant missionary in Thailand.